Praise for *The Way of* T0274780

"Edith Rasell's new book offers a hopeful vision of what the world might look like if we took seriously the prophetic call to economic and social justice. The author has set forth the relevance of ancient biblical ideals to contemporary life on Earth with exceptional intellectual force, practical wisdom, and moral clarity. This important work deserves a widespread and attentive reading."

—John F. Haught, distinguished research professor
of theology, Georgetown University

"Never again wonder if the Bible has something to say about today's economic life. Rasell, an economist, biblical scholar, and activist, has outlined key biblical principles and their relevance for addressing the crisis of poverty and inequality in the nation. *The Way of Abundance* is a must-read for people of faith."

—Kim Bobo, executive director, Virginia Interfaith Center for
Public Policy, and founding director, Interfaith Worker Justice

"Finally, a values-based—even biblically based!—assessment of the economy and how to make it work for all. A masterful work, well written and documented, and thoroughly enjoyable."

—Lawrence Mishel, former president, Economic Policy Institute

"No longer is it a surprise that our kind of global human economy is destructive of the very economy upon which it depends—nature's. Nor is it a surprise that we must find an alternative, perhaps several. As we do so, some will look to sacred Scriptures for the criteria of a just economy, for examples, and for repurposed imagination. Fortunately, *The Way of Abundance* is a deep dive into that project by someone unusually talented in both economics and biblical studies. Get this book and work with it!"

—Larry Rasmussen, Reinhold Niebuhr Professor Emeritus of
Social Ethics, Union Theological Seminary, New York City

"For believers and secular readers alike, Edie Rasell's comprehensive exploration of the biblical roots of economic justice reminds us of the righteousness of this struggle. Her recommendations on taxes reveal the ancient principles behind the tax imperatives of today: use the tax system to relieve poverty and reduce inequality, and tax the wealthy and corporations to pay for the kind of community, society, and planet we all need. Let justice roll, indeed."

—Amy Hanauer, executive director, Institute on Taxation and Economic Policy

"One of the great strengths of this new work by Edie Rasell lies in its innovative interpretive proposals. She builds important bridges that link biblical economy themes with the critique of our current economic predicament. Especially persuasive for the common good (not only the community of faith) is the book's notion of just distribution for thriving abundance. In a time of enormous global inequality and economic disparity, more powerful mechanisms for redistribution of privately hoarded wealth must be found. Rasell's book provides persuasive biblically based warrants for such a central political quest."

—Douglas E. Oakman, professor of religion, Pacific Lutheran University, Tacoma, Washington

"Equipped with a fascinating historical reconstruction of the economic history of Israel and a detailed analysis of our contemporary economic and political situation, Edith Rasell provides a clear vision for what it would mean to embody the Lord's standard of justice in our time. It is a rare thing indeed to find an author gifted in both historical criticism and the finer details of economic policy, but Rasell masters both in this robust call for a more just society."

—D. Glenn Butner Jr., assistant professor of theology and Christian ministry, Sterling College

THE WAY OF ABUNDANCE

THE WAY
OF ABUNDANCE

Economic Justice in
Scripture and Society

Edith Rasell

Fortress Press
Minneapolis

THE WAY OF ABUNDANCE
Economic Justice in Scripture and Society

Scripture quotations are from the New Revised Standard Version of the Bible, copyright © 1989 National Council of the Churches of Christ in the United States of America. Used by permission. All rights reserved worldwide.

Cover design: Brice Hemmer

Print ISBN: 978-1-5064-6982-9
eBook ISBN: 978-1-5064-6983-6

Blessed are those who hunger and thirst for righteousness, for they will be filled.

—Matthew 5:6

Contents

Acknowledgments

I am grateful to the many friends and colleagues who have influenced my thinking and supported my work over the years. I am especially thankful for the people who gave helpful comments on this manuscript including Gloria Albrecht, Eileen Appelbaum, Dean Baker, Brooks Berndt, Mike Fiala, Sue Headlee, Ken Hudson, Cathy Hurwit, Velda Love, Larry Mishel, Christine Moore, Doug Oakman, Larry Rasmussen, Jeff Reiman, Paul Sherry, and Steve Wamhoff.

Introduction

Distressed by poverty in the midst of riches, extreme inequality, and impend-
ing environmental catastrophe, many people know that something is deeply
wrong with our economy. In times of crisis, Christians look to their faith
for guidance. What does the Bible teach us about the economy? What are
God's intentions for our use of the material resources God gives us? What
is a just economy, and how might the US economy move toward greater
justice? As we will see, biblical teaching about the economy includes much
that is unfamiliar to many of us—instructions that go far beyond Jesus's
call to feed the hungry and care for the sick.

Our examination will focus on the Old and New Testament instructions found in the laws of the Pentateuch (the first five books of the Bible),
oracles of the prophets, and teachings and life of Jesus. While this guidance
is focused on economies and societies in the distant past, there are recur-
ring themes and principles whose relevance spans the centuries and can be
used to construct a vision of a just economy today.

We will trace the evolution of the Israelites' economy and society over
the centuries, as described in the biblical narrative and through the tools of
social scientists, and then examine the corresponding evolution of the biblical instruction for creating a just economy. The earliest Israelites living in
Canaan in the twelfth and eleventh centuries BCE, the biblical time of the
judges, were self-sufficient agriculturalists working ancestral land and living
in families and clans with very similar material resources. By the first century CE, the time of Jesus and the Roman control of Palestine, the economy
was characterized by poverty, inequality, indebtedness, commercial abuses,
and the loss of land and livelihood. We will see that as the economy changed
over time and a growing share of Israelites lacked the material resources
necessary to thrive, the biblical teachings on economic justice responded by
providing much greater protections for the vulnerable; enhanced measures

to raise people out of poverty; strengthened provisions to safeguard workers' abilities, through their labor, to provide a flourishing life for themselves and their families; increased prohibitions on fraud, dishonesty, and exploitation in the economic system; and an imperative to resist and overcome oppressive systems. From the perspective of the twenty-first century, the biblical instructions call for economic human rights to be respected and fulfilled, full employment, and a fair economic system that promotes the flourishing of all.

GOD AND OUR MATERIAL WORLD

The Earth Is the Lord's

The biblical writers tell us that everything we have comes from God: "The earth is the Lord's and all that is in it" (Ps 24:1). The creation stories in Genesis are neither historical nor scientific accounts, but they express an ancient people's certainty that God created the earth, the universe, and all living things, including humans. Everything belongs to God. When Moses encounters Yahweh on Mount Sinai, the writers tell us God declared, "Indeed, the whole earth is mine" (Exod 19:5; cf. Exod 9:29). Later Moses reminds the Israelites, "Heaven and the heaven of heavens belong to the Lord your God, the earth with all that is in it" (Deut 10:14). The apostle Paul agrees: "The earth and its fullness are the Lord's" (1 Cor 10:26).

Even from a twenty-first-century scientific point of view, we have to acknowledge that the cosmos was created not by us but by some power we don't understand; let's call it God. All we have comes from God. We are wholly dependent upon the resources of the natural world, which provide our water, food, shelter, clothing, and energy. Our personal gifts *from God*—our mental and physical energy, skills, and ingenuity—are able to turn the things of nature into items we need. But without God's gifts, we could produce nothing. Everything, including our very life, comes from God (see the beautiful, poetic description in Ps 104). Whether considered metaphorically or very concretely, the earth does not belong to us; it belongs to God, as does each one of us.

God Gives Us Abundant Material Resources

For people to thrive, our many needs must be met, including our need for material resources such as food, water, and shelter. God created the material world and called it good (Gen 1:31). The creation of the earth was a gift of abundance from God. The biblical story describes the land given by God to God's people as "flowing streams, with springs and underground waters welling up in valleys and hills, a land of wheat and barley, of vines and fig trees and pomegranates, a land of olive trees and honey, a land where you may eat bread without scarcity, where you will lack nothing, a land whose stones are iron and from whose hills you may mine copper. You shall eat your fill and bless the Lord your God for the good land that he has given you" (Deut 8:7b–10). God gives us abundance—material resources sufficient for all our needs—and with God's blessing, people, creatures, the land, and all creation flourish: "If you follow my statutes and keep my commandments and observe them faithfully, I will give you your rains in their season, and the land shall yield its produce, and the trees of the field shall yield their fruit. Your threshing shall overtake the vintage, and the vintage shall overtake the sowing; you shall eat your bread to the full, and live securely in your land" (Lev 26:3–5). God's intention for our lives, for each one of us and for all creation, is for us to have all we need—not just to survive but to thrive, to live in abundance. The prophet Hosea describes God's reign as a place where all people and creation "flourish as a garden" and "blossom like the vine" (Hos 14:7b). For Jesus, God's reign was like a rich banquet given by a king, with abundant food for the bodies and spirits of people who often had too little (Matt 22:1–10; Luke 14:16–24).[1]

---

1. Please note that while this book references an anthropomorphic deity, this is metaphoric language. The author's view of God is more accurately characterized as infinite, indestructible, transcendent rightness toward which the cosmos is awakening. See John P. Haught, *The New Cosmic Story: Inside Our New Awakening Universe* (New Haven, CT: Yale University Press, 2017). But this is a fairly abstract notion. The rightness that we anticipate and desire and in which we begin to participate—which could also be called the reign of God—is dawning and certainly includes the thriving of all. These images and concepts are often more readily described and grasped through the use of anthropomorphic images, analogies, and metaphors.

God Cares about All Aspects of Life

Abundant life is life lived with God—life lived in God. But God is not concerned with only our spiritual life. God creates us as spiritual beings and also as physical, psychological, emotional, intellectual, artistic, social, and political beings. All of these aspects of life are gifts from God to be used for our own fulfillment and in the service of others. God loves us and seeks our flourishing in all these dimensions, not just the spiritual. In the exodus from bondage in Egypt, God saved bodies as well as souls. Jesus fed and healed bodies even as he also fed and healed souls. Bondage and oppression can be physical as well as spiritual; salvation and deliverance must be as well. Jesus's early followers believed he "came that they may have life, and have it abundantly" (John 10:10). God's vision is for people and all creation to live in the fullness of life, in all our many dimensions.

God's Intentions for God's Resources

Each one of us is present on the planet temporarily. We are aliens and tenants (Lev 25:23), squatters not owners. During this sojourn, we are totally dependent on God's resources. If the earth and all that is in it belong to God, not to us, and if we seek to faithfully live in accordance with God's will, then we need to discern and live out God's wishes for what to do with God's resources. We are accountable to the creator-owner of the resources (Matt 21:33–46; Luke 12:42–48). We bear obligations that shape and limit our choices. As individuals and as a society, we have a responsibility to discern God's intentions for God's planet and God's possessions and then act accordingly: "From everyone to whom much has been given, much will be required; and from the one to whom much has been entrusted, even more will be demanded" (Luke 12:48).

For thousands of years, access to God's resources, and thus to the opportunity to thrive materially, has been shaped by social, economic, and political influences such as landownership, physical force, and gender relations. While God cares for us as individuals, God is also concerned about society; the ways we interact with and care for one another; and how we formulate our rules and social structure to ensure (or not) the flourishing of all people, creatures, and creation. The creator of the cosmos, whose deep caring extends even to a sparrow (Matt 10:29; Luke 12:6), has given us a paradise of abundance. We thwart God's purposes when some of our neighbors receive too small a share of God's resources and fail to thrive as God intends.

God Requires Justice

The Bible tells us repeatedly that God is characterized by justice: "Let those who boast boast in this, that they understand and know me, that I am the Lord; I act with steadfast love, justice, and righteousness in the earth, for in these things I delight, says the Lord" (Jer 9:24). The psalmist writes, "Mighty King, lover of justice, you have established equity; you have executed justice and righteousness in Jacob" (Ps 99:4); "Righteousness and justice are the foundation of your throne; steadfast love and faithfulness go before you" (Ps 89:14; cf. Ps 97:2b); and God "loves righteousness and justice; the earth is full of the steadfast love of the Lord" (Ps 33:5). Note that *righteousness* is another word for *justice*.

God is active in human history doing justice for the oppressed, and God requires justice from us: "He has told you, O mortal, what is good; and what does the Lord require of you but to do justice, and to love kindness, and to walk humbly with your God?" (Mic 6:8). The biblical writers quote Moses, saying, "Justice, and only justice, you shall pursue, so that you may live and occupy the land that the Lord your God is giving you" (Deut 16:20). According to the early church, Jesus began his ministry by announcing, "The Spirit of the Lord is upon me, because he has anointed me to bring good news to the poor. He has sent me to proclaim release to the captives and recovery of sight to the blind, to let the oppressed go free, to proclaim the year of the Lord's favor" (Luke 4:18–19). Jesus was speaking both metaphorically and literally. It was the latter that brought his death by the Roman authoritarian state. The apostle Paul, in his letter to Philemon asking him to free his slave Onesimus, makes clear that being "free" in the spirit is not sufficient. To be a follower of the Way, to do God's will, requires that Onesimus be free in the flesh as well (Phlm 15–16). According to the great twentieth-century Jewish rabbi and scholar Abraham Joshua Heschel, "Justice is not an ancient custom, a human convention, a value, but a transcendent demand, freighted with divine concern."[2] God's love for all requires social justice for all, enacted by all.

2. Abraham J. Heschel, *The Prophets*, vol. 1 (New York: Harper and Row, 1962), 198.

In the United States, when we speak of justice, we are often referring to the criminal legal system, which imposes a penalty on someone found guilty of committing a crime. This is a system of retributive justice; someone who violates the law is subject to a process of retribution that imposes a punishment on the offender.

But retributive justice is just one aspect of a more comprehensive distributive justice where not only punishment but *everything* is distributed fairly, especially those things we prize—income and wealth, health care and education, food and housing, duties and rights, power and opportunities.[3] A just society is characterized by distributive justice. This is a central teaching of both the Old and New Testaments.

Preeminent Old Testament scholar Walter Brueggemann writes that distributive justice is the primary expectation of God: "*Justice is to sort out what belongs to whom, and to return it to them.* Such an understanding implies that there is a right distribution of goods and access to the sources of life. There are certain entitlements that cannot be mocked."[4]

Leading New Testament scholar John Dominic Crossan also sees distributive justice as God's priority: "To be just means to distribute everything fairly. The primary meaning of 'justice' is equitable distribution of *whatever* you have in mind. . . . God's world must be distributed fairly and equitably among all God's people. . . . Do all have enough? Especially that: Do all have enough? Or, to the contrary, do some have far too little while others have far too much? . . . Do all God's children have enough? If not—and the biblical answer is 'not'—how must things change here below so that all God's people have a fair, equitable, and just proportion of God's world?"[5]

God's desire for all people and creation to thrive is to happen through a just distribution of God's material resources. But what distribution is just? What is God's vision? These questions take us into not only theology but also the field of economics.

3. Michael J. Sandel, *Justice: What's the Right Thing to Do?* (New York: Farrar, Straus & Giroux, 2009), 19.
4. Walter Brueggemann, "Voices of the Night—against Justice," in *To Act Justly, Love Tenderly, Walk Humbly: An Agenda for Ministers*, by Walter Brueggemann, Sharon Parks, and Thomas H. Groome (New York: Paulist, 1986), 5–6. Emphasis in the original.
5. John Dominic Crossan, *The Greatest Prayer: Rediscovering the Revolutionary Message of the Lord's Prayer* (New York: HarperCollins, 2010), 2–3. Emphasis in the original.

WHAT IS THE ECONOMY?

The economy, or the economic system, refers to the way we manage the material world. It includes not only the ways in which we produce, distribute, and consume goods (things we can touch, like a car, book, or house) and services (like education, health care, insurance, and haircuts) but also the rules, laws, regulations, practices, and customs that govern this system.

The latter are especially important. Consider production: When something is produced in a factory, office, or wherever people are working, are the workers paid fairly and treated with dignity? Do they have paid sick leave, vacations, pensions, and health insurance? Are the production facility's workers, neighbors, and natural environment protected from any adverse effects of the production process?

Or distribution: How do people gain access to the things they need? Must they buy everything, or are some things given to all or made available at a low cost for those with little money? In other words, who has how much of what? Does everyone have all they need?

And consumption: Do we produce and make available sufficient quantities of all the things that people need? Do we produce junk food or healthy food, private cars or public transportation, affordable housing or McMansions? Do we produce enough quality health care and education for everyone?

The United States is thought of as a "free market" economy. But every economy needs extensive, detailed rules to govern how it functions. A market with no rules would be like the mythical Wild West or some dystopian postapocalyptic future, where society is dominated by the most powerful who coerce and even use lethal force to get what they want. Instead, our society and the economy are governed by rules that shape processes, procedures, and outcomes.

Who gets hired and who doesn't? For what jobs? Who gets a mortgage? At what interest rate? What economic behavior is legal and what is not? What items can receive a copyright or patent and for how long? In the workplace, what constitutes legal pay, benefits, and treatment? Which expenses gain us a tax deduction and which do not? Under what conditions do countries engage in international trade? What degree of risk can banks assume and still retain the promise of a government bailout if they run into trouble? All these issues and many others are shaped by the economic policies, laws, and regulations that govern—and determine the fairness of—our economic system.

If God desires abundant life for all, then our priority for the use of God's material resources is to supply everyone with the resources they need to thrive and to do so in ways that honor creation. Seen through the lens of faith, this is the purpose of the economy. It has no greater priority; there is no larger goal. But is today's economy fulfilling this objective? We know it is not. The economy is designed to primarily serve other purposes: to maximize profit, be efficient, or grow as quickly as possible. But if the economy is to fulfill its purpose, then it must be intentionally shaped through public policy and oversight to achieve this goal.

BIBLICAL TEACHING ON A JUST ECONOMY

God's Vision

The biblical story describes a quest by a group of people who, beginning thousands of years ago, sought to discern and live out God's will not only for their individual lives but also for their life together, their society. We will explore this story to identify the economic instructions given to our ancestors in the Judeo-Christian tradition. Old Testament laws and narratives, the words of the prophets, and the teachings and life of Jesus in the New Testament were God's instructions for transforming ancient economic injustice into justice. These instructions have much to teach us today.

The core of Old Testament instruction is found in the first five books of the Bible—Genesis, Exodus, Leviticus, Numbers, and Deuteronomy—which Christians call the Pentateuch (a Greek word meaning "five books") and Jews call the Torah. The Hebrew word *torah* means "instruction" or "teaching," such as what might be given by a parent to a child. These five books contain what were considered to be divinely inspired laws, narrative stories, and speeches attributed to Moses, the great ancient leader and prophet. The laws and teachings cover many topics, including religious and cultural practices and the structure and conduct of a just society. Our focus will be those concerning the economy.

Theology—our study and understanding of God and therefore of God's law—is specific to a particular time and place. It is unavoidably influenced by the history and culture that shape a society and each individual within it. We see it only in part (1 Cor 13:12). There is little theology that is definitive for all people, times, and places, even the theology of the Bible. We seek to understand the meaning of biblical instruction for its original speakers,

writers, and hearers and then interpret it for today while seeking new revelation and insight. Theologian Paul D. Hanson writes, "The Bible consists
not of words frozen in eternity, but testimonies by a living faith community
of their awareness of living not alone but in the ever-watchful presence of a
loving God. The Word of God is not a set of propositions trumping human
experience and excluding the ongoing exercise of discernment of that loving God in the here and now, but rather the framework of an ongoing conversation between a God continuing to create and to redeem and a people
attentive to God's presence in their midst."[6]

The Law as Gift

We might expect biblical law to be restrictive and oppressive, but that was
not how it was regarded by the biblical writers or ancient Israelites. The
law was a gift, a blessing given by a loving God. It was a guide—a lure
or enticement—to more joyful and fulfilling lives lived in right relationship
with the Creator and with one another. The law was similar to God's other
saving acts, given to establish a society of harmony and justice, a community
in right relationship with God. The law was the road map, the directions,
for seeking and finding God and living out God's vision for society. The law
was so important that over the centuries, the biblical writers described even
its new provisions as coming from the mouth of the great prophet Moses,
God's chosen leader of the exodus from Egypt. The Mosaic law is found
throughout the Pentateuch.

The psalmists describe the law as perfect, good, right, wonderful, righteous, true, sweet, sure, life-giving, and a lamp providing guidance to one's
feet (Pss 1, 19, 119). They proclaim that those who seek to follow the law
find happiness, delight, and peace. Psalm 23, one of the most well-known
and beloved texts in the Bible, tells of the *comfort* derived from God-the-
shepherd's rod and staff, tools used to guide a shepherd's sheep into safe,
life-giving paths. God's law is like a shepherd's tools, given to enhance the
lives of God's people. In a more recent, comprehensive view, the law is
described as "a means by which the divine ordering of chaos at the cosmic
level is actualized in the social sphere, whereby God's will is done on earth
as it is in heaven. . . . The law is a means by which the cosmic and social
orders can be harmoniously integrated, whereby God's cosmic victory can

---

6. Paul D. Hanson, *Political Engagement as Biblical Mandate* (Eugene, OR: Cascade, 2010), 30.

be realized in all spheres of human interaction."[7] Our focus is the law concerning the economy, the instructions or road map showing the way from economic injustice to economic justice. As we will see, God's laws shape the economy to promote material thriving and abundant life.

The law is not the capricious demand of a watchful, angry, judgmental god, although occasionally it may have been regarded as so. Any law that restricts or thwarts something I think I desire can seem odious. But if I step back and reconsider, I may see more clearly. The Israelites sometimes rebelled against the law. But they also knew it was their way to a deeper relationship with God: "Israel wanted nothing so much as communion with Yahweh. . . . Torah obedience corresponds to Israel's true desire. . . . Those who obey are able to participate in the ongoing revolution of turning the world into its true shape as God's creation."[8]

Some of the ancient laws specify practices and prohibitions that today appear pointless and strange. Other provisions fall far short of current standards for justice, just as some of our laws will undoubtedly fall short of more enlightened future standards.[9] Women were subject to patriarchal forms of inequality, abuse, and control. Slavery was normalized. The law is discerned by fallible people with limited vision. Human understanding of God is partial, as is human understanding of God's law. Certainly, Christians today are not bound by the law found in the Pentateuch but seek to live as Jesus did: a life of love and justice centered on God, shaped by the law of the Torah. God's law is not imposed but embraced. To dismiss the law, the law followed by Jesus, is to miss much richness, wisdom, and beneficial instruction.

Evolution of the Law

As we will see, God's vision of economic justice—as embodied in the biblical teaching—is unchanging across the centuries. We will identify the central elements of this vision. But the specific instructions that would transform

7. Terence E. Fretheim, *Exodus*, Interpretation: A Bible Commentary for Teaching and Preaching (Louisville: Westminster John Knox, 1991), 204.
8. Walter Brueggemann, *Theology of the Old Testament: Testimony, Dispute, Advocacy* (Minneapolis: Augsburg Fortress, 1997), 200.
9. The law did have significant flaws—for example, concerning women, immigrants, and slaves. Women were in just about every way subordinate to men. Loans to foreigners carried interest charges and were not automatically canceled after six years (Deut 15:1–3; 23:20). Foreigners, but not Israelites, could be enslaved and inherited as property (Lev 25:44–46), although escaped slaves were not to be returned to their enslavers (Deut 23:15–16).

an unjust economy into one of greater justice are continually altered as a society's economic circumstances change. Thus we will trace the evolution of the Israelites' economy and learn how the law—that is, human understanding of the law—evolved in response. Today, the differences in the major law codes and other instructions in the Bible are obvious. The biblical editors did not try to impose uniformity on the law or the biblical narrative. Rather, the objectives of the earlier law were seen as being fulfilled through its revisions.[10] The new law provided necessary new ways to address new challenges with the objective of reaching the same goal: economic justice.

The practice of reinterpreting the law in light of changing circumstances and new insights, a practice traditionally thought to have originated with Moses, continued over the centuries.[11] The Talmud, a collection of competing interpretations and commentary on the law from around 400 to 600 CE, teaches that "because God has given Israel the Torah, it is now Israel's role to interpret it; in so doing, Israel honors both the Scriptures and God."[12] Jesus participated in this tradition of reinterpretation of the law, and that is also our goal. God's vision of economic justice remains unchanged. But the instructions, the laws that can shape an unjust twenty-first-century economy into one of justice, must be newly discerned. We follow an ancient tradition. The interpretive process continues. We seek God's revelation in our task to discern God's law for today.

The Prophets

In addition to the law, we also find guidance for economic life in the oracles of the classical prophets of the eighth and seventh centuries BCE. They were people who spoke for God, condemning injustice and calling for transformation. To challenge an unjust distribution of material resources and the structures, institutions, and laws that enabled such an economic system was, and continues to be, a controversial, contested, and risky activity. The prophets suffered for their words. To call for justice is to challenge the powerful who benefit from the status quo.

10. Joshua Berman, "Supersessionist or Complementary? Reassessing the Nature of Legal Revision in the Pentateuchal Law Collections," *Journal of Biblical Literature* 135, no. 2 (2016): 211.
11. Amy-Jill Levine, *The Misunderstood Jew: The Church and the Scandal of the Jewish Jesus* (New York: HarperCollins, 2006), 202.
12. Levine, 204.

Jesus's Teachings

Jesus also taught his followers about economic justice. As a first-century Jew, Jesus followed the teachings of the law and the prophets: "Do not think that I have come to abolish the law or the prophets; I have come not to abolish but to fulfill. For truly I tell you, until heaven and earth pass away, not one letter, not one stroke of a letter, will pass from the law until all is accomplished" (Matt 5:17–19; Luke 16:17). Many of the most central concepts of Jesus's teachings, the core of Christianity, are based on the law. What Jesus called the "greatest commandment" comes from the Pentateuch: "'You shall love the Lord your God with all your heart, and with all your soul, and with all your mind.' This is the greatest and first commandment. And a second is like it: 'You shall love your neighbor as yourself.' On these two commandments hang all the law and the prophets" (Matt 22:36–40; Mark 12:28–31; Luke 10:25–28). The command to love God above all else is the first of the Ten Commandments (Exod 20:2–3; Deut 6:4–5), and the instruction to love one's neighbor as oneself is from Leviticus (Lev 19:18). As we will see in chapter 3, Jesus fully upheld the laws concerning the economy and economic justice, and he taught his followers to do so as well.

Jesus also followed in the tradition of making new interpretations of the law. The Gospel writers describe multiple occasions when Jesus challenged the usual understanding of the law by what he said and did: "You have heard that it was said . . . but I say to you . . ." (Matt 5:21–48; Luke 6:27–28; cf. Mark 2:23–28; 3:1–6; Luke 13:10–17). Nonetheless, Jesus and his followers in the early church continued to see the law and the prophets as the key expressions of God's desire for society and for their individual lives: "It is nonsense to speak of the Jewish Jesus abrogating or annulling the Mosaic Law. The Mosaic Law is the given, the sacred canopy under which Jesus and other Palestinian Jews lived and debated the precise understanding and practice of the law."[13]

Paul and the Law

The apostle Paul, a Jew, called the law "holy and just and good" (Rom 7:12). But in the decades after Jesus's death, the apostles determined that gentile followers were not required to obey the Jewish law (Rom 2:12–16).

13. John P. Meier, *A Marginal Jew: Rethinking the Historical Jesus*, vol. 4, *Law and Love* (New Haven, CT: Yale University Press, 2009), 126.

Nonetheless, faithful gentiles "show that what the law requires is written on their hearts, to which their own conscience also bears witness" (Rom 2:15). Paul assumes there is a *"common divine law for all humanity*, with one version written in the promises and traditions of the Jews and the other version unwritten but in the hearts and conscience of the Gentiles."[14] All the followers of Jesus, both Jews and gentiles, are to follow God's law of justice.

Consequences, Not Judgment and Punishment

As we examine the law, we also need to consider what happens when individuals or societies fail to follow the law. Does God punish them? Is misfortune God's punishment for disobedience? This is an important question because there are two contradictory views of God running through the Bible and possibly through our own understanding of God as well.

One view is shown in the book of Joshua, which repeatedly tells a four-stroke cycle of disobedience, followed by punishment from God, followed by repentance, and then, lastly, the restoration of God's blessing. The writers of Joshua understood that God punished disobedience. The contrary view of God is shown in the book of Job, the story of an innocent man who suffers. Misfortune is not due to God's judgment and punishment.

Jesus's view of God was like Job's: a God of unconditional love, compassion, and forgiveness, not judgment and punishment. Jesus's God is one who blesses even the evil and unrighteous with rain and sun for their crops (Matt 5:44–45); his God is the loving, welcoming father of the errant prodigal son (Luke 15:11–32). Jesus and Jesus's God tell us to love even our enemies. If flawed human beings are to love their enemies, surely God loves even those who fall short of God's hopes and expectations. Jesus taught, "Do not judge, and you will not be judged; do not condemn, and you will not be condemned. Forgive, and you will be forgiven" (Luke 6:37; Matt 7:1–2). Crossan argues convincingly that there is no evidence, apart from biblical assertions (like those in Joshua) and human fears, that God ever punishes anyone.[15]

---

14. Marcus J. Borg and John Dominic Crossan, *The First Paul: Reclaiming the Radical Visionary behind the Church's Conservative Icon* (New York: HarperCollins, 2009), 162. Emphasis in the original.

15. John Dominic Crossan, *God and Empire: Jesus against Rome, Then and Now* (New York: HarperCollins, 2007), 73–74. Also see Crossan's *How to Read the Bible and Still Be a Christian: Struggling with Divine Violence from Genesis through Revelation* (New York: HarperCollins, 2015).

God wants only our well-being, our flourishing. We have been provided with guidance to enable this: God's law, the prophets' oracles, Jesus's teachings, and God's ongoing revelations, the insights we glimpse from time to time. God's law is a gift to guide our living and promote our well-being—the path, the way, to justice and peace. God seeks to lead us—to lure and entice us—into a better future. God encourages our cooperation and compliance through enticement, not punishment. God is a teacher and guide, a shepherd, and a lover who wants a relationship, not a punisher or judge searching out our faults.

However, we live in a world that works in particular ways, with "rules" that govern the natural and psychosocial worlds. The law "is a discernment of the reality of things."[16] When a mother tells her child not to touch a hot pot but the child does so anyway, the child's burn is not punishment for disobedience but the consequence of the world's laws—consequences the mother desired her child to avoid by following her instructions given in love. Jump off a cliff, treat people badly, or spew enormous quantities of greenhouse gases into the atmosphere and the laws governing our world predict dire consequences.[17] These outcomes are not God's punishment but the consequences of our unwise actions and failures to fully respond to God's enticement.

OVERVIEW OF THE BOOK

The first three chapters of the book examine three different time periods in the Judeo-Christian tradition. Chapter 1 explores the ancient Israelites' settlements in Canaan in the time of the judges, before the monarchy, in the late thirteenth through eleventh centuries BCE. Drawing on research from the social sciences and the biblical narrative, we examine the economic conditions during this time and the ancient teachings found in Exodus that were responses to those conditions. Chapter 2 explores the economy during the time of the monarchy, particularly in the eighth through seventh centuries BCE, and the economic instructions found in the oracles of the classical

16. Brueggemann, *Theology of the Old Testament*, 598.
17. For example, see Chalmers Johnson, *Blowback: The Costs and Consequences of American Empire* (New York: Henry Holt, 2000).

prophets and the laws and narratives of Leviticus and Deuteronomy.[18] Chapter 3 examines first-century CE Palestine and the economic life of the Israelites under the Romans. The economic instructions primarily come from the four Gospels' descriptions of Jesus's life and teachings. In chapter 4 we outline the characteristics of a just economy—the biblical understanding of God's intentions for the economy and for God's material resources.

Then we turn to today's economy. Chapter 5 evaluates the US and (briefly) the global economies to determine how we measure up when evaluated against the characteristics of a just economy. In chapter 6 we explore some of the changes needed in economic policies and institutions as well as in our personal practices that could move the economy toward greater justice. We continue the ancient tradition of discerning new laws that will guide society to economic justice.

This book is an exploration of the Bible, sacred scripture in the Judeo-Christian tradition. But its conclusions are rooted more fundamentally in the belief that the God of the cosmos, the God of love and justice, desires human thriving and the thriving of all creation. This view is common to all the major faiths. The vision of a just economy presented here might be a starting point for conversations to discern a more broadly shared vision embraced by a diverse community of people of faith and justice seekers.

A NOTE ON METHODOLOGY

This book links biblical law to particular time periods, a methodology that may initially be a concern. The dating of the law codes and narratives in the Pentateuch is uncertain. Moreover, since the codes draw on older traditions and were repeatedly rewritten and redacted after they were initially conceived, how can any particular law code or provision be coupled with a relatively specific period of time?

We recognize that the codes reflect and respond to specific economic conditions. The Ten Commandments and Covenant Code are generally thought to predate the Holiness and Deuteronomic Codes. The Decalogue is considered the oldest law, possibly used in the covenant renewal ceremonies of the tribal federation. The Covenant Code reflects a settled agricultural

---

18. This law originated during the monarchy or in the postexilic period when the economic conditions were similar.

society of largely self-sufficient communities, conditions found during the time of the tribal federation and during the early monarchy. Unlike the other two codes, it does not, for example, address commercial abuses (false weights and measures) or payment of wages. This is consistent with a very early dating of the Covenant Code to when most people were still farming ancestral land, not working for wages on others' estates, and still producing most of what they needed, not purchasing it through market transactions.

The dating of the Holiness and Deuteronomic Codes is uncertain, but they certainly were later than the Covenant Code. Many scholars believe they reached their final form during the exile or within the next few centuries. These two later codes (and the oracles of the prophets) refer to conditions that existed during the monarchy—although not only during the monarchy—and refer to conditions after the exile as well.[19] These codes reflect a time when the largely egalitarian economy of the tribal federation had changed into one characterized by poverty, inequality, loss of land and livelihood, commercial and structural abuses, and economic insecurity—changes well documented by the social sciences as well as the biblical narrative.

The conclusions of this book and its methodology do not depend on precise dating of the codes. Worsening economic injustice led to changes in the biblical teaching that, in response to the new injustices, nearly exclusively go in one direction: toward much greater protections of the poor; enhanced measures to raise people out of poverty; prohibitions on commercial fraud and structural economic injustices; and the provision to return ancestral land (along with livelihood and the opportunity to thrive) to its original owners or, in the absence of that option, provide a living wage job for everyone who needed one.

The biblical instruction—the law, oracles of the prophets, and teachings of Jesus—that provided the road map to guide society from economic injustice to justice changed over time to reflect new economic realities. But God's vision of economic justice and the characteristics of a just economy remained unchanged.

---

19. Nehemiah describes the ongoing problems of debt, loss of land, interest charged on loans, debt bondage, and onerous taxes and tributes (Neh 5:1–13).

Chapter 1

ANCIENT ISRAELITES IN CANAAN

Our examination begins with the ancient Israelites, who, in the mid-thirteenth century BCE, settled in the highlands of Canaan, the land we today call Palestine and Israel.[1] This society was foundational for much that came later, not only in terms of genealogy and geography, but also for the relationship the Israelites established with their God, Yahweh, and their ethos of justice.

UNDERSTANDING THE OLD TESTAMENT

To understand the story of the ancient Israelites, we must first understand the origins of the Old Testament. This collection of ancient books does not contain the transcribed words of God written down by people who somehow heard or knew exactly what God was saying or thinking. The Bible is the inspired work of wise and insightful human beings, but it inevitably reflects the limitations of human understanding and the biases held by human societies and individuals.

---

1. In the period of time covered by this book, the geographic area where the events occurred had multiple names. For the sake of simplicity, I will use the following: Premonarchical Israel was located in Canaan. The monarchies were located in Judah and Israel or, more broadly, in Palestine. During the centuries before and after the time of Jesus, I use the term *Palestine*, the name used by Roman writers, including Herodotus, Ovid, Pliny, and the Jewish historian Flavius Josephus.

The Old Testament narrative describes people who live in specific times and places and engage in particular activities, but for the most part, these accounts are not *history* as we use that term today. Historical accuracy was not the goal of the writers. They were concerned with what they considered much more important tasks: to understand their God called Yahweh and their relationship with Yahweh, to explore how Yahweh acted in history, and to learn what Yahweh wanted from them. The Old Testament is valued as sacred Scripture because it reveals truths about God. Truth can be conveyed through story and myth as much as through the recording and retelling of actual events.

There are historical elements in the Old Testament narrative, memories rooted in events and preserved through oral traditions over many generations until they were written down and included in the biblical story. But when we view the Old Testament as history, we find many contradictions and inconsistencies within the Old Testament itself and between the biblical accounts and the findings of archaeologists, anthropologists, historians, ethnographers, Bible scholars, and other social scientists who have studied this era. This is not surprising, since many of the stories and much of the apparently historical narrative describe a time that precedes the advent of writing in Israel. For the ancient Israelites, the truth of the biblical narrative rested not on historical accuracy but on the insights it provided.

The texts are thought to have been written down at various times spanning hundreds of years, possibly beginning as early as the ninth century BCE. Then they were repeatedly rewritten and reedited by many different authors and editors over additional centuries. During this very long writing and editing process, changes were made to the text in response to new insights and revelations from Yahweh and to speak to new conditions in society. According to Walter Brueggemann, "It is likely that the imaginative freedom of interpreting Israel was not greatly informed by or restrained by 'what happened.'" Rather, the process was one of "interpretive imagination," the creation of an "alternative narrative account of reality with YHWH as its Subject."[2] Nonetheless, the text tells how an ancient people, as early as the late second millennium BCE, was able to hear and embrace a call from God to be a society characterized by justice, including economic justice.

---

2. Walter Brueggemann, *An Introduction to the Old Testament: The Canon and Christian Imagination* (Louisville: Westminster John Knox, 2003), 96.

THE STORY IN THE HEBREW BIBLE

We begin by reviewing the biblical story of the origins of the Israelites. Our abbreviated account starts in Canaan with Joseph and his jealous brothers who sell him into slavery in Egypt. Some years later, a famine strikes Canaan, and some of Joseph's eleven brothers go to buy grain in Egypt. There they encounter Joseph, who has become a high official working for the pharaoh. There is forgiveness and a family reunion, and soon Joseph's whole family leaves Canaan to settle in Egypt. Generations pass. The foreigners "multipl[y] and gr[o]w exceedingly strong" until the pharaoh, afraid of the numerous and powerful Israelites, enslaves them "and [makes] their lives bitter with hard service . . . and in every kind of field labor" (Exod 1:7, 13–14).

The oppressed Israelites cry out to Yahweh, who resolves to free them. Under the leadership of Moses and due to Yahweh's multiple interventions—plagues, afflictions, and ultimately the deaths of all the Egyptians' firstborn children—Pharaoh finally releases the Israelites from slavery. But Pharaoh soon changes his mind and sends his army out to bring them back. So Yahweh intervenes again as the waters of the Reed Sea[3] are parted just long enough to allow the Israelites to pass through on dry ground and then come flooding back to drown Pharaoh's army as it pursues them on the same path. Thus some two million to three million Israelites (Num 1:20–47) begin a forty-year journey through the desert wilderness to their new life in the promised land, a land flowing with milk and honey, a place—unlike Egypt—where they may have abundant life.[4]

The Israelites have barely begun their long journey when they arrive at Mount Sinai and have a transformative encounter with Yahweh. Using Moses as a messenger, Yahweh proposes an agreement, a covenant, with the Israelites.[5] If they will worship Yahweh before all other gods and follow Yahweh's laws and commandments, then Yahweh will bless them,

---

3. The ancient Hebrew biblical text calls the body of water the Reed Sea. But this was mistranslated as the Red Sea in a third-century BCE Greek translation, and the mistranslation remains common today.

4. The totals in Numbers include only men and may have been exaggerated by later writers. The biblical account is not history.

5. The special relationship between Israel and Yahweh at this time was probably not called a covenant or seen as a formal covenantal structure. The term used here refers to the intentional relationship of commitment and obligation between Yahweh and Israel. The concept

cause them to flourish, and establish them as a priestly kingdom and holy
nation (Exod 19:3–6). The Israelites agree, establishing the covenant as
they consent to follow Yahweh's instructions, commandments, and laws
(Exod 19:7–8; 24:3).

After journeying through the desert wilderness for forty years, the Israelites finally arrive at the promised land, the land of Canaan. But before set-
tling down, they must first kill or expel the existing inhabitants. According to
the book of Joshua, the Israelites engage in a series of brutal, bloody battles
where whole towns of people are slaughtered in a campaign of terror. With
Yahweh's help, in less than five years, the Israelites conquer the whole territory of Canaan (Josh 10:40–42; 11:16–23; 21:43). Or maybe they didn't.
There are passages in Joshua and Judges that acknowledge that much of
the land remained in the hands of the Canaanites despite many battles over
many years (Josh 13:1). Joshua and Judges even offer contradictory accounts
of which cities are conquered by the Israelites and which are not.[6]

Both Joshua and Judges report that the conquered lands are distributed among the tribes of Israel (Josh 13–19). A large tribe is given a large
allotment, while a small tribe receives a small one, and within each tribe,
a large clan receives a large portion of land and a small clan a small one.
The exact parcel to be received is determined by lot, thus allowing Yahweh
to determine the final, equitable distribution (Num 26:52–56; 33:54; Josh
14:2; 18:6, 8, 10; 19:51). This random apportionment by lot, outside human
influence, was believed to be controlled by God, thus ensuring its fairness
and responsiveness to divine purposes.

THE STORY ACCORDING TO THE SOCIAL SCIENCES

We now take a second look at the origins of the Israelites and their arrival
in Canaan, this time basing our story on the information gained from the
work of scholars using the tools of the social sciences. We are exploring
these origins in depth because they are key for understanding the covenantal

of a formal covenant was probably not used among the Israelites until the eighth or seventh
centuries BCE.

6. Some cities listed in Joshua as conquered—for example, Jerusalem, Taanach, Dor,
Megiddo, and Gezer (Josh 12:7–24)—are listed in Judges as not conquered (Judg 1:21,
27–29).

relationship between the ancient Israelites and Yahweh, the significance of the laws they believed originated with Yahweh, and their commitment to a just society. We begin by identifying the portions of the biblical story that are confirmed or contradicted by the scientific evidence. But first a word of caution: there is still much scholarly debate about these matters. Few experts unquestioningly accept the biblical story, but there remains much debate about what replaces it.

The Bible tells us that Joseph's extended family left Canaan during a famine and moved to Egypt. Scholars today confirm that ancient Canaanites did move to Egypt during times of famine, including during the second millennium BCE, the time period of the biblical story.[7] During that time, there were Canaanites enslaved in Egypt and forced to work on building projects; small groups of them occasionally escaped into the Sinai desert on a route that could lead them to Canaan. So the basic elements of the Exodus story—the enslavement of Canaanites in Egypt and their escapes—are consistent with historical evidence.

Scholars believe that if there had been an exodus of Egyptian slaves who eventually became the Israelites living in Canaan, it would have happened during the thirteenth century BCE.[8] For most of that century, Egypt was ruled by Rameses II, who engaged in a massive building program for which he used forced labor, especially from foreigners. Mudbricks made with straw were the standard building material, consistent with the biblical story.

But although there are extensive Egyptian records covering this period, there is no record of a large, highly noteworthy number of slaves ever leaving Egypt at any time. There is no mention of a leader named Moses, nor a time of plagues, the deaths of firstborns, or the defeat of the Egyptian army in the Reed Sea. Scholars have been unable to identify a sea with reeds that could be the body of water crossed by the fleeing Israelites. What we call today the Red Sea is too large and too wide and has no reeds.

7. Amihai Mazar, "The Patriarchs, Exodus, and the Conquest Narratives in Light of Archaeology," in *The Quest for the Historical Israel: Debating Archaeology and the History of Early Israel*, by Israel Finkelstein and Amihai Mazar, ed. Brian B. Schmidt, Invited Lectures Delivered at the 6th Biennial Colloquium of International Institute for Secular Humanistic Judaism (Atlanta: Society of Biblical Literature, 2007), 57–65.

8. Nahum M. Sarna and Hershel Shanks, "Israel in Egypt," in *Ancient Israel: From Abraham to the Roman Destruction of the Temple*, 3rd ed., ed. Hershel Shanks (Washington, DC: Biblical Archaeology Society, 2011), 46.

Nonetheless, there is reason to think a parting of waters that permitted slaves to escape might have actually happened. This event is memorialized in one of the oldest texts in the Bible, the Song of the Sea (Exod 15:1–18), thought to date to the late twelfth or early eleventh century BCE, or within a few generations of when the event would have happened.[9] So while the Reed Sea has never been identified and the accuracy of the story cannot be verified, the Song of the Sea is a very early testimony of an event in which Yahweh intervened to liberate and save people fleeing oppression.

Scholars doubt a group of two to three million people spent forty years traveling through the desert wilderness. There are no traces of a large number of travelers moving through the desert, where the very dry conditions would have preserved evidence of their passing.[10] Scholars also doubt the Mount Sinai experience actually happened as described in Exodus and other books in the Pentateuch.[11] A mountain in a location that fits the biblical story has never been identified.[12] Some biblical descriptions of the forty-year journey do not even mention an encounter with God on Mount Sinai or any other mountain (Exod 15; Num 33; Deut 6:20–24; 26:5–9; Josh 24:2–13; Judg 11:12–23; Pss 78; 105; 106; 135; 136). This is a highly significant omission given this encounter's central importance to Israelites' formation as a people, their religious life, and their covenantal relationship with Yahweh.[13] Even the ancient Song of the Sea makes no mention of the mountaintop encounter with Yahweh.

Regardless of historical accuracy, the story of the exodus has inspired oppressed people for centuries. Yahweh took a side in the struggle between the enslaved Israelites and the oppressive Pharaoh, intervening in support of liberation, freedom, and material abundance. Revolutionary change is possible. God does not necessarily support the status quo. Yahweh was

---

9. Frank Moore Cross, *Canaanite Myth and Hebrew Epic* (Cambridge, MA: Harvard University Press, 1973), 124; Sarna and Shanks, "Israel in Egypt," 37.

10. Baruch Halpern, "The Exodus from Egypt: Myth or Reality?," in *The Rise of Ancient Israel*, by Hershel Shanks et al. (Washington, DC: Biblical Archaeology Society, 1992), 87–113.

11. See Frank Crüsemann, *The Torah: Theology and Social History of Old Testament Law*, trans. Allan W. Mahnke (Minneapolis: Fortress, 1996).

12. Sarna and Shanks, "Israel in Egypt," 54.

13. Some scholars believe that the early Israelites had some sort of religious experience connected to an unknown and unidentified mountain that would explain the centrality of the Sinai/Horeb story. See Sarna and Shanks, 55.

concerned to save not just souls but bodies as well. God cares how people, in all their dimensions, fare in this world.

Few scholars today support the story told in Joshua of a rapid, total conquest of Canaan.[14] There is no archaeological evidence supporting the destruction of multiple towns or cities around the time when the Israelites would have arrived during the second half of the thirteenth century. The ancient cities of Jericho, Ai, Gibeon, Lachish, and nearly all the others mentioned in the conquest story have been located and excavated; the archaeological evidence provides little support for a historical conquest of Canaan by the Israelites.[15]

For example, consider Jericho, where the Bible reports the walls fell down in response to a trumpet blast (Josh 6:1–21). Archaeologists have determined that Jericho was destroyed, probably due to earthquakes, about one thousand years before the Israelites would have arrived in Canaan.[16] Many of the locations mentioned in the Bible as sites of conquest and destruction were either uninhabited during the time of the conquest or not destroyed.[17] Moreover, any cities that were destroyed during the presumed time of the arrival of the Israelites in Canaan may not have fallen at the hands of invading Israelites. To summarize, the archaeological evidence does not support the story of rapid conquest and widespread destruction of the Canaanite people that is given in Joshua. However, archaeological evidence does show that a few cities were destroyed in the eastern region of Palestine in the time period consistent with the arrival of a new people we call the Israelites.[18] We return to this below.

There likely are fragments of historical memories and oral tradition contained in the biblical stories of the exodus, wilderness journey, and conquest of Canaan. Moses is an Egyptian name, for example. The people fleeing Egypt endured a long, hazardous journey during which, the story tells us, Yahweh provided food—quail and manna—and water flowed from rocks (Exod 16; 17:1–7). Or maybe Yahweh repeatedly and profoundly fed the

14. Joseph A. Callaway and Hershel Shanks, "The Settlement in Canaan," in Shanks, *Ancient Israel*, 62.

15. Israel Finkelstein and Neil Asher Silberman, *The Bible Unearthed: Archaeology's New Vision of Ancient Israel and the Origin of Its Sacred Texts* (New York: Simon & Schuster, 2001), 73.

16. Callaway and Shanks, "Settlement in Canaan," 63; Finkelstein and Silberman, *Bible Unearthed*, 82.

17. Amihai Mazar, "Patriarchs," 61–62.

18. Callaway and Shanks, "Settlement in Canaan," 64.

travelers with hope and assurance during their difficult journey. The story's
lack of factuality in no way reduces its importance as an illustration of the
travelers' dependence on God and God's response of abundant love. In any
case, the story of the exodus, wilderness journey, encounter with Yahweh on
Mount Sinai, and conquest of Canaan—whether factual or not—became
the Israelites' foundational myths.

New Settlers in the Highlands of Canaan

We now turn to the story of the origins of Israel generally supported by
mainstream Jewish and Christian scholars. Archaeological investigations
show many new settlements in the highlands of Canaan in the late thirteenth
century BCE.[19] What had been a very sparsely settled area became, over a
few generations, a dense network of thriving highland agricultural communities. These settlers became the people we today identify as the ancient
Israelites, devoted to Yahweh and a just society.[20] Some of these newcomers
arriving from the east probably fought with the Canaanites and destroyed
a few of their cities. Moreover, a few centuries after the hill country settlements were established, the settlers expanded into the lowlands, where they
battled with their neighbors. Despite the ongoing conflict, the Canaanites
were not eliminated from the area, and as the biblical story relates, the Israelites continued to be tempted by their gods and customs. The Israelites also
fought the Philistines (the giant Goliath, felled by David and his slingshot,
was a Philistine) who had settled to their southeast on the Mediterranean
coast and were expanding into their territory.

Who were these new settlers called the Israelites? If they were not the
two to three million people who had fled Egypt, where did they come from,
and why did they come? There is still much scholarly debate about the
settlers, but there is some consensus around the following three origins.[21]

---

19. Callaway and Shanks; Finkelstein and Silberman, *Bible Unearthed*, 107.
20. Social scientists have documented "a clear continuity of material culture from these
early Iron Age hill-country settlements to the later centuries of the Iron Age, when this area
was the center of an Israelite monarchy." Callaway and Shanks, "Settlement in Canaan," 70.
21. Shanks, *Ancient Israel*; Finkelstein and Silberman, *Bible Unearthed*; William G. Dever, *Who
Were the Early Israelites and Where Did They Come From?* (Grand Rapids, MI: Eerdmans, 2003);
Shanks et al., *Rise of Ancient Israel*; Israel Finkelstein and Amihai Mazar, *Quest for the Historical Israel.*

First, many of the new settlers were seminomads who moved with the seasons, herding sheep and goats on both the eastern and western sides of the Jordan River. For reasons currently unclear, they decided to end their nomadic lifestyles and settle down. Included among them may have been members of the Shasu people, who lived in Edom, southeast of Canaan, and who may have brought with them their god called Yahweh, the name used by the ancient Israelites for their God.[22] Some of the most ancient biblical texts depict Yahweh as coming from Edom, also called Seir (Deut 33:2; Judg 5:4).

The second group of probable highland settlers was people who had escaped from slavery in Egypt, bringing a devotion to their justice-loving God who had liberated them from bondage.

Third, some of the settlers were probably peasants fleeing oppressive conditions in the lowland city-states of Canaan, where society was characterized by autocratic domination, severe social stratification, poverty, and extreme economic inequality.[23] Each of the city-states was ruled by a king, a warlord, who heavily taxed the population and required men to provide military service and free labor for his building projects. The king and a few wealthy elites owned most of the land and received most of the society's wealth. The huge majority of the lowland population lived as agricultural workers. Some were peasants farming their own land, but many others were slaves, tenant farmers, or day laborers who had no land and worked the large estates owned by the city-state kings and elite. This population had little to lose and much to gain by moving to the largely unsettled frontier in the highlands.

Highland Society

Within a few generations, the new settlers established some 250 to 350 thriving communities.[24] A typical highland settlement was the home of a clan, a group of extended families, composed of some 100 to 300 individuals.[25]

22. Callaway and Shanks, "Settlement in Canaan," 79.
23. Dever, *Who Were the Early Israelites?*, 184; Norman K. Gottwald, *The Tribes of Yahweh: A Sociology of the Religion of Liberated Israel, 1250–1050 BCE* (Maryknoll, NY: Orbis, 1979).
24. Finkelstein and Silberman, *Bible Unearthed*, 107, 109; Dever, *Who Were the Early Israelites?*, 97.
25. Finkelstein and Silberman, *Bible Unearthed*, 108.

They farmed and herded on land that belonged to the clan, not to individuals or families, and was passed down within the clan across generations.[26] Each settlement was largely self-sufficient. People cooperated to provide mutual support and practiced reciprocal sharing of needed resources. Reciprocity and mutual support were central features of village life and would continue to be so for centuries.

Unlike the lowland city-states, the Israelites' highland society was characterized by socioeconomic and political equality among families and clans. Within families, women were subordinate to men, and some people were held in debt bondage or slavery. But among families and clans was a remarkable degree of economic equality. The houses were of a similar type and roughly the same size; there were no special, larger structures that might have housed the wealthy or a military, political, or religious elite. There were no elaborate public structures, no elaborate burial practices that might have celebrated an elite, and no luxury items or status goods. The highlanders "developed an ethos of simplicity and egalitarianism" and refrained from the practices of the lowland city-states, where luxury goods "were of tremendous social importance and were probably used in rites of exclusion and inclusion."[27] The society was patriarchic but had no stratification into upper or lower economic or political classes. It was very different from Canaanite society in the lowlands: "The differences [in the archaeological findings] at these small hill-country hamlets and sites in the lowlands, often within walking distance from highland sites, are remarkable and do seem to designate a 'boundary' that may have resulted from social, economic, or ideological differences with the lowlands and some of the larger settlements in the highlands. Such cultural variation or diversity, situated side by side, cannot be explained as simply different lifestyles. There seems to be a deliberate isolation and separation of the inhabitants of the [lowland city-states] and the smaller [highland] village sites."[28]

26. Rainer Albertz, *From the Beginning to the End of the Monarchy*, vol. 1 of *A History of Israelite Religion in the Old Testament Period*, trans. John Bowden (Louisville: Westminster John Knox, 1994), 73.

27. Avraham Faust, *Israel's Ethnogenesis: Settlement, Interaction, Expansion and Resistance* (Oakville, CT: Equinox, 2006), 227.

28. Ann E. Killebrew, *Biblical Peoples and Ethnicity: An Archaeological Study of Egyptians, Canaanites, Philistines, and Early Israel, 1300–1100 BCE* (Leiden, Netherlands: Society of Biblical Literature, 2005), 13–14.

The highland society was a kinship-based tribal society. No one became disproportionately wealthy, because members of a clan were obligated to care for one another, uphold the welfare of fellow kinsmen, and love their kinsmen as they loved themselves:[29] "The wealth and social resources of [ancient] Israel are understood not in privativistic or acquisitive ways, but as common resources that are to be managed and deployed for the enhancement of the community by the enhancement of its weakest and most disadvantaged members."[30] When a society is able to produce more than what is needed to keep everyone alive, it must decide who is going to get the additional output; most societies succumb to inequality and hierarchy.[31] But the highland settlements maintained their egalitarian ethos even as they produced more material resources than they needed for mere survival. Their choice to distribute their additional resources in ways that maintained households' basic equality differed from the choices made by most other societies at that time (or any time).

Within a geographic region, multiple clans formed a tribe. Together the highland tribes formed what we can call a tribal federation. The tribes and tribal federation had no hereditary leadership, such as a chief or king. Yahweh was their king. Decisions were made by a gathering of the heads of clans.[32] The villages were not fortified, and there were no professional soldiers or standing army. If the need arose, all able-bodied men were expected to fight under a leader, a "judge," who would be selected based on merit, not inherited status. Judges also provided civic leadership and counsel. At least one judge, Deborah, was a woman (Judg 4–5). A judge's authority and standing were temporary and not passed on to his or her children.[33]

A People Israel

Just a few decades after their arrival in the highlands, the diverse settlers coalesced into a unique, ethnically identifiable people. Despite their extremely

29. Frank Moore Cross, *From Epic to Canon: History and Literature in Ancient Israel* (Baltimore: Johns Hopkins University Press, 1998), 4.
30. Brueggemann, *Theology of the Old Testament*, 422.
31. Gerhard E. Lenski, *Power and Privilege: A Theory of Social Stratification* (Chapel Hill: University of North Carolina Press, 1984).
32. Albertz, *From the Beginning*, 73–74.
33. The only exception to the absence of hereditary roles was the priesthood. Priests were members of the tribe of Levi.

diverse backgrounds, they created a common identity that distinguished them from the Canaanites of the lowland city-states. They were bound together through their kinship ties; common stories of origin; commitment to their common God, Yahweh, and Yahweh's law; and rejection of the Canaanite gods and culture.[34]

Kinship Ties

Despite the very diverse origins of the highland settlers, their clans, tribes, and tribal federation were, surprisingly, rooted in kinship. Bible scholar Frank Moore Cross points out that the highland settlers employed "legal mechanisms or devices—we might even say legal fictions—by which outsiders, non-kin, might be incorporated into the kinship group. Those incorporated, an individual or a group, gained fictive kinship and shared the mutual obligations and privileges of real kinsmen. . . . Such individuals or groups were grafted onto the genealogies and fictive kinship became kinship of the flesh or blood."[35]

Even the tribal federation was a kinship organization of families and tribes with common ancestors who were created or somehow identified within genealogies: "Such genealogies are in substantial part constructs, based as much on [fictitious kinship] as real kinship, and the genealogies tend to be fluid, shifting to reflect social and historical changes and developments."[36]

Common Stories of Origin

As the diverse group of settlers interacted and became new kinfolk to one another, not just their ancestors and genealogies, but also their epics and myths were reshaped to become shared stories of origin.[37] Common sagas

---

34. The process that creates the core ideology of a distinct ethnic group often rests on common stories of origin, religious experiences, genealogies, and enemies. These elements were present in the emergence of the people known as Israel. See Killebrew, *Biblical Peoples*, 149, 184.

35. Cross, *Epic to Canon*, 7. Also see Lester L. Grabbe, *Ancient Israel: What Do We Know and How Do We Know It?* (New York: T&T Clark, 2007), 105.

36. Cross, *Epic to Canon*, 12.

37. It was common for a newly forming nation-state in eighteenth-century Europe to "invent a common history, telling tales about a shared past, tying together ribbons of facts and myths" to unite the diverse people residing within the newly formed political entity. See Jill Lepore, *This America: The Case for the Nation* (New York: Liveright, 2019).

and shared memories (whether actual or not) form a group's common identity. In time, all the settlers were heirs of Joseph, their ancestor who left Canaan for Egypt, whose descendants had been liberated from slavery and brought back to their ancestral promised land with the help of Yahweh: "In the national lore, *all* Israelites came from Egypt and wandered in the desert. This is surely not the case. But some did."[38]

A group of escaped Egyptian slaves, led by Yahweh, entered Canaan and "formed the nucleus around which the early Israelite [tribal federation] took shape and expanded, and from whom 'all Israel' took their identity and institutions. This is the testimony of the archaic hymns and the historical basis of the early epic" that we read in the Hebrew Bible.[39] The exodus from Egypt "coded certain common values into the culture. All Israel shared the background of the ancestors—all Israel had been slaves in Egypt. Whatever one's biological ancestry, to be an Israelite meant that one's ancestors—spiritual or emotive or collective ancestors—had risen from Egypt to conquer Canaan."[40] Israel's ancient stories—the promises made to the patriarchs, victory of Yahweh over the Egyptians, creation of the people Israel at Sinai, and the conquest of Canaan—are not history but nonetheless "preserve more or less accurate reflections of the social institutions, especially the religious lore of the old time of which they sing."[41] Moreover, the Exodus story would likely not have survived if it had not contained important truths for the early Israelites, if it had not spoken importantly to the people in the highland villages who had "pharaohs" of their own—the Canaanites and Philistines around them—whom they needed to resist.

The stories bound together and created a common identity for this diverse group of highland settlers who became deeply committed to one another, Yahweh, and their land. Their national story of promise, liberation, and conquest "justified the Israelite land claims in Canaan—became a call to arms, a doctrine of Manifest Destiny, for a people newly arrived."[42] Their mythical heritage "legitimize[d] the land claims" of the tribal

---

38. Callaway and Shanks, "Settlement in Canaan," 79. Emphasis in the original.

39. Cross, *Epic to Canon*, 51–52.

40. Halpern, "Exodus from Egypt," 88.

41. Cross, *Epic to Canon*, 51.

42. Halpern, "Exodus from Egypt," 107.

federation and justified the frequent battles the Israelites fought against their neighbors to protect their land.[43]

The highlanders who had fled poverty and oppression found abundance in the highlands of Canaan, enough for all their needs. These diverse settlers, whom we now call the Israelites, interpreted this experience as the fulfillment of their myths of origin, the stories of promises made by God to their common (fictive) ancestors. The highlands of Canaan became the promised land, their gift from God. The promised land is not a specific geographic area but a metaphor for abundance given by God. Centuries later, as the land held by the Israelites expanded under the monarchs, so too did the boundaries of the promised land.

The God Yahweh

The Israelites' cohesiveness and ethnic identity also stemmed from their shared devotion to Yahweh, the liberating, justice-seeking God who freed slaves, supported liberated captives on a long and difficult journey through the wilderness, and brought them to a land of freedom and abundance, a truth-filled story even if not a factual event.

Yahweh was different from the gods worshiped by the Canaanites and the Israelites' other neighbors. Often those gods (as interpreted by priests employed by the king and other elites) supported the hierarchical and oppressive status quo and legitimized religious, economic, political, and social structures that were destructive to human thriving. But Yahweh was a god of freedom, unbound by social conventions and the established order, who did not hesitate to disrupt an abusive reality to liberate people into freedom and abundance. From the earliest formation of the Israelite religion, Yahweh brought liberation from oppression, not legitimation of oppression: "This starting point explains the bias against domination, transcending present social circumstances, which was to become established time and again in the history of Israelite religion."[44]

The Mosaic Covenant: A Commitment to Yahweh

There was one additional, highly important factor binding together the diverse highland settlers: the covenant between themselves and Yahweh that, according to their stories, had been mediated by Moses on Mount Sinai.

---

43. Cross, *Epic to Canon*, 47.
44. Albertz, *From the Beginning*, 47.

This agreement imposed obligations on and promised benefits to both parties. For their part, the Israelites agreed to worship Yahweh above all other gods, including the Canaanites' gods, and to live as Yahweh instructed, obeying all Yahweh's laws and commandments concerning proper worship and just socioeconomic practices. The covenant committed the Israelites to Yahweh, to one another, and to a "systematic, ethically and religiously based, conscious rejection of many cultural traits" found in Canaan's lowland city-states and throughout the ancient Middle East at that time.[45]

The other half of the covenant was Yahweh's promise to the Israelites. If they followed Yahweh's laws and commandments, they would be Yahweh's treasured possession, a priestly kingdom and holy nation, enjoying abundance and well-being (Exod 19:5–6; cf. Deut 7:12–16). Yahweh desired the Israelites to thrive; Yahweh's laws taught them how to make that happen. The covenant had both religious and socioeconomic components. Unlike their ancient Near Eastern neighbors, the Israelites believed a right relationship with Yahweh did not depend solely on the correct enactment of and participation in religious rites. Even more important was the requirement for social justice.

The commitment to Yahweh meant a rejection of the gods of empire, wealth, oppression, and exploitation: "There is a close link between theological vision and sociological organization. . . . When the 'new' God of freedom and justice is accepted as covenant partner, the totalitarian, hierarchical social order is no longer necessary or viable."[46] Both idolatry and injustice stem from the same origin: from loving something else more than Yahweh. The worship of Yahweh was based on a vision and experience of liberation and abundance. To worship and serve Yahweh was to do justice.

The covenant was "utterly giving and utterly demanding."[47] It provided guidelines for structuring a just and faithful society and for living a faithful life of justice. The covenant helped create a people whom we call the Israelites. It bound clans into tribes and bound the tribes to the federation and to Yahweh. It acknowledged and celebrated the centrality of Yahweh to the

---

45. George Mendenhall, *The Tenth Generation: The Origins of the Biblical Tradition* (Baltimore: Johns Hopkins University Press, 1973), 12.

46. Walter Brueggemann, "Trajectories in Old Testament Literature and the Sociology of Ancient Israel," in *A Social Reading of the Old Testament*, ed. Patrick D. Miller (Minneapolis: Augsburg Fortress, 1994), 19–20.

47. Brueggemann, *Theology of the Old Testament*, 419.

Israelites' social, economic, political, and religious life. It marked them as different from their neighbors and formed a central element of their identity that extended over centuries.

Scholars believe the tribes and federation periodically engaged in covenant renewal celebrations centered on Yahweh. The Israelites' story of exodus, the wilderness journey, and the conquest of the land of promise under the liberating power and guidance of Yahweh was recited and reenacted prior to a reaffirmation of their covenantal bonds: "The central or constitutive element in the early cult was the dramatic reenactment, by recital and ritual acts, of the events of the Exodus and Conquest. This reenactment . . . may be seen as the primary or initial movement in a covenant-renewal ceremony . . . in which the basis of the community's common life and institutions is restored or renewed."[48] The book of Joshua describes two occasions that might be covenant-renewal ceremonies (Josh 8:30–35; 24).[49] The Ten Commandments (Exod 20:1–17), likely one of the most ancient components of Yahweh's law, may have been reaffirmed during the rites of covenant and covenant renewal.[50] The short, easy-to-remember statements (ten commandments to be remembered on ten fingers) were designed for and shaped by oral recitation.

So while there probably was no actual encounter on Mount Sinai with Yahweh, the tribes did encounter Yahweh when they regularly came together to publicly renew their covenant vows. The stories that developed about an encounter with Yahweh—on a mountaintop or in a covenant commitment ceremony in the Canaan highlands—helped create and shape the people called Israel, their religious beliefs, and their commitment to justice.

The egalitarian, kinship-based, nonhierarchical covenantal society of a people committed to Yahweh, to one another, and to justice, became normative for Israel, the standard against which Israelites' future societies would be judged.[51] Over the centuries, as rising social complexity, the establishment of the monarchy, growing wealth and poverty, and imperial conquest brought inevitable changes, the memory of the covenantal society—the

---

48. Cross, *Canaanite Myth*, 79.

49. Also see Deut 26:16–19; 27:1–26; 29:10–13; 31:9–13; 2 Kgs 23:1–3.

50. Cross, *Epic to Canon*, 20; Walter J. Harrelson, *The Ten Commandments and Human Rights*, rev. ed. (Macon, GA: Mercer University Press, 1997), 25. The form used at that time probably was not the version found in Exod 20.

51. Cross, *Epic to Canon*, 17.

commitment to Yahweh and Yahweh's law of justice—remained central to the ethos of the Israelites.

The Origins of Justice

The Israelites were not the only people in the ancient Near East who were concerned with justice. Their neighbors, including Mesopotamia and Egypt, also had law codes specifying just social practices—for example, to care for the poor and marginalized.[52] But the Israelites' beliefs were not simply borrowed or acquired from their neighbors. The highland settlers made justice a more central focus of their society and a defining characteristic of their God. Unlike their Near Eastern neighbors, they believed Yahweh required them to create and maintain a just society. They believed Yahweh's laws and commandments specified economic and social practices that, if followed, would lead to such a society. These laws evolved over the centuries, but they originated among the new settlers in the Canaan highlands.

It is probably impossible to fully identify the origins of the Israelites' uniquely compelling concern for justice, but two factors give us some clues. First, the ancient Israelites knew Yahweh as a justice-loving, compassionate, and liberating God, possibly through an experience of liberation from slavery in Egypt or a new life of wholeness in the highlands of Canaan. They understood their God wanted people to create a just society that promoted human thriving. The Israelites' foundational story of origin—of slaves liberated from bondage by Yahweh and brought home to abundance in the promised land—rooted their society in a covenant with the justice-loving god Yahweh and a commitment to liberation, equality, and thriving.

Second, many of the highland settlers had left oppressive conditions in Canaan's lowlands and in Egypt. They sought to live free of these injustices in their new society. They valued equality and resisted hierarchy and domination in their economic, political, and social lives. Moreover, clan-based tribal societies traditionally place obligations on their members to care for one another. The highland society was established under this kinship ethos

---

52. Robert Gnuse, *No Other Gods: Emergent Monotheism in Israel, Journal for the Study of the Old Testament* Supplement Series 241 (Sheffield, England: Sheffield Academic, 1997), 249, 256; Michael Walzer, *In God's Shadow: Politics in the Hebrew Bible* (New Haven, CT: Yale University Press, 2012), 22.

of compassion and care and continued to preserve it as their circumstances changed.

God did not hand down stone tablets inscribed with the Ten Commandments on Mount Sinai or meet with Moses and the Israelites to give them their law codes. The laws and commandments were the product of the Israelites' discernment of the desires of the justice-loving Yahweh received through what could be called the gift of divine revelation. Their experiences of and beliefs about Yahweh led them to hear the call to create a just society free of the oppressive conditions they had fled in Canaan's lowlands and in Egypt.

THE ECONOMY IN ANCIENT ISRAEL

Our focus is the economy and Yahweh's laws that shaped it. To begin, we summarize some of the key economic features of the covenantal society. Most importantly, everyone had access to land that was held by and passed down through clans, groups of extended families, whose members worked it together. At that time, people working the land, in partnership with people working in their homes, would have produced essentially everything they needed from the resources provided by their land: food, housing, clothing, fuel, and economic security. No one was rich, but no one lacked essential material resources because every family worked their land and produced what they needed.

Each extended family and clan recognized their responsibility to ensure the well-being of all their members. Households engaged in mutual support and reciprocal exchanges with their neighbors. The ones who gave assistance at one point in time might become the recipients of aid at another time. People were far from rich, but when they had excess, they shared it with those in need. Consequently, the society was remarkably egalitarian. No one was wealthy. That is, no family had more land than they needed or failed to share their excess. The distribution of resources was so fair and provided such abundance that they believed God must have guided the allotment of land.

YAHWEH'S LAW

The seemingly idyllic economy did not just happen without intention. It was shaped by what the Israelites understood to be Yahweh's instructions to them, the law, and their commitment to live out divine intentions. These laws are found in the Pentateuch. The oldest laws, those that address the society of the highland settlements, are in the book of Exodus and include the Ten Commandments (Exod 20:2–17) and the laws in Exodus 20:22–23:33, called the Covenant Code. They originated prior to or soon after the formation of the monarchy in the late eleventh century BCE.[53] The laws initially were an oral tradition passed down across generations until they were eventually written down. They reflect their ancient origin and address problems that would have arisen in a settled agricultural society where people engaged in little commerce. We examine only the laws concerning broad economic issues.[54]

We begin with an examination of the first of the Ten Commandments: "I am the Lord your God, who brought you out of the land of Egypt, out of the house of slavery; you shall have no other gods before me" (Exod 20:2–3). This law, and the relationship with Yahweh that it requires, had important implications for the economy and society. This is the most important commandment according to Jesus, followed closely by the second, to love your neighbor as yourself (Matt 22:36–40; Mark 12:28–31; Luke 10:25–28).

The covenant required primary allegiance to Yahweh. But competing with Yahweh for primacy were the Canaanite gods, the gods of the city-states from which many of the hilltop settlers or their ancestors had fled. The hierarchical pantheon of Canaanite gods, as interpreted by the Canaanite priests who were—as is too often the case—allies of the elites, was the model and source of legitimation for the hierarchical Canaanite society. Worshipping Canaanite gods meant affirming a Canaanite society of rich and poor, powerful and powerless, domination and oppression. The Canaanites were not just another ethnic group but an alternative ideology that posed a threat to Israelite's faith and commitment to justice.[55] The first

---

53. Cross, *Epic to Canon*, 20; Dale Patrick, *Old Testament Law* (Atlanta, GA: John Knox, 1985), 65; Fretheim, *Exodus*, 239–40.

54. Numerous laws in Exodus also address potential conflicts over property, including theft, negligence, and damage done by farm animals.

55. Brueggemann, *Introduction to the Old Testament*, 122.

commandment addresses more than the religious question of which god one will serve. It also specifies society's fundamental structure and character. Fidelity to Yahweh and to Yahweh's law required fidelity to Yahweh's justice. The Bible reports that the Canaanites' gods and way of life—centered on hierarchy, control by elites, and acquisitiveness—repeatedly tempted the Israelites away from their commitment to Yahweh and Yahweh's vision for society. We face and often succumb to those same temptations today.

POVERTY

We now turn to the law addressing poverty. In Exodus, there is no explicit obligation in the law to relieve poverty. However, we know the clan-based society embraced the social ethos of responsibility for clan members' welfare, practiced as mutual support and sharing of material resources.

Widows and Orphans

The law did provide explicit protection to the categories of people most likely to fall outside a clan's supportive network: widows and orphans (fatherless children) whose standing within an extended family might fall with the death of the husband and father. The law specified that these potentially marginalized people were entitled to special protection; violators were threatened with severe punishment: "You shall not abuse any widow or orphan. If you do abuse them, when they cry out to me, I will surely heed their cry; my wrath will burn, and I will kill you with the sword, and your wives shall become widows and your children orphans" (Exod 22:22–24). If the person who had been their closest connection to an extended family died, they could not be shunned or expelled and must continue to share in the clan's resources.

Parents

In a similar manner, the fifth commandment obligates families to care for the elderly: "Honor your father and your mother, so that your days may be long in the land that the Lord your God is giving you" (Exod 20:12). Adult children were to provide for their parents in their old age or disability when they could no longer care for themselves, regardless of the elders' ability to contribute to the family's material resources through their labor. Within the extended family, they were to continue to be treated with respect and receive all they needed. The commandment does not direct anyone to obey or be subordinate to their parents. It does not even say to love them, which in any case can hardly be done on command. But elders, even when unable to work, are to be honored and supported.

Lending and Collateral

If a family fell on hard times, they could borrow, and charging interest on these loans was prohibited: "If you lend money to my people, to the poor among you, you shall not deal with them as a creditor; you shall not exact interest from them" (Exod 22:25). Interest on loans was a familiar concept and probably common on commercial loans.[56] But when people's well-being was at risk, interest was prohibited. Unique among the cultures of the ancient Near East, the Bible bars interest charges.[57] Giving a loan to someone in need was perceived not as a favor bestowed but as payment on an insurance policy; we might term it "paying it forward." One who gives a loan today may be in need of one tomorrow. People could rely on the support of others. The encouragement to lend and prohibitions on interest ensured that those with resources to spare could not expand their wealth at the expense of others who were in need.

Lenders often required collateral on loans that would be forfeited if the loan was not repaid. But to protect the poorest borrowers, there were restrictions on the way collateral was held and collected: "If you take your neighbor's cloak in pawn [as collateral], you shall restore it before the sun goes down; for it may be your neighbor's only clothing to use as cover; in what else shall that person sleep? And if your neighbor cries out to me, I will listen, for I am compassionate" (Exod 22:26–27). In all loan arrangements with the poor, the lender is instructed to be compassionate.

56. Patrick, *Old Testament Law*, 86–87.
57. Joshua A. Berman, *Created Equal: How the Bible Broke with Ancient Political Thought* (New York: Oxford University Press, 2008), 96–97.

Bondage Lasts Six Years Only

A poor family in need of a loan might pledge a family member as collateral. If the debt was not repaid, the family member would serve the creditor as a bound laborer, in bondage due to debt. When the debt was repaid, the bound laborer was released. But if the debt was not paid, these laborers were to be released, debt-free, after six years of service (Exod 21:2).

Sabbath Year

The law obligated every Israelite clan to observe the Sabbath Year, one year out of every seven when the land as well as people and work animals were to rest: "For six years you shall sow your land and gather in its yield; but the seventh year you shall let it rest and lie fallow, so that the poor of your people may eat; and what they leave the wild animals may eat. You shall do the same with your vineyard, and with your olive orchard" (Exod 23:10–11). No crops were planted, and no crops, vineyards, or orchards were to be harvested in the usual comprehensive manner. But food could still be gathered from the fields where seeds had sprouted and grown as well as from the untended trees and vines. The produce of the earth was for everyone to eat: the landholder, the poor, and domestic and wild animals. Just as God fed animals in the wild that did not plant or tend any food crops, so also did God feed people. During the Sabbath Year, the poor shared in the produce of the land, for the land belongs to God, who desires that everyone be fed.[58] The Sabbath Year was a spiritual practice that also relieved poverty and boosted yields in non-Sabbath years.

Scholars believe that during the early centuries in the life of the Israelites, the timing of the Sabbath Year was determined by each landholder. It was not observed on the same year throughout the land, so every year some land would be fallow and provide food for the poor to access.

Did the Sabbath Year originate from the practical observation that crop rotation and periodic fallow fields led to higher subsequent yields? Probably not. An extended family of agriculturalists could have fallowed one-seventh of its land each year and planted the other six-sevenths, thus never having a year with no harvest. This would have provided the same effect on yields,

---

58. Robert Gnuse, *You Shall Not Steal: Community and Property in the Biblical Tradition* (Maryknoll, NY: Orbis, 1985), 32.

but not on the spiritual lives of family members. It would not have enacted
the radical dependence on God and God's promise of abundance that the
true Sabbath Year required.

Summary

Before examining the law governing other aspects of the economy, we summarize the law's provisions concerning poverty and protections for the vulnerable in the covenantal society:

- Potentially vulnerable people—widows, orphans, and elders—who
  might fall outside the protective encircling of a family were not to be
  excluded but were to share in the family's or clan's bounty.
- Poverty was a constant threat, even within an economy that might
  be seen as somewhat close to ideal.
- The poor were to be provided loans, but to ease their burden, no
  interest would be charged.
- The obligation to help the poor falls on everyone, not just the most
  affluent members of the clan or community. There were no rich.
  Everyone who could do so, who was not in need, was obligated to
  help those who were.
- The help given to the poor not only is what we would term charity
  but often includes new opportunities and second (and third) chances.
  The poor were offered loans even though they might not be able to
  repay them. Bound laborers were released after six years, no matter
  the size of their outstanding debt.

LIVELIHOOD AND THRIVING

Some laws addressed conditions related to work and livelihood. Every
extended family had land, and adults worked either directly on the land
or in transforming the land's produce into food, clothes, and other needed
items. Each family through their work was able to produce all they needed.
They had abundance.

Sabbath Day

On a farm, the work never stops. Worry, uncertainty, and careful stewardship could easily push people to work long hours every day. But Yahweh
required (or gave the gift) that one day in seven was to be a day of rest, a
time of renewal:[59] "Remember the sabbath day, and keep it holy. Six days
you shall labor and do all your work. But the seventh day is a sabbath to the
Lord your God; you shall not do any work—you, your son or your daughter,
your male or female slave, your livestock, or the alien resident in your towns.
For in six days the Lord made heaven and earth, the sea, and all that is in
them, but rested the seventh day; therefore the Lord blessed the sabbath
day and consecrated it" (Exod 20:8–11; 23:12; 31:12–17). The Sabbath Day
posed two obligations. First, all people, and animals as well, were to cease
working. Work was not to define them, nor was productive economic activity intended to be the chief focus of life. Second, the Sabbath Day brought
a focus on Yahweh. It is "consecrated," a "Sabbath to the Lord." The Sabbath sets within "the patterns of daily life a time that is open to God," a
regular time to celebrate the glory of God, a visible sign of the covenant.[60]

Coveting

The tenth commandment prohibits coveting: "You shall not covet your
neighbor's house; you shall not covet your neighbor's wife, or male or
female slave, or ox, or donkey, or anything that belongs to your neighbor"
(Exod 20:17). Since the eighth commandment (examined below) addresses
theft, the focus of this one is not action but strong desire or craving for
something that might lead to action.

Let us consider two different scenarios. In one, my neighbor has something that I or my family lacks and needs. My desire for the item is sparked
not by my neighbor's possession of it but by our need. I suggest this is not

---

59. The Sabbath was observed even during the very important and extremely busy seasons
of plowing and harvest (Exod 34:21).
60. Patrick Miller, *The Ten Commandments*, Interpretation: Resources for the Use of Scripture
in the Church (Louisville: Westminster John Knox, 2009), 131–32.

the situation described in the commandment. Desiring material necessities that I lack is not covetous.[61]

In a second scenario, my neighbor's item is a bigger, better, fancier, newer version of what I already have, unnecessary but very desirable. Or possibly what I want is not yet in my neighbor's home, but I have seen it advertised. This commandment tells me that if my needs are met, I have enough. I am to be satisfied and not seek more. This commandment prohibits acquisitiveness and conspicuous consumption. God is forbidding the practice of "keeping up with the Joneses." If we ignore this commandment, consumerism easily becomes a form of idolatry, a way to gain and establish our ultimate worth, and our possessions become idols, the source of false meaning in our lives.

We make the following conclusions about livelihood and thriving in the covenantal society. Every clan had land, which meant everyone had work—a livelihood—that collectively provided all the family needed and enabled it to thrive. If there were shortfalls, neighbors would offer assistance. But even in a time and place of little excess and with few resources to fall back on, the primary focus of the economy, astonishingly, was *not* to produce as much as possible. The Sabbath Day and especially the Sabbath Year ensured this. There were higher, more important goals. Nor were people to acquire as much as they could. They were to share with those in need. They were not to covet, not to seek more than they truly needed.

THE ECONOMIC SYSTEM

We now examine the laws that governed the very rudimentary economic system.

Stealing

The eighth commandment prohibits stealing: "You shall not steal" (Exod 20:15). At first glance, this prohibition seems quite straightforward: do not take other people's possessions. But this simple commandment carries additional implications. In the highland communities, many resources were

---

61. As we see in chapter 3, some religious authorities teach that taking a needed item from someone who has excess is not theft.

held in common, including lands used for grazing, water sources, and even flocks.[62] Taking more than one's share of communal possessions was considered theft. This prohibition ensured that all people had access to the things they needed to thrive. Common lands, herds, and water were to be used, shared, and preserved to meet the needs of everyone.

Corruption, Bribes, Honesty

A just society depends on honest interactions and transactions. The ninth commandment forbids lying, especially in judicial proceedings: "You shall not bear false witness against your neighbor" (Exod 20:16). The law also prohibits corruption and the perversion of justice, especially when it will exploit or abuse the poor: "You shall not pervert the justice due to your poor in their lawsuits" (Exod 23:6). Bribes are also banned: "You shall take no bribe, for a bribe blinds the officials, and subverts the cause of those who are in the right" (Exod 23:8). If bribes were effective, they would sway judicial decisions toward the one who could afford to pay them, another disadvantage to the poor.

Immigrants

There is one other category of people for whom the law repeatedly requires special protection and care. These are the people whom the biblical writers call foreigners, aliens, and strangers. We might also call them immigrants or guest workers. They were people from other places who chose to live among the Israelites: "You shall not wrong or oppress a resident alien, for you were aliens in the land of Egypt" (Exod 22:21; 23:9). According to Old Testament scholar Frank Crüsemann, "The rights of aliens, the poor and other exploited people are demands of God to his people that have the same importance as the basic religious principles of the exclusive veneration of God."[63]

---

62. Gnuse, *You Shall Not Steal*, 6.
63. Crüsemann, *Torah*, 191.

Chapter 2

THE TIME OF THE MONARCHY

We now move forward a few hundred years to the eighth and seventh centuries BCE, the time of the monarchy. Our goal is to identify the changes that occurred in society and the economy during the time since the tribal federation and then to examine how the law and the prophets' instructions responded. As we have seen, the law expressed the Israelites' discernment of their obligations to God under the covenant. As the economy changed, so did the provisions of the law that were needed to transform the unjust economy into a just one. Tracking these changes will allow us to identify the characteristics of a just economy—the endpoint toward which the law, the prophets, and Jesus's life and teachings point in each of the eras we examine. We now resume the story of the Israelites in Canaan, drawing on both the biblical tradition and the social sciences.

The settlers prospered in the years following their arrival in the Canaanite highlands. The population grew and created additional settlements in new territory, which brought increasing conflict with their neighbors. The biggest threat came from the Philistines, who attempted to take land held by the Israelites. The dispersed settlements, which had been largely self-sufficient and autonomous, became increasingly interrelated. Near the end of the eleventh century, the pressure of these challenges led to a change in the structure of Israelite society. In order to better respond to the military threats and more ably administer their increasingly complex and interdependent society, the Israelites decided they needed a king.

As described in the book of 1 Samuel, this decision was controversial. The prophet Samuel warned of the abuses that a king would inflict on his people: "He will take the best of your fields and vineyards and olive orchards and give them to his courtiers. He will take one-tenth of your grain and of your vineyards and give it to his officers and his courtiers. He will take your male and female slaves, and the best of your cattle and donkeys, and put them to his work. He will take one-tenth of your flocks, and you shall be his slaves" (1 Sam 8:14–17). Despite Samuel's dire predictions, the Israelites were not deterred. So Samuel anointed the first king, Saul, who began his reign at the end of the eleventh century BCE.

THE ECONOMY UNDER THE MONARCHY

The monarchy brought many changes; what Samuel foretold came to pass. Like most kings, the kings of Israel and Judah (the northern and southern kingdoms) lived in palaces and engaged in lavish lifestyles. They built fortifications and monumental structures. They constructed new cities with prestigious amenities while expanding and refurbishing old ones. They conscripted men into armies that conquered other territories, including fertile valleys of rich agricultural lands. All of this created huge financial burdens that largely fell on peasant farmers. In addition, military service and unpaid forced labor on construction projects (1 Kgs 5:13–18; 12:1–20) took men away from their work, threatening the viability of their farms and land tenure.[1] The monarchic economy achieved its aims through "a combination of coercive political power and exploitative economic power. . . . Economic exploitation became more and more important as the economic demands of the monarchy undermined the viability of families and their mutual support in village communities."[2]

The vast majority of the population continued to farm their plots of land with a goal of self-sufficiency. But international trade was increasing, and with it came rising demand for high-value agricultural goods that could be shipped long distances by sea. Grains, olives for oil, and grapes for wine were grown on large estates, processed, and sold throughout the eastern

---

1. Some of this discontent is expressed in the story of Jeroboam's challenge of Rehoboam (1 Kgs 12:1–15).
2. Richard A. Horsley, *Covenant Economics: A Biblical Vision of Justice for All* (Louisville: Westminster John Knox, 2009), 57.

Mediterranean.[3] Commercial agriculture became a new source of income and greatly increased the value of land. Land was the source of profit, and the king and other elites wanted more of it. The kings confiscated land, taking it from peasants. However, there was a more insidious but effective way for the wealthy to enlarge their estates.

The Role of Debt

For peasant farmers, land was life, the opportunity for well-being. Given the lack of alternative livelihoods, the loss of one's land meant a near-certain descent into poverty, from which there was little chance of escape. But farming is inherently precarious. Farmers contend with adverse weather, pests, illnesses of people or work animals, and other misfortunes that can strike at any time, threatening crops and a farm family's subsistence. When Israelite farmers fell on hard times, whatever the cause, survival sometimes forced them to borrow until the next harvest when they could repay their loan. By one estimate, a Palestinian peasant farmer would have likely been forced to go into debt if more than one in four harvests failed.[4] Given the region's arid land, uncertain rainfall, and myriad other possible adverse events, farmers could easily encounter a four-year period with more than one crop failure and would need to borrow in order to survive until the next harvest.

Creditors, who increasingly were not peasant farmers next door but wealthy people with money to lend and a desire for additional land, required collateral. Often a peasant farmer's only collateral, or possibly the only collateral acceptable to a lender, was land. If all went well, the debt was repaid. But if borrowers could not pay their debts, they could lose some or all of their land. Life then became even more precarious. In the worst case, a creditor foreclosed on a debtor's farm and evicted the family from ancestral land. As small peasant farmers lost their land, the estates of their wealthy creditors expanded.

The use of debt to acquire land and wealth is a very old as well as very contemporary tactic. According to anthropologist David Graeber, "For

3. Finkelstein and Silberman, *Bible Unearthed*, 159, 273.
4. Eugen Wirth, *Agrargeographie des Irak* (Hamburg: Instituts für Geographie und Wirtschaft-geographie der Universität Hamburg, 1962), 20–21. Cited in Jacob Milgrom, *Leviticus 23–27: A New Translation with Introduction and Commentary*, Anchor Bible 3B (New York: Doubleday, 2000), 2191.

thousands of years, the struggle between rich and poor has largely taken the form of conflicts between creditors and debtors—of arguments about the rights and wrongs of interest payments, debt peonage, amnesty, repossession, restitution, the sequestering of sheep, the seizing of vineyards, and the selling of debtors' children into slavery."[5]

In his best-selling history of the Pilgrims, *Mayflower: Voyage, Community, and War*, Nathaniel Philbrick describes how the Pokanoket Indians, just fifty years after the settlers began arriving in Plymouth, became alarmed by their rising numbers and dominance and refused to sell them more land. The newcomers, determined to obtain more land, quickly devised another way to acquire it: they made loans to the Pokanoket and used land as collateral. Then the Pilgrims foreclosed on the debt: "It may have been true that from a strictly legal standpoint there was nothing wrong with how Winslow and the other Plymouth officials acquired large amounts of Pokanoket land. And yet, from a practical and moral standpoint, the process removed the Indians from their territory as effectively—and as cheaply—as driving them off at gunpoint."[6]

In Palestine, land foreclosures created landless peasants. Some became tenants on their own land, where the added requirement to pay rent increased their burdens. Moreover, tenants were often forced to grow crops for export rather than the food they needed to survive, which they were forced to purchase. This left them at risk of being sold adulterated grain and cheated with dishonest weights and measures. Others of the newly landless worked as wage-earning day laborers, often on the estates of the wealthy during planting and harvest times when the need for extra workers peaked. They also needed to purchase their food.

As we follow the economic history of the Israelites under the monarchs and into the time of Jesus, we will see how debt—in particular the debts incurred by peasants that led to foreclosure and the loss of land—brought increasing poverty and suffering to masses of previously self-sufficient, thriving farm families. This process continued to wax and wane during the time of the monarchy, leaving ever-larger numbers of dispossessed people. Increasingly, land belonged "to the king and his nobility rather than to the kin group. . . . Reversion to the Canaanite system of land tenure, according to which land was owned by the king and a few nobles,

---

5. David Graeber, *Debt: The First 5,000 Years* (Brooklyn, NY: Melville House, 2011), 8.
6. Nathaniel Philbrick, *Mayflower: Voyage, Community, War* (New York: Viking, 2006), 214–15.

which Samuel feared when he warned the people of the dangers of the monarch (1 Sam 8:10–17), was realized by the land-accumulating activity of the kings of Israel."[7] By the time of Jesus in the first century CE, relatively few people remained peasant farmers on ancestral land.

Decline of Covenantal Society

New economic developments fundamentally changed the covenantal society. Both the northern and southern kingdoms became more prosperous. But the near universal thriving of the premonarchy era, when everyone was responsible for the well-being of their neighbors, was upended. Increasingly, society became characterized by hierarchy, domination, poverty for many, a precarious livelihood for many others, and extreme wealth for a very few. Abuse of the poor, loss of land, exploitation of workers, fraudulent commercial transactions, and dishonest judicial proceedings became more common. The societal commitment to justice weakened. People could no longer depend on receiving what they needed from a neighbor; many neighbors had little to spare. In the monarchical economy, "covenantal and kinship institutions that flourished in the days of the [tribal federation] were in part displaced by royal institutions and in part transmuted into new forms, maintaining some continuity with federation values and social structures but reshaped to conform to a monarchical superstructure."[8]

In both the northern and southern kingdoms, the monarchic political structure continued until these nations were eventually conquered by more powerful neighbors. The northern kingdom, Israel, fell to Assyria in 721 BCE, and Judah, the southern kingdom, was conquered by Babylon in 587 BCE. In 539 BCE, fifty years after the fall of Jerusalem, King Cyrus of Persia captured Babylon and allowed the exiled Israelites to return to Jerusalem. As we will see, the oppressive economic conditions persisted.

THE RESPONSE: THE PROPHETS AND THE LAW

The injustices under the monarchs led to two responses, both of which were seen as originating with Yahweh: the prophecies of the classical prophets

---

7. Milgrom, *Leviticus 23–27*, 2243–44.
8. Cross, *Epic to Canon*, 20.

of the eighth and seventh centuries and new laws believed to originate with Yahweh. We begin with the prophets.

The Prophets

The prophets were men (there may have been women as well) who believed themselves called, even compelled, to be the voice of God: to hear God's words and then proclaim them to the people of Israel and Judah. But the prophet was more than a mouthpiece: "In speaking, the prophet reveals God. . . . In his words, *the invisible God becomes audible.* He does not prove or argue. . . . The authority of the prophet is in the Presence his words reveal. There are no proofs for the existence of the God of Abraham. There are only witnesses. . . . The prophet is a witness, and his words a testimony— to *His* power and judgment, to *His* justice and mercy."[9] A prophet partici- pates in God's passion for justice.

The prophets had a four-part message. First, they charged the Israelites in the northern and southern kingdoms with failing to keep their prom- ises to Yahweh and breaking their covenant. Their central indictment— God's central indictment—was the Israelites' failure to love God above all else and obey God's law requiring social and economic justice: "Hear, O heavens, and listen, O earth; for the Lord has spoken: I reared children and brought them up, but they have rebelled against me. . . . They have rejected the instruction of the Lord of hosts, and have despised the word of the Holy One of Israel" (Isa 1:2; 5:24b). The prophets charged the whole Israelite society with disobedience. But they focused on the king and other wealthy elites who were abusing the poor, taking land from peasant farm families, exploiting workers, cheating in commercial transactions, and participating in dishonest judicial proceedings. The prophets were critical of a system that allowed some to feast while others were hungry, some to be wealthy while others were poor.

Because the prophets called for a radical reordering of society and an end to domination and exploitation, their message threatened the elites who engaged in and benefited from injustice. The prophets' calling was difficult and dangerous. Jeremiah received a death threat (Jer 26:11), faced an assas- sination attempt (Jer 11:18–22), spent time in the stocks (Jer 20:2), and was thrown down a dry well (Jer 38:6). He repeatedly lamented his call

9. Heschel, *Prophets*, 1:22. Emphasis in the original.

to be a prophet but found he could not stop speaking (Jer 20:7–11). Amos was accused of conspiring against the king and advised to flee the country (Amos 7:10–13). Jeremiah reports that the prophet Uriah, under threat of death, fled to Egypt, where he was found, brought back to Judah, and killed (Jer 26:20–23). The Gospel writers tell of Jesus's repeated references to prophets who were killed by the wealthy and powerful people they criticized (Matt 5:12; 23:29–35; Luke 11:47–50; 13:34).

The second part of the prophets' message was a call for repentance and obedience to the covenant. Hosea called, "Return, O Israel, to the Lord your God, for you have stumbled because of your iniquity" (Hos 14:1). Jeremiah did likewise: "Return, faithless Israel, says the Lord. I will not look on you in anger, for I am merciful, says the Lord; I will not be angry forever" (Jer 3:12). The prophets sought to reconcile humans and God: "For if you truly amend your ways and your doings, if you truly act justly one with another, if you do not oppress the alien, the orphan, and the widow, or shed innocent blood in this place, and if you do not go after other gods to your own hurt, then I will dwell with you in this place, in the land that I gave of old to your ancestors forever and ever" (Jer 7:5–7).

Third, they told of God's coming judgment (Amos 5:21–24) and warned that continuing on the present course was leading to God's punishment: "Therefore because you trample on the poor and take from them levies of grain, you have built houses of hewn stone, but you shall not live in them; you have planted pleasant vineyards, but you shall not drink their wine. For I know how many are your transgressions, and how great are your sins" (Amos 5:11–12). According to Abraham Joshua Heschel, "The divine [laws] are not mere recommendations for man, but express divine concern, which realized or repudiated, is of personal importance to Him."[10]

As discussed in the introduction, one biblical understanding of God is as a judge and disciplinarian who punishes disobedience. This view, which is prominent in the oracles of the prophets, may be due at least in part to the writers and editors who continued to revise the words of the prophets during and after the fall of Judah, the destruction of Jerusalem, and the Babylonian exile. They sought to understand how God could have allowed such a catastrophe to happen and came to interpret it as punishment for their disobedience to the covenant (2 Kgs 24; Jer 25:1–14). Today we understand

10. Heschel, 1:24.

it as the consequence of Palestine's unfortunate geographic location as a vulnerable neighbor to larger, more powerful, land-hungry empires.

The fourth part of the prophets' message was an assurance of God's faithfulness to Israel, regardless of whatever was coming in the near term: "[The Israelites] shall again live beneath my shadow, they shall flourish as a garden; they shall blossom like the vine, their fragrance shall be like the wine of Lebanon" (Hos 14:7). God would, at some future time, bless the Israelites with abundance and peace. Amos also voiced the promise: "The time is surely coming, says the Lord, when . . . I will restore the fortunes of my people Israel, and they shall rebuild the ruined cities and inhabit them; they shall plant vineyards and drink their wine, and they shall make gardens and eat their fruit" (Amos 9:13–14).

The prophets repeatedly warned that worship had little significance unless it was rooted in social and economic justice: "I hate, I despise your festivals, and I take no delight in your solemn assemblies. Even though you offer me your burnt offerings and grain offerings, I will not accept them; and the offerings of well-being of your fatted animals I will not look upon. Take away from me the noise of your songs; I will not listen to the melody of your harps. But let justice roll down like waters, and righteousness like an ever-flowing stream" (Amos 5:21–24).

Devotional practices, sacrifices, songs of praise, and worship rituals were empty unless accompanied by social justice. Micah articulated what must have been a common question and then provided the answer: "'With what shall I come before the Lord, and bow myself before God on high? Shall I come before him with burnt offerings, with calves a year old? Will the Lord be pleased with thousands of rams, with ten thousands of rivers of oil? Shall I give my firstborn for my transgression, the fruit of my body for the sin of my soul?' He has told you, O mortal, what is good; and what does the Lord require of you but to do justice, and to love kindness, and to walk humbly with your God?" (Mic 6:6–8).

The prophets' call for justice and their criticism of cultic practices were not a condemnation of worship but a matter of relative emphasis.[11] Worship was central to their relationship with Yahweh. But so was the practice of justice. Worship without justice was offensive to Yahweh. Isaiah spoke God's warning: "When you stretch out your hands, I will hide my eyes from you; even though you make many prayers, I will not listen; your hands are

11. Meier, *Marginal Jew*, 4:44.

full of blood. Wash yourselves; make yourselves clean; remove the evil of your doings from before my eyes; cease to do evil, learn to do good; seek justice, rescue the oppressed, defend the orphan, plead for the widow" (Isa 1:15–17). God desires sincere worship that expresses itself in justice and compassion toward one's neighbor.

The Law

The second response to the social and economic injustices under the monarchy was new law. Priests and scribes, possibly influenced by the prophets' oracles, sought God's revelations and worked to discern new laws to guide society from injustice to justice, from disobedience to faithfulness. The Israelites continued to see their law as a gift from God, as instructions to shape a holy and just society.

The law in Exodus had nurtured a settled, egalitarian agricultural society of largely self-sufficient communities. But those very ancient laws did not address many of the abuses that had arisen in the monarchical economy, such as false weights and measures, delayed and unpaid wages, and widespread loss of ancestral land. New threats to well-being required new laws. The instructions for creating a just economy had to be revised, created anew by God to fit the new circumstances, and discerned anew by God's people.

The laws that originated during the time of the monarchy are found today in the books of Leviticus (chapters 17–26, called the Holiness Code) and Deuteronomy (the Deuteronomic Code, chapters 12–26, and the speeches of Moses). *Deuteronomy* means "second law"; it was always seen as a retelling and reinterpretation (for the seventh century BCE) of the older law in Exodus. Deuteronomy 5:1–21 is largely a restatement of the Ten Commandments. The biblical writers depict all these laws as originating centuries earlier with Moses on Mount Sinai (called Horeb in Deuteronomy), emphasizing their importance as a revelation from God transmitted to Israel by the great prophet Moses. Again we see that for God, a just society had religious significance, and doing justice was a central element of religious practice. We begin by examining the response to the rise in poverty from the prophets and the law.

POVERTY

The Prophets

The prophets spoke God's searing indictments of those who oppress the poor and vulnerable:

> For scoundrels are found among my people; they take over the goods of others. Like fowlers they set a trap; they catch human beings. Like a cage full of birds, their houses are full of treachery; therefore they have become great and rich, they have grown fat and sleek. They know no limits in deeds of wickedness; they do not judge with justice the cause of the orphan, to make it prosper, and they do not defend the rights of the needy. Shall I not punish them for these things? says the Lord, and shall I not bring retribution on a nation such as this? (Jer 5:26–29)

The prophets' outrage—God's outrage—is shown in their disturbing imagery. Micah is particularly graphic: "Listen, you heads of Jacob and rulers of the house of Israel! Should you not know justice?—you who hate the good and love the evil, who tear the skin off my people, and the flesh off their bones; who eat the flesh of my people, flay their skin off them, break their bones in pieces, and chop them up like meat in a kettle, like flesh in a caldron. Then they will cry to the Lord, but he will not answer them; he will hide his face from them at that time, because they have acted wickedly" (Mic 3:1–4). Isaiah also spoke forcefully of God's anger: "The Lord enters into judgment with the elders and princes of his people: It is you who have devoured the vineyard [Israel]; the spoil of the poor is in your houses. What do you mean by crushing my people, by grinding the face of the poor? says the Lord God of hosts" (Isa 3:14–15).

Amos condemns those who "sell the righteous for silver, and the needy for a pair of sandals—they who trample the head of the poor into the dust of the earth, and push the afflicted out of the way" (Amos 2:6b–7a). He continues, "Alas for those who lie on beds of ivory, and lounge on their couches, and eat lambs from the flock, and calves from the stall; who sing idle songs to the sound of the harp, and like David improvise on instruments of music; who drink wine from bowls, and anoint themselves with the finest oils, but they are not grieved over the ruin of Joseph! Therefore they shall now be the first to go into exile, and the revelry of the loungers shall pass away" (Amos 6:4–7).

These are powerful indictments. The prophets did not soften their message to avoid offending the powerful. They were not afraid to clearly and defiantly side with the poor (and with God) in opposition to the wealthy abusers. For them, there was no middle ground, no compromise with injustice. The stakes for both the rich and the poor were too high.

The Law

The new law in Leviticus and Deuteronomy—including the teachings depicted by the writers as spoken by Moses—provides both continuity with the law of Exodus and new, enhanced protections and expanded support for the poor.

Continuity

The two new law codes and teachings reiterated many of the protections of the poor that had been central to the law in Exodus:

- The nonpoor were to lend to the poor and charge no interest; Deuteronomy makes lending and giving to the poor an obligation, not an optional response (Deut 15:7–11; 23:19–20; cf. Lev 25:36–37; Ps 15:5; Neh 5:7–11).
- Lenders' access to borrowers' collateral was restricted. The types of collateral to be safeguarded were expanded from the borrower's cloak (Deut 24:12–13, 17) to also include a mill or upper millstone necessary to grind grain to make flour for bread, a major component of peasants' diet (Deut 24:6). Taking a mill or millstone would be equivalent to "taking a life in pledge." The lender was also prohibited from entering a borrower's home to take the collateral, providing protection for the dignity of the poor (Deut 24:10–11).
- Widows and orphans continued to receive special protections (Deut 10:17–18; 14:29; 24:17; 26:12–13; 27:19).
- Everyone was obligated to honor (and care for) one's parents (Deut 5:16).

Extensions of the Law
The new laws added significant new provisions to relieve the suffering associated with poverty and encourage sharing.

Gleaning
A new protection given to anyone who was poor, landless, or an immigrant was the right to glean food from farmers' fields. To glean was to enter private property—fields, orchards, and vineyards—and eat. Farmers were required to harvest with gleaners in mind. The landholder was not to harvest too comprehensively and leave too little for the gleaners: "When you reap the harvest of your land, you shall not reap to the very edges of your field, or gather the gleanings of your harvest. You shall not strip your vineyard bare, or gather the fallen grapes of your vineyard; you shall leave them for the poor and the alien: I am the Lord your God" (Lev 19:9–10; 23:22; Deut 24:19–22).

Gleaning was not theft; it was not wrong. Blocking the access of the poor to glean was wrong. Since Yahweh owned all land, there was not a large difference between being a landholder and being landless. In the new law, "both groups are seen as two different kinds of sojourners with different degrees of access to property. [The right to glean] relativizes [private property] claims."[12] Both those with and those without land were dependent on God for food and all material resources. They did not confront one another with competing claims to material resources but shared what God provided.

Portuguese Nobel laureate José Saramago provides a more modern tale of gleaning in his 1980 novel, *Raised from the Ground*. Set in the early years of the twentieth century during a time of political repression and economic distress in Portugal, on a dark night when there is no food in the house, a father and son go to pick up acorns fallen from trees on private property. The father assures his son, "Picking up acorns from the ground isn't stealing, and even if it was, hunger is a good enough reason to steal, he who steals out of hunger will find forgiveness in heaven, I know that isn't quite how the saying goes, but it should, and if I'm a thief because I stole some acorns, then so is the owner of the acorns, who neither made the earth nor planted

12. Jonathan Burnside, *God, Justice, and Society: Aspects of Law and Legality in the Bible* (New York: Oxford University Press, 2011), 220.

the tree nor tended it."[13] Unfortunately, the pair are caught by guards and punished. God's reign is not yet fully present.

Tithe to the Poor
There was a second way in which the law expanded the opportunities for the poor to access food. Every third year, all farm households were obligated to bring a tithe (one-tenth) of their entire harvest to be stored in a central location, where it could be accessed and eaten during the year by the poor, immigrants, and priests who had received no land allotment: "Every third year you shall bring out the full tithe of your produce for that year, and store it within your towns; the Levites [priests], because they have no allotment or inheritance with you, as well as the resident aliens, the orphans, and the widows in your towns, may come and eat their fill so that the Lord your God may bless you in all the work that you undertake" (Deut 14:28–29).

Only after providing for those who, for whatever reasons, were unable to provide for themselves can we expect God to bless us with abundance:

> When you have finished paying all the tithe of your produce in the third year (which is the year of the tithe), giving it to the Levites, the aliens, the orphans, and the widows, so that they may eat their fill within your towns, then you shall say before the Lord your God: "I have removed the *sacred* portion from the house, and I have given it to the Levites, the resident aliens, the orphans, and the widows, in accordance with your entire commandment that you commanded me. . . . Look down from your holy habitation, from heaven, and bless your people Israel and the ground that you have given us, as you swore to our ancestors—a land flowing with milk and honey." (Deut 26:12–13, 15; emphasis added)

The portion of the harvest given to support the poor and landless was "sacred," set apart and dedicated to God and God's purposes, as is the share of our taxes that does the same.

---

13. José Saramago, *Raised from the Ground*, trans. Margaret Jull Costa (Boston: Houghton Mifflin Harcourt, 2012) 330–31.

Release of Bound Laborers with Resources

As in Exodus, the law in Deuteronomy calls for laborers in debt bondage to be released after six years of work (Deut 15:12–15; cf. Neh 5:1–5; Jer 34:14).[14] Deuteronomy provides an important additional protection for the newly released laborers. A former master could not send his released laborer off empty-handed but was told, "Provide liberally out of your flock, your threshing floor, and your wine press, thus giving to him some of the bounty with which the Lord your God has blessed you" (Deut 15:4). This provision of the law helped the newly released laborer avoid a return to poverty.

The law also makes clear that even though the term *slave* is used in Exodus and Deuteronomy in reference to Israelites, in fact, Israelites cannot be enslaved by other Israelites. They had been enslaved in Egypt before being redeemed, freed by Yahweh for all time. Thus they are servants of God and cannot be enslaved to other Israelites (Lev 25:39–42, 55). "I am the Lord your God who brought you out of the land of Egypt, to be their slaves no more; I have broken the bars of your yoke and made you walk erect" (Lev 26:13).

Debt Cancellation

Under the monarchy, the problem of debt, the loss of land and livelihood, and economic destitution had become so severe that debt cancellation was instituted for the first time: "Every seventh year you shall grant a remission of debts. And this is the manner of the remission: every creditor shall remit the claim that is held against a neighbor, not exacting it of a neighbor who is a member of the community, because the Lord's remission has been proclaimed" (Deut 15:1–2). Debt cancellation became an important component of the Sabbath Year.

Debt remission or cancellation removed a lien either on a peasant's land, which could lead to foreclosure, or on a person, which could end in bondage.

---

14. Leviticus (25:35–43, 47–55) describes various scenarios related to redemption of kin. If one clan member indebted to another was unable to repay a debt, he remained bound until the Year of Jubilee, which could be as many as forty-nine years in the future. This contradicts the simple provisions in Deuteronomy and Exodus that freed bound laborers after six years of service (Exod 21:2; Deut 15:12–15). We have noted that as the egalitarian economy of the tribal federation became increasingly unjust under the monarchies, the law became progressively more protective of the vulnerable and provided additional routes by which the poor could once again thrive. This provision in Leviticus, which is contradicted by the one in Deuteronomy, is the only exception to this trend.

It gave debtors a fresh start and prevented destitution and the creation of a permanent underclass of the poor. These benefits to individuals and society were more important than the enforcement of a contractual obligation to repay a debt. Moreover, lenders were warned they should not hesitate to make a loan even if the seventh year was near: "Be careful that you do not entertain a mean thought, thinking, 'The seventh year, the year of remission, is near,' and therefore view your needy neighbor with hostility and give nothing; your neighbor might cry to the Lord against you, and you would incur guilt" (Deut 15:9). Lending to those in need was an obligation that could not be set aside out of fears concerning repayment and the approach of the Sabbath Year's debt cancellation.

The cancellation of debt and release from debt bondage were not only practiced in Israel. They occurred infrequently and at the whim of the king in other areas of the ancient Near East as well.[15] But only in Israel were they a regular occurrence and a binding obligation for every Israelite, as required by Yahweh.

Protection of the Vulnerable

Importantly, the law provided protection for people at the times when they were most vulnerable. If someone needed essential material resources, such as food, and was forced to borrow, he might easily be compelled to agree to exploitative conditions. But the provisions of the law addressed precisely these occasions by limiting the labor and resources that could be extracted from vulnerable people. Interest could not be charged on loans even if a desperate borrower might have been willing to pay it. Debt and bondage were to end after six years, even if a poor borrower could have been compelled to agree to a longer term. The law placed restrictions on a creditor's access to a debtor's collateral precisely because a desperate borrower could not have required them of a lender.

The law did not recognize what we today call freedom (or liberty) of contract.[16] That is, the law prohibited some contracts to which two parties might otherwise have consented because they were exploitative. The law

---

15. Milgrom, *Leviticus 23–27*, 2168; Graeber, *Debt*, 65.
16. See Samuel Bagenstos, *Lochner Lives On: Lochner Presumption of Equal Power Lives in Labor Law and Undermines Constitutional, Statutory, and Common Law Workplace* (Washington, DC: EPI, October 7, 2020); and Jack Beatty, *The Age of Betrayal: The Triumph of Money in America, 1865–1900* (New York: Alfred A. Knopf, 2007).

recognized that "free" markets were riddled with coercion and that despairing and desperate people could not make free choices; they were not free. God's law requires society to protect the vulnerable.

Sabbath Year

The new law continued the obligation to observe the Sabbath Year (Lev 25:1–7). No crops were planted, and all people, including the poor and landless, ate from what grew in the fallow and untended fields, orchards, and vineyards. As we have seen, during the time of the monarchy, the Sabbath Year was also the time of debt cancellation and release of bound laborers. Biblical writers confirm that the Sabbath Year was observed during at least some periods of Israel's history (Neh 10:31). By the mid- or late-monarchical era, it was celebrated at the same time throughout the land.[17]

The Sabbath Year continued to be a time of universal rest and provision of food to all. But unavoidably, less food was produced than in other years. People were forced to trust that they would have the food they needed and that Yahweh would be with them during what could be difficult times. The Sabbath Year was a bold affirmation that maximizing agricultural output was not an economic or social goal, even in a society that may have, at times, faced food scarcity. There were higher values, including rest, a deepening relationship with Yahweh, and the enjoyment of life, even if it meant living with fewer material resources. To thrive and live in abundance did not mean to focus on maximizing society's wealth or a family's possessions. The production of material goods, even food, was subordinated to living with the recognition that life is about much more than possessions and that all material resources depend on God.

Eradication of Poverty

There is one more very important teaching about poverty in the book of Deuteronomy. The writers of the book place it within a speech given by Moses as the Israelites prepare to cross the Jordan River and enter the promised land at the end of their long wilderness journey. These passages are the clearest and most detailed discussion of poverty in the Old Testament and form the basis for Jesus's teaching as well. This is the biblical mandate concerning the poor:

---

17. Gnuse, *You Shall Not Steal*, 33; Jacob Milgrom, *Leviticus 17–22: A New Translation with Introduction and Commentary*, Anchor Bible 3A (New York: Doubleday, 2000), 1391.

There will, however, be no one in need among you, because the Lord is sure to bless you in the land that the Lord your God is giving you as a possession to occupy, if only you will obey the Lord your God by diligently observing this entire commandment that I command you today. . . . If there is among you anyone in need, a member of your community in any of your towns within the land that the Lord your God is giving you, do not be hard-hearted or tight-fisted toward your needy neighbor. You should rather open your hand, willingly lending enough to meet the need, whatever it may be. . . . Give liberally and be ungrudging when you do so, for on this account the Lord your God will bless you in all your work and in all that you undertake. *Since there will never cease to be some in need on the earth, I therefore* command *you, "Open your hand to the poor and needy neighbor in your land."* (Deut 15:4–5, 7–8, 10–11; emphasis added)

Let's go through this carefully. Moses begins by declaring that there will be no one in need because God's abundance provides enough for all to thrive—if we obey God's law. But then Moses acknowledges that there will be people in need. Stuff happens. Some people will always be falling into poverty. Therefore, we must always be giving—opening our hands, our hearts, our wallets, and our social safety nets; sharing liberally and ungrudgingly; generously giving enough to meet the need. It could not be clearer. For Moses (and the writers of Deuteronomy), giving was not optional, not something to do when we're having a good day and feeling flush. It was obligated by God. Read again the last sentence in the passage above: "Since there will never cease to be some in need on the earth, I therefore *command* you, 'Open your hand to the poor and needy neighbor in your land'" (Deut 15:10–11). Moses is commanding this behavior. This is the law of God.

Poverty eradication does not happen once and for all. Misfortune is constantly befalling our neighbors and ourselves. Rather, through the ceaseless, open-handed sharing of God's resources, need is transformed into plenty and misery into flourishing.

God's abundance is enough for all our needs. There is no scarcity. But the problem in Israel under the monarchs and still the problem today is poverty in the midst of abundance, the maldistribution of God's material resources. Moses promised abundance "if only you will obey" God's law. As we will see below, Jesus made a similar declaration, asserting that God provides abundantly and no one needs to worry about having enough if we make seeking God's reign our priority (Matt 6:25–33; Luke 12:22–31). God's law is the way of abundance.

According to Walter Brueggemann, "If we are to identify what is most characteristic and most distinctive in the life and vocation of this part-ner [Israel] of YHWH, it is the remarkable equation of love of God with love of neighbor, which is enacted through the exercise of distributive jus-tice of social goods, social power, and social access to those without lever-age; those without social leverage are entitled to such treatment simply by the fact of their membership in the community. . . . Israel, as a community under obligation [to YHWH], is indeed a community of social revolution in the world."[18]

LIVELIHOOD AND THRIVING

To avoid poverty, people must be able to work and support themselves and their families at a level that allows them to thrive. They must have a liveli-hood that enables thriving. In the highland covenantal society, every clan had a landholding, passed down through generations, which enabled family members to produce all the material resources they needed, including food, shelter, clothing, and fuel. Everyone contributed their labor to support a thriving family.

During the time of the monarchy, agriculture continued to be the only possible means of support for the vast majority of the population. But a growing number of peasant farm families had lost their ancestral land. Family self-sufficiency and economic security—which always depended on numerous factors affecting crops, herds, workers, and in times of need, the generosity of neighbors—were replaced by poverty and precariousness. The rising value of land, due to the opportunities for commercial agricul-ture and international trade, created the incentive for creditors to put land at risk and foreclose on it. Preventing the loss of ancestral land was essen-tial for keeping families out of poverty; returning the dispossessed to their land was the most important way—nearly the only way—to end poverty and return a family to a life of thriving.

18. Brueggemann, *Theology of the Old Testament*, 424.

The Prophets

Peasant families' loss of land to their wealthy creditors did not go unnoticed by the prophets. Micah declared, "Alas for those who devise wickedness and evil deeds on their beds! When the morning dawns, they perform it, because it is in their power. They covet fields, and seize them; houses, and take them away; they oppress householder and house, people and their inheritance" (Mic 2:1–2). Isaiah also denounced the large landholders who drove small farmers off the land and announced God's threat of punishment: "Ah, you who join house to house, who add field to field, until there is room for no one but you, and you are left to live alone in the midst of the land! The Lord of hosts has sworn in my hearing: Surely many houses shall be desolate, large and beautiful houses, without inhabitant" (Isa 5:8–9).

The Law: Continuity and Extensions

To promote thriving, the law continued to obligate everyone to observe a Sabbath Day of rest each week (Lev 23:3; Deut 5:12–15) and to prohibit coveting (Deut 5:21). The new law extended the protections of peasant landholdings, including provisions for the return of land that had been lost.

Land May Not Be Bought and Sold

The most basic protection against the loss of land was the prohibition on its purchase and sale. The Israelites believed that everything, including land, belonged to God. Since God owned the land and had allotted it to clans, it was to remain with the clans. Landholders were tenants on the land allotted to them by God. Land could not be bought or sold, although it could be leased: "The land shall not be sold in perpetuity, for the land is mine; with me you are but aliens and tenants" (Lev 25:23). Within an extended family, land was an eternal inheritance, an everlasting assurance of economic security. The belief that land was inalienable, not to be sold or even given away, was strongly held (1 Kgs 21). Given the prohibition against land sales, the primary means by which land changed hands was through confiscation by the king and foreclosure on unpaid debt that had been secured with land.

Redemption of Land

A new provision to preserve a clan's landholding was the obligation to redeem land that was lost by one's kin. If a farm family was forced to sell a portion of its land to pay a debt, then one of their kin was obligated to buy the land (redeem it) so it stayed within the clan: "If anyone of your kin falls into difficulty and sells a piece of property, then the next of kin shall come and redeem what the relative has sold" (Lev 25:25; cf. Ruth 4:1–6; Jer 32:6–15).

The Jubilee Year

Among the multiple provisions in the law that safeguarded ancestral landholdings—the prohibition on the sale of land, the cancellation of debt, prohibition on interest, the obligation of redemption, and prohibitions on fraud—the greatest protection against the permanent loss of ancestral land was the Year of Jubilee (Lev 25:8–17). The Jubilee Year occurred every fiftieth year, after seven seven-year cycles of Sabbath Years. It was a time of liberation, especially liberation from poverty among those who had lost their land. The Jubilee Year began with trumpet blasts and the proclamation of liberty: "You shall have the trumpet sounded throughout all your land. And you shall hallow the fiftieth year and you shall proclaim *liberty* throughout the land to all its inhabitants. It shall be a jubilee for you: you shall return, every one of you, to your property and every one of you to your family" (Lev 25:9b–10; emphasis added).

It was truly a time of rejoicing. As in any Sabbath Year, debts were canceled, bound laborers freed, and farms fallowed as people and animals rested from their labor. But during the Year of Jubilee, the year of liberation, rural land that had been lost by the original landholder for any reason was returned.[19] The foundation of liberty was land and the abundance it signified and enabled. God's generosity in giving the land and the requirement that an extended family could not lose their land ensured that everyone would have abundance, livelihood, and economic security. Liberty and freedom were possible only when one's material needs were assured.

The Jubilee and Sabbath Years were divinely ordained, regularly occurring acts of justice and liberation that permanently improved the economic condition of the poor. These social obligations were not acts of charity performed by the "haves" to temporarily ease the distress of the "have-nots" but justice-making institutions and structures embedded in society. Ensuring

---

19. The Jubilee provisions did not protect urban property from being sold and lost; God owned the land but not cities, which were created by humans (Lev 25:29–34).

everyone's needs were met, that everyone was able to thrive, was a concern of God and an obligation of society.

Scholars do not know whether the Jubilee requirement to restore land to original landholders was ever practiced. Unfortunately, people and societies sometimes fail to do the will of God. But we do know with certainty that the return of land and all it provided to a farm family was part of God's law, one component of God's intentions for a first-millennium BCE just economy. Even if the Jubilee was never practiced, we cannot ignore this law and its teaching. The laws in the Pentateuch were the road map for moving from an unjust economic system to one that embodied God's vision of justice. Not following all the road map's directions did not indicate the instructions were incorrect or signify the ultimate destination was the wrong one. It just meant people would not get to where they hoped to go, society would not arrive at the destination God envisioned for it. The Jubilee Year was a critically important (although, unfortunately, probably never enacted) way for people to regain their land and other material essentials. It was an important component of a just economy. The Jubilee Year as well as many other provisions of the law placed limits on material inequality.

THE ECONOMIC SYSTEM

The Prophets

The prophets condemned greed, dishonesty, fraud, and corruption: "From the least to the greatest of them, everyone is greedy for unjust gain; and from prophet to priest, everyone deals falsely" (Jer 6:13). Even people singled out by God for special care—widows and orphans—were targets of exploitation. All the prophets criticized greed and the maltreatment of the most vulnerable: "Everyone loves a bribe and runs after gifts. They do not defend the orphan, and the widow's cause does not come before them" (Isa 1:23b; cf. Isa 5:20a, 23, 25; Jer 5:28b; Mic 7:3). Society's elites were singled out for criticism: "Hear this, you rulers of the house of Jacob and chiefs of the house of Israel, who abhor justice and pervert all equity, who build Zion with blood and Jerusalem with wrong! Its rulers give judgment for a bribe, its priests teach for a price, its prophets give oracles for money; yet they lean upon the Lord and say, 'Surely the Lord is with us! No harm shall come upon us.' Therefore because of you Zion shall be plowed as a field;

Jerusalem shall become a heap of ruins, and the mountain of the house a wooded height" (Mic 3:9–12).

Political leaders, the writers of laws and statutes, were also corrupt and condemned: "Ah, you who make iniquitous decrees, who write oppressive statutes, to turn aside the needy from justice and to rob the poor of my people of their right, that widows may be your spoil, and that you may make the orphans your prey! What will you do on the day of punishment, in the calamity that will come from far away? To whom will you flee for help, and where will you leave your wealth, so as not to crouch among the prisoners or fall among the slain?" (Isa 10:1–4a).

The prophets also criticized merchants' use of dishonest weights and measures. Food, seed, and many other goods were purchased by weight or volume. Dishonest weights and measures would shortchange buyers, who received less than they paid for, and advantage sellers, who were paid for more than they actually sold. Moreover, when families were forced to borrow foodstuffs, the amount they borrowed—that is, the size of their debt—would have been measured by these same fair (or biased) weights and measures. In addition, grains might have been adulterated with inedible and infertile husks and chaff.

The prophets spoke of these abuses: "Hear this, you that trample on the needy, and bring to ruin the poor of the land, saying, . . . 'We will make the ephah small and the shekel great, and practice deceit with false balances, buying the poor for silver and the needy for a pair of sandals, and selling the sweepings [chaff] of the wheat.' The Lord has sworn by the pride of Jacob: Surely I will never forget any of their deeds" (Amos 8:4, 5b–7).[20] Also from Micah: "Can I [God] tolerate wicked scales and a bag of dishonest weights? Your wealthy are full of violence; your inhabitants speak lies, with tongues of deceit in their mouths. Therefore I have begun to strike you down, making you desolate because of your sins" (Mic 6:11–13).

The Law

Laws originating during the monarchic period addressed the rise in corruption, fraud, bribery, and other distortions of justice, restating provisions of

---

20. The ephah is a dry measure equal to about four-fifths of a bushel. The shekel is a coin and also a unit of measurement equal to about eleven grams or slightly less than half an ounce. A "great" shekel would have been one that was heavier than the official one.

the earlier law in Exodus and extending the law in new directions to cover new economic abuses that had arisen since the time of the tribal federation.

Continuity

The law in Exodus had specifically prohibited the bribing of judges and other officials, and this was also emphasized in the new law codes. Judges and officials "shall render just decisions for the people. You must not distort justice; you must not show partiality; and you must not accept bribes, for a bribe blinds the eyes of the wise and subverts the cause of those who are in the right. Justice, and only justice, you shall pursue, so that you may live and occupy the land that the Lord your God is giving you" (Deut 16:18–20; cf. Lev 19:15; Deut 10:17). The eighth commandment was restated: "You shall not steal" (Lev 19:11, 13; Deut 5:19).

Extensions of the Law

Honest Commercial Practices

The new law addressed the problem of dishonest weights and measures: "You shall not have in your bag two kinds of weights, large and small. You shall not have in your house two kinds of measures, large and small. You shall have only a full and honest weight; you shall have only a full and honest measure" (Deut 25:13–15a). The writers of Leviticus also criticized dishonest practices: "You shall not cheat in measuring length, weight, or quantity. You shall have honest balances, honest weights, an honest ephah, and an honest hin:[21] I am the Lord your God, who brought you out of the land of Egypt. You shall keep all my statutes and all my ordinances, and observe them: I am the Lord" (Lev 19:35–37). Again, "you shall not deal falsely; . . . You shall not defraud your neighbor" (Lev 19:11b, 13a).

The new law also prohibited moving stones and other markers indicating the boundaries of ancestral landholdings: "You must not move your neighbor's boundary marker, set up by former generations, on the property that will be allotted to you in the land that the Lord your God is giving you to possess" (Deut 19:14).

Prompt Payment of Workers' Wages

In the tribal federation, working for wages was uncommon. But as peasants lost their land and the elites' landholdings grew, people needed jobs, and

---

21. A hin is a liquid measure equal to approximately one gallon.

laborers were needed to work the estates. The new laws included provisions concerning wages. Workers were to be paid daily and fairly. Even to hold a worker's wages into the evening was wrong, since poor laborers and immigrants needed each day's wages to buy each day's necessities: "You shall not withhold the wages of poor and needy laborers, whether other Israelites or aliens who reside in your land in one of your towns. You shall pay them their wages daily before sunset, because they are poor and their livelihood depends on them; otherwise they might cry to the Lord against you, and you would incur guilt" (Deut 24:14–15). Or briefly, "You shall not keep for yourself the wages of a laborer until morning" (Lev 19:13c).

No One Is above the Law
Everyone was obligated to follow the law. No one, not even the king, was above the law. But because the king's wealth and power might have made him especially susceptible to disobedience, and because of his critically important role in society, the king most of all had to know and follow the law: "[The king] shall have a copy of this law [the book of Deuteronomy] written for him in the presence of the Levitical priests. It shall remain with him and he shall read in it all the days of his life, so that he may learn to fear the Lord his God, diligently observing all the words of this law and these statutes, neither exalting himself above other members of the community nor turning aside from the commandment, either to the right or to the left, so that he and his descendants may reign long over his kingdom in Israel" (Deut 17:18b–20).

Strangers, Foreigners, and Aliens
The new law continued the obligation placed on Israelites to care for and not abuse the non-Israelites who lived among them, called foreigners, aliens, and strangers. They were to be treated fairly: "When an alien resides with you in your land, you shall not oppress the alien" (Lev 19:33). But the new law went much further: "The alien who resides with you shall be to you as the citizen among you; you shall love the alien as yourself, for you were aliens in the land of Egypt: I am the Lord your God" (Lev 19:34; Deut 10:19).

There was to be "one law" for citizens and aliens alike (Lev 24:22; Deut 1:16; 10:17–19; 24:17; 27:19; cf. Num 15:16, 29). Aliens were to be allowed to rest on the Sabbath and during the Sabbath Year (Lev 16:29; Deut 5:14). Aliens enjoyed the right to glean as Israelites did (Lev 19:10; 23:22; Deut 24:19–21), and the food collected in every third year's tithe was available to the poor, including aliens (Deut 14:28–29; 26:12–13). No one, not even the king, was above the law, and no one, not even a foreigner, was below it.

Love of Neighbors

It is important to note that it was during this time of growing poverty, rising inequality, loss of ancestral land, and rising economic insecurity that the law stipulated what may be the most sweeping and rigorous protection of the vulnerable: "You shall love your neighbor as yourself: I am the Lord. You shall keep my statutes" (Lev 19:18b–19a). Jesus identified this law in Leviticus as the second most important, exceeded only by the command to love God with all our being (Matt 22:34–40; Mark 12:28–31; Luke 10:25–28).

Ultimately, the law cannot anticipate and legislate against all possible adverse circumstances and conditions that people might encounter. To ensure abundant life for all people and creation, society and all its members must go deeper than the letter of the law: "The written law is a witness to an unwritten law. The [law] can be understood as testimony to the justice and righteousness God requires of God's people. If one were to adopt this perspective, one would be bound not to the actual provisions of the law but to the principles and values informing them. The search for God's will would be grounded in the God already known, yet open to new insight into the order of justice and right that is the norm of all law."[22] In regard to material well-being and economic justice, this might be summed up as loving all our neighbors as we love ourselves, loving as God does.

22. Patrick, *Old Testament Law*, 253–54.

Chapter 3

JESUS AND ROMAN PALESTINE

PALESTINE UNDER THE ROMAN EMPIRE

We now move forward in time another six hundred to seven hundred years to the first century CE, the time of Jesus. Palestine had been under the control of the Roman Empire since 63 BCE. Herod the Great, whom Rome appointed king in 37 BCE, used terror and brutality to promote the empire's economic and political interests as well as his own. After Herod's death in 4 BCE, Rome divided Herod's kingdom into smaller territories and appointed Herod's son Herod Antipas to rule Galilee. Judea and its capital, Jerusalem, were ruled by a series of Roman governors, including Pontius Pilate.

First-century Palestinian society was characterized by a strict social, economic, and political stratification; its key characteristic was marked inequality. There were essentially two classes, two opposing societies. The wealthy, ruling elite—1 to 2 percent of the population—included the ruler of the region, his family, close friends, key government officials, the high priests, and a few wealthy landholders and merchants.[1] Many of this elite group were Romans, but it included Israelites also. These people held all political and economic power, prestige, and privilege. The institutions of government were used by the elite to protect their privileged position and extract wealth from those who produced it, the nonelites, including some

---

1. Estimates of the size of social classes are from Richard L. Rohrbaugh, "The Jesus Tradition: Gospel Writers' Strategies of Persuasion," in *The Early Christian World*, 2nd ed., ed. Philip Esler (New York: Routledge, 2017) 169–96.

people who were thriving and many more who were poor. About 10 percent of the population—unemployed day laborers, artisans with too little work, tenant farmers, and the sick and disabled—were utterly destitute. Some were unable to work. But many simply had no land and no job: "Agrarian societies usually produced more people than the dominant classes found it profitable to employ. . . . The problem was not that agrarian economies could not support larger populations, but rather that they could not do so without reducing, and ultimately destroying, the privileges of the upper classes."[2]

The majority of the population lived in rural areas and primarily worked in agriculture. Some peasant farm families lived as they had for centuries, working their small plots of land to provide subsistence for themselves. But by the first century CE, many peasants had lost their ancestral land and, if still working in agriculture, were tenant farmers or day laborers who struggled to obtain the minimum food, shelter, and clothing necessary to sustain life. Among the peasant families who still had land, the primary cause of poverty was not low production but the high taxes, rents, and other assessments that took away much of what they produced. Many nonagricultural rural workers such as artisans were former peasants or descendants of peasants who had lost their land and were often more destitute than peasant landholders.

In summary, the population in Roman-occupied Palestine was subjected to a political, economic, and social system that transferred wealth in the form of agricultural produce as well as money from the nonelites to the elites. Periodically, the Israelites revolted against Rome; each time they were brutally crushed. The revolt in 4 BCE sparked by the death of Herod the Great was ended when Roman legions slaughtered, enslaved, and crucified the rebels and burned their cities, including Sepphoris, located four miles from Nazareth.[3] The revolt in 66–70 CE began with the burning of debt records[4] and ended with Rome's sacking of Jerusalem, destruction of the Jerusalem Temple, and the murder, enslavement, and expulsion of the Jerusalem population.

2. Lenski, *Power and Privilege*, 281–82.
3. Crossan, *God and Empire*, 109.
4. Josephus, *War* 2.427, cited in Douglas E. Oakman, *The Political Aims of Jesus* (Minneapolis: Fortress, 2012), 66.

HEROD THE GREAT AND HEROD ANTIPAS

Herod the Great and his son Herod Antipas had an enormous influence on life in Palestine. Upon his appointment, Herod the Great took control of land held by previous kings and also confiscated more land held by small farmers, creating additional landless peasants. Ultimately, Herod the Great and later his son Antipas owned between one-half and two-thirds of all land that they ruled.[5]

Herod the Great and Antipas had huge expenses. They enjoyed opulent lifestyles, maintained a standing army, and engaged in massive, expensive building projects. Herod the Great built a nearly impregnable clifftop fortress at Masada and multiple palace-fortress complexes, including the Herodium near Jerusalem, the largest palace in the world at the time.[6] Herod the Great and his successors also rebuilt the Jerusalem Temple and the massive stone platform on which it stood, the Temple Mount. Building began in 19 CE and extended over eighty years; it was ongoing during Jesus's life (John 2:20).

Both Herod the Great and Antipas also built cities. During the time of Herod the Great, more than 90 percent of the population of Palestine resided in rural areas.[7] There were few cities, but they housed most of the elite and the Roman political, military, and economic administrative apparatus. The people and administrative structures in cities controlled the rural, agricultural lands surrounding them. A more extensive network of cities not only displayed a ruler's status and wealth but also allowed more intensive oversight of rural producers and control over their agricultural output.

Herod the Great's largest building project was the Mediterranean coastal city of Caesarea Maritima and its harbor, the most technologically advanced in antiquity.[8] It quickly became a major port for exporting agricultural products from Palestine to locations throughout the Mediterranean world, promoting the further growth of commercial agriculture. Antipas

---

5. Harold W. Hoehner, *Herod Antipas: A Contemporary of Jesus Christ* (Cambridge: Cambridge University Press, 1972), 70.

6. Magen Broshi, "The Role of the Temple in the Herodian Economy," *Journal of Jewish Studies* 38 (1987): 31.

7. Ekkehard W. Stegemann and Wolfgang Stegemann, *The Jesus Movement: A Social History of Its First Century*, trans. O. C. Dean Jr. (Minneapolis: Fortress, 1999), 42.

8. Broshi, "Temple," 31.

built or rebuilt the Galilean cities of Tiberias and Sepphoris, accelerating social and economic stratification in Galilee. The administrative apparatus newly located in these cities enhanced the extraction of resources and money from the peasants of Galilee.[9]

THE ECONOMY

Taxes

The imperial rule of Herod the Great and his successors was extremely expensive. Some of the costs were covered by the sale of agricultural products grown on the rulers' estates. But many of the expenses were borne by the nonelites. Experts are not certain of the total amount of taxes and tribute assessed on producers, but huge sums were extracted to support elites in Rome; regional administrators such as Herod the Great, Herod Antipas in Galilee, and Pontius Pilate in Judea; and local elites. Tribute sent to Rome totaled one-quarter of the harvest every other year.[10] Herod the Great took an estimated 25 to 33 percent of Palestinian grain and half of all the fruit produced each year in addition to other assessments.[11] In a typical agrarian society like Roman Palestine, the nonelite 90 percent of the population is estimated to have retained only one-third to one-half of what they produced.[12] In all, taxes were an "unbearable burden" for many families already struggling to survive.[13] In addition, nonelites were forced to work, without pay, on a ruler's building projects or in logging, stone quarrying, mining, or the military. This meant men had less time to work their own land or earn money to survive. Nonelites lived near or below a subsistence level not because they produced so little but because so much was taken from them by the elites: "In the Mediterranean societies of the Roman empire, it was above all the redistribution system that established and stabilized the enormous concentration of *power and wealth* in the relatively small upper class in urban centers, but at the same time held the great mass of the population

9. Jonathan L. Reed, *Archaeology and the Galilean Jesus: A Re-examination of the Evidence* (Harrisburg, PA: Trinity International, 2000), 219.

10. Horsley, *Covenant Economics*, 83.

11. Broshi, "Temple," 31.

12. Lenski, *Power and Privilege*, 228.

13. Stegemann and Stegemann, *Jesus Movement*, 119.

in poverty and made it ever poorer, especially in the country. . . . The taxes and rents from the rural producers flowed into the cities and above all into the hands of the elite."[14]

Commercial Agriculture and a Monetized Economy

In addition to the onerous tax burden, other changes in the economy made life more difficult for rural producers. One of these was the monetization of the economy. Until the end of the first century BCE, there was little money in circulation in rural Palestine, and most people had little use for it.[15] Debts, rents, and even taxes were calculated as quantities of agricultural products and paid out of a farmer's harvest. But under Herod the Great, peasants were increasingly required to pay their taxes, rent, debt, and other assessments in cash crops—grain, olives for oil, and grapes for wine—or in cash earned from the sale of these crops. Herod the Great's new port on the Mediterranean, Caesarea Maritima, facilitated the export of grain, oil, and wine to cities throughout the eastern Mediterranean. The increased opportunity for gaining wealth spurred elites' desire for land and cash crops to export.

Traditionally, small peasant farm families grew the crops they needed to survive. They planted diverse crops not only to meet their needs but also as a way to spread the required labor, especially for planting and harvesting, more evenly over the year and to reduce their risk. If some crops succumbed to adverse weather events, pests, and crop diseases, others might survive. But the need to grow cash crops was incompatible with the traditional practice of growing diverse ones.

The monetization of the economy and cash cropping increased the inherent risk of farming. It also meant that peasants had to purchase, instead of grow, a rising share of what they needed. These commercial transactions became traps in which they could be cheated by landlords, creditors, tax assessors, and merchants. Monetization of the economy enhanced the power of the elites and further eroded peasants' ability to be self-sufficient and thrive. It also sparked a rising tide of debt, foreclosure, and eviction.

---

14. Stegemann and Stegemann, 37. Emphasis in the original.
15. Douglas E. Oakman, *Jesus and the Peasants* (Eugene, OR: Wipf & Stock, 2008), 57, 68–69.

Debt

For hundreds of years, peasant farmers in Palestine had been threatened by debt, and many had lost their land through foreclosure. Now the monetization of the economy, along with commercial agriculture, cash cropping, and international trade—developments that had begun during the monarchy and now accelerated under Rome—heightened the threat to small farmers' viability. Rising numbers of peasant farm families were forced to borrow to pay their financial obligations or obtain the food they needed to survive until the next harvest. Elites were very willing to make loans at interest rates ranging from 60 to 200 percent.[16] Prohibitions on interest were often ignored. If the loan was repaid, the lender received a nice profit. If a defaulting borrower had used land as collateral, he could be evicted or legally redefined as a tenant.[17] Land lost by peasants through debt was incorporated into their creditors' estates. The indebtedness of peasant farmers and the loss of their land are hallmarks of this era.[18]

As noted, peasants who lost their land faced dire consequences. They could become tenant farmers, possibly on land they had previously owned, or agricultural wage laborers. Both options usually led to deeper poverty. In addition to taxes and tribute, tenants owed rent, either a fixed amount (paid in agricultural produce or money) or a predetermined share of the harvest, typically 25 percent to 50 percent.[19] Day laborers were not assured of work, and without work, they had no income and probably no food. Other landless peasants moved to cities, where they sought to eke out a living as day laborers or artisans.

The abolition of debt was a frequent revolutionary slogan in ancient times, often accompanied by a demand for land redistribution.[20] Peasant uprisings often began with the burning of debt records, as happened in Judea in 66 CE: "For the last five thousand years, with remarkable regularity, popular insurrections have begun the same way: with the ritual destruction

16. William R. Herzog II, *Parables as Subversive Speech: Jesus as Pedagogue of the Oppressed* (Louisville: Westminster John Knox, 1994), 161.

17. See K. C. Hanson and Douglas E. Oakman, *Palestine in the Time of Jesus*, 2nd ed. (Minneapolis: Fortress, 2008), 142.

18. Stegemann and Stegemann, *Jesus Movement*, 112.

19. Stegemann and Stegemann, 44; Lenski, *Power and Privilege*, 228; David A. Fiensy, *Christian Origins and the Ancient Economy* (Eugene, OR: Cascade, 2014), 8.

20. Oakman, *Jesus and the Peasants*, 13.

of the debt records—tablets, papyri, ledgers, whatever form they might have taken in any particular time and place."[21] The destruction of debt records has happened in nearly every major peasant revolt in history. Debt relief and a more equitable distribution of landownership (today called land reform) were the main demands made by peasants in agricultural societies in the past and are still the cry today in places around the world where poor people depend on small plots of land for food, shelter, clothing, and economic security.[22]

In first-century Palestine, wealth was largely derived from the sale of agricultural products. An increase in one's wealth was nearly impossible except through an enlargement of one's estate. Cash cropping and increased opportunities for export raised land values. Since peasants would not readily sell their land, debt was an important mechanism through which elites expanded their estates. Instead of seeing land as a gift from God, owned by God and not something to be bought and sold, elites considered it a commodity to be acquired, if necessary, through foreclosure.

But as the elites grew wealthier, the nonelites sank further into poverty. Throughout human history up until the nineteenth century, the economy and the population grew at about the same slow rate; the per capita output of material resources remained essentially unchanged.[23] From one generation to the next, the standard of living remained the same, although it might vary from year to year depending on harvests, pestilence, and other factors. No one had more material resources than his or her parents did. Anthropologists call this a "limited good" economy.[24] In such circumstances, there is only one way to increase one's standard of living: take resources from

21. Graeber, *Debt*, 8.

22. Information about twenty-first-century farmers' struggles can be obtained from La Via Campesina (https://viacampesina.org/en/), a self-described international movement bringing together millions of peasants, small- and medium-size farmers, landless people, rural women and youth, Indigenous people, migrants, and agricultural workers from around the world.

23. Thomas Piketty, *Capital in the Twenty-First Century*, trans. Arthur Goldhammer (Cambridge, MA: Harvard University Press, 2014), 99; Angus Maddison, *The World Economy* (Paris: OECD, 2006), table 1–2.

24. Paul Trawick and Alf Hornborg, "Revisiting the Image of Limited Good: On Sustainability, Thermodynamics, and the Illusion of Creating Wealth," *Current Anthropology* 56, no. 1 (February 2015): 1–27; George Foster, "Peasant Society and the Image of Limited Good," *American Anthropologist* 67 no. 2 (1965): 293–315.

someone else. One person can have more only if someone else has less. Among peasant villagers in the limited good society of first-century Palestine, to acquire an increased amount of possessions or money was considered not only dishonorable but exploitative: "An honorable man would thus be interested only in what was rightfully his and would have no desire to gain anything more, that is, to take what was another's. Acquisition was, by its very nature, understood as stealing."[25] The growth in wealth among the elite was matched by the growth in poverty among the rest of the population. It was also seen by many of the nonelite as immoral.

Breakdown of the Village Economy

The economic condition of many agricultural workers—landholders, tenants, and day laborers—hovered around subsistence. Landholders were more likely to be able to meet their needs, while tenants and especially day laborers may have often had less than they needed. Village households continued to engage in mutual support and reciprocal exchanges with neighbors in need, being the giver of assistance at one point in time and the recipient in another (Luke 11:5–13).[26] Those with material resources in excess of what they needed shared with those who had too little. Loans—of food, seeds, draft animals, and possibly money—were often made, free of interest charges. Debts were often canceled after six years. This was not a system in which neighbors made a profit off one another. But under Roman domination, this system of reciprocity and mutual cooperation was breaking down. The growth in debt, loss of land, increased inequality, and rising poverty weakened traditional village life. There were rising numbers of rural peasants with needs and fewer with excess to share.

The heavy tax burden, monetization of the economy with opportunities for fraudulent commercial transactions, and the increase in commercial agriculture with pressure on peasants to grow cash crops all contributed to making the lives of nonelites more difficult. Subsistence became increasingly

25. Bruce J. Malina and Richard L. Rohrbaugh, *Social-Science Commentary on the Synoptic Gospels* (Minneapolis: Fortress, 1992), 48.
26. See Hanson and Oakman, *Palestine*, 116; Richard A. Horsley and Neil Asher Silberman, *The Message and the Kingdom: How Jesus and Paul Ignited a Revolution and Transformed the Ancient World* (Minneapolis: Fortress, 1997), 54–55; and Stegemann and Stegemann, *Jesus Movement*, 17.

out of reach. More peasant farm families were forced to borrow and lost their land. People became even more impoverished. The economic changes imposed by Rome meant "the complete dislocation of peasant life, family support, and village security."[27] The rich got richer, and the poor became poorer. This was the context for Jesus's ministry.

THE MINISTRY OF JESUS OF NAZARETH

Jesus was born during the final days of the reign of Herod the Great, probably about 4 BCE. He grew up in Nazareth, a modest village of two hundred to four hundred peasants located in the region of Galilee. According to the Gospel writers, he was a carpenter (Mark 6:3), the son of Joseph the carpenter (Matt 13:55). More accurately, Jesus might be described as a handyman or jack-of-all-trades.[28] Both Jesus and his father were village artisans, landless peasants, poor men from a poor family that may have lost their land in a previous generation through debt and foreclosure. An artisan earned about a denarius a day, enough to support a family just above destitution. Maybe Jesus had known hunger. He recognized that daily bread could not be taken for granted (Matt 6:9–13; Luke 11:2–4).

Jesus probably could neither read nor write. Scholars estimate that just 3 percent of people in first-century Palestine could read, a skill acquired by only a few elite aristocrats, scribes, and other experts.[29] Nonetheless, Jesus knew the Hebrew Scriptures very well and was unafraid to challenge scribes, priests, Pharisees, and other learned scholars.

Jesus lived and participated in an oral culture. He was a good speaker who created engaging and stimulating parables, aphorisms, and stories. His message was primarily shared with the peasant farmers, agricultural workers, and fishers who lived in Galilee. Jesus knew their hardships, toil, and fears, and many of his stories and parables reflect the culture and values of these rural people. He spoke to his listeners' spiritual needs, and he also

---

27. John Dominic Crossan, *The Birth of Christianity* (New York: HarperCollins, 1998), 330.

28. The Gospel writers use the Greek word *tektōn*, which is often translated as "carpenter" but would more accurately be translated as "handyman" or "jack-of-all-trades." William R. Herzog II, *Jesus, Justice, and the Reign of God* (Louisville: Westminster John Knox, 2000), 98.

29. John Dominic Crossan and Jonathan L. Reed, *Excavating Jesus: Beneath the Stones, behind the Texts* (New York: HarperCollins, 2001), 30–31.

spoke to their everyday concerns for food, work, and well-being. People were attracted to Jesus. They sought him out, followed him, became his disciples, and remembered what he said. They saw God in him.

As we have seen, Jesus, a Jew, was dedicated to the law found in the Pentateuch and to the oracles of the prophets: "Do not think that I have come to abolish the law or the prophets; I have come not to abolish but to fulfill" (Matt 5:17).[30] He called people to follow the law (Matt 19:16–22; Mark 10:17–22; Luke 18:18–25).

Jesus taught his followers about God and God's law as it had been understood and handed down across the generations. But in the tradition of Israelites who lived in the centuries before him, Jesus also taught new understandings of the ancient teaching, interpretations that addressed the specific conditions of his day and more fully revealed God's vision for his society.

The Reign of God: Jesus's Vision of God's Just Society

According to Luke, Jesus began his ministry in a synagogue in Nazareth by quoting the prophet Isaiah: "The Spirit of the Lord is upon me, because he has anointed me to bring good news to the poor. He has sent me to proclaim release to the captives and recovery of sight to the blind, to let the oppressed go free, to proclaim the year of the Lord's favor" (Luke 4:18–19).

Jesus's early followers experienced his ministry as rooted in this Scripture, which proclaimed good news to the poor. Jesus was speaking to the economically poor of Galilee, sharing the message that God sought their release from the bondage and oppression of poverty and unmet needs. Jesus

---

30. Of the words attributed to Jesus in the Gospels, scholars believe some likely originated with him and others probably did not. I do not distinguish between these. Teachings that did not originate with Jesus express beliefs about him and his message that were held by his early followers. The Gospel writers felt free, even mandated, to adapt and change the received tradition to apply it to their current circumstances. Some traditions, parables, stories, and pronouncements may have been preserved simply because they originated with Jesus. But most of the narratives were included because they provided important *contemporary* guidance. This becomes very obvious when we compare the Gospel narratives, which differ markedly even when presenting the same event (e.g., Jesus's birth and death) or teachings. See Robert W. Funk, Roy W. Hoover, and the Jesus Seminar, *The Five Gospels: The Search for the Authentic Words of Jesus* (New York: Macmillan, 1993); Meier, *Marginal Jew*, vol. 4; and John P. Meier, *A Marginal Jew: Rethinking the Historical Jesus*, vol. 5, *Probing the Authenticity of the Parables* (New Haven, CT: Yale University Press, 2016).

was also speaking to the spiritually poor. God desired human liberation from all that holds people captive.

The "year of the Lord's favor" is the year of Jubilee, the time when liberty is proclaimed throughout the land, a time of special care for the poor, food for the hungry, and rest for people, animals, and land. Debts are canceled, bound laborers freed, and ancestral lands returned to their original owners. It is a time of restoration, liberation, and abundance.

In the law, the Jubilee Year happened every fifty years. But Jesus understood that abundance and liberation were to happen every year, including this year, and every day. The good news that Jesus proclaimed was the news of God's reign of justice and peace happening right here, right now. The Year of Jubilee begins today: "The kingdom of God is among you" (Luke 17:20–21). It is not coming violently or at some unknown time in the future. But like a tiny mustard seed sowed in a field or a bit of yeast mixed with flour (Matt 13:31–33; Mark 4:30–32; Luke 13:18–21), it is already among us, growing quietly but steadily as increasing numbers of people deepen their relationship with God, choose to live as Jesus did, and participate in God's reign.

The reign of God, also called the kingdom of God or the kingdom of heaven by the Gospel writers, is Jesus's understanding of God's intentions for society, God's vision for God's world, here and now. The reign of God is where God's will is done, "on earth, as it is in heaven" (Matt 6:10). Jesus taught his listeners about the reign of God and told a number of stories and parables about it to demonstrate how life on earth would be lived if we put into practice God's intentions for a just society and a just economy. Through Jesus's teachings and the way he lived his life, he taught his followers to live as participants in God's reign. After his death, his followers were called people of the Way (Acts 9:2; 18:25–26; 19:9, 23; 22:4; 24:14, 22). As we seek to more faithfully and fully participate in God's reign here and now, we are journeyers on the Way.

We now examine characteristics of the reign of God as Jesus taught and lived them. Our focus continues to be teachings that address the economy: poverty, wealth, and the use and distribution of material resources; livelihood and the ability of workers to support themselves and their families in lives of thriving; and the structures and institutions of the economy. Jesus's teachings, his description of the reign of God on earth, are instructions for transforming injustice into justice.

The Reign of God: Love

The foundation of God's reign is love: love of God, love of neighbor, and even love of enemy. Central to Jesus's life and teaching was what Christians call the Greatest Commandment: "'You shall love the Lord your God with all your heart, and with all your soul, and with all your mind.' This is the greatest and first commandment. And a second is like it: 'You shall love your neighbor as yourself'" (Matt 22:36–39; cf. Mark 12:29–31; Luke 10:25–28; John 13:34; Gal 5:14; Phil 2:4; Jas 2:8). Jesus is quoting Deuteronomy 6:5 (to love God) and Leviticus 19:18 (to love our neighbors): "On these two commandments hang all the law and the prophets," he said (Matt 22:40).

The love Jesus commanded is not a feel-good or sentimental type of love. It is love that promotes thriving and abundant life. It is love put into practice as justice. It is an obligation to embody justice in our *personal* interactions and behaviors and, just as important, to ensure that our *economic, political,* and *social* structures, institutions, and policies are rooted in and promote justice. In fact, Jesus *spoke* very little about love. In the Gospel of Mark, for example, Jesus teaches the Greatest Commandment to his listeners, but throughout the rest of the Gospel, the word *love* is never spoken again by Jesus.[31] But while he speaks little about love, he frequently speaks about justice, and his life manifests his commitment to love God and everyone and to do justice. To be a follower of Jesus is to live and love as he did.

Jesus's love of God guided his life and ultimately led to his death. Only by loving God above all else and placing this relationship at the center of his life was Jesus able to fulfill his calling. Loving God means putting God's vision for society and love for God's people, creatures, and creation before all other lesser gods. Loving God and neighbor means participating in the reign of God on earth.

Jesus taught that we are to love people we do not even like, to even love our enemies (Matt 5:44; Luke 6:27, 35). He is telling us to model our behavior on God's. God is as kind to the ungrateful and the wicked as to anyone else (Luke 6:35b), and God sends rain and sun—necessary for crops, food, and well-being—to the evil and the good, the righteous and the unrighteous (Matt 5:45). Jesus does not command us to like or feel positive emotions toward enemies or anyone else. Rather, we are to *do good* to them

---

31. Meier, *Marginal Jew*, 4:481.

(Luke 6:27b). This love is an obligation to be fulfilled, a commitment that followers of Jesus seek to enact: "If you love those who love you, what credit is that to you? For even sinners love those who love them. If you do good to those who do good to you, what credit is that to you? For even sinners do the same. . . . But love your enemies, do good" (Luke 6:32–33, 35a).

But what does it mean to love my neighbor as myself? Who is my neighbor? When Jesus was asked this question, he responded by telling the parable of the Good Samaritan (Luke 10:29–37). While traveling from Jerusalem to Jericho, a man is attacked by bandits and left at the roadside. A priest and a Levite pass by but ignore the injured man. Then a Samaritan, a member of an ethnic group regarded by Israelites as enemies, comes along. He stops, cares for the man's wounds, takes him to an inn, and pays the innkeeper to look after him. This Samaritan is a neighbor to the injured enemy. The Samaritan recognizes the injured man as his neighbor. The relationship of neighbor is not erased by ancient enmity, racial-ethnic animosity, opinions about worthiness, personal dislike, or any other factors. According to Jesus, the relationship of neighbor and the obligations inherent in that relationship cannot be rejected or ignored.

Even unknown strangers are our neighbors. For Jesus, welcoming the stranger is as important as giving food to the hungry and drink to the thirsty (Matt 25:31–46). In the Bible, a stranger is often an immigrant. For Paul, one of the characteristics of a follower of Jesus was extending hospitality to strangers (Rom 12:13).

The Reign of God: Abundance

Jesus described the reign of God as a banquet to which everyone is invited (Luke 14:15–24; cf. Isa 25:6; Matt 22:1–14). In God's reign, the material needs of all are met. Mohandas Gandhi, the Mahatma or "Great Soul" who led India's mid-twentieth-century nonviolent campaign for independence, reportedly noted, "There are people in the world so hungry that God cannot appear to them except in the form of bread." Material abundance—enough for all our needs—is a central characteristic of God and God's reign.

The Feeding of Thousands
The four Gospels include multiple stories describing "miraculous" feedings of crowds of people who gather in remote areas to listen to Jesus (Matt

14:15–21; 15:32–38; Mark 6:34–44; 8:1–9; Luke 9:12–17; John 6:1–13).
Each has a similar story line.

Thousands of people gather in a remote, deserted area to hear Jesus's
teachings. Many hours pass, and they grow hungry. Jesus feels compassion
for them and tells the disciples he wants to feed everyone. The disciples'
responses vary from skepticism to incredulity. How can that happen? They
suggest sending the people away to buy food in nearby villages. But Jesus
wants to feed the people right on the spot. He knows that God will provide,
and maybe he wants to show the disciples and all the gathered people that
they can trust God's abundance and even serve as God's instruments in sharing that abundance. The disciples gather together all the food they have, just
a few loaves of bread and fish—far too little to feed the thousands who are
gathered. But Jesus invites the crowd to sit down on the grass. Then he takes
the food, blesses it, breaks it up, and shares it with the crowd. (The Gospel
writers describe Jesus's use of this same four-part formulation in the Last
Supper; it is the language we use today in our celebrations of the Eucharist.)
The crowd eats. All are filled and there is food left over. There is abundance.
Passing our food and all our material gifts through the reign of God—to
abide by God's laws, to live out God's intentions for us, to share our material
resources—is to live with abundance. What the disciples had initially viewed
as a shortage is, within the reign of God, found to be abundance.

The multiplication of the loaves and fishes in these parables can be interpreted either supernaturally or more prosaically. It does not matter whether
food for all was produced through a miraculous act performed by God or
by the rural folks themselves who, heading out for the day to a deserted
area, had the good sense to take along some food. Jesus's point is to describe
the abundance found within the reign of God. God provides abundance.
Everyone has abundance when people share.

Daily Bread

According to Jesus, God wants us to have the material resources we need
to thrive. In the Lord's Prayer (Matt 6:9–13; Luke 11:2–4), he instructs the
disciples, poor peasants, and fishers to ask for daily bread. God will provide
(Matt 7:7–11). The request is not for *my* daily bread but *our* daily bread.
God's abundance is for all, to be shared among all.

In Nazi Germany in the late 1930s, Dietrich Bonhoeffer wrote about the
linked spiritual and physical commitment that is embodied in the sharing
of bread:

> The table fellowship of Christians implies obligation. It is *our* daily bread that we eat, not my own. We share our bread. Thus we are firmly bound to one another not only in the Spirit but in our whole physical being. The *one* bread that is given to our fellowship links us together in a firm covenant. Now none dares go hungry as long as another has bread, and he who breaks this fellowship of the physical life also breaks the fellowship of the Spirit. . . . So long as we eat our bread together we shall have sufficient even with the least. Not until one person desires to keep his own bread for himself does hunger ensue.[32]

We cannot profess a spiritual commitment to a neighbor if we do not also enact the parallel commitment to ensure our neighbor's material well-being.

Eucharist

In our thanksgiving meal, Communion, or Eucharist, we may experience God's care for our physical as well as spiritual well-being. In the Eucharist, we participate in one of Jesus's many meals with his disciples including the Last Supper and the feeding of thousands of people in the wilderness. It is a foretaste of the rich banquet to which everyone is invited that is the reign of God.

At God's table, all are invited, all are welcome, all are worthy and deserving. The food needed for life is taken, blessed by our thanksgiving to God, broken in preparation for sharing, and given to all. All receive without payment the bread and drink we need: "Ho, everyone who thirsts, come to the waters; and you that have no money, come, buy, and eat! Come, buy wine and milk without money and without price" (Isa 55:1). God satisfies our physical as well as our spiritual needs. In our thanksgiving meal, we live out God's vision: everyone is filled with God's abundant resources, regardless of who they are and what they possess. For a moment, we enact and collectively embody God's reign of justice, which overpowers all scarcity and division.

Don't Worry

Jesus repeatedly taught that God provides all we need, just as God provides all that is needed by the lilies of the field and birds of the air. Furthermore,

---

32. Dietrich Bonhoeffer, *Life Together* (New York: Harper & Row, 1954), 68–69. Emphasis in the original.

even King Solomon in all his glory was not clothed as beautifully as a lily. Jesus taught that we are surrounded by God's abundance, freely and generously given. We don't need to worry about our needs being met. Our flourishing is assured. God provides (Matt 6:25–33; Luke 12:22–31).

However, in Jesus's day, like today, there were many people who did not have enough to eat and lacked other necessities. How could Jesus tell them not to worry? How can Jesus tell us today not to worry? Insight into Jesus's understanding comes in the last line of this teaching: "Strive first for the kingdom of God and [God's] righteousness [justice], and all these things will be given to you as well" (Matt 6:33). If we strive first to live in God's reign, to live out God's intentions for our society, we will find that God's abundance is enough for all our needs. No one would have to worry. There would be abundance for all.

But are there really sufficient material resources in the world today for all to thrive or is this just a glib claim without a basis in reality? Consider the worldwide problems of hunger and food scarcity. Even though hundreds of millions of people around the globe are hungry and millions die every year from inadequate nutrition, experts say there is no global food shortage. More than enough food is produced to feed everyone, but shockingly, one-third of the world's food is wasted every year.[33] If just *one-fourth* of the *wasted food* were recovered and actually eaten, it would feed all the eight hundred million who are chronically hungry.[34] In the United States, although more than thirty-seven million people were food insecure in 2018,[35] our grocery store shelves were overflowing. Hunger in the United States and around the world stems from multiple causes, but a food shortage is not one of them. According to Eric Holt Giménez, executive director of Food First, "Hunger is caused by poverty and inequality, not [food] scarcity."[36] God has given us

33. Food and Agriculture Organization of the UN, *Global Food Losses and Food Waste—Extent, Causes and Prevention* (Rome: FAO, 2011), 4.
34. UN Development Program, *Human Development Report 2016: Human Development for Everyone* (New York: UNDP, 2016), 29–30.
35. Coleman-Jensen et al., *Household Food Security in the United States in 2018*, Economic Research Report no. 270 (Washington, DC: US Department of Agriculture, Economic Research Service, September 2019), table 2. A household that is food insecure experiences a lack of access, at times, to enough food for an active, healthy life for all household members and limited or uncertain availability of nutritionally adequate foods.
36. Eric Holt Giménez, "We Already Grow Enough Food for 10 Billion People—and Still Can't End Hunger" Huffington Post, May 2, 2012, updated December 18, 2014.

abundance. Now it is up to us to make sure that it is equitably shared to meet the needs of all God's people.

But we also note: it is possible, and increasingly common, for human action and inaction to destroy God's resources and thus potentially negate God's promise of abundance. Already much of creation is threatened. Human destruction of the planet's natural resources and generative capacity endangers many of God's creatures and much of creation. Homo sapiens will not uniquely escape this fate (indeed, some of our human neighbors have already succumbed) unless we greatly change our acquisitive behaviors, more clearly distinguish our needs from our wants, more carefully discern our God-given obligations to our neighbors of all species, more lovingly care for the planet, and more faithfully do God's will. We explore the climate crisis more fully in chapters 5 and 6.

The Reign of God: Inclusivity and a Great Reversal

Jesus taught that in the reign of God, all are welcome. He lived out this inclusivity in many ways but especially in his table fellowship, where everyone was invited. There are twenty-five references in the Gospels to Jesus's unusual dinner partners, who included all varieties of "sinners" (Mark 2:15–17).[37] The parable of the great banquet (Luke 14:15–24; cf. Matt 22:1–14) illustrates the radical inclusiveness that defines the kingdom of God.

But God's reign is not only inclusive. It is also characterized by the reversal of our usual hierarchies, the upending of our typical social, economic, and political ordering: "The last will be first, and the first will be last" (Matt 20:16; Mark 10:31; Luke 13:30). Those who are least welcome in our communities—the destitute, the poor, people of color, immigrants, people with mental illness or physical disabilities, anyone who is not exclusively heterosexual, and others of our marginalized sisters and brothers—are the most welcome in God's reign and receive special care and blessings. The prophets and the psalmists tell of God's anger over society's mistreatment of the poor: "'Because the poor are despoiled, because the needy groan, I will now rise up,' says the Lord; 'I will place them in the safety for which they long'" (Ps 12:5).

---

37. Walter Wink, *The Human Being: Jesus and the Enigma of the Son of Man* (Minneapolis: Fortress, 2002), 87.

Beatitudes

According to Jesus, God is biased *in favor of* the poor: "Blessed are you who are poor, for yours is the kingdom of God. . . . Blessed are you who are hungry now, for you will be filled" (Luke 6:20–21; cf. Matt 5:3, 6). In God's reign, the poor and destitute receive God's special blessing.

Luke and Matthew contain somewhat different versions of these two beatitudes or blessings. In Luke, the "poor" and "hungry" are blessed, while Matthew writes of blessings for the "poor *in spirit*" and those who "hunger and thirst *for righteousness.*" Was Jesus pronouncing God's blessing on people whose material and physical needs were unmet, as described in Luke, or was his concern for his listeners' spiritual well-being, as Matthew describes? Many scholars think Jesus was talking about the economically poor and physically hungry, but because Jesus's radical embrace of the poor and destitute was hard for his early followers to accept, in Matthew's Gospel, Jesus's blessing of the poor and hungry was spiritualized and softened.[38]

But Jesus possibly (probably?) used both formulations. He was certainly concerned about the materially poor and repeatedly affirmed and showed God's special care and love for them. But Jesus was also concerned for the poor in spirit and those who sought righteousness and justice. The physical and spiritual well-being of everyone was important to Jesus, even as the economically poor were a specific priority of the reign of God. All people, the poor and nonpoor, are encouraged to participate in God's reign.

It can be hard for relatively well-off people in the Global North to learn of God's special care for the poor. In the last decades of the twentieth century, liberation theologians described God's "preferential option for the poor," a formulation that was controversial, especially among people who were not poor. The Peruvian theologian Gustavo Gutierrez wrote, "God has a preferential love for the poor not because they are necessarily better than others, morally or religiously, but simply because they are poor and living in an inhuman situation that is contrary to God's will."[39] Or according to

38. R. Alan Culpepper, "The Gospel of Luke: Introduction, Commentary, and Reflection," in *New Interpreter's Bible* (Nashville: Abingdon, 1995), 9:143; Fred B. Craddock, *Luke*, Interpretation: A Bible Commentary for Preaching and Teaching (Louisville: Westminster John Knox, 1990), 89; Funk, Hoover, and Jesus Seminar, *Five Gospels*, 138–39. Funk et al. note that the wording in Luke is also found in the earlier *Gospel of Thomas*, logion 54.
39. Gustavo Gutiérrez, *On Job: God-Talk and the Suffering of the Innocent*, trans. Matthew J. O'Connell (Maryknoll, NY: Orbis, 1987), 94.

the great Black liberation theologian James H. Cone, "The overwhelming weight of biblical teaching . . . is upon God's unqualified identification with the poor precisely because they are poor."[40] The liberation theologians are reminding us of what Jesus taught his followers some two thousand years ago. God has a special concern and blessing for the poor: "Blessed are you who are poor."

Lazarus

The reversal that characterizes God's reign and God's special care of the poor are central to the story Jesus told of a rich man "who feasted sumptuously every day" while Lazarus, his poor and hungry neighbor, spent his days seated near the rich man's home, hoping to be given a few crumbs to eat (Luke 16:19–31). Both men eventually die, and surprisingly, Jesus relates that Lazarus is in heaven with Abraham, the Israelite patriarch, while the rich man is tormented in Hades. We might initially view the rich man as blessed by God while Lazarus, apparently, was not. In the first century and in the twenty-first, the rich are often admired, celebrated, and even seen as people who enjoy God's favor (Jas 2:1–9) while the poor are often assumed to be violating the rules and suffering God's punishment. But this parable puts an end to these assumptions. In God's reign, our hierarchies are reversed, status is redefined. Would we have recognized the true value of Jesus, the low-wage, illiterate, poor brown man of Nazareth? Or would we have wondered, "Can anything good come out of Nazareth?" (John 1:46).

The Reign of God: Do Not Judge, All Are Worthy

What would we have thought if we had seen poor Lazarus sitting all day, every day, outside the rich man's house? A panhandler? A lazy loafer? Why doesn't he get a job? We would judge and probably condemn him. But Jesus says, "Do not judge, and you will not be judged; do not condemn, and you will not be condemned" (Luke 6:37; cf. Matt 7:1). In a rich country, it is hard to avoid the nearly automatic assumption that poor people must have done something wrong: they should have remained in school, worked harder, avoided pregnancy, and stayed out of jail and off drugs. We assume, we judge, that their behaviors and choices have made them unworthy and

40. James H. Cone, *A Black Theology of Liberation*, 20th anniversary ed. (Maryknoll, NY: Orbis, 1991), 117.

undeserving of material resources. But our judgments about the causes of poverty are often wrong, as we will see in chapter 5. Moreover, Jesus calls us to cease judging our neighbors altogether.

According to Jesus, God sees all people as deserving of material abundance, even those who err and have not yet repented of their wrongs. This is the God who makes the "sun rise on the evil and on the good, and sends rain on the righteous and on the unrighteous" (Matt 5:45) and "is kind to the ungrateful and the wicked" (Luke 6:35) as well as to the grateful and the good. Material abundance is not dependent on being worthy. God gives to everyone, without conditions, independently of anyone's prior performance or expected future response. No one, even someone who violates God's will, is barred from accessing needed material resources. Neither must anyone repent or make restitution before their material needs are met. Certainly, there are consequences for violations of God's law. And repentance (a change of heart, a return to God) is essential for the full restoration of relationships among people and with God. But according to Jesus, God's material abundance is for everyone, no exceptions.[41] All people, made in the image and likeness of God, deserve their share of God's resources. Everyone has a *right* to live in material abundance.

The Prodigal Son

We hear this teaching again in the parable of the Prodigal Son (Luke 15:11–32). Jesus tells the story of a wealthy man's younger son who obtains his inheritance from his father and goes to live in a distant land. After he squanders all his money in dissolute living, the country is stricken with famine, and the son is forced to take a job feeding pigs. One day he realizes the pigs are eating better than he is. He decides to return home, apologize, throw himself on his father's mercy, and ask to work as a hired hand on his father's farm where he will at least have enough to eat. So he returns home. As he approaches, his father spies him in the distance and runs to embrace and kiss him. By the time the son apologizes, the father is already preparing

---

41. Moreover, on a purely practical level, repentance and a return to one's true self are more likely to happen when one's material needs are met. For example, Housing First advocates have shown that homeless people, like all people, "need the safety and stability of a home in order to best address challenges and pursue opportunities." US Interagency Council on Homelessness, *Deploy Housing First Systemwide* (Washington, DC: US Interagency Council on Homelessness, August 15, 2018), https://www.usich.gov/solutions/housing/housing -first/.

to dress him in his best robe, place a ring on his finger, and host a feast of welcome and rejoicing.

The parable illustrates God's forgiveness and the joyful welcome and restoration given to someone who returns to God (Matt 18:12–14; Luke 15:3–10).[42] But it is important to recognize that the father's loving response does not rest on whether or not the son apologizes and shows proper remorse for his errors. The son is repentant (Luke 15:18–19), but when the father glimpses him in the distance, he does not know whether the son's return indicates a change of heart or just a desire for regular meals. But whatever the reason and despite the son's poor decisions and destructive behaviors, the father's love and desire for relationship continued while the prodigal was gone and, when he returned, were manifest even before the son apologized. Repentance is necessary to fully restore broken relationships, but God's love and blessings, including God's material resources, do not depend on it. They are not just for the "good" and "righteous" but for everyone, even those who have not yet repented. Forgiveness is freely given, not earned or deserved.[43]

God's Generosity

The prodigal son had an older brother who remained at home throughout the years of his younger brother's absence, working hard and obeying his father. The older son, who is dutiful but shows little affection for this father, resents the generosity and lavish welcome given his brother. One scholar describes the older brother as harshly judgmental, coldly self-righteous, distrustful of judicial leniency, and embittered with victimhood.[44] Unfortunately, many of us may also manifest these harsh, judgmental traits. The older brother displays none of the welcome, forgiveness, or generosity of the father. Each of us is called to mirror the nature of God, the father figure in this story, and to turn away from those characteristics we share with the older brother. We are called to be generous and forgiving in our sharing and personal interactions and to turn away from harsh judgment.

42. Luke placed the parable of the prodigal son immediately after two other parables about finding something that was lost, a sheep (Luke 15:3–7) and a coin (Luke 15:8–10). All these parables portray God seeking after those who are lost and rejoicing when they are found.
43. Jesus also declared a paralyzed man to be forgiven prior to his repentance (Matt 9:1–8; Mark 2:1–12; Luke 5:17–26; John 5:1–18). See Wink, *Human Being*, 78.
44. Christopher D. Marshall, *Compassionate Justice: An Interdisciplinary Dialogue with Two Gospel Parables on Law, Crime, and Restorative Justice* (Eugene, OR: Cascade, 2012), 234–39.

Jesus also told a parable about a vineyard owner's generosity toward his laborers (Matt 20:1–15). The workers who worked a full day and were paid for a full day resent the owner's generosity with those who worked only part of the day but received a full day's pay. Is there no material reward for doing more, doing better, doing right? Apparently, God knows people have different gifts, travel diverse routes, and confront different life situations that impact their behaviors and contributions to society. But God is generous and intends for everyone to thrive and share fully in God's material resources.[45]

Brueggemann notes, "Justice as hoped for by Israel . . . is not simply a retributive arrangement whereby each receives what is 'deserved,' but rather a radical notion of distributive practice that gives to each one what is needed . . . in order to live a life of well-being."[46]

The Reign of God: Share and Relieve Need

Jesus was well aware of the poverty and unmet needs of many people living under Roman occupation, especially in rural Galilee. Village life extending back to the covenantal society was based on cooperation and mutual support. Jesus's teachings reiterated the provisions of the law that called for the sharing of material resources and also extended neighbors' obligations to one another.

Give

Throughout Roman Palestine, especially in rural areas, most people were barely getting by, living at or barely above subsistence. But still Jesus urges his listeners, primarily poor Galilean peasants, to give food to the hungry, drink to the thirsty, clothes to the naked, care to the sick, and visits to those in prison (Matt 25:31–46). Jesus was clear about the obligation—placed even on those who were nearly impoverished themselves—to help those who were in need: "Give to everyone who begs from you, and do not refuse anyone who wants to borrow from you" (Matt 5:42; Luke 6:30). Yes, the rich were to give to the poor. But so was anyone who had any material resources beyond what they needed.

---

45. See the story about David in 1 Sam 30:1–25.
46. Walter Brueggemann, *The Covenanted Self: Explorations in Law and Covenant*, ed. Patrick D. Miller (Minneapolis: Augsburg Fortress, 1999), 49.

Lend

The law in the Pentateuch obligates those with any excess to lend to the poor and charge no interest. Jesus expanded this obligation teaching his listeners to even drop their expectation of being repaid: "If you lend to those from whom you hope to receive, what credit is that to you? Even sinners lend to sinners, to receive as much again. But love your enemies, do good, and lend, expecting nothing in return" (Luke 6:34–35).

Cancel Debt

Jesus also encouraged debt cancellation. Since the time of the monarchy, debt and foreclosure had driven increasing numbers of peasants off their ancestral lands into poverty, a problem that grew worse under Roman occupation. Many of Jesus's stories and parables addressed the problem of debt. In the law, debt relief was to happen after six years. But in Jesus's vision of God's reign, liberation from debt, jubilee, was to be a daily event. In the Lord's Prayer Jesus taught his listeners to ask for debt cancellation and commit to canceling the debts of others: "Forgive us our debts, as we also have forgiven our debtors" (Matt 6:12).

This portion of the Lord's Prayer in the Gospel of Luke reads "forgive us our sins, for we ourselves forgive everyone indebted to us" (Luke 11:4). Scholars believe Jesus's original language is better represented in the text in Matthew that uses the language of debt[47] although during his ministry he may have used both versions. The prayer seems to establish a parallel between our forgiveness of another's monetary debts (and sins) and God's forgiveness of our sins.

Jesus also told a parable about a king who was owed a huge sum of money by a servant (Matt 18:23–35). When it became clear the servant would be unable to repay him, the king canceled the entire debt. But when that servant encountered someone who owed him a much smaller amount that could not be repaid, he had the debtor thrown into prison. The newly debt-free servant refused to cancel the debt he was owed.

---

47. Funk, Hoover, and Jesus Seminar, *Five Gospels*; Crossan, *Greatest Prayer*; John S. Kloppenborg, *Q, the Earliest Gospel: An Introduction to the Original Stories and Sayings of Jesus* (Louisville: Westminster John Knox, 2008). In Aramaic, the language Jesus spoke, the same word (hôbâ) is used for debt and for sin. Douglas E. Oakman, *Jesus, Debt, and the Lord's Prayer: First-Century Debt and Jesus' Intentions* (Eugene, OR: Cascade, 2014), 75.

When the king finds out, he reverses his act of debt cancellation and punishes the servant. Debt cancellation, forgiveness, or grace from the "king" or from God comes with the obligation to extend grace and forgiveness to others, including the cancellation of monetary debt.

The Poor Will Always Be with Us

Is there a contradiction between Jesus's teaching about our obligation to relieve and eliminate poverty through gifts and loans and the comment attributed to him, "you always have the poor with you" (Matt 26:11; Mark 14:7; John 12:8)? The Gospel writers tell of a woman who interrupts a dinner party to anoint Jesus with expensive ointment (Matt 26:6–13; Mark 14:3–9; Luke 7:36–50; John 12:1–8). Some guests question the waste; the ointment should have been sold and the money given to the poor. But Jesus affirms what she has done, adding, "For you always have the poor with you, and you can show kindness to them whenever you wish, but you will not always have me."[48]

Jesus appears to say we don't need to put too high a priority on relieving poverty. It is an impossible task since the poor will always be with us. He almost seems to be saying, don't worry about them too much because, after all, there is not much we can do. Over the centuries people have used this passage to excuse inaction and desultory efforts toward poverty relief. But this is a misunderstanding of Jesus's words.[49]

The phrase "you always have the poor with you" echoes the statement attributed to Moses in Deuteronomy 15:11, which *begins* like the passage in Mark, "there will never cease to be some in need on the earth." But Moses *continues*, "I therefore command you, 'Open your hand to the poor and needy neighbor in your land.'" Like Moses, Jesus recognizes that misfortune happens. Despite God's abundance and even under the best of circumstances, people will inevitably fall into poverty due to illness, accidents, unwise choices, bad luck, abuse by others, and larger social forces such as recessions, lack of good jobs, and unjust institutional structures. The poor

---

48. Some scholars believe these words were never spoken by Jesus. Funk, Hoover, and Jesus Seminar, *Five Gospels*.

49. Also see Liz Theoharis, *Always with Us? What Jesus Really Said about the Poor* (Grand Rapids, MI: Eerdmans, 2017).

will always be with us. But so too will be our obligation to eradicate poverty, obligations placed on us by Jesus and by God.

Jesus Did Not Ask His Followers to Live in Poverty

Before ending this discussion of poverty we need to address one final concern. In a familiar story known by most Christians, Jesus tells a rich man who wants to live a faithful life to sell all he owns and give the money to the poor (Matt 19:16–22; Mark 10:17–22; Luke 18:18–23). We examine this story in more detail below. But our question now is whether Jesus/God expects faithful people to live in poverty—that is, to have unmet material needs. To be faithful, must everyone give away *all* they have? The answer is no. God's vision, Jesus's vision, is for everyone to thrive with all the material resources they need and for no one to be poor.

When Jesus sent out his disciples to minister to the Galileans, he told them to take nothing extra with them: no bread, no money, no bag for carrying extras, and not even a second tunic for warmth at night (Matt 10:9–10; Mark 6:8–9; Luke 9:3; 10:4). They were to rely on the community for their survival and well-being. But did they take enough? Was Jesus teaching his closest followers to live in poverty with material needs that went unmet? When Jesus later asked whether they lacked anything on their journey, they replied, "No, not a thing" (Luke 22:35). In response, Jesus did not tell them to take even less with them on their next journey! They had little but, with the support of the community, they had enough to meet all their needs. Jesus wanted them to have no excess. He also wanted them to have enough to meet their needs, to thrive, just as we are all called to thrive. We are not called to live in poverty with unmet needs. We are called to give our excess to those who need it. We are called to carefully discern the difference between our needs and our wants. And like Jesus's disciples on the road, we may find that even though we have little, we lack nothing, we have enough to thrive, we have abundance.

The Reign of God: Treat Others as God Treats Us

The "Golden Rule" is often considered the essence of Jesus's teachings: "Do to others as you would have them do to you" (Matt 7:12; Luke 6:31; cf. Luke 6:37–38). It is important to realize both what this Rule is saying and what it is not. The Golden Rule does not call for conventional fairness and reciprocity. It does not teach me to treat others as they treat me if that means I respond to mistreatment with mistreatment and treat with compassion only those who show compassion to me. It does not mean to give to others in proportion to what I receive from them.

Instead, we are called to treat others as God/Jesus treats us: "This is my commandment, that you love one another as I have loved you" (John 15:12):

> But I say to you *that listen*, love your enemies, do good to those who hate you, bless those who curse you, pray for those who abuse you. . . . Give to everyone who begs from you; and if anyone takes away your goods, do not ask for them again. . . . If you love those who love you, what credit is that to you? For even sinners love those who love them. If you do good to those who do good to you, what credit is that to you? For even sinners do the same. If you lend to those from whom you hope to receive, what credit is that to you? Even sinners lend to sinners, to receive as much again. But love your enemies, do good, and lend, expecting nothing in return. Your reward will be great, and you will be children of the Most High; for he is kind to the ungrateful and the wicked. Be merciful, just as your Father is merciful. (Luke 6:27–28, 30, 32–36, emphasis added; Matt 5:42–44, 46–48)

Applied to the realm of economics and material resources, we are to share God's resources with all God's people and creation. Material abundance is not something earned but given by God to everyone; we are called to enact it: "When you give a luncheon or a dinner, do not invite your friends or your brothers or your relatives or rich neighbors, in case they may invite you in return, and you would be repaid. But when you give a banquet, invite the poor, the crippled, the lame, and the blind. And you will be blessed, because they cannot repay you, for you will be repaid at the resurrection of the righteous" (Luke 14:12–14).

The Reign of God: Livelihood

Over many centuries including the first, people worked the land to produce what they needed. Thriving depended on access to land; economic justice required every family to have secure access to land. Land was so essential to well-being that the Israelites believed it was not owned or controlled by people but by God and at some earlier time God had fairly apportioned it to provide abundance to every extended family. According to the prophet Micah, in God's reign, every family dwells securely under *their own* vines and fig trees—that is, on their own land (Mic 4:4). Through their own efforts, they thrive.

The central importance of land is reflected in the law codes, the biblical instructions for creating and maintaining a just economy. But in the first century CE, most people did not have land and were not going to be getting any. If God's vision is for everyone to be able to work and support a thriving family, how was this to happen without land? Did Jesus provide any teaching about this? He did in the parable of the vineyard owner and his workers (Matt 20:1–15).

This parable is one of Jesus's descriptions of the reign of God, the kingdom of heaven. The central figure is a landowner whose behavior and teachings provide insights into God's character and show how life on earth would be lived if we put into practice God's intentions for a just society and a just economy. In this parable Jesus describes a vineyard owner who goes to the marketplace early in the morning and hires workers, promising to pay each of them a denarius, a small silver coin that was the standard daily wage, sufficient for a family's food and other necessities for the day. Over the course of the day, the landowner returns to the marketplace four more times, the last is at 5 p.m., and each time he encounters unemployed laborers looking for work. Each time he hires everyone he finds, promising to pay them "whatever is right." At the end of the day, the owner pays all the workers the same wage, a denarius, including those who worked just part of the day. The ones who had worked since early morning receive what they had been promised but they protest, arguing that anyone who worked just part of the day should not receive the same pay as those who worked the whole day. But the vineyard owner tells a grumbling worker, "Friend, I am doing you no wrong; did you not agree with me for the usual daily wage? Take what belongs to you and go; I choose to give to this last the same as I give to you. Am I not allowed to do what I choose with what belongs to me? Or are you envious because I am generous?" (Matt 20:13–15).

Some interpreters of this parable turn aside from the question of whether the workers' pay was fair or not and see the story solely within a spiritual context: God treats every believer identically, giving each one the same "reward," no matter how early or late in life they became a follower of Jesus. While this interpretation is certainly valid, it sidesteps the parable's instructions about economic practices in God's reign on earth, here and now.

The parable shows that, in the reign of God, work is both a right and a responsibility. The vineyard owner repeatedly hires all the unemployed workers he encounters, giving everyone the opportunity to work and earn a wage. Work is also a responsibility. The vineyard owner calls everyone who is idle to come and work. He doesn't give them money, which they need, but a job. In God's reign, and in a just economy, each of us has the right and responsibility to share our labor *with* society.

In addition, each of the workers, like each of us, has the opportunity (the right) to receive *from* society what they need to thrive, purchased by the money they earn, which is sufficient for their needs. In the parable, all the workers, regardless of their exact contributions, receive the usual daily wage, enough to purchase their daily necessities. The laborers work for different lengths of time. Some may also work more quickly than others or have more prior experience and skill tending vines and picking grapes. But the vineyard owner ignores these differences and pays each worker the same amount of money. Making sure that each worker and his family have enough to meet their needs is more important than providing additional income to those who work longer, harder, or more skillfully. The factor determining each worker's pay is not the differences in the labor each provided but what the worker and the worker's family need to thrive. Everyone receives a first-century living wage. Some people, then and now, may share their gifts, their work, through paid employment, while others may do so through unpaid work such as caring for children and elders, studying, or doing other things to support and enhance the well-being of people and creation.

The Reign of God: Taxes

The Gospel writers report that the authorities became increasingly concerned about Jesus's opposition to the abusive Roman domination of society (Mark 11:18; 12:12; Matt 21:15–16, 45–46; Luke 13:31; 19:47–48; 20:19). But they hesitated to confront him directly because he was so popular with the people. In an effort to undermine his support, they send someone to ask a question about taxes: Is it permissible, under Jewish law, to pay taxes to the emperor? (Matt 22:15–22; cf. Mark 12:13–17; Luke 20:19–26)? They think they have him. If he says "Pay the tax," he will be viewed as supporting a brutal occupying power and lose support among his followers. If he says "Don't pay the tax," he could be arrested and imprisoned or worse. But Jesus avoids the trap, saying, "Give to the emperor the things that are the emperor's, and to God the things that are God's" (Mark 12:17). He advises them neither to pay nor not to pay. Instead, he poses a quandary that all his followers, then and now, need to answer for themselves: What belongs to God and what belongs to the powers of the domination society?[50]

In the first century, coins were issued by Rome to enable a monetized economy, to facilitate the extraction of taxes and tribute, and to promote the spread of commercial agriculture that benefitted large landholders.[51] Coins bore the image of the emperors and certainly belonged to them. It is significant that Jesus did not possess a coin but had to ask someone to hand him one. Apparently, he was either too poor to have money or made a point not to use it. He did not participate in the cash economy.

But money brought greater poverty to peasant farmers. Money and the monetized economy had nothing to do with God's reign as it was lived out in the rural villages through the sharing of necessities between people who had enough and those who did not. In Caesar's system, people with no land and no money did not share in God's abundance. Jesus was not calling for the nonpayment of taxes, but he was calling his followers to avoid participating in Caesar's unjust economic system of oppression.

What does it mean to give to God the things of God? The things of God include those material goods that enable one another's well-being, such as the sacred tithe given to support the landless poor (Deut 26:12–13). To give these things to God is to share God's resources, the material goods necessary for thriving, among neighbors—those who have enough and those who do not. Jesus is telling his listeners to continue to live out their covenant of social justice, mutual aid, and reciprocity, to hold fast to their commitment to God's vision of a just society.

Caesar's empire is one of poverty and wealth, excess and unmet needs. Caesar's empire rests on the idols of materialism, consumerism, nationalism, militarism, hatred, and greed. Jesus taught his followers to give their allegiance to God and God's reign, not to Caesar and Caesar's values. We cannot serve God and Caesar (Matt 6:24; Luke 16:13).

---

50. For more about the domination society, see Walter Wink, *Engaging the Powers* (Minneapolis: Fortress, 1992).

51. Douglas E. Oakman, *Jesus and the Peasants* (Eugene, OR: Wipf & Stock, 2008), 93.

The Reign of God: Immigrants Are Welcome

Like the law in the Pentateuch, Jesus taught that immigrants are to be loved and cared for. For Jesus, faithful care of the poor included welcoming the stranger, the non-Israelite, the immigrant (Matt 25:35, 43–44). Paul also saw extending hospitality to strangers as an important characteristic of a follower of Jesus (Rom 12:13). The early church shared this view: "Do not neglect to show hospitality to strangers, for by doing that some have entertained angels without knowing it" (Heb 13:2).

The Reign of God: Excess Is Shared

Jesus spent time with the poor and with the rich. He liked the rich and the poor and offered everyone his friendship, respect, and love. But Jesus repeatedly criticized the rich, warning them of the need to give away their excess to the poor (Matt 19:16–30; Mark 10:17–27; Luke 18:18–30). In Jesus's Sermon on the Plain, he speaks of God's special blessing given to the poor, hungry, sad, and other hurting people. Then he lists the "woes" that fall on the rich and those who are full: "Woe to you who are rich, for you have received your consolation. Woe to you who are full now, for you will be hungry" (Luke 6:24–25). Wealth was often obtained by exploiting or abusing others, through either illegal means or practices that were legal but immoral and prohibited under the Law of Moses. But Jesus makes no careful distinction based on the sources of one's wealth.[52] Possession of wealth is wrong.

"Truly I tell you, it will be hard for a rich person to enter the kingdom of heaven. Again I tell you, it is easier for a camel to go through the eye of a needle than for someone who is rich to enter the kingdom of God" (Matt 19:23–24; cf. Mark 10:23–25; Luke 18:24–25). Note, Jesus does not say rich people are going to hell or that God will punish them. He says it is hard for a rich person to participate in God's reign here and now on earth, as hard as it is for a camel to go through the eye of a needle. So is there any hope for the rich? Yes, Jesus said, because "for God all things are possible" (Matt 19:26; Mark 10:27; Luke 18:27).

---

52. He may have thought that wealth could only be acquired through unjust means.

What Accounts for Jesus's View of the Rich?

Jesus's teachings about wealth likely grew out of what he identified as the Greatest Commandment: to love God above all else (including wealth and possessions) and to love our neighbors as much as we love ourselves (Matt 22:36–39; Mark 12:29–31; Luke 10:25–28). Peasants were to freely share with (give to) their neighbors in need. Wealthy elites were to share (give away) their excess. Holding on to wealth while others have unmet needs reveals one's attachment to wealth. It displays a love of wealth that exceeds love of neighbor and love of God. Possessing wealth is idolatry and a barrier to participation in the reign of God.

The rich would participate in the reign of God when they repented—that is, returned to right relationship with God, gave away their wealth, and addressed any harm their acquisitiveness had caused. Luke tells the story of Jesus's encounter with Zacchaeus, a rich tax collector (Luke 19:1–10). If he was like a typical tax collector at that time, Zacchaeus not only collected assessed taxes but also extorted additional money for himself. When Zacchaeus seeks out Jesus, climbing a tree in order to better see him as he passes by, Jesus responds with a challenge. He calls Zacchaeus to come down from the tree and hurry home because Jesus is coming right over to his house. Yikes! During their face-to-face encounter, Zacchaeus vows to give away half of all he owns to the poor and repay fourfold those he has defrauded. Jesus announces that salvation has come to his house; Zacchaeus is participating in the reign of God.

In an encounter with a rich man who asks Jesus how to be a faithful Jew, Jesus advises him to obey what we today call the Ten Commandments. But Jesus adds one additional command, "You shall not defraud" (Mark 10:19), possibly based on the law in Leviticus: "You shall not defraud your neighbor" (Lev 19:13a). Apparently, Jesus felt this was important additional advice for this wealthy man. Jesus clearly disapproved of acquiring wealth through exploitation, extortion, or any unfair or dishonest means. But Jesus's concern with wealth extended far beyond how it was acquired. Jesus repeatedly emphasized the barrier created by possessions and wealth—no matter how they were obtained—and the need to seek God's reign before all else— that is, to give excess resources to needy neighbors.

Fertile Field

In one parable Jesus describes people's diverse responses to hearing the word of God (Matt 13:3–9, 18–23; Mark 4:2–9, 13–20; Luke 8:4–15). Some hearers are fertile ground; they respond to the word and bear fruit. But others are infertile ground: "As for what fell among the thorns, these are the ones who hear; but as they go on their way, they are choked by the cares and riches and pleasures of life, and their fruit does not mature" (Luke 8:14). Wealth interferes with hearing and responding to the invitation to participate in God's reign.

God's Banquet

Jesus describes the reign of God as a great banquet to which all are invited (Matt 22:1–10; Luke 14:16–24). But when the dinner hour arrives, the rich are too busy to come and instead send the host their excuses: "The first said to him, 'I have bought a piece of land, and I must go out and see it; please accept my regrets.' Another said, 'I have bought five yoke of oxen, and I am going to try them out; please accept my regrets'" (Luke 14:18–19). Clearly, these are not poor peasants living on the edge of subsistence but people with resources. So the host instructed his servant to instead invite "the poor, the crippled, the blind, and the lame. . . . None of those who were [initially] invited will taste my dinner" (Luke 14:21, 24). The rich were too concerned with their possessions, too busy with all they owned, to accept the invitation to the banquet, to the reign of God.

Hoarding

Like the wealthy farmer who planned to build larger barns to hold all his goods (Luke 12:16–21), Jesus suggests the rich are too concerned with accumulating treasures and too little concerned with seeking God's reign. Someone who hoards material resources is hindered from fully embracing God's vision: "Do not store up for yourselves treasures on earth, where moth and rust consume and where thieves break in and steal; but store up for yourselves treasures in heaven, where neither moth nor rust consumes and where thieves do not break in and steal. For where your treasure is, there your heart will be also" (Matt 6:19–21). Jesus warned against holding on to more than we need: "Take care! Be on your guard against all kinds of greed; for one's life does not consist in the abundance of possessions" (Luke 12:15).

The Reign of God Is Worth All We Have

Jesus told two parables illustrating that participation in God's reign was worth everything we have, worth giving away all our excess: "The kingdom of heaven is like treasure hidden in a field, which someone found and hid; then in his joy he goes and sells all that he has and buys that field. Again, the kingdom of heaven is like a merchant in search of fine pearls; on finding one pearl of great value, he went and sold all that he had and bought it" (Matt 13:44–46). Full participation in the reign of God is worth my spending (giving away) all my unnecessary material resources in order to "purchase" it. We need not worry about being in need: "Do not be afraid, little flock, for it is your Father's good pleasure to give you the kingdom. Sell your possessions, and give alms" (Luke 12:32–33a).

Attachment to Wealth

But is wealth—resources and possessions in excess of what one needs to thrive—*always* a barrier to participation in the reign of God? A common view today, at least among those with excess, is that Jesus criticized *attachment* to wealth, not the (mere) *possession* of wealth: so long as wealth is acquired without overt exploitation, is not used to abuse, and is not an attachment, it is not a problem.

What was Jesus's message? Certainly, Jesus would criticize abusive means of obtaining or using wealth including ways that are legal but block people or creation from thriving. In addition, attachment to anything, including wealth, is a violation of the first commandment. If God comes first and all else is secondary, then we are called to release *all* attachments including those to wealth.

But what might Jesus say about the mere possession of excess material resources, more than I need to thrive? He would say give it to those in need. If I possess excess, more than I need, while my neighbors, including other species and creation, lack necessities, then I am not loving my neighbors. I am not giving to everyone who asks as Jesus taught (Matt 5:42; Luke 6:30) nor opening my hands to my poor and needy neighbors as Moses commanded (Deut 15:11). *Possession* of wealth while others have unmet needs is evidence of my attachment to it. It is idolatry. It reveals how little I love my neighbors and how little I love God.

In the twenty-first century as in the first, God provides abundance, enough for all our needs. But neither God nor the planet can provide all we want. If I consume or hoard excess beyond what I need, resources are taken away from those who do have needs. Today, my life of excess means others continue to have too little and the ecosystem continues to be overused and destroyed.

A Controversial Parable

The Parable of the Talents (Matt 25:14–28; Luke 19:11–27) is one of Jesus's more perplexing parables. It appears in both Matthew and Luke in somewhat different versions. Here we examine the text in Matthew.

A rich man goes away and entrusts three servants with different amounts of money. The first was given five talents, a huge sum equivalent to what thirty thousand laborers would earn in one day. The second servant was given two talents (a day's wages for twelve thousand laborers) and the first received just one talent.[53] The two servants with the most money use it to make more; each one doubles his wealth. The third buries his money in the ground to keep it safe (an accepted practice among peasants) until he can give it back to his master.

When the rich man returns home he praises and rewards the two servants who doubled their money or, rather, doubled the rich man's money. The third servant returns his one talent and explains that he did not use it to make more because of the master's harsh and dishonest business practices: reaping where he did not sow and gathering where he did not scatter seed. The rich man never disputes these accusations. But he criticizes the servant for not at least giving the money to bankers who would pay interest on it. Then he berates the servant, calling him wicked, lazy, and worthless, and severely punishes this whistleblower who spoke the truth about his master and his profitmaking practices.[54]

A common interpretation of this parable identifies the rich man as Jesus: formerly here, now gone, but returning in the future. In the meantime, everyone has been given skills that they are to use to the fullest as they seek God's reign. Those who do so will be rewarded when Jesus returns. Anyone who fails to use their skills and talents for good will be punished. But a number of scholars dispute this interpretation.[55] Why would Jesus, the master, be

---

53. Scholars believe this parable is the origin of the English word for abilities (talents) but that it did not have this meaning in the first century.

54. Herzog, *Parables*, 150–68.

55. Malina and Rohrbaugh, *Social-Science Commentary*; Herzog, *Parables*, 150–68.

described as harsh and dishonest? Why would he endorse the payment of interest in violation of the law and his own teaching? Why would he encourage the accumulation of wealth?

To understand the parable we need to listen with the ears of first-century peasants.[56] They would have affirmed the actions of the "disobedient" third servant who criticized his master's abusive and dishonest practices and safe guarded his master's wealth but did not increase it. They understood that one person's increase in possessions and wealth was possible only if another person's decreased. Jesus's listeners would also have readily recognized the first two servants who collaborated with the dishonest, greedy master to build wealth; they dealt with them every day.

The parable describes forms of exploitation that were destroying the traditional village economy and the lives of peasants: the use of money to make more money, the charging of interest, collaboration with elites in the exploitation of peasants, and the amassing of wealth and possessions, which drained resources away from those in need. Like all of Jesus's parables, its purpose is to instigate introspection and thoughtful reflection on faithful responses to life's challenges. The parable is an indictment of the rich. It calls for a return to traditional village values of reciprocity and mutual assistance and away from the monetized economy of commercial agriculture. It also presents Jesus's listeners with a challenge, one he is facing in his own life: whether to accept oppression and collaborate with oppressors or resist and face potentially dire consequences.

A Parable Used to Justify Inequality

This controversial parable is used by extreme free market Christians to justify inequality.[57] In this interpretation, the servants are endowed by their master (Jesus/God) with diverse abilities (represented by varying amounts of money), which give them differing degrees of success in increasing their master's wealth. They are rewarded by their master in proportion to the financial gains they make. In this interpretation, the parable shows us God's will for a world where people of varying abilities are rewarded by the market

56. For a searing contemporary telling and interpretation of this parable, see the novel by Kenyan Ngũgĩ wa Thiong'o, *Devil on the Cross* (Portsmouth, NH: Heinemann, 1987).

57. For example, see Anne R. Bradley, *Income Inequality and the Parable of the Talents* (Tysons, VA: Institute for Faith, Work, and Economics, May 24, 2012).

(an "earthy construct, given to us by God"[58]) with differing amounts of money and possessions. Therefore, income and wealth inequality are God's will, determined by the God-given market, and reflecting an inequality in God-given talents.

This interpretation of the parable omits some highly significant details in the story, mentioned above, that invalidate these conclusions. But a hugely flawed component of the argument is the view that market "rewards" or outcomes—that is, workers' pay, benefits, and job opportunities—are approved by God. This is a reversal of biblical economic teaching. The market does not ensure that everyone thrives nor even that most people do. Biblical teaching rejects the notion that one's material resources should be linked to skills and abilities. If God blesses the evil and the good, and the righteous and the unrighteous with equal material resources, then surely God also equally blesses those with differing gifts and talents.

Moreover, researchers have clearly and repeatedly shown that workers' market outcomes ("rewards") are influenced by myriad factors *unrelated to skills and abilities* including racism, sexism, region of the country and the industry in which one works, the size of the firm, the degree of concentration and monopoly power held by firms in the industry, whims of supervisors, general availability of good jobs, other family responsibilities that claim a worker's time and efforts, luck, and public policies governing international trade, the right to form unions, minimum wages, overtime, and taxes, to name just some of the many factors that advantage and disadvantage workers and result in huge pay differences that have no relationship to their qualifications. God's will in regard to many of these factors would likely favor greater equalization of pay and benefits, not inequality.

The Institute for Faith, Work, and Economics—whose funders reportedly include the Koch brothers[59]—promotes the use of this parable to justify and even celebrate inequality. This organization and other extreme free market Christian think tanks oppose unions and seek to shrink government and end the publicly funded social safety net. They argue that income

58. Anne R. Bradley, *Why Does Income Inequality Exist?—Part Two* (Tysons, VA: Institute for Faith, Work, and Economics, June 5, 2012).
59. The website for the Institute for Faith, Work, and Economics is https://tifwe.org/. Charles Koch is a billionaire oil-baron philanthropist, as was his brother David, who died in 2019. Mariya Strauss, "'Faith-Washing' Right-Wing Economics: How the Right Is Marketing Medicare's Demise," *Public Eye*, Fall 2015.

inequality is "a manifestation of the Biblical principle of uniqueness,"[60] the God-established proper reward for each person's unique skills and abilities.[61] We examine inequality in greater depth in chapter 5. But to suggest that God approves of poverty-level wages and the other life-damaging features of many jobs that leave workers and their families with unmet material needs violates fundamental biblical economic teaching.

Prosperity Gospel

Despite Jesus's repeated criticisms of the rich and his calls to give our excess money and possessions to the poor, a reportedly 17 percent of Christians today are adherents of the prosperity gospel.[62] They believe wealth is desirable and evidence of a special blessing from God. It can be attained by anyone who properly and faithfully pursues the prosperity gospel's path.

But this belief is the reverse of Jesus's message. Possessions and wealth beyond what one needs to thrive are barriers to participation in God's reign, evidence of attachment to wealth that interferes with our love of God and love of neighbor. God desires everyone to thrive. But poverty happens and abusive economic systems perpetuate it. God's special blessing is for the poor.

What about the Rich Today?

The Jesus described in the Gospels is not an ascetic. He likes to party, get together with friends, and go out to dinner. Jesus liked the rich; he loved them (Mark 10:17–22). Neither in Jesus's day nor today are the rich necessarily bad people! In the United States, most high incomes and wealth are acquired through legal, not illegal, means and destructive inequality is primarily due to bad laws and regulations, not bad people.

But we can be sure Jesus would have been dismayed by the number of possessions—things, services, and experiences—many of us have today, far beyond what we need to thrive. He would have counseled strongly against consumerism. How each of us relates to stuff is a spiritual practice. It is also an existential challenge. Today, not only are our souls at stake, but so

---

60. Bradley, *Income Inequality*.

61. Also see Peter Montgomery, "Biblical Economics: The Divine Laissez-Faire Mandate," *Public Eye*, Spring 2015; Strauss, "'Faith-Washing.'"

62. David Van Biema and Jeff Chu, "Does God Want You to Be Rich?," *Time*, September 10, 2006.

is the future of the planet. By giving up our excess, we become free for the discipleship of Jesus and new life in God's reign, right here and right now.

Meritocracy

In the United States today, some people get rich through illegal means, but most of the wealthy earn their money legally (although possibly through abusive or exploitative ways) or inherit it from others who did. The United States is seen as a meritocracy where people get ahead and earn rewards in direct proportion to their individual efforts and abilities. Someone with more talent, skill, and willingness to work hard—that is, with greater merit—earns more money, advances further, and generally has more prestige, status, and wealth than someone with less merit.

But the rhetoric of meritocracy hides the large extent to which success and failure often hinge decisively on factors completely outside an individual's control and have nothing to do with talent, skill, or hard work. For example, the financial and educational attainment of one's parents matters hugely as does prejudice and disadvantage related to race, sex, class, religion, national origin, sexual orientation, and appearance. Many of the wealthy work hard but so do very many of the middle class and poor. Many of the wealthy are talented but so are many of the nonwealthy. Hard work and ability are no guarantee of success and may even fail to keep someone out of poverty.

Overall the biggest influence on anyone's success and financial standing is luck: the luck of where you are born, your health and genetic endowment, the family in which you are raised and its assets, your access to good education and health care, and opportunities that you sought out or stumbled into and where they led, often for reasons unrelated to you. Even if talent and hard work alone determined material success, luck would still be important since you were very lucky to inherit and grow up in an environment that nurtured those traits in you.[63]

The United States is very far from being a true meritocracy.[64] But is meritocracy our goal, our ideal? Certainly, a society that distributes resources based on merit is much better than one in which resources are distributed based on power and domination. But even the best meritocracy

---

63. Robert H. Frank, *Success and Luck* (Princeton, NJ: Princeton University Press, 2016).
64. Michael J. Sandel, *The Tyranny of Merit: What's Become of the Common Good?* (New York: Farrar, Straus & Giroux, 2020).

falls very far short of the biblical understanding of a just economy in which *everyone* is deserving of and receives the resources necessary to thrive in the society in which they live. Possession of wealth, of excess, when others are in need cannot be justified by merit, hard work, or luck. God's just economy is not a meritocracy. Certainly, a person's skills and attributes are important determinants of their most appropriate and effective roles in the economy, in society, in politics, and even in the family. But leaders are to serve. All people deserve respect. God's material resources are for everyone: "The wealth and social resources of Israel are understood not in privatistic or acquisitive ways, but as common resources that are to be managed and deployed for the enhancement of the community by the enhancement of its weakest and most disadvantaged members."[65]

What about equality of opportunity, a condition not present in the United States but often presented as our goal, an ideal for society? To enact true equality of opportunity, the lifting up of the disadvantaged (and relative lowering of the advantaged) would need to begin before conception, generations before. But even this impossible to achieve equality of opportunity fails Jesus's call for the last to be first.

I need to remember that my wealth is not mine; everything belongs to God. I am not even responsible for my wealth. It is largely a matter of luck. I must heed the warning that the ancient writers of Deuteronomy included in the instructions Moses gave to the Israelites as they entered the Promised Land.

> Take care that you do not forget the Lord your God, by failing to keep his commandments, his ordinances, and his statutes, which I am commanding you today. When you have eaten your fill and have built fine houses and live in them, and when your herds and flocks have multiplied, and your silver and gold is multiplied, and all that you have is multiplied, then do not exalt yourself, forgetting the Lord your God. . . . Do not say to yourself, "My power and the might of my own hand have gotten me this wealth." But remember the Lord your God, for it is he who gives you power to get wealth, so that he may confirm his covenant that he swore to your ancestors, as he is doing today. If you do forget the Lord your God and follow other gods to serve and worship them, I solemnly warn you today that you

---

65. Brueggemann, *Theology of the Old Testament*, 422.

shall surely perish. Like the nations that the Lord is destroying before you, so shall you perish, because you would not obey the voice of the Lord your God. (Deut 8:11–14, 17–20)

How Much Is Enough?

In the twenty-first century in the United States, what resources are necessary to thrive, and what is excess? How much is too much? These are incredibly important questions requiring repeated, prayerful discernment over the course of one's life. This discernment must, at a minimum, take into account an accurate and deep awareness of how our neighbors near and far are faring: people, creatures, plants, rivers, lakes, forests, oceans, wetlands, and all creation. Through prayerful introspection, awareness of the state of our neighbors of all kinds throughout the world, consultation with a community of friends, and deep trust in God's abiding love, we seek to discern God's will. But take care: "For us well-off Christians, sin is not principally personal or sexual; rather, it is our refusal to acknowledge our terror at the prospect of the systemic economic changes needed for the just and sustainable distribution of the world's goods to all people and other creatures."[66] Facing my fear, I hold tight to the conviction that God is love and wills abundant life for me: "This I know, that God is for me" (Ps 56:9b).

We also need to acknowledge that in the United States, unfortunately, wealth is necessary to thrive. Our flawed public policy choices make some amount of wealth a prerequisite for thriving. Wealth would be much less necessary and more people would thrive if housing, childcare, and all levels of education were affordable; health insurance provided more comprehensive coverage and served as a true bulwark against financial hardship; and Social Security benefits, unemployment support, paid time off, and income for those unable to work were less meager. But instead of providing universal services and a safety net that truly meets our needs, as a society, we have chosen the route of privatization. In the absence of a universal personal infrastructure of support and opportunity, we are too often forced to rely on our personal wealth, something many people lack. A just society, committed to the common good, would not make wealth a prerequisite for obtaining

---

66. Sallie McFague, *Life Abundant: Rethinking Theology and Economy for a Planet in Peril* (Minneapolis: Fortress, 2001), 204.

what anyone needs to thrive. Rather than striving to provide everyone with wealth, we must ensure that thriving does not depend on it.

Consumerism

Jesus cautions us about our attraction to possessions and money: "No one can serve two masters; for a slave will either hate the one and love the other, or be devoted to the one and despise the other. You cannot serve God and wealth" (Matt 6:24; Luke 16:13). To serve God, to make God our "master" and to serve no others, is to say "no" to stuff, to wealth, to excess, and to all the other potential masters who seek our allegiance.

Anyone with two masters has divided loyalty. A paramount commitment to God and God's vision for the world is incompatible with a similar commitment to building wealth and accumulating possessions. To make wealth or anything other than God a primary focus of one's life is to place God second. Wealth becomes idolatry, something that we grasp to find fulfillment, meaning, and joy.

The most deceptive master of them all, my false self, plays on my self-doubt and insecurities to encourage me in wrong directions. But I need not worry. My inherent value, my worthiness, is already established and affirmed through God's unconditional love. Idols, on the other hand, provide "rewards" only to those who earn them by buying and owning the right things. The biblical writers tell us that our identity stems from our relationship with God. We are people of God, made in the image of God. Our meaning in life and our joy stems from how we live out our journey as people of the Way, how we as individuals and as a society strive to walk through the narrow gate (Matt 7:13–14; Luke 13:24), choose the way of life (Deut 30:19–20), and carry the "light burden" of participating in God's reign on earth (Matt 11:28–30). None of this is advanced by anything we can purchase in a Mall or even online.

Jesus and the Rich Man

As he was setting out on a journey, a man ran up and knelt before him, and asked him, "Good Teacher, what must I do to inherit eternal life?" Jesus said to him, "Why do you call me good? No one is good but God alone. You know the commandments: 'You shall not murder; You shall not commit adultery; You shall not steal; You shall not bear false witness; You shall not defraud; Honor your father and mother.'" He said to him, "Teacher, I have kept all these since my youth." Jesus, looking at him, loved him and said, "You lack one thing; go, sell what you own, and give the money to the poor, and you will have treasure in heaven; then come, follow me." When he heard this, he was shocked and went away grieving, for he had many possessions. (Mark 10:17–22)

Mark tells of a rich man who came to Jesus asking "what must I do to inherit eternal life?" (cf. Matt 19:16–22; Luke 18:18–23). What should I do to live more faithfully? How can I participate in the reign of God here and now? Jesus advises him to follow the Ten Commandments and other Jewish laws and the man replies he has been doing so all his life. Mark writes that at that point in the conversation Jesus looks at the rich man and loves him. Jesus turns to this man and sees a good person who has been faithfully following his religious teachings. The rich are not bad people.

But then Jesus invites the rich man to enter into a deeper relationship with him and with God. Jesus invites the rich man to sell all he has, give the money to the poor, and come, follow him and participate in the reign of God. This is difficult for the rich man to hear. He is shocked and goes away grieving. He keeps his riches. The end.

Or maybe not. Let's consider whether there might be more to this story. Yes, the man was shocked and grieved by Jesus's request, a tough thing for anyone to hear. But this man was a seeker. He had, after all, gone to where Jesus was hanging out, got dust and dirt on his rich robes, and rubbed shoulders with the poor people who followed Jesus. He sought out this rabbi, this prophet, because he was looking for something more than just a comfortable and somewhat superficial life. He was on a journey, searching for how to live more faithfully. Not unlike many of us.

So after the encounter, he went home, shocked and grieving. But some time later he started to think about what Jesus had said. He had experienced a powerful presence. He continued to feel Jesus's love. He continued to hear Jesus's call to deeper relationship and more faithful living.

After a few days passed, or maybe a few weeks or months or years, bit by bit he started down a new path toward greater commitment. He became more generous, more giving, freer with his possessions. Maybe he didn't ever give away all his wealth but maybe he did give away some of it, maybe most of it. Maybe he started hanging out, sometimes, with the Jesus crowd. As time went by, maybe he became more and more committed to this deeper, more faithful path.

Many of us, like the rich man with too much stuff, are seeking to be more faithful followers of Jesus, in deeper relationship with God. Jesus is looking at us with eyes filled with love and, at the same time, calling us to greater faithfulness. God does not ask anyone to live in misery, without the material resources they need. But each of us is called to seek, to trust, and to journey deeper.

The Reign of God: Overcome Oppression

Jesus's stories and parables address a distant and unfamiliar time in the past. We can easily miss their radical economic significance. His teaching was "designed to stimulate social analysis and to expose the contradictions between the actual situation of its hearers and the Torah of God's justice. . . . [His teaching] could incite peasants and villagers to social unrest or even revolt."[67] Jesus was a nonviolent threat to the Roman domination system.[68]

Luke anticipates the great economic, social, and political reversal that characterizes God's reign and Jesus's life and teaching by placing a radical song on the lips of Jesus's pregnant mother. Mary's song, the *Magnificat*, is a very early Christian hymn that Luke incorporates into the first chapter of his Gospel (Luke 1:46–55). It powerfully expresses the hope of the Jesus followers in the decades after his death for revolutionary social change. God "has brought down the powerful from their thrones, and lifted up the lowly; he has filled the hungry with good things, and sent the rich away empty" (Luke 1:52–53). These are not references to a spiritual upheaval nor is the language metaphorical. The Jesus followers believed, based on what Jesus had taught and revealed to them, that this was God's intention for the world.

Scholars believe Mary's song is based on Hannah's song (1 Sam 2:1–10), another hymn of praise and expectation sung by a pregnant woman, the mother-to-be of Samuel, a prophet and key figure in Israel's journey. She sings of a world that incarnates God's vision, where "the bows of the mighty are broken, but the feeble gird on strength," where "those who were full have hired themselves out for bread, but those who were hungry are fat with spoil," a world where God has raised the poor from the dust and lifted the needy from the ash heap. These hymns describe the coming of God's

67. Herzog, *Parables*, 28.
68. See Walter Wink, *Engaging the Powers: Discernment and Resistance in a World of Domination* (Minneapolis: Fortress, 1992).

reign. The domination system has been reversed: the first are last, the last are first. The hungry are full, the poor have abundance.

Jesus was an evangelist, urging a deeper commitment to God and God's reign. He also engaged in works of compassion and mercy like healing the sick. But Jesus was also doing the work of justice, seeking to change (redeem) unjust systems, institutions, and structures. He is the Savior of the world, not just of individuals (John 4:42; 1 John 4:14). Jesus lived out God's will for the world by seeking the transformation of people *and society*, a nonviolent transformation enacted through prayer, enlightened daily practices, and social struggle: "The gospel is not a message of personal salvation *from* the world, but a message of *a world transfigured, right down to its basic structures*."[69] Jesus was not crucified by Rome because he called people to love God, be kind, and share possessions but because he challenged Rome's abusive structures and practices.

Jesus showed his opposition to Roman rule and Roman values throughout his ministry. Then in the week before Passover, one week before he was killed, he traveled to Jerusalem where the crowds celebrated his entry into the city. On the next day, "Jesus entered the temple and drove out all who were selling and buying in the temple, and he overturned the tables of the money changers and the seats of those who sold doves. He said to them, 'It is written, "My house shall be called a house of prayer"; but you are making it a den of robbers'" (Matt 21:12–13; Mark 11:15–17; Luke 19:45–46; John 2:13–16). According to Luke and many scholars today, this was the key event that led the religious and political authorities to kill him.

To grasp the significance of Jesus's action, we need to understand the role played by the Jerusalem Temple in Jewish life. The temple was the main site of religious practice and central to Jesus's faith; he had come to Jerusalem to celebrate Passover in the temple. But the temple was also the center of Judea's economic and political life. The chief priests of the Jerusalem Temple were chosen by the Rome-appointed rulers of Judea, and they collaborated with the Roman rulers to administer the territory. The temple functioned "as an instrument of imperial legitimation and control of a subjected people."[70] In the first century, the economic and political power

---

69. Wink, 83. Emphasis in the original.
70. Richard A. Horsley, *Jesus and the Spiral of Violence: Popular Jewish Resistance in Roman Palestine* (Minneapolis: Fortress, 1993), 287.

structure in Judea was controlled by Rome and the Rome-appointed rulers, but it was mediated through the temple authorities.

Jesus was not upset about the commercial activities taking place in the Temple.[71] But he was very disturbed by the activities of the temple priests. When Jesus charged that the temple had become a "den of robbers" he was not saying that robbery was happening within the temple. Rather he was charging that the temple was the robbers' den, the place where the robbers—the priests—stayed. Jesus's charge "indicted the temple authorities as robbers who collaborated with the robbers at the top of the imperial domination system. They had made the temple into a den of robbing and violence. Jesus's action was not a cleansing of the temple, but an indictment of the temple."[72] Jesus did not deny the temple's central importance to his faith. It was because the temple was of such great religious significance that its association with corruption and collaboration was so troubling. Jesus's challenge to the temple authorities was a challenge to the collaboration system that facilitated the empire's control of Palestine. Jesus's actions in the temple were symbolic, a demonstration of the cleaning and overturning of the domination system that was needed.

We know that Jesus was trying to change an oppressive system and not just evangelizing, teaching and healing because he was *crucified* by the *Romans*. Crucifixion was a form of execution used by Rome against those who challenged imperial rule through acts of rebellion, such as treason or military desertion.[73] If Jesus had been a nonthreatening religious figure teaching love and sharing, he would not have been crucified by Rome: "The cross was the consequence of the practice of liberation."[74]

"Christ crucified," a concept central to the apostle Paul's theology and Christology, has both personal and political significance.[75] It is personal in

71. Marcus J. Borg, *Jesus: Uncovering the Life, Teachings, and Relevance of a Religious Revolutionary* (New York: HarperCollins, 2006), 234; Marcus J. Borg and John Dominic Crossan, *The Last Week: What the Gospels Really Teach about Jesus's Final Days in Jerusalem* (New York: Harper-Collins, 2006), 48.

72. Borg, *Jesus*, 235.

73. Slaves who persisted in running away were probably also crucified; murderers may have possibly been as well. The "bandits" crucified beside Jesus would have been "social bandits" or guerilla fighters. Hanson and Oakman, *Palestine*, 87; Borg and Crossan, *First Paul*, 131, 147.

74. Leonardo Boff, *Passion of Christ, Passion of the World*, trans. Robert R. Barr (Maryknoll, NY: Orbis, 2001), 129.

75. Borg and Crossan, *First Paul*, 136.

that each of us is called to die to our false self, die to the normalcy of the domination system, and die to the Siren call of materialism and consumerism. But "Christ crucified" is also an economic and political call to each of us to stand against injustice, inequality, poverty, and domination, a call to nonviolently act for justice without fear of the consequences. God's reign calls for both our personal and political participation.

That Jesus was a threat to Rome is also shown in the writing of the Roman historian Tacitus in his *Annuals* written in 109 CE: "Christus, from whom the name had its origin, suffered the extreme penalty during the reign of Tiberius at the hands of one of our procurators, Pontius Pilatus, and a deadly superstition, thus checked for the moment, again broke out not only in Judaea, the first source of the evil, but also in the City [Rome], where all things hideous and shameful from every part of the world meet and become popular."[76] Tacitus records the common view among Roman elites that the "superstition" begun by Christus was "evil," "hideous," and "shameful." This Christus did not just go around doing good. The Roman elites viewed him as a threat to the empire: "A Jesus whose words and deeds did not threaten or alienate people, especially powerful people, is not the historical Jesus."[77]

TEACHINGS FROM OUR CHRISTIAN HERITAGE

We continue to explore Jesus's teaching but now through the writings and interpretations of his other followers.

The Early Followers of Jesus

After Jesus's death, small communities of his followers gathered together regularly to remember his life and teachings and to worship God. These new congregations of Jesus followers included poor people, wealthy people, and everyone in between. In some congregations, people sold their private property and shared the proceeds among all the members: "The whole group of those who believed were of one heart and soul, and no one claimed private ownership of any possessions, but everything they owned was held

---

76. Tacitus Cornelius, *The Annals* 15.44.4, quoted in Oakman, *Jesus, Debt*, 9–10.
77. Meier, *Marginal Jew*, 5:17.

in common. . . . There was not a needy person among them, for as many as owned lands or houses sold them and brought the proceeds of what was sold. They laid it at the apostles' feet, and it was distributed to each as any had need" (Acts 4:32, 34–35; cf. Acts 2:44–47a). Poor and destitute members of the community who lacked material necessities did not have to wait to receive (or not) the merciful assistance of others. Instead, the community pooled its resources to be used for the good of all. This radical sharing did not mean that everyone ended up living in poverty; quite the contrary, it meant they all had enough.

Many of the early communities of Jesus followers continued to struggle over issues of wealth. The author of First Timothy, thought to be writing in the 110s, warned, "Those who want to be rich fall into temptation and are trapped by many senseless and harmful desires that plunge people into ruin and destruction. For the love of money is a root of all kinds of evil, and in their eagerness to be rich some have wandered away from the faith and pierced themselves with many pains" (1 Tim 6:9–10).

The writer of James admonishes members of the early Jesus movement that rich and poor are equally worthy of respect (Jas 2:1–9). To treat a rich person with more courtesy and honor than a poor one is to "make distinctions" among ourselves and become "judges with evil thoughts." To treat the poor as lesser or to be partial to the rich is to commit sin and transgress God's law.

In Paul's second letter to the Corinthians, he asks them to donate money to poor Christians in Jerusalem. He writes, "I do not mean that there should be relief for others and pressure on you, but it is a question of a fair balance between your present abundance and their need, so that their abundance may be for your need, in order that there may be a fair balance. As it is written, 'The one who had much did not have too much, and the one who had little did not have too little'" (2 Cor 8:13–15). Paul instructs the Corinthians on the importance of a "fair balance" where no one has either too much or too little. Those who have excess now are called to share with those who have needs now. Later, the direction of this exchange may be reversed. His description recalls the village economy of mutual support and reciprocal sharing. Paul also quotes the instructions found in Exodus regarding how the ancient Israelites in the wilderness were to share the manna God provided (Exod 16:18).

The Church in Its First Centuries

The leaders of the Christian church in its first few centuries continued to stress the obligation to share. One person's excess was theft from someone who had too little.

Basil the Great (330–379 CE), bishop of Caesarea (located in present-day Turkey) and considered a saint in the Roman Catholic Church, wrote, "Will not one be called a thief who steals the garment of one already clothed, and is one deserving of any other title who will not clothe the naked if he is able to do so? That bread which you keep, belongs to the hungry; that coat which you preserve in your wardrobe, to the naked; those shoes which are rotting in your possession, to the shoeless; that gold which you have hidden in the ground, to the needy. Wherefore, as often as you were able to help others, and refused, so often did you do them wrong."[78]

According to Ambrose (333–397 CE), bishop of Milan, when people with more than they need give to others who have less than they need, they are doing no more than returning to the poor what is rightfully theirs: "Not from your own do you bestow upon the poor man, but you make return from what is his. For what has been given as common for the use of all, you appropriate to yourself alone. The earth belongs to all, not to the rich."[79]

Augustine (354–430 CE), Bishop of Hippo in northern Africa and a recognized saint in the Roman Catholic Church, taught "the superfluous things of the wealthy are the necessities of the poor. When superfluous things are possessed, others' property is possessed."[80]

SUMMARY

Jesus's teachings and lived embodiment of God's reign show us God's intentions for our use of God's material resources. Jesus reiterated and extended

---

78. Basil of Caesarea, *Homilia in illud Lucae, "Destruam . . . ,"* 7, PG 31:276, trans. John A. Ryan, quoted in Charles Avila, *Ownership: Early Christian Teaching* (Eugene, OR: Wipf & Stock, 1983), 50.

79. Ambrose of Milan, *De Nabuthe*, 11, PL 14:747, trans. Martin R. P. McGuire, quoted in Avila, *Ownership*, 66.

80. Augustine of Hippo, *Enarratio in Psalmum CXLVII*, 12, PL 37:1922, quoted in Avila, 113.

the law's obligations placed on those with excess to help those with material needs: to give, lend without expectation of being repaid, and cancel debts. As we share God's material resources and enable all to thrive, we participate in the reign of God here and now.

Everyone is worthy and deserving of God's abundance. The poor are the most deserving of all; they are under God's special blessing and protection. The last shall be first. We are not to judge who is deserving of God's resources, given by God to everyone. No one needs to be poor or even worry about being in need. God's abundance is enough to provide for the needs of all. If we participate in the reign of God, if we live within a community of loving, sharing people committed to God and to our neighbors (of all species and throughout creation), then God's material gifts ensure abundance.

We have seen that access to land—to food, shelter, clothing, and economic security—and to a livelihood that enabled thriving are central to the vision of economic justice. But over the centuries as growing numbers of peasants lost their land, farming was no longer an option for most people. Jesus articulated a new component of God's vision for universal thriving: everyone has a job that pays enough for a working family to thrive. In God's reign, everyone has the opportunity and obligation to contribute their labor to society and to receive all they need from society.

Abuses large and small riddle the economic system and create barriers to thriving. Jesus criticized exploitative practices, challenged abusive authority, acted to end oppression, and sought a society where everyone thrived, even at the cost of his life. We are called to do likewise.

Chapter 4

ELEMENTS OF A JUST ECONOMY

In our examination of these three eras, we have seen that as the economic conditions experienced by the huge majority of Israelites worsened across the centuries, human discernment of the law and Jesus's teachings responded with more expansive and comprehensive protections against poverty and exploitation and with new opportunities to thrive. In each era, changed economic circumstances necessitated new instructions to guide society to the same destinations: a just distribution of God's resources, just livelihoods for God's people, and a just economic system. We now identify three core characteristics of this just economy:

- the thriving of all people and creation;
- a job for everyone who is available to work that pays a wage large enough to support a thriving family; and
- an economic system that is fair, protects the vulnerable, promotes the thriving of all, and is kept on course through the active engagement of justice-seeking people.

Today we face an additional crisis that was unknown to our biblical ancestors: unsustainable economic activity and use of the natural world. Sustainability is now a fourth core characteristic of a just economy. We will examine what this means for us in chapters 5 and 6.

We now explore each of these characteristics.

THRIVING PEOPLE AND CREATION

One of the most important characteristics of a just economy is that everyone thrives. A just distribution of resources means that no one lacks what they need. No one is poor. Everyone lives in abundance. Everyone whose material needs are met lives in the fullness of (material) life.

Today there are people with unmet material needs. They are the poor. They are not sharing in abundant life. There are also those with enough, whose material needs are satisfied, who live in abundance. And there are some who have more than they need, who have excess. These are the rich, who have an obligation to share their excess so everyone has enough, so everyone thrives. Although this is not our usual definition or image of the rich, it seems to be the biblical one.

Efforts to Relieve Poverty Are Unending

We have seen in all three of the eras we examined, under very different economic circumstances and structures, that people fall into poverty. Poverty happens. Thus, the task of restoring the poor to thriving lives never ceases.

All People with Excess Are Obligated to Help

In a just economy, the responsibility to help the poor falls on everyone with any excess. The most affluent have the heaviest obligations, but anyone who has excess—who is rich—is to help the poor. Society gathers resources from the rich to use for this purpose.

All the Poor Receive Help

Nowhere in the biblical instructions—not during the tribal federation, under the monarchy, or in Jesus's life or teachings—are distinctions made among the poor. No one is worthy or unworthy. All are deserving. Anyone who is poor—that is, anyone in need—is to be helped, regardless of whether the impoverishment occurred due to circumstances outside someone's control (like the destruction of one's crops or the lack of a job) or due to bad choices and factors that might have been avoided.

The Poor Receive New Opportunities to Thrive

The relief of poverty has two components. First, immediate needs are addressed. Material resources and money are shared, given, and loaned, interest-free. No one makes money off the poor. Second, poor people have a path along which they can move from poverty to abundance. Debts are canceled. Bound laborers are freed and provided with resources to enable a new start. Land is redeemed and returned. People who have been captured by poverty have new opportunities to thrive through their own efforts. They have second, third, and fourth chances—even seventy-times-seven new chances (Matt 18:21–22).

Poverty Eradicated

In a just economy, while poverty is constantly appearing, it is also constantly being eliminated. No one lives in persistent poverty. There is no one in need. Poverty is eradicated. God's intention for the use of God's resources—the fullness of life for all people and creatures—is fulfilled. The economy achieves its purpose of providing the material resources people need.

All People Have Rights to Material Resources

The biblical instructions repeatedly show that all people have rights—rights that do not depend on deservedness or worthiness—to society's material resources: the right to land, to access food collected in the third-year tithe, to eat food growing on private land during the Sabbath Year, to have a job and receive wages that support a family, and to glean on private land that has not been fully harvested. Everyone had access to the produce of the land. If there was food in the fields, vineyards, and orchards, the landless poor ate alongside the landholders. The poor had no need to beg. As Saint Basil taught, "That bread which you keep, *belongs to* the hungry . . . that gold which you have hidden in the ground, to the needy" (emphasis added). Looking through the lens of the twenty-first century, we could say the law established a right to food, land (and thus housing, clothing, and fuel), livelihood, leisure, economic security, and all the material resources necessary to thrive. The law shows "that God's claim on redeemed slaves constitutes their *right* to the means of life. This right supersedes the right to land and produce."[1]

Private Property

In thinking about the biblical stance toward private property, we start with the realization that God owned the land, the means of production and essential foundation of abundant material life during the biblical era. Land-holders were God's tenants, and their rights over their landholdings were limited. Universal thriving and access to essential resources superseded private property rights. In addition, land could not be bought and sold; it was not a commodity. The distribution of essential resources was too important to be determined in a market.

Enough: No to Endless Economic Growth and Exploitation of Nature

Maximizing output or seeking the fastest pace of economic growth are not the primary goals of a just economy. The Israelites observed the Sabbath Day, when no work was done. During the Sabbath Year and Year of Jubilee, no crops were planted. This was not a strategy that would maximize output or the landholders' gains; those were not the goals of the just economy. Instead, through steady but unharried labor, farm families produced enough for themselves and others who needed resources. The psalmist reminds us that our material abundance and economic security ultimately depend on God, not on our own efforts to acquire more and more: "Unless the Lord builds the house, those who build it labor in vain. Unless the Lord guards the city, the guard keeps watch in vain. It is in vain that you rise up early and go late to rest, eating the bread of anxious toil; for he gives sleep to his beloved" (Ps 127:1–2). During the Sabbath Day, Sabbath Year, and Jubilee Year, not only did people rest, but so did animals and even the land. Nature was not to be exploited to boost the material resources available to people. God's reign is one of abundance and sharing, not scarcity and competition.

---

1. M. Douglas Meeks, *God the Economist: The Doctrine of God and Political Economy* (Minneapolis: Augsburg Fortress, 1989), 87. Emphasis added.

LIVELIHOOD: JOBS FOR ALL THAT ENABLE THRIVING

The law included many provisions intended to maintain peasants on their ancestral land and return land that was lost to its ancestral owner. Peasant families working their own land could provide themselves with material abundance, and it was essentially the only way they could do so. The law's focus on land reflects its essential importance. But in first-century Palestine, when most peasant families no longer held any land, Jesus continued to affirm God's vision for livelihood and thriving. Since land could no longer serve as the foundation of a flourishing life, Jesus taught that in the reign of God, everyone would have a job that paid enough to support a thriving family.

In a just economy, everyone available to work has both the right to a job and the responsibility to work. According to Pope John Paul II, "Work is a good thing for man—a good thing for his humanity—because through work man not only transforms nature, adapting it to his own needs, but he also achieves fulfilment as a human being and indeed, in a sense, becomes 'more a human being.'"[2]

Moreover, each worker needs and deserves a wage sufficient to support a thriving family. We could call this the right to a job at a living wage. But what is an appropriate wage? In a market economy, labor is sold by workers and purchased by employers in a system governed by supply and demand. But labor has meaning and value apart from its market price.

As we have seen in the biblical instructions, key material resources such as land and food were of such great importance that their prices and distribution were not to be determined within a market of buying and selling. Land and food were not commodities.[3] Neither is human labor a commodity.

Wages (and the benefits received as part of a compensation package) carry significance for fairness and human dignity. A wage cannot solely be a free market–determined price that is paid for work. The International Labor Organization—an agency of the United Nations that brings together governments, employers, and workers to examine issues related to employment—has long affirmed that labor is not a commodity, and its price (the wage)

---

2. John Paul II, *Laborem Exercens* (Rome: Libreria Editrice Vaticana, September 14, 1981), section 9.

3. This term is also used in a narrower sense to mean "undifferentiated products" such as corn or soybeans, but here it refers to everything exchanged in a market.

cannot be determined solely through a process of supply and demand.[4] Workers need jobs and are vulnerable to being forced to agree to an unacceptable wage. A just economic system protects workers against wages and working conditions that are harmful to human dignity and well-being.

THE ECONOMIC SYSTEM PROTECTS THE VULNERABLE AND PROMOTES UNIVERSAL THRIVING

At the most basic level, a just economy is characterized by honesty, fair practices, and the absence of bribery, theft, and corruption. We have seen how the biblical teachings sought to combat the deceitful practices of the past.

A just economy also provides protections for the vulnerable, including people experiencing material need or those who fear they soon might be. The needs of these vulnerable people and of their loved ones can compel them to accept unjust conditions in order to obtain needed resources—for example, to work for wages that are too low or borrow under terms that are too onerous. The biblical instructions closed off many of these possibilities by banning interest on loans, canceling debt and bondage after six years, and placing restrictions on creditors' access to collateral. The biblical teachings do not recognize freedom of contract. Abusive, exploitative agreements are prohibited. Everyone who works full time receives a wage sufficient for all their material needs. No one who works is poor.

We saw in chapter 1 that to take more than one's share of our common resources was seen as a form of theft. Certainly, in the twenty-first century, this means we cannot overuse the planet's resources and leave others—now or in the future—with too little.

Some people argue that free market capitalism is the source of economic freedom and a prerequisite for political freedom. But this is certainly not the biblical view. Someone ensnared in poverty is not free; their choices are extremely restricted. Moreover, for survival, they may be forced to make a choice among very limited, onerous, or even harmful options. Such a choice is not freely made but imposed on them by need. A just economy provides protections for the vulnerable, and those with wealth and power are not free to exploit the less powerful.

---

4. International Labor Organization, *Global Wage Report 2016/17* (Geneva: ILO, December 15, 2016), 2.

In a just economy, the same rules apply to everyone. The rich and the poor receive equal treatment under the law, as do immigrants, strangers, foreigners, and aliens who are to be loved like any neighbor, loved like oneself. Even someone as powerful as a king is to receive equal treatment under the law.

Economic justice is to go beyond a strict accounting of lending and borrowing, beyond a calculation of what is earned and who is deserving. All are worthy of living in the fullness of life, without exception, with no preconditions. The last are to be first. Justice is to ensure that all have what they need to thrive. A just economic system ensures this just distribution.

SEEK TO OVERCOME OPPRESSION AND PARTICIPATE IN GOD'S REIGN

A just economic system relies on the active engagement of justice-seeking people to eliminate oppression. The prophets spoke God's indictments of economic injustice and suffered for doing so. Jesus lived in ways that eroded the hierarchy of social standing and power, and he called for a more equitable distribution of resources. He challenged Roman oppression and Judean collaboration with it. Jesus's ministry was a threat to the powers of his day and brought about his crucifixion by Rome. Jesus is our personal Lord and Savior, showing us the ways of personal liberation, return from exile, and communion with God. Jesus is also our economic, political, and social Lord and Savior, showing us the paths of economic, political, and social liberation and the way of nonviolent resistance to injustice.[5]

It is structures, laws, systems, and institutions—powers and principalities—that oppress. Individuals are their agents. According to Brazilian liberation theologian Leonardo Boff, "We labor under an illusion if we hope to join battle against the evil of the world with a blind, vengeful assault on individuals. . . . These persons are not the producers of the drama; they are but players on the stage. The more profound drama is social reality itself. It is the very structure of the system that is wicked."[6] But, at the same time, individuals are responsible for what they do or fail to do. We are to take Jesus as our model: "He had no intention of resigning himself to, or

---

5. See Borg and Crossan, *Last Week*, 215.
6. Boff, *Passion*, 125.

compromising with, any [unjust or exploitative] situation merely in order
to survive. He remained faithful to his truth to the end, heedless of any
danger. . . . He lives and acts despite death. If death must come, let it come,
but the vitality and inspiration of his life is not the fear of death: it is commitment to his Father's will . . . [and] to a message of liberation for a world
of brothers and sisters."[7] Jesus saves us by providing a model for us to follow.

Faithful people participate in the reign of God. They seek to overcome
oppressive and exploitative structures and institutions that fail to promote
the thriving of all people and creation. They work with God to cocreate a
just economy and a just society.

7. Boff, 64.

Chapter 5

BIBLICAL ECONOMIC JUSTICE AND TODAY'S ECONOMY

We now examine the US economy (and take a brief look at the global economy as well) through the lens of our four criteria for economic justice:

- Are all people and creation thriving?
- Does every adult who is available to work have a job that pays a family-supporting wage?
- Is the economic system fair and free of oppression, does it protect the vulnerable and promote universal thriving, and are justice-seeking people actively engaged to make and keep it so?
- Is the economy operating sustainably, in a manner that ensures abundant life for people and other beings indefinitely into the future?

This chapter was written before and during the early months of the coronavirus pandemic. The economy is in flux. But longstanding unjust, destructive trends continue: poverty in the midst of plenty, extreme inequality, poverty-wage jobs, abusive economic structures, and an unsustainable economy. We address what could be done to enhance economic justice in chapter 6.

MANY ARE NOT THRIVING

The most important characteristic of a just economy is that everyone thrives. But in the United States, despite a level of material abundance that would be incomprehensible to people in the past, tens of millions of people are not thriving. The reason is not scarcity; there is no shortage of resources. People are not hungry because the grocery stores are empty. The lack of afford-able housing is not due to a scarcity of building materials. People are failing to thrive because our resources, God's resources, are not justly distributed. Some have too little, while others have more than they need. We are not sharing as we are called to do. High and growing inequality are the defining characteristics of the US and global economies.

Income Inequality

Income and the material resources that money can buy are very unequally distributed. The skewed distribution means tens of millions are unable to pur-chase what they need. In 2019, the poorest one-fifth of households in the United States had an average income of $15,286, too little to support a life of thriving, while average income among the top 5 percent was thirty times as much, $451,122.[1] Among the middle 20 percent of households, income aver-aged $68,938. Over half of all income (52 percent) goes to the one-fifth of households with the highest incomes. Just 3 percent goes to the lowest-income fifth. In recent decades, the households at the top of the income distribu-tion have been pulling away from those in the bottom and the middle. The rich have gotten richer, but the incomes of most others have stagnated or even fallen, not just in the United States, but in many countries around the world.

This was not always the case. In the first few decades after World War II, income was rising faster for people in the bottom and middle of the distribu-tion than at the top. Between 1946 and 1980, incomes among the bottom 90 percent more than doubled, up by over 100 percent.[2] (See the two bars on the left in figure 5.1a. The horizontal line marks a doubling of income.

---

1. Jessica Semega et al., *Income and Poverty in the United States: 2019*, Report no. P60-270 (Wash-ington, DC: US Bureau of the Census, September 2020), table A-4.
2. Thomas Piketty, Emmanuel Saez, and Gabriel Zucman, "Distributional National Accounts: Methods and Estimates for the United States," *Quarterly Journal of Economics* 133, no. 2 (2018): table II.

All incomes are adjusted for inflation.) Income among the top 1 percent rose about half as fast, up 47 percent over the period. Income inequality was shrinking. Income equality was rising.

The trend was a good one, but not everyone was equally able to benefit. African Americans, other people of color, and women continued to face barriers to full participation in society and the economy. But even these disadvantaged groups saw improvements. While the median African American family income was, and still is today, lower than the median white family income, in the postwar decades, it grew more rapidly. It began to catch up. (The median is the number in the middle of a distribution: half of all households have income below the median, and half have one that is higher.)

But then things changed. Starting in the late 1970s, the trend toward greater income equality was reversed, and despite occasional fluctuations, inequality has steadily increased ever since.

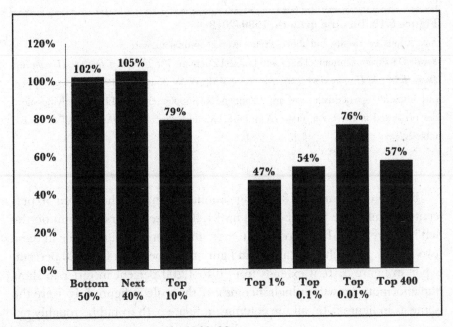

Figure 5.1a. Income growth, 1946–80

Note: Adults age twenty and above. Pretax average annual income.

Source: Data from Thomas Piketty, Emmanuel Saez, and Gabriel Zucman, "Distributional National Accounts: Methods and Estimates for the United States," *Quarterly Journal of Economics* 133, no. 2 (2018): table II.

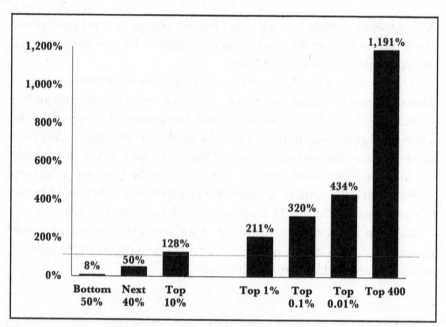

Figure 5.1b. Income growth, 1980–2018

Note: Adults age twenty and above. Pretax average annual income.

Source: Data from Emmanuel Saez and Gabriel Zucman, *The Triumph of Injustice: How the Rich Dodge Taxes and How to Make Them Pay* (New York: W. W. Norton, 2019), Technical Appendix, https://www.taxjusticenow.org/#/appendix. Supplementary tables underlying statistics presented in the book, https://eml.berkeley.edu/~saez/SZ2019AppendixTables.xlsx, table A2.

Between 1980 and 2018, average annual income for the bottom 50 percent of adults rose just 8 percent, up $1,400.[3] See the first column on the left in figure 5.1b. (It is important to note the difference in the scale in these two figures. The left vertical axis in figure 5.1a goes from 0 to 120 percent, while in figure 5.1b, it extends from 0 to 1,200 percent in order to show the enormous growth in high incomes. If the scale in figure 5.1b were the same as in figure 5.1a, all the columns in figure 5.1b would be roughly ten

3. Emmanuel Saez and Gabriel Zucman, *The Triumph of Injustice: How the Rich Dodge Taxes and How to Make Them Pay* (New York: W. W. Norton, 2019). Online supplement at https://www.taxjusticenow.org/#/appendix; supplementary tables underlying statistics presented in the book, tables A1 and A2, https://eml.berkeley.edu/~saez/SZ2019AppendixTables.xlsx.

times higher, showing the true huge differences between them.) This meager 8 percent increase *over thirty-eight years* was the average: some people saw somewhat larger gains, and others had smaller gains and even declines. Living standards for fully half the population essentially stopped rising. They were left behind. The next higher-income 40 percent of adults had gains of 50 percent over those thirty-eight years. While substantially better than for the bottom 50 percent, these gains are still far lower than those received by people at the top of the income ladder. Note again the horizontal line that marks a doubling of income (a 100 percent increase).

While most people saw their incomes stagnate, a few saw their incomes soar. Among the top 1 percent, average income roughly tripled (up 211 percent), rising from $480,000 to $1.5 million. But the real gains went to people even higher up the income ladder. Average income among the top one one-hundredth of 1 percent (some twenty-four thousand adults) rose to $33 million, up over fivefold. Among the top four hundred adults, average annual income rose over 1,000 percent and in 2018 exceeded $500 million. In 2018, nearly half (47 percent) of all income went to the top 10 percent, up from 35 percent in 1980.[4] The nation's growing economy no longer benefits everyone, certainly not the bottom half of adults. The gains are increasingly captured by people at the very top. Income inequality is high and rising in many countries around the world, but it is higher in the United States than in any other major industrialized nation.[5]

This forty-year trend of rising inequality has severely impacted the bottom 50 percent, who, between 1980 and 2018, saw their share of all national income fall from 19.7 percent to 12.7 percent. At the same time, the top 1 percent saw their share rise from 11.2 percent to 20.5 percent.[6] See figure 5.2. The dollar value of this shift is huge. If the bottom 50 percent had received the same share of national income in 2018 as they did in 1980, each adult would have received an additional $5,135 in income that year.[7]

This reversal in income growth, from rising equality to rising inequality, was not inevitable. A growing *national* income means *every person's* income

4. Saez and Zucman, https://eml.berkeley.edu/~saez/SZ2019AppendixTables.xlsx, tables A1 and A2.

5. World Bank, "Data," accessed November 23, 2021, https://data.worldbank.org/indicator/SI.POV.GINI. Comparisons made based on the Gini index.

6. Saez and Zucman, *Triumph of Injustice*, figure 1.1.

7. Saez and Zucman, https://eml.berkeley.edu/~saez/SZ2019AppendixTables.xlsx, table A1.

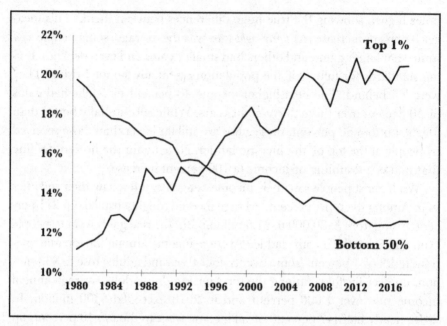

Figure 5.2. Shares of national income, bottom 50 percent and top 1 percent, 1980–2018.

Source: Data from Emmanuel Saez and Gabriel Zucman, *The Triumph of Injustice: How the Rich Dodge Taxes and How to Make Them Pay* (New York: W. W. Norton, 2019), Technical Appendix, https://www.taxjusticenow.org/#/appendix. Supplementary tables underlying statistics presented in the book, https://eml.berkeley.edu/~saez/SZ2019AppendixTables.xlsx, table A1.

could also grow. Between 1949 and 1980, per capita gross domestic product (GDP)—a measure of the nation's affluence and its ability to ensure that everyone thrives—more than doubled, up 115 percent over thirty-one years.[8] As we have seen, this growth was broadly shared, as income for the bottom 90 percent also more than doubled. After 1980, the economy continued to grow, although more slowly than in the previous three decades (we return to this point later), and by 2018, it had nearly doubled again, up 90 percent over thirty-eight years. But this growth was not shared. It was captured

8. Federal Reserve Economic Data, Federal Reserve Bank of St. Louis, US Department of Commerce Bureau of Economic Analysis, "Real Gross Domestic Product per Capita (A939RX0Q048SBEA)," accessed May 21, 2020, https://fred.stlouisfed.org/series/A939RX 0Q048SBEA.

primarily by high-income households. In both periods, the potential existed for a near doubling of incomes. But in the last forty years, the nation's growing abundance has been largely captured by people at the pinnacle of the income distribution.

The rise or fall in household income across decades is reflected in the rise or fall in living standards across generations. The United States is seen as the land of opportunity, where children can rise above the economic status of their parents. But in recent decades, this has become more of a dream than a reality. Millions of adults today have smaller incomes (adjusted for infla-tion) and a lower standard of living than their parents did at the same age.[9] Among children born in 1940, 92 percent had higher incomes than their parents.[10] But among children born in 1984, just half achieved this goal. In a true land of opportunity, a nation's growing affluence would provide plentiful possibilities for a child's standard of living to rise above the level of their parents.

The high level of income and wealth inequality harms us all, even apart from the destructiveness caused by poverty. In a highly unequal society, chil-dren from *all* backgrounds, on average, do less well in school than their counterparts in more equal societies.[11] People of *all* socioeconomic levels, on average, have worse health than those living in more equal societies.[12] A high degree of inequality brings heightened anxiety about social status, an increased focus on consumerism and competition for status, higher levels of stress, more mental illness, and less social cohesion and support for the common good.[13]

9. Michel Hout, "Social Mobility," in *State of the Union, Pathways 2019* (Stanford, CA: Stan-ford University Press, 2019).

10. Raj Chetty et al., "The Fading American Dream: Trends in Absolute Income Mobility since 1940," *Science* 356, no. 6336 (April 28, 2017).

11. Richard Wilkinson and Kate Pickett, *The Spirit Level: Why Greater Equality Makes Societies Stronger* (New York: Bloomsbury, 2009); Richard Wilkinson and Kate Pickett, "The Spirit Level Authors: Why Society Is More Unequal Than Ever," *Guardian*, March 9, 2014.

12. National Research Council and Institute of Medicine, *US Health in International Perspective: Shorter Lives, Poorer Health*, ed. Woolf Steven H. and Laudan Aron (Washington, DC: National Academies Press, 2013); James Banks et al., "Disease and Disadvantage in the United States and England," *Journal of the American Medical Association* 295, no. 17 (2006): 2037–46; Wilkin-son and Pickett, *Spirit Level*.

13. Wilkinson and Pickett, *Spirit Level*; Richard Wilkinson and Kate Pickett, *The Inner Level: How More Equal Societies Reduce Stress, Restore Sanity and Improve Everyone's Well-Being* (New York: Penguin, 2019).

There is nothing inevitable about high inequality or the nation's reversal from growing equality to growing inequality. It was a choice, largely driven by changes in economic policies that many of us did not realize we were making. The economy is not fully under our control, but we can choose our economic policies, institutions, and structures. We can select ones that exacerbate inequality or reduce it. For many years, standard economic thinking warned that public policies designed to reduce inequality would harm the economy. Now further study has found that interventions to reduce inequality do not harm the economy but strengthen it.[14] We can create a system of distributive justice so that all may thrive as the biblical teachings instruct.

Wealth Inequality

Wealth is the value of all the assets someone owns—the balances in checking and savings accounts, equity in a home, a pension, and financial assets such as stocks, bonds, and other financial instruments—minus debt. In the United States today, wealth is necessary for thriving. It provides the opportunity to attend college, buy a home, or start a business and helps families weather emergencies such as the loss of a job or a large medical expense.

Unfortunately, wealth is even more unequally distributed than income. In 2018, the wealthiest 10 percent (average wealth $2.6 million) owned 71 percent of the nation's wealth, leaving the bottom 90 percent with just 29 percent.[15] The bottom half of all adults owned less than 1 percent of the nation's wealth. The wealthiest one-tenth of 1 percent (240,000 adults, average wealth over $70 million) own as much as the bottom 80 percent; their share of the nation's wealth rose from 7 percent in 1980 to 19 percent in

14. Joseph E. Stiglitz, *The Price of Inequality: How Today's Divided Society Endangers Our Future* (New York: W. W. Norton, 2012); Jonathan Ostry, Andrew Berg, and Charalambos G. Tsangarides, "Redistribution, Inequality, and Growth" (staff discussion note, Washington, DC: International Monetary Fund, 2014), 4; Josh Bivens, *Progressive Redistribution without Guilt: Using Policy to Shift Economic Power and Make US Incomes Grow Fairer and Faster* (Washington, DC: EPI, June 9, 2016).

15. Saez and Zucman, *Triumph of Injustice*, supplementary tables underlying statistics presented in the book, table A1, https://eml.berkeley.edu/~saez/SZ2019AppendixTables.xlsx. Also see Jesse Bricker et al., "Wealth and Income Concentration in the SCF: 1989–2019," Board of Governors of the Federal Reserve System, FEDS Notes, September 28, 2020, https://doi.org/10.17016/2380-7172.2795.

2018. The wealthiest 400 people (average wealth $6.7 billion) own more than the bottom 60 percent (144 million adults). The trend in wealth ownership mirrors the trend for income: growing equality in the post–World War II decades followed by growing inequality after about 1980.

Despite its prominence in the media, the stock market has little impact on the wealth of most households. In 2019, nearly half of all households (47 percent) owned no stocks or mutual funds, either directly or in a retirement fund.[16] Among families with stocks, the median value among the top 10 percent was $439,000, dwarfing the holdings of the bottom 50 percent ($10,000) and even those of the upper-middle income 40 percent ($40,000).[17] In 2016, the least wealthy 90 percent of households owned just 7 percent of all stocks and mutual funds, while the top 10 percent owned 93 percent; the wealthiest 1 percent owned over half (53 percent).[18]

There is also a very large racial and ethnic wealth gap. In 2019, median wealth among white families ($188,000) was nearly eight times that of Blacks ($24,000) and over five times that of Hispanics ($36,000).[19] Homeownership, the most common way for the middle class to accumulate wealth, has been largely closed off to African Americans and many people of color for most of our nation's history.[20] Racial discrimination in housing continues.[21] In addition, exclusionary zoning—for example, bans on multifamily housing, low-rise apartment buildings, accessory homes, and small lot sizes—drives up the price of housing, reduces the nation's stock of affordable homes, and perpetuates income-based residential segregation.[22]

16. Neil Bhutta et al., "Changes in US Family Finances from 2016 to 2019: Evidence from the Survey of Consumer Finances," *Federal Reserve Bulletin* 106, no. 5 (September 2020): box 5.

17. Bhutta et al., box 5.

18. Edward N. Wolff, "Household Wealth Trends in the United States, 1962 to 2016: Has Middle Class Wealth Recovered?" (working paper no. 24085, NBER, Cambridge, MA, November 2017): table 10.

19. Bhutta et al., "Changes in US Family Finances," table 2.

20. Richard Rothstein, *The Color of Law: A Forgotten History of How Our Government Segregated America* (New York: Liveright, 2017).

21. For example, see Chicago Lawyers' Committee for Civil Rights, *2018 Fair Housing Testing Report* (Chicago: CLCCR, 2018), https://bit.ly/2CpI4rG.

22. Richard D. Kahlenberg, *An Economic Fair Housing Act* (New York: Century Foundation, August 3, 2017).

Tens of Millions Are Poor

Despite the nation's affluence, high inequality leaves tens of millions of people with unmet material needs. They are not thriving; they are poor. Our economy violates God's intentions for God's material resources. But in the United States, poverty is defined in a much more restricted way than in our biblically based description. Today, someone is considered to be poor only if their annual household income falls below the official poverty threshold that varies by family size and composition. In 2019, a family of two adults and two children with an annual income below $25,926 was considered poor, as was a single person living on less than $13,300 a year.[23] Fully thirty-four million people (10.5 percent of our population) lived in poverty in 2019. This was the lowest level of poverty ever observed since the federal government began collecting these data in 1959. (Note that this was before the coronavirus pandemic.) This was very good news and shows the importance of the persistent low level of unemployment we experienced in the latter years of the 2010s. Moreover, even in a time of record-low unemployment, as in 2019, nearly half of the poor (45 percent) were extremely poor, living on *less than half the poverty-level income*—that is, less than $12,963 a year for a family of four.[24] The median household income in 2019 was $68,703. People living in poverty are living far below what is typical. They are not thriving but living under harmful and demeaning material circumstances.

Millions of people continue to be trapped in poverty despite our nation's rising affluence. The trend was very different during the 1960s and into the early 1970s, when even poor households had strong income gains, as shown in Figure 5.1a. The nation's poverty rate fell dramatically, from 22.4 percent in 1959 to 11.1 percent in 1973.[25] *Shockingly, until 2019, the poverty rate had never again fallen as low as it was in 1973, even though the per capita GDP has risen over threefold since 1959.* If the nation's growing prosperity had continued to be broadly shared after 1973, official poverty as defined by the government

---

23. Semega et al., *Income and Poverty: 2019*, 55 and table B-1.
24. Semega et al., table B-3.
25. Unfortunately, there are few comparable data on poverty prior to 1959.

would have been eliminated by the early 1990s.[26] Poverty is worse in the United States than in thirty-four other industrialized countries.[27]

The characteristics of the officially poor may be surprising if one believes common myths. Among the poor, whites are the largest racial/ethnic group (43 percent of all the poor), followed by Hispanics (29 percent), African Americans (24 percent), and Asians (4 percent).[28] However, within a racial or ethnic group, whites are less likely to be poor than are people of color. In 2019, just 7 percent of whites were poor, while poverty afflicted 23 percent of Native Americans and Alaskan Natives, 19 percent of African Americans, 17 percent of Native Hawaiians and Pacific Islanders, 16 percent of Hispanics, and 7 percent of Asians.[29] So while a plurality of the poor are white, poverty disproportionately afflicts people of color.

Looking more deeply, we find additional unfounded myths. If our thirty-eight million poor neighbors were represented by one hundred people, thirty-one would be children, thirteen would be seniors, and the other fifty-five would be adults ages eighteen to sixty-four.[30] Among the working-age adults would be twenty who work, eleven with disabilities, eight students, eight caregivers, four early retirees, and two who are unemployed and looking for work. Just two would fall outside these categories. It appears the huge majority of poor adults are probably doing just what they think they need to be doing, things we would probably affirm and celebrate. It is an indictment of our economy and our country that they cannot do these things and thrive.

Why are so many people floundering, living in poverty, and failing to thrive? Too often we look for some reason innate to the person, like their home environment, race, ethnicity, or culture. But these explanations don't fit the facts. Poverty is not a condition that only or even primarily affects people with certain traits. *The majority of Americans* (59 percent) *will live in*

26. Elise Gould, *No Matter How We Measure Poverty, the Poverty Rate Would Be Much Lower If Economic Growth Were More Broadly Shared* (Washington, DC: EPI, January 15, 2014).

27. OECD iLibrary, "Poverty Rate," accessed April 26, 2019, https://doi.org/10.1787/0fe1315d-en. Poverty is defined as a household income below half the median, 2014–17.

28. Semega et al., *Income and Poverty: 2019*, table B-1.

29. US Bureau of the Census, "American Community Survey," table S1701, accessed October 6, 2020.

30. Lauren Bauer, *Who Was Poor in the United States in 2017?* (Washington, DC: Brookings Institution, January 3, 2019). Data for 2017.

official poverty at some point in their adult lives, including 53 percent of whites and 91 percent of African Americans, 59 percent of women and 56 percent of men, and 39 percent of white males with a high school diploma or more education.[31] Some 45 percent of all adults will use a means-tested government program restricted to people in need at some time during their prime working years, ages twenty to sixty.[32] If floundering and poverty were due to a personal failing—laziness, a poor work ethic, flawed choices, inability to defer gratification, or whatever—then it would have to be a very common one, afflicting much of the population.

Remember that the biblical writers do not differentiate among poor people based on the reasons they are poor. Regardless of its cause, poverty is to be relieved. Everyone is worthy; all are deserving of needed resources. Higher wages and more work hours would enable some of the poor to escape poverty. Others have restrictions on the number of hours they can work or may not be able to work at all due to disability or conflicting responsibilities. In a just economy, those unable to work receive the support they need to thrive.

Our national tragedy of childhood poverty is especially destructive, and it is also costly. In 2019, nearly 10.5 million children, or about one in every seven, were poor by the official definition.[33] Roughly one in three children will experience poverty sometime during childhood.[34] Children of color are more likely to be poor than white children, and child poverty is more prevalent in the United States than in other high-income nations. Children growing up poor experience stress and have stressed parents. They are less likely to graduate from high school and attend college. They have fewer job opportunities and lower earnings as adults. They have poorer mental and

31. Mark R. Rank, *One Nation, Underprivileged: Why American Poverty Affects Us All* (New York: Oxford University Press, 2005), tables 4.1, 4.3, and 4.4. Data for other races and ethnicities are not available.
32. Mark R. Rank, Thomas A. Hirschl, and Kirk A. Foster, *Chasing the American Dream: Understanding What Shapes Our Fortunes* (New York: Oxford University Press, 2014), table 3.1, 37. Means-tested programs include food stamps (SNAP), Medicaid, TANF/ Aid to Families with Dependent Children, SSI, General Assistance, housing assistance, or other cash or in-kind welfare program.
33. Semega et al., *Income and Poverty: 2019*, table B-1.
34. Katherine Magnuson and Elizabeth Votruba-Drzal, "Enduring Influences of Childhood Poverty," in *Changing Poverty, Changing Policies*, ed. Maria Cancian and Sheldon Danziger (New York: Russell Sage Foundation, 2009), 153–79.

physical health. The nation's failure to end child poverty tragically wastes talent and lives. It also costs nearly $1 trillion annually, largely due to the loss of poor children's future economic productivity and increased expenses for health care and crime.[35] Many programs that provide the poor with food, housing, medical care, or income support have been shown to improve children's well-being and future success.[36] Every dollar spent on reducing childhood poverty could save the country at least seven dollars in future costs avoided.[37] Our failure to end poverty, especially childhood poverty, is not only immoral but also financially wasteful.[38]

Tens of Millions More with Unmet Needs

Our sisters and brothers with incomes low enough to place them among the officially poor face severe hardship. But the official poverty threshold is too low. Tens of millions of families with incomes above the poverty level also have unmet material needs. They are not thriving. Researchers generally agree that families need incomes of at least twice the poverty level for a minimally adequate standard of living, or $51,852 for a family of four in 2019.[39] By this standard, 26 percent of the population, or over eighty-five million people, had incomes too low to thrive in 2019.[40] This assessment of poverty is probably closer to the biblical one.

For many of our neighbors with unmet material needs, deprivation is multidimensional. Too little income often means too little food, housing that

---

35. Michael McLaughlin and Mark R. Rank, "Estimating the Economic Cost of Childhood Poverty in the United States," *Social Work Research* 42, no. 2 (June 2018): 73–83. Data for 2015. Also see Mark R. Rank, "The Cost of Keeping Children Poor," *New York Times*, April 15, 2018.
36. National Academies of Sciences, Engineering, and Medicine, *A Roadmap to Reducing Child Poverty*, Consensus Study Report (Washington, DC: National Academies Press, 2019).
37. Jorge Luis García et al., "Quantifying the Life-Cycle Benefits of a Prototypical Early Childhood Program" (working paper 23479, NBER, Cambridge, MA, issued June 2017, revised February 2019).
38. For an overview, see Jason DeParle, "How to Fix Child Poverty," *New York Review of Books*, July 23, 2020.
39. For the minimal income needed to thrive for a range of family types and sizes and in a variety of locations, see the EPI Family Budget Calculator (https://www.epi.org/resources/budget/) and the Living Wage Calculator from the Massachusetts Institute of Technology (https://livingwage.mit.edu/).
40. Semega et al., *Income and Poverty: 2019*, table B-3.

is too expensive and substandard, and restricted access to education and health care. We briefly review some aspects of material deprivation faced by many people in the United States. Remember, the conditions described here in the late 2010s, prior to the coronavirus pandemic, reflect a time in the United States when poverty and other forms of deprivation were *lower* than usual.

Food

In 2018, some twenty-six million adults and eleven million children could not consistently afford sufficient, healthy food.[41] Among these food-insecure people, hunger was not a rare occasion but, on average, present during seven months of the year. Just 30 percent of these families had incomes below the poverty level. The other 70 percent were not considered to be poor by the official definition. Hunger exists even though millions of people participate in food assistance programs. The main program, the Supplemental Nutrition Assistance Program (SNAP), formerly called food stamps, helped over thirty-six million people in 2019 with an average benefit of $130 a month per person, or about $1.44 per meal.[42] Yes, all these people were in need and eligible for this support. A federal government study found that less than 1 percent of participants were ineligible for the support they received.[43]

Federal spending on feeding programs totaled $92 billion in 2019.[44] In addition, many charitable organizations, including churches, synagogues, mosques, temples, food banks, and community meal programs, provide food to those who lack it. Feeding America reports distributing $86 million in grants to food banks in 2019, serving more than forty million people in every county in the nation.[45] Something is seriously wrong with our economy— with our use and distribution of God's resources—when millions of people need assistance to buy and obtain food but millions are still hungry despite

41. Coleman-Jensen et al., *Household Food Security*, table 2.

42. US Department of Agriculture Food and Nutrition Service, "Supplemental Nutrition Assistance Program Participation and Costs," accessed December 2, 2021, https://www.fns .usda.gov/sites/default/files/resource-files/SNAPsummary-11.pdf.

43. US Department of Agriculture Food and Nutrition Service, *What Is FNS Doing to Fight SNAP Fraud?* (Washington, DC: USDA, June 27, 2019).

44. US Department of Agriculture Food and Nutrition Service, "Annual Summary of Food and Nutrition Service Programs," accessed December 2, 2021, https://www.fns.usda.gov/ sites/default/files/resource-files/annual-10.xls.

45. Feeding America, *2019 Annual Report* (Chicago: Feeding America, 2020).

such aid. Remember that this was in 2019, before the onset of the pandemic and at a time when the economy was relatively strong.

Housing

On any night in 2019, more than half a million people (568,000) were homeless.[46] Over the course of a year, the number who are homeless at some point is likely in the millions. Being homeless is not only a barrier to thriving but also a threat to life. Homeless people have higher rates of illness and die on average twelve years sooner than the nonhomeless population.[47] An important cause of homelessness is the nation's extreme shortage of affordable housing. Among eleven million renter households with extremely low incomes, there are only thirty-seven units of affordable and available housing for every one hundred families.[48] They are forced to pay more than they can afford or be homeless. Most of these families spend at least half of their income on housing, and one in four spends more than 70 percent.[49] Unaffordable rents leave too little income for food, transportation, health care, and other expenses. This precariousness means that even a small reduction in income can lead to eviction and potential homelessness. In 2016, some nine hundred thousand renter households were evicted, an event that creates long-lasting financial, social, emotional, and legal consequences.[50] Despite the shortage of affordable housing, three out of four low-income households that are eligible to receive federal housing assistance do not receive it

46. US Department of Housing and Urban Development, *The 2019 Annual Homeless Assessment Report to Congress, Part 1* (Washington DC: US Department of HUD, January 2019).
47. National Health Care for the Homeless Council, *Homelessness and Health: What's the Connection?* (Nashville: NHCHC, February 2019).
48. National Low Income Housing Coalition, *The Gap: A Shortage of Affordable Rental Homes* (Washington, DC: NLIHC, March 2019). Extremely low-income households have incomes at or below either the poverty guideline or 30 percent of the median family income in the metropolitan or nonmetropolitan area, whichever is higher.
49. Eviction Lab, Princeton University, "Why Eviction Matters, Eviction Impact," accessed March 10, 2020, https://evictionlab.org/why-eviction-matters/#eviction-impact. Also see Matthew Desmond, *Evicted: Poverty and Profit in the American City* (New York: Crown, 2016); and Joint Center for Housing Studies of Harvard University, *The State of the Nation's Housing 2019* (Cambridge, MA: Harvard University Press, 2019).
50. Eviction Lab, Princeton University, "Why Eviction Matters, Affordable Housing Crisis," accessed March 10, 2020, https://evictionlab.org/why-eviction-matters/#affordable-housing-crisis.

because our housing support programs are chronically underfunded.[51] Even middle-income households face a shortage of affordable housing.[52]

Lack of Economic Security

Many households lack economic security. In an April 2019 Gallup poll, 40 percent of Americans said they were barely making ends meet or were running up debt.[53] Such tight finances provide few opportunities to save. In 2018, four in ten adults (39 percent), if faced with an unexpected expense of $400, would not be able to cover it from savings or with a credit card that would be fully paid off when due.[54] Incomes are also growing increasingly precarious. Over a two-year period, one-quarter of families experienced a drop in income of at least 40 percent.[55]

Debt

As the biblical writers understood, debt is always risky. But today, a lack of legal protections leaves low-income borrowers subject to particularly abusive lending practices. Payday, auto title, and other small-dollar loans carry interest rates that may exceed 300 percent.[56] These debt traps are designed to force borrowers into repeat loans on which they pay billions of dollars in interest and fees. Payday loans can end in bankruptcy; one in nine people with an auto title loan has their car repossessed.[57] The student loan program is poorly administered, is riddled with abuse, and weighs down borrowers for decades. Some forty-five million people have student loan debt that averages

51. Will Fischer and Barbara Sard, *Chart Book: Federal Housing Spending Is Poorly Matched to Need* (Washington, DC: CBPP, March 8, 2017).

52. National Low Income Housing Coalition, *Out of Reach 2019* (Washington, DC: NLIHC, 2019).

53. V. Lance Tarrance, *Despite US Economic Success, Financial Anxiety Remains* (Washington, DC: Gallup, July 12, 2019).

54. Board of Governors of the Federal Reserve System, *Report on the Economic Well-Being of US Households in 2018* (Washington, DC: Federal Reserve, May 23, 2019).

55. Pew Charitable Trusts, *The Precarious State of Family Balance Sheets* (Philadelphia: Pew, January 29, 2015).

56. Federal Trade Commission, *Consumer Information, Car Title Loans* (Washington, DC: FTC, July 2014).

57. Pew Charitable Trusts, *Auto Title Loans: Market Practices and Borrowers' Experiences* (Philadelphia: Pew, March 25, 2015), 13.

$33,000.[58] In early 2020, two in five student loan borrowers were in default or delinquent.[59] In many cases, even institutions using deceptive and abusive practices are protected, while struggling borrowers receive little help.

Health Care

Americans have shorter lives and more premature deaths from preventable conditions than people in other wealthy nations.[60] But the United States also spends much more on health care than do other countries: 50 percent more than Germany and France, 57 percent more than Canada, and 72 percent more than the United Kingdom.[61] Moreover, while other countries spend less, they provide universal health care. In the United States, some twenty-six million people had no health insurance in 2019, many of whom were low-wage workers.[62] The uninsured have poorer health and shortened lives.[63]

But the most important factor influencing health and longevity is *not* health care. Access to medical care and its quality account for only 10 to 20 percent of all the modifiable factors that contribute to a population's health outcomes.[64] The greatest impact, the other 80 to 90 percent, comes from what are called the social determinants of health. These include social and economic factors like education, income, and family support; health behaviors, including the use of tobacco, alcohol, and drugs as well as diet and exercise; and the physical environment, including air and water quality and housing. The reason our nation's health expenditures are so

58. Zach Friedman, "Student Loan Debt Statistics in 2019: A $1.5 Trillion Crisis," *Forbes*, February 25, 2019.

59. Center for Responsible Lending, *Student Debt Cancellation Is Essential to Economic Recovery from COVID-19* (Washington, DC: Center for Responsible Lending, April 9, 2020).

60. Roosa Tikkanen and Melinda K. Abrams, *US Health Care from a Global Perspective, 2019: Higher Spending, Worse Outcomes?* (New York: Commonwealth Fund, January 30, 2020).

61. OECD Data, "Health Spending," accessed February 11, 2020, https://data.oecd.org/healthres/health-spending.htm.

62. Katherine Keisler-Starkey and Lisa N. Bunch, *Health Insurance in the United States: 2019*, Report no. P60-271 (Washington, DC: US Bureau of the Census, September 15, 2020), table 1.

63. Steffie Woolhandler and David U. Himmelstein, "The Relationship of Health Insurance and Mortality: Is Lack of Insurance Deadly?," *Annals of Internal Medicine* 167, no. 6 (September 19, 2017): 424–31.

64. Sanne Magnan, "Social Determinants of Health 101 for Health Care: Five Plus Five," *NAM Perspectives*, Discussion Paper, Washington, DC: National Academy of Medicine, October 9, 2017, https://doi.org/10.31478/201710c.

high and produce such poor outcomes is our failure to adequately address these social determinants of health.

Certainly, access to quality health care matters. But poverty and disadvantage, regardless of insurance coverage, are bad for one's health. The poor live shorter lives and have more illness and disability than comparable people who are not poor.[65]

Paid Time Off

Fully thirty-one million workers (22 percent or nearly one-quarter of the workforce) have no paid sick leave or paid holidays, and thirty-three million have no paid vacation.[66]

Nonstandard Employment

Gig workers, temps, independent contractors, and on-call and contract workers earn less and have fewer benefits than they would in standard jobs, and they often work fewer hours than they would like.[67] For example, at Google, over half the employees are temps and contract workers, employed at Google but not working for Google.[68] They are paid less and have poorer benefits than the Google employees they work beside. Many of the workers in nonstandard jobs have unpredictable work schedules that make their incomes uncertain and variable but also make a second job, schooling, or scheduled childcare nearly impossible. People who work part time, either by choice or because nothing else is available, are paid 20 percent less per hour, on average, than a full-time employee who does the same work.[69]

65. Irma T. Elo, "Social Class Differentials in Health and Mortality: Patterns and Explanations in Comparative Perspective," *Annual Review of Sociology* 35, no. 1 (2009): 553–72.

66. US Department of Labor, Bureau of Labor Statistics, *Employee Benefits in the United States—March 2020* (Washington, DC: BLS, 2020).

67. Arindrajit Dube and Ethan Kaplan, "Does Outsourcing Reduce Wages in the Low Wage Service Occupations? Evidence from Janitors and Guards," *Industrial and Labor Relations Review* 63, no. 2 (January 2010): 287–306; Lawrence F. Katz and Alan B. Krueger, "The Rise and Nature of Alternative Work Arrangements in the United States, 1995–2015" (working paper no. 22667, NBER, Cambridge, MA, September 2016).

68. Daisuke Wakabayashi, "Google's Shadow Work Force: Temps Who Outnumber Full-Time Employees," *New York Times*, May 28, 2019.

69. Lonnie Golden, *Part-Time Workers Pay a Big-Time Penalty* (Washington, DC: EPI, February 27, 2020).

Education

Education is a necessary foundation of individual thriving and essential for a flourishing society, a strong economy, and a vibrant democracy. But not all students equally benefit from the nation's investment in education. Research repeatedly finds that funding levels impact student achievement and education outcomes.[70] But most states fail to adequately fund schools serving their most impoverished children.[71] Social class, not cognitive abilities or effort, is the most significant predictor of educational success.[72] In addition, segregation in schools lowers achievement, hinders success in college, and reduces future employment opportunities and incomes of students of color.[73] After some progress in the 1960s and 1970s, racial segregation in public schools has increased in recent decades. Segregation by race and class is now the norm in K–12 education.[74] Many low-income families, unable to afford a computer or internet access, are excluded from online educational opportunities, job searches, and other activities that are a customary part of life today.

Higher education provides opportunity for some but is skewed to advance the already advantaged. Eighth graders from lower-income families with high test scores are less likely to complete college than are students with low test scores from high-income families.[75] Just 32 percent of students with parents who have the lowest incomes attend college, compared to 95 percent of those with parents with the highest.[76]

70. Bruce D. Baker, *Does Money Matter in Education?*, 2nd ed. (Washington, DC: Albert Shanker Institute, 2016).

71. Bruce D. Baker et al., *The Real Shame of the Nation* (New Brunswick, NJ: Education Law Center and Rutgers Graduate School of Education, 2018).

72. Emma García and Elaine Weiss, *Education Inequalities at the School Starting Gate: Gaps, Trends, and Strategies to Address Them* (Washington, DC: EPI, September 2017).

73. Gary Orfield et al., *Harming Our Common Future: America's Segregated Schools 65 Years after Brown*, Civil Rights Project (Los Angeles: University of California Press, May 10, 2019).

74. Emma García, *Schools Are Still Segregated, and Black Children Are Paying a Price* (Washington, DC: EPI, February 12, 2020).

75. Lawrence Mishel et al., *The State of Working America*, 12th ed. (Ithaca, NY: Cornell University Press, 2012), Figure 3O.

76. Raj Chetty et al., "Mobility Report Cards: The Role of Colleges in Intergenerational Mobility" (working paper no. 23618, NBER, Cambridge, MA, July 2017): appendix figure 1; Saez and Zucman, *Triumph of Injustice*, 214.

Early Childhood Education and Childcare

Quality childcare and early childhood education are vitally important for a child's future. Some affluent families enroll their children in top-rated programs even before they are born. But the benefits of these services are especially important for less advantaged children who, by nine months of age, are falling behind their more affluent peers in cognitive development, general health, and social-emotional development,[77] all areas that are improved by high-quality early childhood education programs.[78]

Just 67 percent of all three- to five-year-olds in the United States are enrolled in early childhood education, far fewer than the 100 percent enrollment in France, 97 percent in Germany, and 94 percent in the United Kingdom.[79] Public funding is essential so that children of all backgrounds may benefit from quality programs.

Childcare of all types is expensive, hard to find, and too often of poor quality. In thirty-five states, families pay more for childcare than for mortgages,[80] and in no state does the average cost of infant or toddler care meet the federal definition of affordable childcare—that is, available for no more than 7 percent of a family's annual income.[81]

Retirement

Working families, caught between stagnant wages and high costs, are saving too little for retirement. While many employers sponsor and contribute to workers' pension plans, many others do not. In 2021, 28 percent of workers were employed in firms with no pension plan, and just 56 percent of all workers were participants in an employer-sponsored plan.[82]

---

77. Tamara Halle et al., *Disparities in Early Learning and Development: Lessons from the Early Childhood Longitudinal Study—Birth Cohort* (Bethesda, MD: Child Trends, June 2009).

78. OECD, *Starting Strong 2017: Key OECD Indicators on Early Childhood Education and Care* (Paris: OECD, 2017), 31.

79. OECD, *Starting Strong 2017*, table 1.1.

80. Shael Polakow-Suransky, "How to End the Child-Care Crisis," *New York Times*, May 24, 2019.

81. Simon Workman and Steven Jessen-Howard, *Understanding the True Cost of Child Care for Infants and Toddlers* (Washington, DC: Center for American Progress, November 15, 2018).

82. US Department of Labor, Bureau of Labor Statistics, "Retirement Benefits: Access, Participation, and Take-Up Rates" in *National Compensation Survey: Employee Benefits in the United*

In recent decades, employer pension plans have become less generous as firms have shifted from traditional plans that guarantee a certain income in retirement to defined contribution plans like 401(k)s that provide no guarantees.[83] Instead, retirement income depends on the size of contributions made to the plan by the employer and employee and the investment savvy of the worker-investor. In most of these plans, an employer contribution depends on an employee first making their own personal contribution, something many workers cannot afford. For all these reasons, most workers have too little in retirement savings.

Defined contribution plans reflect the nation's wage inequality. Among families with a head of household aged thirty-two to sixty-one, the median retirement account was valued at $7,800 in 2016. Meanwhile, a family in the top 10 percent had accumulated over $320,000, and a family in the top 1 percent had more than $1.6 million.[84] Even among families near retirement (with a household head aged fifty-six to sixty-one), the median value of retirement accounts averaged just $21,000, and over a third of these families (38 percent) had no account at all. Given the low balances in retirement accounts, the Social Security program is critically important for seniors. One-third of senior households receive 90 percent or more of all their income from Social Security.[85]

Racism

One other factor influences economic outcomes and leaves many people unable to thrive: racism, white supremacy, discrimination, xenophobia, white privilege, and the many other biased practices and policies that have led to higher rates of poverty and socioeconomic disadvantage among Native Americans, African Americans, Hispanics, immigrants, Muslims, and other

States, March 2021 (Washington, DC: BLS, September 2021), accessed November 23, 2021, table 1, https://www.bls.gov/news.release/ebs2.t01.htm.

83. US Department of Labor, Employee Benefits Security Administration, *Private Pension Plan Bulletin, Historical Tables and Graphs, 1975–2017* (Washington, DC: DOL, September 2019), table E4, https://www.dol.gov/sites/default/files/ebsa/researchers/statistics/retirement-bulletins/private-pension-plan-bulletin-historical-tables-and-graphs.pdf.

84. Monique Morrissey, *The State of American Retirement Savings* (Washington, DC: EPI, December 10, 2019).

85. Social Security Administration, *Income of the Aged Chartbook, 2014*, Pub. no. 13-11727 (Washington DC: SSA, April 2016).

groups marginalized by dominant white culture. Racism and white supremacy are social evils. They are not only historical realities, but they continue
to have huge impacts today. Racism is a multilayered system embedded in
our culture, economy, and law and all aspects of society that disadvantages
people of color, especially African Americans.[86] It is not an event but a social
structure into which we are all socialized. The nation, and white Americans
in particular, must actively work to end this oppression.

The success achieved by some people of color in rising above the harmful effects of racism is not evidence of the absence of severe racial barriers. People of color and other marginalized groups are disadvantaged
in housing and wealth creation; education; access to loans and insurance;
health care; hiring, promotions, and pay; interactions with law enforcement;
fairness before the law; and just about every other aspect of well-being,
including the right to life itself.[87]

An Inadequate Safety Net

Before moving on, we need to note that the social safety net, while inadequate, does relieve at least some of the needs of millions of people. In 2017,
the various means-tested programs lifted thirty-six million people out of
official poverty, reducing the count of the officially poor by nearly half.[88] But
these programs are insufficient.

Consider the main welfare program providing cash assistance, Temporary Assistance for Needy Families (TANF). In 2017, fewer than one-quarter
of families living in official poverty (23 percent) received TANF benefits.
In sixteen states, 10 percent or fewer of all poor families received TANF.[89]

86. Robin DiAngelo, *White Fragility: Why It's So Hard for White People to Talk about Racism* (Boston: Beacon, 2018).
87. For example, see Michelle Alexander, *The New Jim Crow: Mass Incarceration in the Age of Col-
orblindness* (New York: New Press, 2010); Rothstein, *Color of Law*; Eric Foner, *Forever Free: The
Story of Emancipation and Reconstruction* (New York: Alfred A. Knopf, 2005); Ibram X. Kendi,
Stamped from the Beginning: The Definitive History of Racist Ideas in America (New York: Nation,
2016); and Colin Gordon, *Race in the Heartland* (Washington, DC: EPI, October 10, 2019).
88. Danilo Trisi and Matt Saenz, *Economic Security Programs Cut Poverty Nearly in Half over Last
50 Years* (Washington, DC: CBPP, November 26, 2019).
89. Ife Floyd, Ashley Burnside, and Liz Schott, *TANF Reaching Few Poor Families* (Washington,
DC, CBPP, November 28, 2018).

Moreover, the benefit level is so low that in almost every state, it leaves a family of three below *half* the poverty-level income.[90]

In addition to TANF, there is only one other federal cash assistance program.[91] People who are unable to work and have very low incomes and few assets may qualify for Supplemental Security Income (SSI). SSI provides benefits, averaging $771 per month for an individual and $1,157 for a couple, to some 8.1 million poor people, of whom 86 percent are disabled.[92] Many of these beneficiaries have no other source of income. Their safety net is entirely inadequate.

The Destructiveness of Poverty

Poverty means inadequate food, substandard housing, episodic health care, and restricted educational opportunities. But it is also more than these, as bad as they are. Considered broadly, the poor are unable to consume the goods and services that satisfy basic cultural norms. They fail to "participate in the activities and have the living conditions and amenities which are customary, or are at least widely encouraged or approved, in the societies to which they belong. Their resources are so seriously below those commanded by the average family that they are in effect excluded from the ordinary living patterns, customs, and activities."[93] The poor are outsiders in society. They may appear to others and even feel themselves to be too different, too other, to comfortably participate in many aspects of community life. They are the socially excluded.

Over their life trajectory, these neighbors are limited in what they can do and become not only by money but also due to social exclusion, a condition

---

90. CBPP, *Policy Basics: Temporary Assistance for Needy Families* (Washington, DC: CBPP, February 6, 2020).

91. In 2015, some twenty-six states maintained programs of General Assistance that provided very small cash benefits to adults. Most of these programs were restricted to people considered unable to work due to physical or mental disability. Only eleven states provided General Assistance to able-bodied individuals. See Liz Schott, "State Assistance for Poor Childless Adults Shrinking," *Off the Charts* (blog), CBPP, July 13, 2015, https://www.cbpp.org/blog/state-assistance-for-poor-childless-adults-shrinking.

92. CBPP, *Policy Basics: Supplemental Security Income* (Washington, DC: CBPP, February 6, 2020).

93. Peter Townsend, *Poverty in the United Kingdom: A Survey of Household Resources and Standards of Living* (Berkeley: University of California Press, 1979), 31.

that harms not only these individuals whose lives are stunted but society as well, which is deprived of their contributions. Being among the excluded often means low self-esteem, a lack of control over important decisions, and feelings of alienation and inferiority. It can also bring a sense of shame that expresses itself as despair, depression, withdrawal, suicidal thoughts, and self-loathing.[94] It usually means a failure to live in the fullness of life. In these ways, poverty in a wealthy country like the United States can be just as destructive as the worst poverty anywhere in the world.

According to the United States Conference of Catholic Bishops, "Poverty is not merely the lack of adequate financial resources. It entails a more profound kind of deprivation, a denial of full participation in the economic, social, and political life of society and the inability to influence decisions that affect one's life. It means being powerless in a way that assaults not only one's pocketbook but also one's fundamental human dignity."[95]

Poverty and Despair: The Destruction of Self and Others

Social exclusion, despair, shame, and the loss of one's sense of self-worth can manifest in a variety of ways. In recent years, we have seen it play out as addiction, suicide, hatred, hypermasculinity, misogyny, xenophobia, violence, and terrorism. Between 2014 and 2017, life expectancy at birth in the United States declined.[96] This is a startling finding, since life expectancy had been rising nearly continuously for over one hundred years and seldom falls except during war, a major epidemic, or other calamitous social condition. Deaths among seniors continued to decline during those years, but surprisingly, deaths rose most rapidly among twenty-five- to sixty-four-year-old white men and white women without college degrees. The causes were not the usual ones like cancer and heart disease. Instead, the increase was largely due to the diseases of despair—drug overdose, suicide, and liver disease

---

94. Robert Walker et al., "Poverty in Global Perspective: Is Shame a Common Denominator?," *Journal of Social Policy* 42, no. 2 (April 2013): 215–33.

95. US Conference of Catholic Bishops, *Economic Justice for All: Pastoral Letter on Catholic Social Teaching and the US Economy* (Washington, DC: US Catholic Conference, 1986), 93.

96. National Center for Health Statistics, *Health, United States, 2018* (Hyattsville, MD: National Center for Health Statistics, 2019); National Center for Health Statistics, *Health, United States, 2017*, Special Feature on Mortality (Hyattsville, MD: National Center for Health Statistics, 2018).

related to alcoholism.[97] The death rate from these diseases began rising soon after 2000, the effect of cumulative economic and social disadvantages that have made life unbearable for some: a shortage of good jobs, falling wages, fewer opportunities for achieving even minimal hopes and dreams, and the erosion of social, marital (the marriage rate among this population is much lower than for other groups), and community ties. Add the easy availability of opioids and guns, and the death rate climbs.[98] Poverty, official or biblical, is often deadly, whether the cause is inadequate health care, homelessness, stress, suicide, alcoholism, or drug overdose. In 2018, life expectancy rose due to the decline in opioid deaths.[99] What the future holds is uncertain.

The recent focus on what are relatively small increases in white mortality should not obscure the fact that Blacks live shorter lives, on average, than whites. However, life expectancy is rising more quickly for Blacks than for whites. Between 2000 and 2017, life expectancy for whites rose by 1.5 years, from 77.3 to 78.8, while for Blacks it rose by 3.5 years, from 71.8 to 75.3.[100] Blacks still have shorter life spans than whites, on average, but the gap is shrinking. Hispanics live longer than either whites or Blacks, an average of 81.8 years in 2017.

Despair and social exclusion can also manifest as hatred and violence against others. This is not a new phenomenon. Rising expectations followed by their frustration have historically been a source of revolution and rebellion.[101] The revolutions of the Arab Spring were driven, in part, by the frustrated expectations of young adults who saw few opportunities for work that would enable them to thrive.[102] (In 2020, over 22 percent of fifteen- to twenty-four-year-olds worldwide were not in employment, education, or

97. Anne Case and Angus Deaton, *Mortality and Morbidity in the 21st Century* (Washington, DC: Brookings Institution, March 23, 2017); Anne Case and Angus Deaton, *Deaths of Despair and the Future of Capitalism* (Princeton, NJ: Princeton University Press, 2020).

98. Everytown for Gun Safety, *Firearm Suicide in the United States* (New York: Everytown for Gun Safety, August 30, 2018), https://everytownresearch.org/firearm-suicide/. Half of all suicides are by gun. Two-thirds of deaths by gun are suicides.

99. Sabrina Tavernise and Abby Goodnough, "American Life Expectancy Rises for First Time in Four Years," *New York Times*, January 30, 2020.

100. Elizabeth Arias and Jiaquan Xu, "United States Life Tables, 2017," *National Vital Statistics Reports* 68, no 7 (Hyattsville, MD: National Center for Health Statistics, 2019).

101. James C. Davies, "Toward a Theory of Revolution," *American Sociological Review* 27, no. 1 (February 1962): 5–19.

102. International Labor Organization, *Youth Unemployment in the Arab World Is a Major Cause for Rebellion* (Geneva: ILO, April 2011).

training.[103]) William Schultz, executive director of Amnesty International, points out that among the root causes of international terrorism is a lack of economic opportunity and people's inability to meet their "legitimate aspirations."[104]

In the United States, lack of opportunity and frustrated expectations may also be expressed through hatred and violence turned on others—for example, in the form of armed groups promoting white supremacy and militarized vigilantes at the southern border. Consider the words of Chris Hedges, Pulitzer Prize–winning journalist and graduate of Harvard Divinity School: "The white racists and neo-Nazis may be unsavory, but they too are victims. They too lost jobs and often live in poverty in deindustrialized wastelands. They too are frequently plagued by debt, foreclosures, bank repossessions, and the inability to repay student loans. They too suffer from evictions, opioid addictions, domestic violence, and despair."[105]

Poverty and its accompanying despair, hopelessness, and social exclusion are deadly to oneself and others. African American poet Langston Hughes recognizes this in his 1951 poem "Harlem":

What happens to a dream deferred?

Does it dry up
like a raisin in the sun?
Or fester like a sore—
And then run?
Does it stink like rotten meat?
Or crust and sugar over—
like a syrupy sweet?

103. International Labor Organization, *Global Employment Trends for Youth 2020: Technology and the Future of Jobs* (Geneva: ILO, 2015).

104. Rohan Gunaratna, *Inside Al Qaeda: Global Network of Terror* (New York: Columbia University Press, 2002), 232–33. Also see William Schulz, *Tainted Legacy: 9/11 and the Ruin of Human Rights* (New York: Nation, 2003).

105. Chris Hedges, *America: The Farewell Tour* (New York: Simon & Schuster, 2018), 198. Reportedly, many of the people arrested for their participation in the January 6, 2021, insurrection at the Capitol had a history of financial problems. See Todd C. Frankel, "A Majority of the People Arrested for Capitol Riot Had a History of Financial Trouble," *Washington Post*, February 10, 2021.

Maybe it just sags
like a heavy load.

Or does it explode?[106]

JOBS AND WAGES

We now explore the causes of the rise in inequality, the persistence of poverty, and the increase in despair over the past forty years. These trends have largely been driven by a growth in wage inequality. Many workers are not sharing in the nation's rising prosperity. The United States is failing to fulfill the second criterion of a just economy: not all adults who want a job have one, and many jobs do not pay a family-supporting wage.

The fundamental reason for someone's failure to flourish today in the United States is the shortage of good jobs, and the problem is getting worse, especially for younger workers without a college degree.[107] The most common reason for a family to fall into official poverty is a loss of employment and earnings.[108] Moreover, if someone is unable to work or can only work restricted hours, the safety net too often fails to supply the needed resources to keep the worker and their family above poverty.

Low Wages

We sometimes forget that located squarely in the center of our political democracy (which has always been incomplete and now is increasingly threatened) is a very undemocratic, abusive, hugely important structure

---

106. Langston Hughes, *The Collected Works of Langston Hughes*, vol. 3, *The Poems: 1951–1967*, ed. Arnold Rampersad (Columbia: University of Missouri Press, 2001), 145.

107. David R. Howell, "From Decent to Lousy Jobs: New Evidence on the Decline in American Job Quality, 1979–2017" (working paper, Center for Equitable Growth, Washington, DC, August 2019).

108. Stephanie Riegg Cellini, Signe-Mary McKernan, and Caroline Ratcliffe, *The Dynamics of Poverty in the United States: A Review of Data, Methods, and Findings* (Washington, DC: Urban Institute, January 2008); Mark R. Rank, Hong-Sik Yoon, and Thomas A. Hirschl, "American Poverty as a Structural Failing: Evidence and Arguments," *Journal of Sociology and Social Welfare* 30, no. 4, art. 2.

called the market economy. Here, people are not equal. We do not have equal input into how economic institutions and structures function. A democratic society where *all* are equal and living in liberty cannot be achieved if society lacks a democratic economy that ensures everyone has the material resources they need to thrive. As we have seen, how one fares economically is a matter of life and death, not just in a very poor country far away from the prosperous Global North, but also within this rich nation.

The stagnant *incomes* and the rise in *income* inequality examined earlier are largely due to a forty-year stagnation and, for many, a decline in *wages*, the term used by economists for all the money someone earns by working, whether it is called a wage, salary, commission, earnings, or self-employment income. Most households get all or nearly all of their income from work, and seniors' retirement income is largely dependent on their previous earnings. So for most people, income is primarily determined by wages. Stagnant and falling incomes are largely due to stagnant and falling wages. Unsurprisingly, the trend in wage growth mirrors the trend in income growth.

Just as growth in GDP and national income provides the potential for household incomes to rise, the growth in economic productivity—the total amount of output generated in an average hour of work across the whole economy—provides the potential for workers' compensation (wages and benefits) to rise. Between 1948 and 1979, average compensation for private sector workers categorized as production and nonsupervisory (PNS) workers—roughly the four-fifths of all workers who do not have a four-year college degree—rose 108 percent, more than doubling, closely mirroring the productivity gain of 118 percent.[109] (All compensation data are adjusted for inflation.) The potential for rising compensation among workers across the wage distribution was largely realized. This is shown on the left side of figure 5.3, where hourly compensation and productivity rose in tandem.

But after the 1970s, rising productivity no longer meant rising wages and benefits for many workers. From 1979 to 2020, productivity continued

109. EPI State of Working America Data Library, "Productivity and Hourly Compensation," updated March 2020, https://www.epi.org/data/#?subject=prodpay. There is only one set of wage data that extends into the immediate postwar period: wages for the four-fifths of the private sector labor force classified as production and nonsupervisory workers.

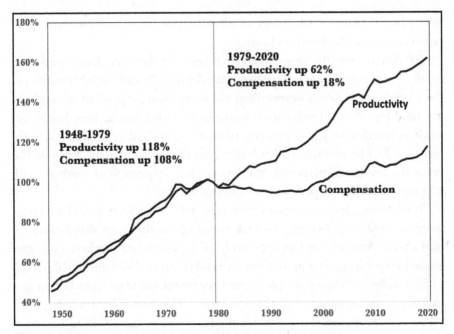

Figure 5.3. Compensation and productivity, 1948–2020

Note: Compensation is wages plus benefits. Productivity is output per hour, the factor that enables wage growth. Hourly compensation of the 82 percent of private-sector workers classified as production and nonsupervisory workers and net productivity of the total economy. The vertical line marks 1979.

Source: Economic Policy Institute analysis of data from the US Departments of Labor and Commerce, State of Working America Data Library, https://www.epi.org/data/#?subject =prodpay.

to rise (up 62 percent), but average compensation for PNS workers nearly flatlined, rising just 18 percent over the four decades.[110] Productivity growth provided the potential for compensation to continue its robust rise, but that did not happen. Flat wage gains explain most of the stagnation in people's incomes. Wage decline and stagnation were especially common in jobs held by men. Shockingly and tragically, in 2019 the median male wage was still

---

110. Note that *compensation* did not rise. The rising cost of fringe benefits like health insurance, which may have squeezed wage growth, is not a factor in the stagnation of compensation.

below its 1978 level.[111] Over half of all men were being paid less than their fathers and grandfathers had been.

As with income, the lower down a worker is on the wage distribution, the smaller their pay increases have been. Between 1979 and 2019, the wage of the worker at the tenth percentile (paid more than 10 percent of workers but paid less than 90 percent of workers, an indication of how low-wage workers fared) rose just 3 percent, from $9.75 to $10.07 an hour, *over the forty years*.[112] The median worker had a gain of just 15 percent. Even workers at the seventieth percentile (paid more than 70 percent of workers) had an increase of just 20 percent over the period.

While wages for the majority rose very little, some workers did see large increases, but it is necessary to look very high in the wage distribution to find them. Among the top one-tenth of 1 percent of workers, average annual wages increased more than fourfold between 1979 and 2018, rising to $2.8 million.[113] Many people at the very top of the wage distribution are executives and managers. In the 350 largest US firms, CEO pay has skyrocketed. Compared to each firm's median worker, these CEOs' pay rose from an average of 20:1 in 1965, to 58:1 in 1989, and to 278:1 in 2018.[114] The highest-paid hedge fund managers take home up to $2 billion in just one year.[115] This is not to suggest that CEOs and hedge fund managers are necessarily bad and greedy people, but our economic system and public policies enable, and even encourage, these very disparate wages.

Over the past four decades, strong productivity gains provided the potential for substantial wage increases for all workers. But just a few already highly paid workers reaped most of the benefits. In addition, a greater share of income has been flowing into firms' profits rather than into employees'

111. EPI State of Working America Data Library, "Median/Average Hourly Wages," updated February 20, 2020, https://www.epi.org/data/#?subject=wage-avg.

112. EPI State of Working America Data Library, "Wages by Percentile and Wage Ratios," updated February 20, 2020, https://www.epi.org/data/#?subject=wage-percentiles.

113. EPI State of Working America Data Library, "Wages for Top 1.0%, 0.1% and Bottom 90%," updated December 2019, https://www.epi.org/data/#?subject=wagegroup.

114. Lawrence Mishel and Julia Wolfe, *CEO Compensation Has Grown 940% since 1978* (Washington, DC: EPI, August 14, 2019). CEO annual compensation includes salary, bonus, restricted stock grants, stock options realized, and long-term incentive payouts for CEOs at the top 350 US firms ranked by sales.

115. Andrew Ross Sorkin, "Bridgewater's Ray Dalio Tops the List of Hedge Fund Manager Compensation," *New York Times*, April 30, 2019.

wages and benefits. Why is this happening? As we will examine below, the growth in inequality that began during the 1970s and continues today was driven by changes in our economic policies.

Unions

In the workplace, two factors greatly influence wages, benefits, and working conditions: workers' bargaining power and public policies. Unions play important roles in both these areas. A lone worker generally has little power in the workplace and must accept whatever pay and working conditions an employer offers. But when workers come together in a union, they can exert pressure for better wages and benefits, negotiate workplace rules and procedures for dealing with problems, and have a voice in workplace decision-making. But the share of the labor force represented by a union has been falling for decades. In 2019, just 12 percent of workers were represented by a union, down from 27 percent in 1973.[116] The fall in union membership and the decline in the power of unions in the political arena are key reasons for the inability of workers to transform rising productivity into rising wages. The fall in middle-class incomes tracks the decline in union membership and the political power of unions.[117]

Unions are good for workers, especially those in the bottom and middle of the wage scale. A worker covered by a union contract earns an average of 13 percent more than a similar nonunion worker and has better benefits.[118] Unions narrow the historic wage disadvantages suffered by women and people of color. When unions are strong, they set a standard for an entire industry or occupation, raising wages for nonunion as well as union workers. Many problems present in workplaces today could be addressed by unions, such as scheduling abuses, lack of paid sick leave, and managers assigning workers too few hours. What prevents union demands from becoming excessive is the realization that each worker's wages and continuing employment depend on their firm's success. Through the process

116. EPI State of Working America Data Library, "Union Coverage," updated January 31, 2020, https://www.epi.org/data/#?subject=unioncov.

117. Ross Eisenbrey, *Middle Class Incomes Suffer without Collective Bargaining* (Washington, DC: EPI, March 4, 2015).

118. Josh Bivens et al., *How Today's Unions Help Working People: Giving Workers the Power to Improve Their Jobs and Unrig the Economy* (Washington, DC: EPI, August 24, 2017). Wage differential for 2011.

of collective bargaining, a firm's union and management seek to find the appropriate balance between the needs of the workers and the needs of the firm. Many mainline Protestant and Catholic bodies have supported trade unions and organizing.[119] In 2017, Pope Francis declared, "There is no good society without a good union."[120]

The decline in union representation has contributed to the growth in inequality. An estimated one-third of the increased wage inequality between middle- and high-wage male workers and one-fifth of the increased wage inequality among females is due to the decline in unions.[121] Among men, the erosion of collective bargaining has been the largest single factor driving a wedge between middle- and high-wage workers.

Almost half (48 percent) of workers say they would vote to form a union if they had the chance.[122] Their right to do so is a fundamental human right. But the right to form a union is only weakly protected in US law, and workers' desires for unions are nearly always thwarted by employers using both illegal practices and legal but "heavy-handed tactics that would be illegal in any election for public office."[123] Employers spend an estimated $340 million each year on "union avoidance advisers."[124] In nearly a third of all union election campaigns, employers are charged with illegal behaviors, including threats, surveillance activities, or harassment. One in five campaigns involves a charge that a worker was illegally fired for union activity. Many workers are afraid to join a union or support an organizing effort.[125] But penalties assessed for illegally interfering with union organizing are minimal and do not deter many employers' illegal practices. In addition, the

119. Interfaith Worker Justice, *What Faith Groups Say about Worker Justice* (Chicago: IWJ, 2011).
120. Junno Arocho Esteves, "Pope Francis: Labor Unions Are Essential to Society," *America Magazine*, June 28, 2017.
121. Bruce Western and Jake Rosenfeld, "Unions, Norms, and the Rise in US Wage Inequality," *American Sociological Review* 76 (2011): 513–37; Mishel et al., *Working America*, table 4.37. Data cover 1973–2007.
122. Bivens et al., *Today's Unions*.
123. Gordon Lafer and Lola Loustaunau, *Fear at Work: An Inside Account of How Employers Threaten, Intimidate, and Harass Workers to Stop Them from Exercising Their Right to Collective Bargaining* (Washington, DC: EPI, July 23, 2020); Lance Compa, *Unfair Advantage: Workers' Freedom of Association in the United States under International Human Rights Standards* (New York: Human Rights Watch, 2000).
124. McNicholas et al., *Unlawful: US Employers Are Charged with Violating Federal Law in 41.5% of All Union Election Campaigns* (Washington, DC: EPI, December 11, 2019).
125. Lafer and Loustaunau, *Fear at Work*.

right to strike over wages and benefits without employer retaliation—a right recognized in US law and international conventions—is essentially nullified, since it is also lawful for US employers to permanently replace striking workers.

Twenty-eight states have so-called right-to-work laws. Proponents claim this legislation prevents someone from being forced to join a union. But this is incorrect, since under federal law, no one can be required to join a union even if they are covered by and benefit from working under a union contract. However, a union is required by federal law to represent and negotiate a contract that covers all workers, whether they are members or not. Federal law also requires both union members and nonmembers working in private firms under a union contract to pay fair-share fees that cover the costs of core union services, such as negotiating the contract. "Right-to-work" legislation nullifies that part of the law, allowing a worker who is covered by a union contract and represented by the union to choose not to pay the fair-share fee. That worker will receive all the benefits of a union contract without having to pay anything to support the efforts that made it happen. Union supporters call this "right-to-freeload" legislation. Right-to-work legislation encourages workers who benefit from a union contract to cease paying for union services, thereby defunding and weakening these important institutions. In 2018, the US Supreme Court ruled that public sector employees nationwide who are covered by a union contract may choose not to pay their fair-share fee.

Unions also promote civic engagement and democratic participation.[126] Historically in the United States and still today in other countries, trade unions are powerful actors in the public arena. The efforts of unions and union members boost voter turnout, provide hands-on support for political candidates, and build political support for issues that benefit workers and working families. The failure to modernize our workplace standards— for example, to increase the federal minimum wage or require paid sick days for all workers—is directly connected to the decline in the strength of the labor movement.

126. Jake Rosenfeld, *What Unions No Longer Do* (Cambridge, MA: Harvard University Press, 2014), 170–71; Bivens et al., *Today's Unions*.

Unemployment

In addition to having a union, a second factor that boosts workers' bargaining power with employers is low unemployment. In recent decades, annual earnings for the bottom 90 percent of workers have risen in a meaningful way *only* when unemployment was at low levels.[127] But in the last forty years, average unemployment has been higher than in the three decades before 1980. After World War II until about 1980, full employment was the norm, but since then it has been rare.[128] This is another factor contributing to slow wage growth.

There is no economic factor that guarantees the number of jobs will equal the number of people who want to work. Even in the strongest economy, not everyone who wants a job has one. In 2013, when unemployment averaged a somewhat elevated 7.4 percent over the year, a new Walmart in Washington, DC, with six hundred job openings received twenty-three thousand applications; job seekers had an acceptance rate of 2.6 percent. It was harder to get a job at Walmart than to get into Harvard (acceptance rate of 5.9 percent).[129] A steady job, even one without top wages or benefits, is sought after by many workers who have even less desirable jobs.

Even when the unemployment rate is low, millions lack jobs. Moreover, the unemployment rate counts only the jobless who are actively looking for work, not everyone who wants a job but, possibly after weeks of fruitless searching, gives up. Joblessness is always more severe than the unemployment rate indicates.

Moreover, employers are more likely to hire whites than equally qualified people of color. So whatever the level of overall unemployment, the rate for African Americans runs about twice the level for whites, and the rate for Hispanics is generally about halfway between the rates for whites and Blacks. This gradient is present at every education level, even for college grads. In February 2020, the unemployment rate was 3.2 percent for

127. Elise Gould, *State of Working America Wages 2019* (Washington, DC: EPI, February 20, 2020), figure D.
128. Josh Bivens and Ben Zipperer, *The Importance of Locking in Full Employment for the Long Haul* (Washington, DC: EPI, August 21, 2018).
129. Christopher Ingraham, "Wal-Mart Has a Lower Acceptance Rate Than Harvard," *Washington Post*, March 28, 2014.

college grads who were Black, 3.0 percent for Hispanics, and 2.2 percent for whites.[130]

A Shortage of Good Jobs

There are too few good jobs, so some people will always be left out. If they are to have any job, they may have to work in one with inadequate pay, few benefits, and little opportunity for advancement. But material hardship is only one part of the destructiveness of these jobs. They are often destructive of a worker's self-worth as well. It is commonly argued that workers are paid for what their labor is worth. Thus a low-wage job must mean a worker contributes very little to society and is less worthy of respect than someone with higher pay. Thank God the pandemic has forced us to recognize the *essential, valuable* work of low-wage workers. Now we need to raise the pay, improve the benefits, and treat with dignity the workers in these jobs as we recognize their inherent worthiness and important contributions. The labor market can be compared to the child's game of musical chairs, structured so there are always too many kids (workers) competing for too few chairs (good jobs).[131]

A Bias in Hiring

During periods when the economy is particularly strong and unemployment low, there are more jobs and more good jobs. Someone who might otherwise have been forced into a poor job or been left unemployed will be hired, maybe even into a good job. But during times when the economy is weaker—and this is the usual situation—there will be fewer good jobs and more unemployment. The workers most often left without a good job or without any job at all are those with lower levels of education, fewer skills, less experience, or more constraints due to family responsibilities or anyone deemed by a potential employer to have fewer positive attributes to bring to the workplace. This is often a very subjective determination, easily influenced by implicit racial or class bias. Workers' characteristics and qualifications that influence hiring are also very dependent on their previous life opportunities and challenges, many of which are largely outside a person's

130. EPI State of Working America Data Library, "Unemployment," updated March 2020, https://www.epi.org/data/#?subject=unemp.
131. Rank, *One Nation, Underprivileged*.

control, such as the quality of their education, opportunities for postsecond-ary schooling, family connections to people who can ease a worker's way into a good job or internship, accessible and reliable transportation, and other factors tightly linked to race and class. When employers have a choice of whom to hire—which is nearly always—they are, statistically, more likely to hire someone who is white and has relatively more education, regardless of whether it is necessary for the job.

More Education Will Not Eliminate Low-Wage Work

We often blame people in low-wage jobs or with no job for their plight: if they just had better skills, had done better in school, or had finished col-lege, then they could get better jobs and would not have stagnant or falling wages. But this misunderstands the problem. Higher educational attainment often can allow an *individual* to move into a better job. But more education does not solve *society's* problem of low-wage work. If every adult had a col-lege degree, we would still have tens of millions of people flipping burgers, cleaning floors, and caring for our elders in nursing homes. There would still be millions of people working in low-paying jobs and failing to thrive. More education can help an individual climb the economic ladder, but it will not fix our economy's problem of low-wage jobs. There will always be jobs on the bottom rungs of the ladder. In a just economy, even these jobs are good ones.

While more skills and additional education or training can often move someone from a lower-paying job into a higher-paying one, this is not a certainty. The educational attainment of the low-wage labor force has risen dramatically in recent decades.[132] But now even a college degree is no guar-antee of a good job or rising wages. In 2018, 43 percent of recent college graduates were working in jobs that did not require a college degree.[133] Even five years after graduation, 29 percent of college grads were still in jobs that did not require a college degree, including 35 percent with degrees in biol-ogy and biomedicine and 18 percent in computer science and engineering. In 2019, a time when the economy was particularly strong, the lower-paid

---

132. Lawrence Mishel, *Low-Wage Workers Have Far More Education Than They Did in 1968, Yet They Make Far Less* (Washington, DC: EPI, January 23, 2014).

133. Preston Cooper, "Underemployment Persists throughout College Graduates' Careers," *Forbes*, June 8, 2018.

half of all workers with a college degree were paid less than in 2000.[134] There is a shortage of good jobs, including for college grads, and even a college degree does not ensure rising wages.

Education does not convert poor-quality jobs into good ones or increase the number of good jobs.[135] To argue that income inequality could be significantly reduced if people only had more education and better skills falsely blames individuals for structural failings of the economy. This pretext allows some pundits, experts, and policy makers to avoid discussing the required changes in public policy that could address the problem but that might offend powerful forces that benefit from the status quo.

Overtime Pay

Another factor contributing to unemployment and wage inequality is Congress's failure to regularly update the eligibility criteria for overtime pay. Requiring employers to pay "time and a half" (1.5 times an employee's regular rate of pay) to some employees who work more than forty hours in a week discourages managers from requiring excessive hours of work and encourages them to instead create jobs and hire additional staff. All hourly workers must be paid time and a half for overtime hours. But so must some salaried workers.[136] In 1975, more than 60 percent of full-time salaried workers were eligible to receive the overtime pay premium because their regular pay was below the legal cap for eligibility. By 2016, the share of full-time salaried workers automatically eligible for overtime pay had dropped to less than 7 percent.[137] This makes it very easy (too easy) for employers to overwork existing salaried employees instead of hiring additional staff and creating new jobs. Policy change to automatically make more salaried workers eligible for overtime pay is necessary but furiously opposed

---

134. Gould, *Working America Wages 2019*, figure S.

135. The only exception would be in the very unlikely situation where a highly educated workforce created a shortage of workers with lower levels of education. This shortage might boost their wages.

136. Salaried workers who are executives or professionals or work in administrative positions with authority over work directly related to general business operations are ineligible for overtime.

137. Celine McNicholas, Samantha Sanders, and Heidi Shierholz, *What's at Stake in the States If the 2016 Federal Raise to the Overtime Pay Threshold Is Not Preserved—and What States Can Do about It* (Washington, DC: EPI, November 15, 2017).

by many employers. The failure to raise the salary cap for eligibility is
costing workers over $1 billion a year in lost overtime pay and lengthening
their work weeks.[138]

Wage Theft

Wage theft is the illegal but common workplace practice of employers' failure to pay workers all the wages they earn—for example, by paying less than
the legally required minimum wage, failing to pay workers (legally eligible
under current law) time and a half for overtime hours, or forcing employees to continue to work after clocking out, thus paying them nothing for
those work hours. In low-wage industries, two-thirds of workers (excluding
managers, professionals, and technical workers) experience wage theft *in any
week* and lose an average of 15 percent of their pay.[139] The total amount lost
by workers is huge and dwarfs other forms of theft. In 2012, for example,
the amount of employer-stolen wages that were recovered and restored to
workers ($933 million) was nearly three times the amount stolen in all bank,
home, street, gas station, and convenience store robberies ($341 million).[140]
While some wage theft can be attributed to employers' mistakes and misunderstanding of the law, most wage theft is intentional.[141] Authorities recover
from employers and return to workers some $1 billion in stolen wages
each year, but employers steal fifty times as much: an estimated $50 billion
a year.[142] Policy makers in some state legislatures have enacted legislation to
rein in wage theft, but much more is needed. Congress must protect workers

138. Heidi Shierholz, *More Than Eight Million Workers Will Be Left behind by the Trump Overtime Proposal* (Washington, DC: EPI, April 8, 2019).
139. David Cooper and Teresa Kroeger, *Employers Steal Billions from Workers' Paychecks Each Year* (Washington, DC: EPI, May 10, 2017); Annette Bernhardt et al., *Broken Laws, Unprotected Workers* (Berkeley: University of California, Los Angeles, Institute for Research on Labor and Employment, 2009).
140. Brady Meixell and Ross Eisenbrey, *Wage Theft Is a Much Bigger Problem Than Other Forms of Theft—but Workers Remain Mostly Unprotected* (Washington, DC: EPI, September 18, 2014).
141. Kim Bobo, *Wage Theft in America: Why Millions of Americans Are Not Getting Paid—and What We Can Do about It* (New York: New Press, 2009), 23.
142. Celine McNicholas, Zane Mokhiber, and Adam Chaikof, *Two Billion Dollars in Stolen Wages Were Recovered for Workers in 2015 and 2016—and That's Just a Drop in the Bucket* (Washington, DC: EPI, December 13, 2017).

against wage theft and penalize violations; in most states, penalties are nearly nonexistent.

Future Jobs

What about the future? Can we reliably assume that without a major over-haul of our public policies, there will be more good jobs and fewer poor-quality ones in the years ahead? Unfortunately, no. According to the US Labor Department, much of the job growth over the next ten years will be in occupations with low wages. Over half of the new jobs will be in just ten occupations, and over 60 percent of these jobs will be in occupations that paid $30,000 a year or less in 2019: home health and personal care aide, fast food worker, restaurant cook, medical assistant, laborer, and mate-rial mover.[143] In 2028, just 38 percent of all jobs will require any education beyond high school, barely up from 37 percent of jobs in 2018.[144] We cannot deceive ourselves into thinking that job trends will solve our economic (and ethical) problem of low wages. Nor will a more highly educated workforce mean living wages for all. To have a society where everyone has the opportu-nity to earn a family-supporting wage, we must ensure that all jobs are good jobs. Workers deserve nothing less.

THE ECONOMY FAILS ON ALL COUNTS

We now examine the third criterion of a just economy. Is the economy fair and are economic interactions free of fraud and corruption? Do we struc-ture the economic system and its rules, practices, and institutions to protect the vulnerable and promote universal thriving? No. In all these ways, the economy fails. While some people may escape the snares of unjust condi-tions, many do not. People of faith are called to participate in the struggle for a just economy.

We recognize the economy is far from being entirely under our control. However, through our economic and other public policies, we have much influence. We have noted that policy changes reversed the postwar trend of

143. US Department of Labor Bureau of Labor Statistics, "Employment Projections: Table 1.4," accessed March 28, 2020, https://www.bls.gov/emp/tables.htm.

144. EPI, *Top Charts of 2019* (Washington, DC: EPI, December 23, 2019), figure 13.

growing equality in wages, income, and wealth to one of growing inequality. We now explore this more fully and examine some of the changes in public policies that are largely responsible for stagnant wages and incomes, the failure to eliminate poverty, and marked growth in inequality. We will gain insights into beneficial policies that we could institute to promote universal thriving; these are more fully examined in chapter 6.

Neoliberal Policies

The new economic policy regime that first gained dominance in the late 1970s and 1980s is variously called neoliberal, supply-side, or market fundamentalism. Neoliberals call for a minimal role for government, tax cuts, deregulation, privatization of public services, and cuts in government programs and services. They argue that freeing corporations to increase profits through deregulation and tax cuts and cutting taxes on the wealthy will boost productive investment, create jobs, raise wages, and grow the economy. It is assumed the rising affluence will trickle down to everyone. Since unions interfere with employers' ability to organize work most efficiently and maximize profits, or so they argue, corporations have not only actively opposed workers' efforts to organize but also engaged in a legal offensive to weaken the rights of unions and workers under the law.[145] Supporters of the neoliberal regime argue that the economic outcomes most beneficial to society—high levels of investment and innovation, rapid productivity and wage growth, and fast economic growth—are achieved by letting the "free" market operate with few constraints.

But deregulation and shrinking the role of government—essentially pulling government out of the economic game—are like removing the referees from a big playoff match. The resulting free-for-all allows the biggest, most ruthless economic actors to overpower and take advantage of smaller, less powerful ones. This battle plays out in workplaces, where workers see their bargaining power, wages, and benefits decline; in the marketplace, where consumers face higher prices, abysmal customer service from megacorporations, and poorer-quality products than they might have had otherwise; and in society, where poverty persists despite unimaginable wealth,

145. Lawrence Mishel, Lynn Rhinehart, and Lane Windham, *Explaining the Erosion of Private-Sector Unions: How Corporate Practices and Legal Changes Have Undercut the Ability of Workers to Organize and Bargain* (Washington, DC: EPI, October 7, 2020).

our infrastructure crumbles, education is defunded, the planet cries out for relief, millions lack health insurance and decent housing, the will of the public is thwarted by corporate and wealthy interests, and despair kills and stunts millions of lives. According to Nobel Prize–winning economist Joseph Stiglitz, "Neoliberalism has encouraged selfishness, and led to pervasive moral depravities, evidenced so clearly by the bankers in the run-up to the Great Recession: a willingness to do almost anything that enhances profits, so long as one could get away with it."[146]

The neoliberal agenda has not worked out as promised. It has instead led to slower economic growth, a decline in productive investment, slower productivity growth, greater economic instability with more booms and busts, and stagnant (or falling) wages and incomes. The economic gains that occurred have primarily been captured by the already wealthy. Most of the neoliberal policies have had the completely predictable—and now realized—outcome of benefiting powerful corporations and wealthy households while harming working families.

Pope Francis is also critical of our neoliberal policies: "Some people continue to defend trickle-down theories which assume that economic growth, encouraged by a free market, will inevitably succeed in bringing about greater justice and inclusiveness in the world. This opinion, which has never been confirmed by the facts, expresses a crude and naïve trust in the goodness of those wielding economic power and in the sacralized workings of the prevailing economic system. Meanwhile, the excluded are still waiting."[147]

Workers, Workplaces, and the Growth of Corporate Power

The neoliberal legislative agenda has gutted labor protections, eroded standards, and blocked efforts to update and extend outdated laws. Neoliberal legislation has negatively impacted a broad array of policies concerning unions, minimum wages, child labor, wage theft, occupational safety, discrimination, sexual harassment, tipped employees, unemployment insurance, overtime pay, employee misclassification, privatization of

146. Joseph E. Stiglitz, *The Welfare State in the Twenty-First Century* (New York: Roosevelt Institute, June 20, 2017), 5.
147. Pope Francis, *Evangelii Gaudium* (Rome: Libreria Editrice Vaticana, November 26, 2013), no. 54.

public services, taxes, and state budgets.[148] It is important to note that policy changes can occur through commission or omission. Failure to update and modernize policies—for example, Congress's failure to increase the federal minimum wage—can be just as damaging as newly enacted policies. To address these problems, often the needed fix is to reverse or update a policy.

Since labor regulations and protections are found in state as well as federal law, the attack on labor has happened in state legislatures as well as in Congress. This state effort was enacted, in part, through the American Legislative Exchange Council (ALEC), an organization that brings together corporate lobbyists and state legislators to write model legislation, bills that legislators may then introduce in their state legislatures. ALEC claims a membership of one-quarter of all state representatives and over two hundred corporations and nonprofit organizations.[149] ALEC also works with a network of sixty-four state-based procorporate think tanks, the State Policy Network. We need to be aware of ALEC and other harmful forces in our states, but the focus here is on federal law.

Corporations, Neoliberalism, and the Economy

The rise in corporate power has harmed workers and consumers. It is also weakening the economy overall, establishing the conditions for future economic malaise and even decline. We examine three ways in which corporations have increased their power (including their power for harm) in the marketplace:

- the increased number and power of megacorporations that stifle competition,
- the financialization of the economy, and
- the current regime of globalization.

The Power of Megacorporations

Our first topic is the growth and power of megacorporations. Optimal outcomes in a capitalist economy—the production of innovative products

---

148. Gordon Lafer, *The One Percent Solution: How Corporations Are Remaking America One State at a Time* (Ithaca, NY: ILR, 2017).

149. American Legislative Exchange Council, *Strategic Plan 2016–2018* (Arlington, VA: ALEC, 2016), 8.

sold at the lowest prices and made by workers who are treated with dignity and whose compensation enables them to share in the nation's growing prosperity—require vigorous competition among many firms within each industry. This is one of the most fundamental principles of capitalism. When just a few megacorporations dominate any sector of the economy, competition is stifled and firms have the power to skew the market to their advantage.[150] A megacorporation with few competitors may dominate its market, but not necessarily because its product is better than those of its competitors. It may just be the result of the megacorporation buying up many of the other firms in its sector, leaving few competitors. This means few product options for consumers and few job options for workers in the industry.

The destructive impact of large firms with too much power in their markets was recognized a century ago. Antitrust laws were passed to block anticompetitive practices, stop mergers and acquisitions that would reduce competition, and break up large firms that lacked competitors. But in recent decades, a lack of antitrust enforcement and regulators' permissive attitude toward mergers and acquisitions have enabled the creation of megafirms with concentrated power within their markets.[151] Even clearly illegal practices are not policed and punished. This is a large and growing problem in the US economy.[152] We all recognize the size and power of the big tech firms. Apple and Google combined provide the software for 99 percent of all smartphone operating systems.[153] Alphabet (Google) is the search engine of some 90 percent of users. Regulators allowed Google, Facebook, Amazon, Apple, and Microsoft to purchase 436 companies in the past ten years, often for the purpose of preventing competition.[154] But the problem is much

---

150. If competition is not possible or too costly, government regulation is needed to push a firm toward optimal outcomes.

151. Gilad Edelman, "The Big Tech Hearing Proved Congress Isn't Messing Around," *Wired*, July 29, 2020.

152. Marshall Steinbaum, Eric Harris Bernstein, and John Sturm, *Powerless: How Lax Antitrust and Concentrated Market Power Rig the Economy against American Workers, Consumers, and Communities* (New York: Roosevelt Institute, March 27, 2018).

153. Open Markets Institute, "America's Concentration Crisis," accessed March 26, 2020, https://concentrationcrisis.openmarketsinstitute.org/.

154. Jonathan Tepper with Denise Hearn, *The Myth of Capitalism: Monopolies and the Death of Competition* (Hoboken, NJ: Wiley, 2019), 106.

broader than big tech. Consider just a few of the very many concentrated industries and megafirms with which we all must do business:

- The four largest food companies control 82 percent of beef packing, 85 percent of soybean processing, 63 percent of pork packing, and 53 percent of chicken processing.[155]
- The five largest US banks held 46 percent of all commercial banking assets in 2017, up from 28 percent in 2000.[156]
- The four largest US airlines (Delta, American, United Continental, and Southwest) control 76 percent of sales of domestic flights.[157]
- Two firms (Home Depot and Lowe's) control 81 percent of home improvement sales.
- Two firms (CVS and Walgreens) control 61 percent of sales in pharmacies and drug stores.
- Two firms (Anheuser-Busch and MillerCoors) have 66 percent of the beer market.
- Three companies now control 98 percent of the US cell phone market.
- In most areas of the United States, there are just a few broadband providers; broadband speeds in the United States are slower and service is more expensive than in many other major industrialized countries.[158]

Market concentration means fewer competitors and higher prices. It cost the nation an estimated $600 billion in 2018, an average of $300 per household each month.[159] The high prices charged by megafirms provide them with excess profits—greater than what would be attained in competitive

155. Robert B. Reich, "The Monopolization of America: The Biggest Economic Problem You're Hearing Almost Nothing About," *Robert Reich* (blog), May 6, 2018, http://robertreich.org/post/173655842990.

156. Federal Reserve Economic Data, Federal Reserve Bank of St. Louis, "World Bank, 5-Bank Asset Concentration for United States," accessed March 26, 2020, https://fred.stlouisfed.org/series/DDOI06USA156NWDB.

157. Unless another attribution is made, these data are from Open Markets Institute, "America's Concentration Crisis."

158. Federal Communications Commission, *International Broadband Data Report*, report no. 6 (Washington, DC: FCC, February 2, 2018).

159. Thomas Philippon, "The US Only Pretends to Have Free Markets," *Atlantic*, October 29, 2019.

markets.[160] But the high profits do not necessarily translate into high levels of investment and innovation, higher-quality products, expanded production, and job creation. Because consumers have few choices, there is less pressure on a firm to spend money to improve its product or even provide good customer service. Instead, megafirms are using much of their excessive profits to fund large dividends to shareholders and buy back stock.[161] This drives up share prices, making money for CEOs and shareholders, but harms both the firm and the economy in the longer term.

Market concentration means lower wages, since fewer employers are competing in an industry to hire or retain workers. Economists estimate this could be the cause of some 30 percent of wage stagnation in recent decades.[162] Monopolized industries contribute to the economic stagnation that characterizes the US economy today: stagnant and falling wages, slow economic growth, low corporate investment, a decline in the creation of new firms, slower growth in productivity, distortions in the allocation of resources, and a less efficient economy.

Financialization of the Economy

A second harmful change impacting the marketplace and our material well-being is the financialization of the economy. In recent decades, the US financial sector and its institutions, elites, markets, and motives have come to dominate the entire economy. The primary purpose of this industry, which includes banking, investment, insurance, and real estate, is to take the savings of households and corporations and channel them into productive uses. But instead of serving the needs of the real economy, the deregulated financial sector is now much more focused on quickly making money from money, through short-term, speculative, and often risky activities. Only an estimated 15 percent of all money flowing through the financial sector

160. Matt Phillips, "Apple's $1 Trillion Milestone Reflects Rise of Powerful Megacompanies," *New York Times*, August 2, 2018.

161. William Lazonick, *Profits without Prosperity: How Stock Buybacks Manipulate the Market, and Leave Most Americans Worse Off* (New York: Institute for New Economic Thinking, April 2014).

162. Efraim Benmelech, Nittai Bergman, and Hyunseob Kim, "Strong Employers and Weak Employees: How Does Employer Concentration Affect Wages?" (working paper no. 24307, NBER, Cambridge, MA, February 2018).

becomes invested in the real economy to fund new ideas or increase the production of existing products.[163]

Today's financial firms often fail to perform the essential but less profitable functions necessary for a healthy economy. Providing capital for long-term investments that lead to improved goods and services, gains in productivity, and rising wages is actually in conflict with the finance sector's primary focus: to produce quick returns for investors. Financial firms' risky practices can crash—and have crashed—the global economy. In the wake of the 2007–8 financial crisis, Congress enacted a number of new regulations and protections. But experts warn that these did not go far enough, and under pressure from financiers, policy makers and regulators have already eased and reversed some of them. A financial sector is essential to a healthy economy. But when it becomes too dominant and too divorced from its fundamental purpose, it is harmful, inhibiting economic growth, misallocating resources, and increasing economic volatility.[164]

Under pressure from Wall Street, the financial sector's quest for high, short-term profits and use of money to make more money have spread to corporations throughout the economy. Nonfinancial firms are increasingly making profits from financial activity—trading financial instruments, hedging, avoiding and evading taxes, and selling financial services such as credit cards and loans—not from producing and selling quality goods and services.

Shareholders have also forced nonfinancial corporations to adopt Wall Street's goal of quick profits. Investments in the real economy that can enable the production of a better good or service require patience from investors. And an investment is risky; some innovations and expansions do not work out as expected. Often a much easier, quicker, and less risky way to raise a firm's share price quarter by quarter (and to meet Wall Street's expectations) is to cut costs through layoffs, outsourcing, and offshoring production to lower-wage workers; cutting back investment; and buying back the firm's own stock. (A Depression-era prohibition on share buybacks—a manipulative practice designed for the sole purpose of raising the share price—was repealed in 1982.) In 2013, Walmart spent $6.6 billion on stock

---

163. Adair Turner, *Between Debt and the Devil: Money, Credit, and Fixing Global Finance* (Princeton, NJ: Princeton University Press, 2015), 7.
164. Gautam Mukunda, "Profits without Prosperity: The Price of Wall Street's Power," *Harvard Business Review*, June 2014.

buybacks. Instead, it could have raised the wages of its 825,000 US employees by $5.13 per hour.[165]

Rising profits are squeezing wages. The entire national income can be considered to be divided into two parts: one received by workers that includes wages and the value of benefits and a second part received by firms as profit, much of which is paid out to owners of capital as dividends, interest, capital gains, and other business income. In recent decades, there have been two important shifts in the distribution of the nation's income. First, as we have seen, within the portion of our nation's income received as wages and benefits, more has been flowing to the highest-paid workers. Second, there has been a decline in the share of national income received as wages and benefits and an increase in the share going to profits and then paid out to owners of capital.[166] This is contributing to the wage and income stagnation experienced by many households.

Financialization is epitomized by private equity (PE) firms, a huge and hugely profitable but little-known part of the financial sector.[167] The PE business model, supporters say, is to buy up underperforming firms, improve operations to make them stronger, and sell them.[168] This does happen sometimes. But more often, the PE practice is to take over a company, load it with

165. Catherine Ruetschlin and Amy Traub, *A Higher Wage Is Possible at Walmart* (New York: Demos, 2014).

166. Federal Reserve Economic Data, Federal Reserve Bank of St. Louis, "University of Groningen and University of California, Davis, Share of Labor Compensation in GDP at Current National Prices for United States," accessed March 23, 2020, https://fred.stlouisfed .org/series/LABSHPUSA156NRUG; Josh Bivens, *The Decline in Labor's Share of Corporate Income since 2000 Means $535 Billion Less for Workers* (Washington, DC: EPI, September 10, 2015).

167. For a relatively short and understandable overview of private equity and hedge fund firms, see *America for Sale? An Examination of the Practices of Private Funds: Hearings before the US House of Representatives Comm. on Financial Services*, 116th Cong., November 18, 2019 (written testimony of Eileen Appelbaum), https://democrats-financialservices.house.gov/ UploadedFiles/HHRG-116-BA00-Wstate-AppelbaumE-20191119.pdf.

168. Eileen Appelbaum and Rosemary Batt, *Private Equity Pillage: Grocery Stores and Workers at Risk* (Washington, DC: Center for Economic and Policy Research, 2018); Robert Kuttner, "Sears Didn't 'Die.' Vulture Capitalists Killed It," Huffington Post, October 15, 2018; David Heath, Mark Greenblatt, and Aysha Bagchi, "Dentists under Pressure to Drill 'Healthy Teeth' for Profit, Former Insiders Allege," *USA Today*, March 19, 2020; Eileen Appelbaum and Rosemary Batt, *Private Equity at Work: When Wall Street Manages Main Street* (New York: Russell Sage Foundation, 2014).

debt (used in part to pay huge fees to the PE firm), sell off its profitable components (further benefiting the PE partners), and then see what happens to the now heavily indebted firm with few assets. The process usually leads to cost cutting, outsourcing, and wage and benefit losses for workers. Too often it ends in bankruptcy, with layoffs, financial losses to legitimate investors, and economic, social, and cultural losses to communities. Just within the retail sector, private equity (not internet sales or bad management decisions) is largely responsible for the bankruptcies of Sears,[169] Toys "R" Us, Shopko, Payless Shoe Source, Charlotte Russe, Bon-Ton, Nine West, David's Bridal, Claire's, and Southeastern Grocers, the parent company of BI-LO and Winn-Dixie.[170]

The demands of financialization for cost cutting and short-term profits and the destructiveness of private equity firms have forced many companies in recent decades to shift their focus from top-quality engineering and innovation to cost cutting and short-term financial performance. Wealth owners have gotten wealthier, but once-leading firms like Kodak, Hewlett-Packard, and others have been turned into second-tier also-rans.[171] One of the latest to be swept into this maelstrom is Boeing.[172] The financialization of the economy is another factor contributing to reduced real investment, slowed productivity growth, and even slower wage growth, as well as slower economic growth and a misallocation of resources.[173] It also raises inequality and increases the likelihood of financial instability and economic crises.

Globalization: The Impact on the United States

We now examine a third important way corporations have boosted their profits and economic power: neoliberal globalization. The increased global economic integration of recent decades is governed by a legal framework rooted in neoliberalism. The same forces that dominate policy making in the United States also rule the international setting. The central organizations

169. Lauren Hirsch, "Sears Sues Former CEO Eddie Lampert, Treasury Secretary Mnuchin and Others for Alleged 'Thefts' of Billions from Retailer," CNBC, April 18, 2019.
170. Stop Wall Street Looting Act of 2019, S. 2155, 116th Congress (2019).
171. Rana Foroohar, *Makers and Takers: The Rise of Finance and the Fall of American Business* (New York: Crown Business, 2016).
172. Mukunda, "Profits without Prosperity."
173. Gerald Epstein and Juan Antonio Montecino, *Overcharged: The High Cost of High Finance* (New York: Roosevelt Institute, July 2016).

governing the process—the World Trade Organization, World Bank, and International Monetary Fund—are dominated by the major industrialized countries and largely reflect the financial and commercial interests of the Global North. Joseph Stiglitz, who served as senior vice president and chief economist of the World Bank, acknowledges that globalization has been "run, to too large an extent, by and for large multinational corporations and financial institutions in the large advanced countries. They were the winners. And much collateral damage occurred as they sought to maximize their winnings."[174]

Our current regime of so-called free trade has shaped an international economic regime that is neither free nor fair. Trade agreements and other international rules have become a way for corporations to gain rights, repeal regulations, and expand opportunities for profit. Under the guise of crafting trade agreements, treaty negotiators are writing and rewriting the rules of the national and international economies behind closed doors and in an undemocratic process. The rhetoric of free trade, similar to the rhetoric about the free market, covers a hidden, forceful, and well-funded effort by international corporations to promote their own interests and profits.

The United States has not been a victim of unfair international trade agreements but is a dominant player in the skewed binational and international rule-making processes. The goals sought by US trade negotiators were achieved spectacularly and are now written in our international agreements. Multinational corporations and financial firms primarily in the Global North have reaped higher profits while workers and consumers around the world and the global environment have been harmed.

The process of globalization did not *have to* lead to our current harmful trends, and reversing these trends would not require the United States to close off economic activity with the rest of the world. It would, however, require a different globalization regime, one based on fair rules that ensure the gains from globalization are shared.

Consider the effect of trade on workers in the United States. Trade theory predicts and our recent history confirms that trade with low-wage countries, while potentially very beneficial to some economic interests, will

174. Joseph E. Stiglitz, *Globalization and Its Discontents, Revisited: Anti-globalization in the Era of Trump* (New York: W. W. Norton, 2018), xxv, 117.

lower the pay of *most* workers, especially those without a college degree.[175] International and national policies could have ensured the gains from trade were broadly shared by workers in the Global North and South. But those policies were not enacted. Similarly, the globalization regime could have included environmental protections and enforcement. It could have mandated the transparency and disclosure necessary to contain tax havens and capital flight. It could have instituted an international tax assessment system to ensure multinational corporations paid fair taxes in all the countries where they operated, contributing to the costs of infrastructure and other services essential to their business operations.[176] None of this was done.

However, our neoliberal globalization regime does provide other special benefits for multinational firms. For example, multinational corporations receive enhanced protections for their investments and profits made overseas, making it easier for these firms to relocate production offshore. Under the provisions of the investor-state dispute settlement (ISDS) process, a foreign corporation may sue a host government if new regulations or protections cause a loss of the firm's expected future profits. For example, a US firm investing in another country can sue the host government for lost future profits arising from newly enacted regulations such as worker or environmental protections. Similarly, foreign firms investing in the United States can sue federal, state, or local governments for lost future profits due to new regulations or protections. All assessed penalties are paid by taxpayers. These disputes are adjudicated by a secret tribunal of three corporate lawyers whose decisions cannot be appealed and on whose authority taxpayers could be required to pay huge sums to foreign corporations.[177] At the end of 2019, over one thousand ISDS cases had been brought worldwide.[178]

This special legal privilege is not a part of any US law; US firms are barred from suing the US government. But by providing enhanced legal protection for foreign assets, the ISDS makes foreign investment much safer

175. Josh Bivens, *Adding Insult to Injury: How Bad Policy Decisions Have Amplified Globalization's Costs for American Workers* (Washington, DC: EPI, July 11, 2017).

176. In 2021, as this book goes to press, a multinational effort is under way to assess a uniform, minimum corporate income tax.

177. Anthony Depalma, "NAFTA's Powerful Little Secret: Obscure Tribunals Settle Disputes, but Go Too Far, Critics Say," *New York Times*, March 11, 2001.

178. UN Conference on Trade and Development, Investment Dispute Settlement Navigator, Investment Policy Hub, accessed June 6, 2020, https://investmentpolicy.unctad.org/investment-dispute-settlement.

and more profitable for multinational firms. The ISDS also makes new regulatory protections potentially more expensive and, therefore, less likely to be enacted.

The neoliberal globalization regime has also forced countries to provide more rigorous and longer-lasting protections for intellectual property. For example, newly developed pharmaceuticals receive extended patent protection, making these drugs more expensive and less affordable for poor consumers and impoverished health care systems while delaying the production of comparable generic versions. Supporters argue that pharmaceutical firms must be able to recover the expense of developing a new drug. But researchers repeatedly have shown that the profits received by drug companies hugely exceed their spending on research. Additional monopoly profits just enrich shareholders and drain resources from people and health systems forced to buy expensive medications.

Another casualty of our skewed globalization regime is the US manufacturing sector. Between 1970 and 1997, employment in manufacturing in the United States was stable, although the share of all employees working in manufacturing declined from 26 to 14 percent and jobs were moving from the US industrial Midwest to the South.[179] Then between 1997 and 2018, the United States lost ninety-one thousand manufacturing plants and nearly five million manufacturing jobs.[180] The key factor behind these losses was not automation (robots) or high, uncompetitive wages but the overvalued dollar.[181] A high value of the dollar compared to other currencies raises the price of US exports, lowers the price of our imports, and makes US manufacturers uncompetitive. For many years the high value of the dollar was maintained through massive currency manipulation by China and

179. Rising demand for products was offset by rising productivity; employment was fairly stable. Data from US Bureau of Labor Statistics, All Employees, Manufacturing (MANEMP), retrieved from FRED, Federal Reserve Bank of St. Louis, https://fred.stlouisfed.org/series/ MANEMP; US Bureau of Labor Statistics, All Employees, Total Nonfarm (PAYEMS), retrieved from FRED, Federal Reserve Bank of St. Louis; January 13, 2021, https://fred .stlouisfed.org/series/PAYEMS.

180. Robert E. Scott, *We Can Reshore Manufacturing Jobs, but Trump Hasn't Done It* (Washington, DC: EPI, August 10, 2020)

181. Scott; Susan N. Houseman, "Understanding the Decline of US Manufacturing Employment" (working paper no. 18-287, Upjohn Institute, Kalamazoo, MI, June 1, 2018); Gwynn Guilford, "The Epic Mistake about Manufacturing That's Cost Americans Millions of Jobs," *Quartz*, May 3, 2018.

other countries.[182] The United States could have taken countermeasures, but it did not do so under the influence of US firms that benefited from the low prices of imports, including Walmart, Apple, and many others. US policy makers put the interests of some multinationals ahead of maintaining a strong manufacturing sector in the United States.

The decline of the manufacturing sector means a loss of good jobs for the nearly two-thirds of the labor force that does not have a college degree. It is also a threat to our national security. In addition, it endangers the economy. Innovation—the birth of new products and processes in energy, pharmaceuticals, cars, computers, or any other industry—is the origin of tomorrow's new and better products and good jobs. It is the foundation of a future strong economy. But to benefit society and provide profit to firms, innovations must be commercialized. Ideas must become prototypes, pilots, and testable demonstrations that are first put into early manufacturing and finally into full-scale commercial production. All these stages of scaling up involve close interactions between innovators and manufacturers. Researchers have found that without a strong manufacturing sector, the United States will lose its ability to innovate and create new products.[183] With the loss of innovation, we will also lose many high-wage, high-value-added jobs and, potentially, the future strength of the economy.

Government Capture

How did the neoliberal regime, with all its destructive economic impacts, come to dominate US policy making? To understand this takeover, we first need to remember our history. One of the progressive triumphs of the twentieth century was to establish government as a counterforce to the brutality of unfettered capitalism. The three midcentury decades of growing equality were the product of Depression-era New Deal legislation, the long struggle of many people for justice, and the shared experiences of the Great Depression and World War II. The postwar decades were far from perfect. New

182. C. Fred Bergsten and Joseph E. Gagnon, *Currency Conflict and Trade Policy: A New Strategy for the United States* (Washington, DC: Peterson Institute for International Economics, June 2017).

183. Suzanne Berger with the MIT Task Force on Production in the Innovation Economy, *Making in America: From Innovation to Market* (Cambridge, MA: MIT Press, 2013); Sridhar Kota and Tom Mahoney, "Reinventing Competitiveness: The Case for a National Manufacturing Foundation," *American Affairs Journal* 3, no. 3 (Fall 2019).

Deal legislation did not go far enough and omitted too many people, and important provisions were already being undone long before the late 1970s. But the economy was moving in the direction of greater equality and more universal thriving. However, in the last forty years, much of this has been reversed. The capture of government by corporations and the wealthy is a key factor behind rising inequality, stagnant wages, the excessive power of corporations, and persistent poverty.

The Origins of Neoliberalism

The roots of neoliberalism go back to the immediate postwar period, but it did not gain much support until the 1970s, a decade when an international oil embargo, inflation, slow economic growth, and a recession seemed to indicate that new economic policies were needed. The post–World War II consensus around the policies responsible for broadly shared prosperity began to crumble, providing an opportunity for neoliberals to step in. With the election of Ronald Reagan in 1980, neoliberal ideas extended their reach into the highest levels of government. In his first inaugural address in 1981, President Reagan proclaimed, "Government is not the solution to our problem; government is the problem."[184] The neoliberal decades were underway. From that time until today, numerous neoliberal policies, large and small, have affected all aspects of our economy, from the workplace to the boardroom and from Main Street to Wall Street.

To bring about changes in policy—changes that advanced their own interests and increased their profits—corporate America embarked on a huge, well-planned, and well-funded effort to influence government. Our attention here will focus on the federal government, although corporations also targeted states. The Business Roundtable, a group of CEOs from the largest US firms, formed in 1972 to promote their common interests. The US Chamber of Commerce, "the voice of American businesses," expanded its membership from 36,000 firms in 1967 to 160,000 in 1980,[185] while the number of corporations with public affairs offices in Washington

---

184. Ronald Reagan, "Inaugural Address," Washington, DC, January 20, 1981, https://www.reaganfoundation.org/ronald-reagan/reagan-quotes-speeches/inaugural-address-2/.

185. Jacob S. Hacker and Paul Pierson, *American Amnesia: How the War on Government Led Us to Forget What Made America Prosper* (Washington, DC: Simon & Schuster, 2016), 201.

grew from 100 in 1968 to more than 500 just ten years later.[186] In 1971, only 175 firms had registered lobbyists in Washington, DC; in 1982, nearly 2,500 did. Donations from corporate political action committees (PACs) for congressional races increased fivefold over the 1970s.[187] Corporate America also worked to expand its influence within the media, think tanks, foundations, universities, and the courts. Neoliberal arguments, usually accompanied by campaign donations, were persuasive to many policy makers in federal, state, and local government. While these policies generally failed to help the economy, the nation, or most people, as we have seen, they certainly helped the finances of corporations and the affluent.

The 2010 US Supreme Court decision *Citizens United v. the Federal Election Commission*, which allowed corporations and other groups to spend unlimited money on elections, provided the spending is not formally coordinated with a candidate, flung wide the already open doors for corporate money to flood into the political process. Corporate largess is not offset by union money as is often implied. Consider spending on federal elections. Between 1990 and 2020, unions spent $1.5 billion, while corporations from just five economic sectors—finance, insurance, and real estate; health care; communications and electronics; energy and natural resources; and agribusiness—spent $13.3 billion, or over eight times as much.[188] These numbers omit spending on lobbyists and contributions to state and local government candidates for office. Opening the floodgates to both corporate and union money in no way ensures a level playing field, even though it is often described that way.

Princeton's Sheldon Wolin writes of "the *political* coming of age of corporate power and the *political* demobilization of the citizenry."[189] Big

---

186. David Yoffie and Joseph L. Badaracco Jr., "A Rational Model of Corporate Political Strategies" (working paper, Division of Research, Harvard Business School, 1984), 2, cited in David Vogel, *Fluctuating Fortunes: The Political Power of Business in America* (New York: Basic Books, 1989), 197.

187. Taylor E. Dark, *The Unions and the Democrats: An Enduring Alliance* (Ithaca, NY: Cornell University Press, 1999), 149.

188. Center for Responsive Politics, "Open Secrets, Influence and Lobbying, Interest Groups," accessed May 27, 2020, https://www.opensecrets.org/industries/. This includes contributions from (1) individuals as well as corporations and unions that give directly from their treasuries to outside groups; (2) PACs, including super PACs; and (3) individuals giving more than $200 to candidates and party committees.

189. Sheldon S. Wolin, *Democracy Incorporated: Managed Democracy and the Specter of Inverted Totalitarianism* (Princeton, NJ: Princeton University Press, 2008), x. Emphasis in the original.

corporations, using the power of both wealth and neoliberal ideology, have largely succeeded in capturing government and parts of the judicial system, repurposing them to serve corporate interests: "One cannot point to any national institution(s) that can accurately be described as democratic: surely not in the highly managed, money-saturated elections, the lobby-infested Congress, the imperial presidency, the class-biased judicial and penal system, or, least of all, the media. . . . The political role of corporate power, the corruption of the political and representative processes by the lobbying industry, the expansion of executive power at the expense of constitutional limitations, and the degradation of political dialogue promoted by the media *are* the basics of the system, not excrescences upon it."[190] Wolin wrote this in the mid-2000s, prior to the *Citizens United* decision. Since then, the situation has only worsened.

An important tactic used by neoliberals is to both discredit government, labeling it inefficient and ineffective, and at the same time capture and use it to promote their agenda. They have succeeded spectacularly. But there are many things that either government does or they don't happen. Too often in recent years, these things are not happening, and we are experiencing the results of their absence: crumbling infrastructure, inadequate and unaffordable education at all levels, too little affordable housing, too much pollution, too little effort to slow greenhouse gas emissions, too much power wielded by corporations, too few protections of workers in their workplaces, and too much instability in the economy and the business cycle. Government done right can protect and advance the common good, including broadly shared prosperity. We saw this in the postwar years, when strong government and sound policies reduced poverty and built a thriving and expanding middle class. We see it now operating in reverse: a weak government, captured by special interests, has allowed the hollowing out of the middle class, a transfer of income and wealth to the very wealthy, and more extreme losses among those who are already poor. A just economy is possible only if the public, using the tool that is government, makes it happen.

190. Wolin, 105, 287.

The Corporate Purchase of Policy Makers and Policy

There is a good reason for the pervasive corporate influence in Washington, DC.[191] Electing the right candidates and lobbying to get the most favorable legislation and regulations are highly profitable. One study by researchers at the University of Kansas found that corporations had a return of more than $220 for each $1 spent on lobbying for an important tax law.[192] For corporations, spending money to influence public policy often entails less risk and can be much more profitable than other forms of investment. Expanding a company, developing a better product, or enhancing the skills of a firm's workforce is expensive and risky. What if the additional products fail to sell or the innovation is a flop? The returns to wealthy corporations on investments in political campaigns and lobbying are often quicker, less risky, and larger than the returns on more traditional investments in the real economy. A shortfall in productive investment is one reason for the dismal track record of the US economy in recent decades.

A close look reveals how moneyed interests are capturing our government. In the 2017–18 election cycle, less than one-half of 1 percent of US adults gave more than $200 to elect or defeat a member of Congress, but together contributions from private individuals exceeded $4 billion.[193] The top forty-four thousand donors (fewer than one-tenth of 1 percent of the adult population) gave more than $2.2 billion, an average of over $50,000 each. Of course, this is not all the money that was spent. Other donors include corporations, trade associations, nonprofit organizations, unions, and PACs. Initial data on the 2020 federal election show spending totaled nearly $14 billion; slightly less than half of that was spent on the race for president and the rest on congressional seats.[194]

A truly democratic election cannot occur within a tsunami of dollars. In all the races for seats in the US Senate and House of Representatives

191. Lee Drutman, *The Business of America Is Lobbying: How Corporations Became Politicized and Politics Became More Corporate* (New York: Oxford University Press, 2015), 3.

192. Raquel Meyer Alexander, Stephen W. Mazza, and Susan Scholz, "Measuring Rates of Return for Lobbying Expenditures: An Empirical Case Study of Tax Breaks for Multinational Corporations," *Journal of Law and Politics* 25, no. 401 (2009).

193. Center for Responsive Politics, "Open Secrets, Donor Demographics," accessed August 17, 2020, https://www.opensecrets.org/overview/donordemographics.php.

194. OpenSecrets.org, *2020 Election to Cost $14 Billion, Blowing Away Spending Records* (Washington, DC: Center for Responsive Politics, October 28, 2020).

between 2008 and 2018, the top spender won more than 75 percent of the time.[195] Rigorous analysis by Princeton's Martin Gilens and Northwestern University's Benjamin Page shows that "economic elites and interest groups can shape US government policy—but Americans who are less well-off have essentially no influence over what their government does."[196] They find that in the United States, "the majority does not rule—at least not in the causal sense of actually determining policy outcomes. When a majority of citizens disagrees with economic elites or with organized interests, they generally lose. . . . When the preferences of economic elites and the stands of organized interest groups are controlled for, the preferences of the average American appear to have only a minuscule, near-zero, statistically non-significant impact upon public policy."[197]

Wall Street is especially adept at using its financial power to influence our elected officials. Going back to at least 1990, the financial sector has been the largest donor in every federal election cycle.[198] In just the 2018 cycle, it gave nearly $1 billion to fund congressional races and the two political parties. No other industrial sector comes anywhere close to matching this level of contributions. In the 2016 and 2018 election cycles, the financial sector alone gave 16 percent of all the money spent in the federal races for Congress and president. In addition, the industry spends tens of millions of dollars each year on lobbyists and the campaigns of state policy makers. Not coincidentally, people from Wall Street and the financial sector occupy top positions in both Democratic and Republican administrations, including secretary of the Treasury. They bring a Wall Street mentality and ethos to public service and the economic policy arena. The big banks are not broken up, mortgage lenders are bailed out while homeowners suffer foreclosure, and Dodd-Frank banking regulations are slowly whittled down:

195. Center for Responsive Politics, "Open Secrets, Did Money Win?," accessed May 12, 2020, https://www.opensecrets.org/elections-overview/did-money-win.

196. Martin Gilens and Benjamin I. Page, "Critics Argued with Our Analysis of US Political Inequality. Here Are 5 Ways They're Wrong," *Washington Post*, May 23, 2016; Martin Gilens and Benjamin I. Page, "Testing Theories of American Politics: Elites, Interest Groups, and Average Citizens," *Perspectives on Politics* 12, no. 3 (2014): 564–81.

197. Gilens and Page, "Testing Theories."

198. Center for Responsive Politics, "Open Secrets, Election Overview, Sector Totals," accessed September 22, 2020, https://www.opensecrets.org/elections-overview/sectors?cycle=2018.

"Whether voters cast their ballots for Clinton, Bush, Obama or Trump, they somehow get Goldman Sachs."[199]

The power of money does not stop once an election is over but continues through the process of lobbying. Between 2014 and 2017, Fortune 100 companies spent $2 billion to lobby Congress on hundreds of pieces of legislation and to influence regulations.[200] In 2019, twelve thousand lobbyists and $3.5 billion were deployed to sway federal legislation and regulatory agencies; some 87 percent of this money came from business, 1 percent from labor unions, and 12 percent from other groups, such as nonprofits and foreign entities.[201] This money is not wasted but often achieves its legislative or regulatory goal. Corporate lobbyists are successful in attaining their aims an estimated eighty-nine times out of one hundred.[202]

Even apart from the corrupting influence of money, a democratic election cannot occur—and voters' preferences for candidates and economic policies are distorted—when some members of the electorate are bound by poverty and face myriad obstacles to participation. Since 2013, when the Supreme Court struck down portions of the 1965 Voting Rights Act, twenty-five states have put in place new barriers to voting, including more restrictive voter ID requirements, reductions in early or absentee voting options and in the number of polling places, and purges of voter rolls.[203] One trend has been positive: at least thirteen states have expanded voting access.[204] Gerrymandering is the practice of placing the boundaries of a candidate's district to favor one political party over another. The Electoral College determines who wins the

199. Robert Kuttner, *Can Democracy Survive Global Capitalism?* (New York: W. W. Norton, 2018), 19.

200. Adam Andrzejewski, "How the Fortune 100 Turned $2 Billion in Lobbying Spend into $400 Billion of Taxpayer Cash," *Forbes*, May 14, 2019.

201. Center for Responsive Politics, "Open Secrets, Lobbying Data Summary," accessed May 12, 2020, https://www.opensecrets.org/federal-lobbying; Center for Responsive Politics, "Open Secrets, Business, Labor & Ideological Split in Lobbying Data," accessed May 12, 2020, https://www.opensecrets.org/federal-lobbying/business-labor-ideological ?cycle=2019.

202. Christine Mahoney, "Why Lobbying in America Is Different," *Politico*, June 4, 2009, updated April 12, 2014.

203. Brennan Center for Justice, *New Voting Restrictions in America* (New York: BCJ, November 19, 2019). Since this study was done in 2019, additional barriers have been erected.

204. Max Feldman and Wendy Weiser, *The State of Voting 2018—Updated* (New York: Brennan Center for Justice, August 3, 2018).

election for president, not the majority vote of the public. These and other practices thwart democracy and must be addressed.

But the flaws in our democracy are much deeper than these grave problems with elections. The real problem is not the outcome of a particular election but the deeper systemic forms of inequality that concentrate political and economic power in the hands of the few at the expense of the many. Most fundamentally, high income and wealth inequality are threats to democracy.[205] Princeton's Jason Stanley observes, "Ever since Plato and Aristotle wrote on the topic, political theorists have known that democracy cannot flourish on soil poisoned by inequality. . . . Extreme economic inequality is toxic to liberal democracy. . . . [It] creates conditions richly conducive to fascist demagoguery."[206]

Despite our flawed elections and the corrosive power of money within the political process, we are thankful for the many elected policy makers and the very many people working in government, our bureaucrats, who are dedicated to the common good. Unfortunately, our faulty system makes their work more difficult.

Militarism

No reflection on the role of government and public spending can omit at least a brief look at the US military. In 2019, the Department of Defense budget totaled $676 billion—a huge amount of money but unfortunately not even close to all our spending on the military, defense, security, cybersecurity, intelligence, and other similar operations. We need to add in funding for Overseas Contingency Operations (money for war fighting); the Department of Veterans Affairs; military pensions paid out of the Department of the Treasury; nuclear bombs budgeted through the Department of Energy; sales of military hardware to foreign governments, including authoritarian regimes like Egypt, funded through the Department of State; some functions of the Department of Homeland Security; and the portion of the interest payments on the federal debt attributable to the military share of previous deficits. These additional costs raised our total military spending to

205. Jacob S. Hacker and Paul Pierson, *Let Them Eat Tweets: How the Right Rules in an Age of Extreme Inequality* (New York: W. W. Norton, 2020).
206. Jason Stanley, *How Fascism Works: The Politics of Us and Them* (New York: Random House, 2018), 76–77, 185.

over $1 trillion in 2019. In total, nearly one-quarter of all our federal spending goes to military purposes.[207]

In 2021, the United States had 1.4 million active-duty military personnel, 800 thousand in the reserves and national guard, and 762,000 civilians who worked for the military.[208] These troops and employees were stationed in over 170 countries around the world and maintained military bases in eighty countries, 40 percent of all countries in the world.[209] Our tax dollars are buying multibillion-dollar aircraft carriers, nuclear bombers at over half a billion dollars each, and the $1.4 trillion program building F-35 stealth fighter jets, which have multiple serious unresolved defects, including, according to the Pentagon, "unacceptable" inaccuracy in the planes' guns.[210] What are we accomplishing?

For decades, the Pentagon has been a morass of waste, fraud, and abuse.[211] It cannot pass an audit.[212] Spending on the military is not only bloated, wasteful, and misdirected, but very little is related to *defense*. According to military professionals, tens of billions could be saved each year with no impact on our ability to robustly defend the country.[213] The War on Terror, begun in the aftermath of September 11, 2001, has cost $6.4 trillion through 2020.[214] But despite the money and tragic loss of life—primarily

207. Mandy Smithberger, "The Pentagon Budget Is Out of Control," *Nation*, March 3, 2020.
208. Defense Manpower Data Center, "Number of Military and DoD Appropriated Fund (APF) Civilian Personnel Permanently Assigned," September 30, 2021. https://dwp.dmdc.osd.mil/dwp/api/download?fileName=DMDC_Website_Location_Report_2109.xlsx&groupName=milRegionCountry.
209. K. K. Rebecca Lai, Troy Griggs, Max Fisher, and Audrey Carlsen, "Is America's Military Big Enough?," *New York Times*, March 22, 2017; Stephanie Savell, "Where We Fight," *Smithsonian*, January 2019. Base locations in 2017–18.
210. Tony Capaccio, "The Gun on the Air Force's F-35 Has 'Unacceptable' Accuracy, Pentagon Testing Office Says," *Time*, January 30, 2020; Hartung and Smithberger, "America's Defense Budget."
211. Walter Pincus, "Defense Procurement Problems Won't Go Away," *Washington Post*, May 2, 2012.
212. Aaron Mehta and Jen Judson, "The Pentagon Completed Its Second Audit. What Did It Find?," *Defense News*, November 16, 2019.
213. William D. Hartung and Mandy Smithberger, "America's Defense Budget Is Bigger Than You Think," *Nation*, May 7, 2019; Craig Whitlock and Bob Woodward, "Pentagon Buries Evidence of $125 Billion in Bureaucratic Waste," *Washington Post*, December 5, 2016.
214. Neta C. Crawford, *United States Budgetary Costs and Obligations of Post-9/11 Wars through FY2020: $6.4 Trillion*, Costs of War (Providence, RI: Brown University Watson Institute, November 13, 2019).

affecting people in other countries—many argue our safety is not improved. Meanwhile, some real needs of the members of the military, their families, and veterans are neglected. For example, families in privatized military housing face mold, rats, and lead paint, and veterans need greater access to mental health services.[215]

The military also plays key roles in the economy. It is a source of enormous profit for the military-security-industrial complex. It also stands ready to enforce US dominance in the neoliberal global economy. Thomas Friedman, *New York Times* columnist, best-selling author, and three-time Pulitzer Prize-winning journalist who celebrates globalization, writes that no major trading partners have gone to war in recent decades due, in part, to the positive interconnections created by globalization. (Of course, the interconnections might have been more positive without the neoliberal policies.) But Friedman also openly acknowledges the threat that stands just behind the "free" trade regime. The absence of war in recent decades "is also due to the presence of American power and America's willingness to use that power against those who would threaten the system of globalization. . . . The hidden hand of the market will never work without a hidden fist. . . . Indeed, McDonald's cannot flourish without McDonnell Douglas, the designer of the US Air Force F-15. And the hidden fist that keeps the world safe for Silicon Valley's technologies to flourish is called the US Army, Air Force, Navy and Marine Corps."[216]

Taxes

For people of faith, sharing God's resources so all people and creation may thrive is a fundamental commitment. Sharing happens in many ways, but we are obligated to participate in organized efforts to support those with material needs (Deut 14:28–29). In a democratic society of 320 million people and a world with more than 7 billion, our sharing is a collective commitment, a common project in which we carefully discern and plan how much money is needed, how it is spent, and how much each one contributes. It happens through the tax system. We begin by examining the current system

215. "Mold, Lead Paint and Rats: Military Families Complain of Unsafe Housing," CBS News, February 13, 2019.
216. Thomas L. Friedman, *The Lexus and the Olive Tree: Understanding Globalization*, rev. ed. (New York: Anchor, 2000), 464.

and explore options for improvement in the next chapter. Jesus taught his listeners to give to God the things that belong to God (Matt 22:15–22). The share of our resources given to those with needs is the "sacred" portion that enables our collective well-being (Deut 26:12–13). Taxes today have little in common with those levied in imperial Rome. Our tax system and budgeting processes are in need of major reform. But a sizable portion of our tax money pays for food, housing, health care, education, and other essential needs of people who otherwise would go without.

Progressive Taxes Are Fair, Just Taxes

One of the most important features of a tax system is who pays and how much—that is, how the tax burden is allocated among people across various levels of income and wealth. Remember that distributive justice is at the heart of the biblical vision of justice. From this perspective, the best system is one that places the greatest tax burden on those with the greatest resources and the lowest burden on those with the least. In the terminology of tax policy, this is called progressive taxation: higher-income taxpayers pay a larger *share* of their income in tax than do middle-income ones, and those in the middle pay a larger share than those with low incomes. The opposite of a progressive system is a regressive one, in which lower-income people pay a higher share of income in tax than people with higher incomes, a description of most sales taxes.[217]

A progressive tax system has many advantages. First, it reduces inequality in post-tax incomes. Second, since lower- and even middle-income people have little money to spare, raising money for the things government must do without creating hardship means getting money from those with excess. This is what happens with progressive taxation. Third, we realize that people with a lot of money have particularly benefited from the goods and services funded by taxes that enable businesses to make a profit: the nation's physical infrastructure that gets firms' products to market, the public education system that provides skilled workers, the judicial system that enforces contracts, a financial system that enables business operations, and many other things. These services and functions are helpful to all of us, but high-income people have especially benefited, and they can contribute proportionally.

217. See Aidan Davis, *Options for a Less Regressive Sales Tax in 2019* (Washington, DC: ITEP, September 26, 2019).

In the United States today, the share of national income paid in taxes of all types is 28 percent. The average among six of our peer nations is over 37 percent.[218] In the United States, the overall tax rate varies only slightly across the income spectrum. The lower-income 70 percent of adults pay 24 to 28 percent of their income in tax, while the higher-income ones pay somewhat more, 28 to 30 percent.[219] Overall, the US tax system is slightly progressive, except for the very top of the income ladder. For the first time in one hundred years, the four hundred highest-income taxpayers now pay a lower share of income in tax (23 percent) than the bottom 50 percent (24.2 percent).[220]

Problems with the Tax System
Too Little Revenue
In 2019, taxes collected by all levels of government totaled about $6 trillion, of which some $3.5 trillion were received by the federal government. For two decades, the tax revenue received by the federal government has been trending downward, measured as a share of the economy. Moreover, the federal government consistently runs a deficit, spending more than it takes in. In 2019, prior to the pandemic, federal revenue from all sources covered just 80 percent of spending, and the government borrowed the rest, nearly $1 trillion. The tax system raises too little money to meet our nation's needs. Small deficits can be good for the economy. Deficits during economic downturns are essential. Large deficits during years when the economy is strong, as have been common in some recent years, can weaken the economy and society.

Most of the states—maybe all—also raise and spend too little. Revenue collected by state and local governments, as a share of GDP, has been largely unchanged over the past thirty years even as needs have increased with population growth and the rising cost of many of the big-ticket items

218. The peer nations are Canada, France, Germany, Italy, Japan, and Great Britain in 2018.
219. Saez and Zucman, *Triumph of Injustice*, 15. Data for 2018. Figures from Saez and Zucman are broadly consistent with other research. See Steve Wamhoff, "Emmanuel Saez and Gabriel Zucman's New Book Reminds Us That Tax Injustice Is a Choice," *Just Taxes* (blog), ITEP, October 15, 2019. Including refundable tax credits in household tax liabilities reduces effective tax rates to 20.2 percent and 22.0 percent in the first and second quintiles in 2019.
220. Saez and Zucman, *Triumph of Injustice*, 22.

purchased by states, such as health care and education.[221] While our discussion here is focused on the federal government, the problem of too little revenue afflicts all levels of government. The problems arising from too little money are exacerbated by a second problem that is just as severe: misdirected spending.

Tax Cuts

The federal government's revenue shortfall is due in part to multiple tax cuts enacted in recent decades. Changes in tax law between 2001 and 2018 reduced federal revenue by $5.1 trillion over the period, resulting in spending cuts and larger deficits.[222] Nearly two-thirds of these tax cuts benefited the one-fifth of households with the highest incomes, and the top 1 percent received 22 percent; the one-fifth of households with the lowest incomes received just 3 percent of the cuts. Tax cuts have contributed to the rise in inequality, the shortfall in government revenue, and the increase in the federal debt. In 2018, some two-thirds of the national debt was due to tax cuts and the unfunded wars fought since 9/11.

Lack of Progressivity

The largest single tax is the federal individual income tax, which is a progressive tax. The bottom 20 percent of taxpayers, on average, receive tax credits and refunds that exceed taxes owed; middle-income taxpayers pay an average of 3.6 percent of income in tax; and the top 20 percent pay 15.4 percent.[223] In addition to income taxes, everyone with income from working owes payroll taxes for Social Security and Medicare. The lower-income four-fifths of adults pay more in payroll tax than income tax.[224]

Most other taxes—particularly state and local taxes, such as sales tax and state income taxes—are either flat (everyone pays the same share of

221. CBO Budget and Economic Data, "Historical Budget Data, Table 4," accessed April 24, 2020, https://www.cbo.gov/system/files/2020-01/51134-2020-01-historicalbudgetdata .xlsx; Saez and Zucman, *Triumph of Injustice*, table A3.

222. Steve Wamhoff and Matthew Gardner, *Federal Tax Cuts in the Bush, Obama, and Trump Years* (Washington, DC: ITEP, July 11, 2018).

223. Tax Policy Center, "Table 20-0037: Average Effective Federal Tax Rates, by Expanded Cash Income Percentile, 2019," February 26, 2020, accessed October 20, 2020, https:// www.taxpolicycenter.org/model-estimates/baseline-share-federal-taxes-february-2020/ t20-0037-average-effective-federal-tax.

224. Saez and Zucman, *Triumph of Injustice* and online supplement.

income in tax) or regressive.[225] The progressivity of the federal income tax partially offsets the regressivity in other parts of the tax code. We must never exchange the progressive federal individual income tax for a flat tax as some propose.[226]

While the federal individual income tax is progressive, it is much less progressive than it was in the past. Between 1930 and 1980, the top marginal income tax rate averaged 78 percent.[227] In 2019, it was 37 percent. But because of various tax breaks, tax avoidance measures, and illegal tax evasion, most high-income taxpayers do not pay the statutory rate. A better way to evaluate a tax burden is to calculate the share of income someone actually pays in tax, the effective tax rate. This fraction has also been falling for decades. Taxpayers with income of $1 million or more[228] paid an effective tax rate of 51 percent in 1955, 38 percent in 1985, and just 26 percent in 2015.[229] In addition to federal individual income taxes, high-income households also bear most of the burden of the corporate income tax, and the very wealthy pay estate taxes. But these taxes are also riddled with loopholes and have been cut in recent years.

In the last few decades, as income has increasingly flowed to households at the very top of the economic ladder, changes in tax rates and tax law have not shifted a proportionally greater tax obligation onto them. The opposite has happened, as their taxes have been cut. Thus governments are starved for money, common projects that could enhance our well-being go unfunded, and inequality has worsened. Higher tax rates on high-income households need to be restored.

One important reason for the lack of progressivity in federal taxes is the low tax rates individuals pay on their income from capital: interest, dividends, capital gains, rents, corporate profits, and business income. The economy-wide tax rate on capital is 26 percent, while the tax on labor income is higher: 29 percent.[230] Most capital is owned by the wealthy, but the bottom

225. Meg Wiehe et al., *Who Pays: A Distributional Analysis of the Tax Systems in All 50 States*, 6th ed. (Washington, DC: ITEP, 2018).

226. Simplification of the tax code could be achieved as easily with the current progressive tax as with a flat one.

227. Saez and Zucman, *Triumph of Injustice*, 24.

228. In the top one one-hundredth of 1 percent in 2005 and 2015.

229. Tax Policy Center, "Effective Tax Rate by AGI, 1935–2015," accessed October 20, 2020, https://www.taxpolicycenter.org/file/182421/download?token=oPN7UniL.

230. Saez and Zucman, *Triumph of Injustice*, figure 5.1.

90 percent receive nearly all their income from working. The different tax treatment of labor income (earnings) compared with capital income is the primary reason Warren Buffett pays a smaller share of his income in taxes than does his secretary.[231] One important tax reform, discussed below, is to equalize the tax rates paid by individuals on their labor and capital incomes.

We often hear the neoliberal argument that cutting taxes on capital (wealth) will spur more investment, leading to greater innovation, faster productivity growth, higher wages, and faster economic growth. But this is a myth, as has been shown repeatedly in the wake of recent tax cuts. Over the past one hundred years, lower taxes on capital have not been shown to stimulate investment, and higher taxes do not reduce it.[232] A lower tax on capital increases the income of the rich, reduces government revenue, and has little impact on investment. It is just another windfall for the affluent.

Tax Expenditures

We now turn to the second major problem within our system of taxing and funding: misdirected spending. We have already briefly touched on wasteful and harmful military spending. We now examine an extremely important but fairly unfamiliar aspect of the tax code: tax expenditures. These are special provisions, often called tax breaks, that reduce a taxpayer's liability (and reduce government revenue) in return for what are deemed to be socially desirable activities, such as making an investment, contributing to a retirement plan, buying a home, or raising children. Tax expenditures are a form of government spending and, like any government spending, are ultimately paid for by tax increases elsewhere in the tax code, cuts in spending, or increased borrowing. And just like direct spending, tax expenditures have huge implications for economic fairness. *We explore tax expenditures because they are little understood, extremely expensive, and largely benefit affluent households.* We may view some tax expenditures as accomplishing important goals, while others do not. Our concern is whether these expenditures promote the common good and, if so, whether a tax expenditure is the best way to achieve the desired goal.

231. Chris Isidore, "Buffett Says He's Still Paying Lower Tax Rate Than His Secretary," CNN Money, March 4, 2013, https://money.cnn.com/2013/03/04/news/economy/buffett -secretary-taxes/index.html. This interview was prior to the 2017 Trump tax cuts favoring the wealthy.
232. Saez and Zucman, *Triumph of Injustice*, 103.

The over two hundred tax expenditures in the federal tax code are estimated to have cost $1.8 trillion in 2020, equal to all the revenue collected through the federal individual income tax and half of all federal revenue.[233] Tax expenditures are approximately equal to all the discretionary spending that is heatedly debated during the budget authorization process each year plus interest payments. States also enact tax expenditures that can total over half of their income tax revenue; the problems in the states mirror those at the federal level.[234]

Tax expenditures are heavily skewed to benefit the highest-income taxpayers. Among tax expenditures claimed by individuals through the income tax system in 2019, one quarter of the money (24.1 percent) went to the top 1 percent of taxpayers, about the same share as went to the bottom 60 percent (24.5 percent).[235] See figure 5.4. Nearly half of the benefits (45.8 percent) went to the top 10 percent. The top 20 percent received 58.8 percent of the benefits, the bottom 20 percent just 4.3 percent.

Overall, tax expenditures are more costly than all the spending programs targeted to those in need. In the 2019 federal budget, spending on all safety net programs totaled $810 billion.[236] Tax expenditures totaled $1.6 trillion,

233. CBO Budget and Economic Data, *The Budget and Economic Outlook: 2020 to 2030* (Washington, DC: CBO, January 28, 2020), chapter 1.

234. Carl Davis, *State Itemized Deductions: Surveying the Landscape, Exploring Reforms* (Washington, DC: ITEP, February 5, 2020); Aravind Boddupalli, Frank Sammartino, and Eric Toder, "States Adopt Some Federal Tax Expenditures and Add Others," *TaxVox: State and Local Issues* (blog), Tax Policy Center, January 24, 2020, https://www.taxpolicycenter.org/taxvox/states -adopt-some-federal-tax-expenditures-and-add-others.

235. Daniel Berger and Eric Toder, *Distributional Effects of Individual Income Tax Expenditures after the 2017 Tax Cuts and Jobs Act* (Washington, DC: Tax Policy Center, June 4, 2019), table 2. This analysis omits business taxes, which would tilt the distribution even more toward high-income taxpayers, and payroll taxes which also skew to favor people with higher incomes but less so than do other tax expenditures.

236. CBPP, *Policy Basics: Where Do Our Federal Tax Dollars Go?*, updated ed. (Washington, DC: CBPP, April 9, 2020). Safety net programs include Medicaid; the Children's Health Insurance Program; Affordable Care Act subsidies; Temporary Assistance for Needy Families; the refundable portions only of the Earned Income Tax Credit and Child Tax Credit; Supplemental Security Income; unemployment insurance; and various forms of in-kind assistance for low-income people, including SNAP (food stamps), school meals, low-income housing assistance, childcare assistance, help meeting home energy bills, and various other programs, such as those that aid abused or neglected children.

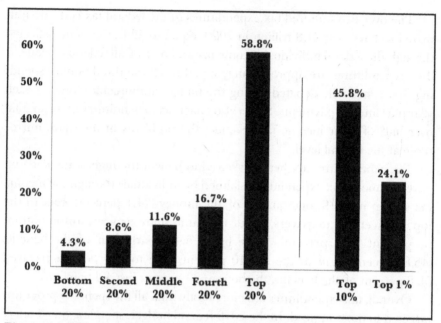

Figure 5.4. Who benefits from tax expenditures, 2019

Note: Shares of dollars spent, nonbusiness individual tax expenditures.

Source: Data from Daniel Berger and Eric Toder, *Distributional Effects of Individual Income Tax Expenditures after the 2017 Tax Cuts and Jobs Act* (Washington, DC: Tax Policy Center, June 4, 2019), table 2.

or roughly twice as much. Tax expenditures for the top 20 percent alone totaled some $700 billion.

Legislation to enact a tax expenditure is easier for Congress to pass than legislation establishing a spending program. A tax expenditure can be described as an ever-popular tax cut and appears in budget projections only indirectly as reduced future revenue. Unlike discretionary spending, which is automatically examined annually during the budgeting process, tax expenditures are largely hidden from view, seldom reevaluated by Congress, and automatically continue until the law is changed. Two very similar forms of government spending appear in the federal budget in very different ways. Direct spending, which includes many safety net programs, is very visible and subject to annual appropriations and review. Tax expenditures that disproportionately benefit the affluent are hidden in the budget and seldom reexamined. If budget cuts are necessary, it is usually direct spending, including the safety net, that gets the ax, not tax expenditures.

We now examine some specific tax expenditures in the individual income and payroll tax systems:[237]

- *Employees do not pay income or payroll tax on the value of their employers' contributions to health insurance premiums (tax revenue lost in 2019: $280 billion).* Receiving health insurance through an employer is a good thing. But workers with this benefit enjoy a sizable boost to their pay—health insurance—on which they pay no income or payroll tax. Workers who do not receive this benefit pay taxes on all their earnings and, if they purchase health insurance, can deduct from their income only the amount paid for premiums and other out-of-pocket medical expenses that exceed 10 percent of their adjusted gross income, and then only if they are among the one in eight taxpayers who itemize deductions. Otherwise, they pay tax on all their income, including what they pay for health insurance. Just over 12 percent of this tax expenditure benefit went to the 40 percent of people with the lowest household incomes, while some 70 percent of the benefit went to the 40 percent of people with the highest.

- *Workers do not pay income or payroll tax on their contributions to retirement plans (tax revenue lost in 2019: $276 billion).* Contributing to a retirement plan is a good thing. But a household that can afford to contribute (sometimes a large amount) gets a break on their income and payroll taxes, while those who cannot afford contributions pay tax on all their earnings. They are effectively subsidizing the savings of the more affluent. Nearly 60 percent of this benefit went to the 20 percent of households with the highest incomes. Just 15 percent went to the bottom 60 percent.

- *The Earned Income Tax Credit (tax revenue lost in 2019: $70 billion).* This is a very important wage supplement provided to low-wage workers who, depending on their earnings and family size, receive a single lump sum amount each year in which they qualify. Fully 81 percent of this benefit was received by the 40 percent of taxpayers with the lowest incomes. Is this the best way to assist these low-wage workers?

- *The Child Tax Credit of up to $2,000 per qualifying child (tax revenue lost in 2019: $118 billion).* This benefit is provided to parents raising children. For poor parents, eligibility for this benefit and its amount are limited by family earnings. One-third of all children are ineligible for full benefits—including over half of all Black and Latinx children and 70 percent of children in single-parent families—largely because their families earn too little.[238] Only 2 percent of all children are in families with incomes that are too high ($200,000 for single head of household; $400,000 for couples) to qualify for the benefit.

- *Homeowners may deduct from their taxable income their mortgage interest payments on loans up to $750,000 (tax revenue lost in 2019: $28 billion).* Homeowners also are exempted from paying capital gains tax on the sale of a principal residence (tax revenue lost in 2019: $35 billion). The combined loss of revenue from these two tax breaks totaled $63 billion. The federal government provides this subsidy to promote homeownership. Over 60 percent of the benefit went to the highest-income 20 percent of taxpayers. Contrast this with the $53 billion budgeted in 2020 to support housing for low-income, disabled, and elderly households and homeless people.[239] Is this the best use of our federal tax dollars?

- *Most owners of capital pay a lower tax rate on their capital gains received on assets held for over a year than on their wages (tax revenue lost in 2019: $140 billion).* Dividends and capital gains on assets held longer than one year are taxed at a lower rate (20 percent) than the likely tax rate these wealthy, high-income individuals would pay on earnings (37 percent). Since the top 10 percent own 93 percent of stocks and 71 percent of all wealth, they gain the most from this tax break. In 2019, the top 10 percent received over 90 percent of this benefit; 75 percent flowed to the top 1 percent.

Many of the goals promoted by tax expenditures are good ones, but providing a tax break is seldom the best way to accomplish it. There is also the question of our priorities. When many of our neighbors are in need, should

238. Sophie Collyer, David Harris, and Christopher Wimer, "Left Behind: The One-Third of Children in Families Who Earn Too Little to Get the Full Child Tax Credit," Center on Poverty and Social Policy at Columbia University, Poverty and Social Policy Brief 3, no. 6 (May 13, 2019). Note, the temporary Child Tax Credit provided through Covid relief legislation is available in full to all children except those in the highest-income families.
239. National Low Income Housing Coalition, *Advocates Secure Increased Funding in Final FY20 Spending Bill* (Washington, DC: NLIHC, December 16, 2019).

the nation devote hundreds of billions of dollars each year to support more affluent households? There is also an issue of hypocrisy. How can I continue to enjoy my tax breaks while also calling for an end to government support for my needy neighbors?

Corporate Income Tax

Corporations pay corporate income tax, a tax on their profits. The statutory tax rate has steadily declined from about 50 percent in the 1950s through the 1970s, to 35 percent in the 1990s, and finally to 21 percent in 2017, where it remains. The decline in the tax rate has reduced corporate tax payments. The corporate income tax brought in less than one-fourth as much revenue in 2018 as in the 1960s, measured as a share of national income, and corporate taxes accounted for just 6.1 percent of all federal revenue in 2018 compared with 20.6 percent in 1962.[240] The 2017 tax cut alone caused federal corporate tax revenue to fall from $252 billion in 2017 to $138 billion in 2019.[241]

Many corporations pay much less than the statutory rate due to tax expenditures, tax avoidance measures like the use of offshore tax havens, and illegal tax evasion. Corporate tax expenditures incentivize a variety of activities, many of which provide no benefit to the economy, including deductions from profits of the cost of stock options at the time they are exercised,[242] deductions for the depreciation of equipment at a faster pace than the equipment actually wears out,[243] and others. Consequently, many huge, highly profitable corporations pay little or no tax. Among 379 profitable Fortune 500 firms in 2018, 91 paid no tax, including Dow-DuPont, Murphy Oil, Amazon, Chevron, Halliburton, Starbucks, FedEx,

240. Saez and Zucman, *Triumph of Injustice*, figure 4.

241. Federal Reserve Economic Data, Federal Reserve Bank of St. Louis, "US Dept. of Commerce Bureau of Economic Analysis, Federal Government: Tax Receipts on Corporate Income," accessed April 27, 2020, https://fred.stlouisfed.org/series/FCTAX.

242. See Elise Bean, Matthew Gardner, and Steve Wamhoff, *How Congress Can Stop Corporations from Using Stock Options to Dodge Taxes* (Washington, DC: ITEP), December 10, 2019.

243. See Steve Wamhoff and Richard Phillips, *The Failure of Expensing and Other Depreciation Tax Breaks* (Washington, DC: ITEP, November 19, 2018); and Matthew Gardner and Steve Wamhoff, *Depreciation Breaks Have Saved 20 Major Corporations $26.5 Billion over Past Two Years* (Washington, DC: ITEP), June 2, 2020.

Eli Lilly, Duke Energy, and CenturyLink.[244] Another fifty-six firms paid less than 5 percent of their profits in tax. Overall, the average effective tax rate among these huge, profitable firms was not the statutory rate of 21 percent but 11.3 percent.[245] In 2012, 19.5 percent of all large profitable firms paid no federal corporate income tax.[246]

Corporations benefit greatly from all the things that society provides: an educated and skilled workforce; infrastructure that enables commerce; talented scientists and engineers to innovate and develop new products; a judicial system to enforce their contracts; and the products of government-funded research and development, including the internet, the global positioning system, touchscreen displays, voice recognition technology, and many breakthrough pharmaceutical, biotech, and cybersecurity innovations. Corporations need to pay taxes if for no other reason than that their profits depend on all the things that government does.

Maintaining the Integrity of the Tax System

The tax system is the most important way in which we the people come together to fund the things we want to do. Tax fairness and integrity at all levels are essential. We each need to be committed to paying our share of needed revenues and have confidence that our neighbors are doing the same.

But some corporations and households pay less tax than they owe due to tax avoidance and illegal tax evasion. Tax cheating is not uncommon and is practiced to some extent by people at all income levels. But most taxpayers have little opportunity to cheat. Their income is reported directly to the IRS by employers, banks, investment companies, and pension funds. In 2018, people in the bottom 90 percent of income earners evaded an estimated 11 percent of their taxes.[247] But tax evasion becomes more common in higher-income households, and the problem is getting worse.[248] In 2018,

244. Matthew Gardner, Lorena Roque, and Steve Wamhoff, *Corporate Tax Avoidance in the First Year of the Trump Tax Law* (Washington: DC: ITEP, December 16, 2019).

245. Gardner, Roque, and Wamhoff, *Corporate Tax Avoidance*.

246. US Government Accountability Office, *Most Large Profitable US Corporations Paid Tax but Effective Tax Rates Differed Significantly from the Statutory Rate*, GAO-16-363 (Washington, DC: GAO, published March 17, 2016, publicly released April 13, 2016).

247. Saez and Zucman, *Triumph of Injustice*, figure 3.1.

248. Andrew Johns and Joel Slemrod, "The Distribution of Income Tax Noncompliance," *National Tax Journal* 63, no. 3 (September 2010): 397–418; Annette Alstadsæter, Niels

the highest-income US taxpayers evaded an estimated 24 percent of their taxes, totaling billions of dollars.[249]

A global industry has arisen to help corporations and individuals avoid and evade taxes using offshore bank accounts, exotic trusts, and a worldwide web of tax havens, secrecy jurisdictions, and hidden shell corporations. Details about these practices are well known, for example, through the leaked Panama Papers: the 11.5 million documents from Mossack Fonseca, a Panama-based international law firm and the world's fourth-largest provider of offshore services.[250] In the service of wealthy clients, this firm created over three hundred thousand shell corporations (existing only on paper) to enable clients to evade taxes and international sanctions.

The goal of some multinational corporations is to avoid paying taxes anywhere. Poor nations and wealthy ones are deprived of needed tax revenues. Developing countries are losing at least $100 billion each year in corporate tax avoidance.[251] US multinational firms book nearly 60 percent of their foreign profits in low-tax countries, primarily Ireland and Bermuda, where they do little or no business. In total, about 20 percent of all US corporate profits are booked in tax havens.[252] This shift—on paper—causes the United States to lose about 15 percent of corporate income tax revenue each year.[253]

The Internal Revenue Service

The Internal Revenue Service (IRS) is charged with enforcement of our federal tax code. Most importantly, enforcement promotes voluntary compliance by giving taxpayers the confidence that everyone is paying their fair

Johannesen, and Gabriel Zucman, "Tax Evasion and Inequality," *American Economic Review* 109, no. 6 (2019): 2073–2103.

249. Saez and Zucman, *Triumph of Injustice*, figure 3.1.

250. Luke Harding, "What Are the Panama Papers? A Guide to History's Biggest Data Leak," *Guardian*, April 5, 2016.

251. UN Conference on Trade and Development, *World Investment Report, 2015: Reforming International Investment Governance* (Geneva, UNCTAD, 2015), 200; Oxfam International, *Reward Work, Not Wealth* (Oxford: Oxfam International, January 2018).

252. Gabriel Zucman, *The Hidden Wealth of Nations* (Chicago: University of Chicago Press, 2015).

253. Saez and Zucman, *Triumph of Injustice*, 77; Gabriel Zucman, *Taxing Multinational Corporations in the 21st Century* (Economics for Inclusive Prosperity, February 2019), https://econfip.org/policy-briefs/taxing-multinational-corporations-in-the-21st-century/.

share. The IRS needs to be adequately funded to carry out its mission. Currently, it is not.

The IRS estimates that some $400 billion owed in taxes is not collected each year, largely due to the underreporting of income by some wealthy individuals and corporations.[254] This equals about one-fifth of all the individual income taxes the IRS does collect. In a 2020 report, the inspector general for tax administration, a Department of the Treasury watchdog, identified nearly nine hundred thousand high-income households that had not filed taxes between 2014 and 2016 whose cases were not being pursued by the IRS and who, together, owed an estimated tax of $45.7 billion.[255]

These problems could be tackled by IRS agents doing more audits. But Congress has steadily been cutting the IRS budget, down 20 percent between 2010 and 2018, with the biggest cuts falling on enforcement.[256] During that period, the share of individual income tax returns examined by the IRS fell by nearly half (46 percent), and the share of corporate income tax returns examined fell by over one-third (37 percent).[257] The IRS software system dates from the 1960s; it is reported to be the oldest in the federal government.[258] Cutting the IRS budget to save money is false economy. The Congressional Budget Office estimates that a $40 billion increase in funding for IRS examinations and collections would return $103 billion.[259]

254. US Government Accountability Office, *Tax Gap: IRS Needs Specific Goals and Strategies for Improving Compliance*, GAO-18-39 (Washington, DC: GAO, published October 31, 2017, publicly released November 30, 2017); Natasha Sarin and Lawrence H. Summers, "Shrinking the Tax Gap: Approaches and Revenue Potential," *Tax Notes*, November 18, 2019.

255. Treasury Inspector General for Tax Administration, *High-Income Nonfilers Owing Billions of Dollars Are Not Being Worked by the Internal Revenue Service*, ref. no. 2020-30-015 (Washington, DC: US Department of the Treasury, May 29, 2020).

256. CBO Budget and Economic Data, "Increase Appropriations for the Internal Revenue Service's Enforcement Initiatives," in *Options for Reducing the Deficit: 2019 to 2028* (Washington, DC: CBO, December 13, 2018).

257. CBO Budget and Economic Data, *Trends in the Internal Revenue Service's Funding and Enforcement* (Washington, DC: CBO, July 8, 2020).

258. Natasha Sarin and Lawrence H. Summers, "Understanding the Revenue Potential of Tax Compliance Investment" (working paper no. 27571, NBER, Cambridge, MA, July 2020).

259. CBO, *Trends*.

Other experts predict even higher returns of from $4 to $10 for each additional dollar spent.[260]

Some of the neoliberal support for tax cuts and hostility to government carries over to hostility to the IRS, manifested as budget cuts imposed by Congress. Wealthy households and corporations in particular benefit from the reduction in audits. Audit rates for people with incomes of $1 million or more have fallen by nearly three-quarters, from 8.4 percent in 2010 (32,494 audits) to 2.4 percent in 2019 (13,946), and for corporations with at least $20 billion in assets, down from 98 percent to 50 percent.[261]

Globalization and the Global South

God's intention for the use of God's resources certainly includes the well-being of people throughout the world. We take a brief look at what is happening to our neighbors in the Global South. Although the economic contexts in the Global North and South are very different, many of the same neoliberal policies are used, and the regions share many of the same problems: poverty, inequality, and economic systems that fail to promote thriving.

Tens of millions of people in the Global South have been harmed by the neoliberal globalization regime. Sweatshop working conditions are abusive and even deadly. Imports of subsidized corn and other grains from the Global North have bankrupted traditional farmers and forced them off their land. Environmental destruction from poorly regulated mining, oil extraction, logging, and commercial activities sickens millions and destroys the natural systems on which people, plants, and animals rely. Rapid inflows and panic-driven outflows of capital (money) destabilize economies and cause deep recessions. Privatization of water, education, and health care

260. John N. Koskinen, "Prepared Remarks of John A. Koskinen Commissioner Internal Revenue Service before the Urban-Brookings Tax Policy Center" (speech, Urban-Brookings Tax Policy Center, Washington, DC, April 8, 2015); Dennis J. Ventry Jr., "Why Steven Mnuchin Wants a Stronger IRS," *New York Times*, March 27, 2017; Sarin and Summers, "Understanding the Revenue."

261. Internal Revenue Service, SOI Tax Stats, "Examination Coverage: Recommended and Average Recommended Additional Tax after Examination—IRS Data Book Table 17b," accessed December 14, 2020, https://www.irs.gov/statistics/soi-tax-stats-examination -coverage-recommended-and-average-recommended-additional-tax-after-examination-irs -data-book-table-9a.

make them unaffordable. The end of subsidies for food and other essentials required by neoliberal trade agreements can worsen living standards and deepen poverty. Local firms and industries are put out of business by multinationals.

While a country's gains from international economic activity may exceed its losses, the gains often flow primarily to the already affluent. Inequality grows. Poor countries may become permanently locked into a low level of economic development, producing and exporting labor-intensive products that are low tech and low wage. When international trade and investment extend into locations that do not have the legal and regulatory framework present in high-income countries that could protect workers, the environment, agricultural resources, landownership, and cultural traditions, the needed legislation is seldom enacted. Sub-Saharan Africa has possibly been the region most damaged by neoliberal policies that have produced a quarter century of stagnation, deindustrialization, and continued impoverishment.[262]

Every country has its own unique circumstances that impact its economy and its people's living standards, including its natural resources, political institutions, economic structures, and historical trends. But economic policies matter a lot. The neoliberal policies that now govern the economies of most countries have slowed the eradication of poverty, worsened inequality, and enhanced the power of multinational firms.

The divide separating globalization's winners and losers does not primarily fall between countries or between the Global North and South. The line dividing winners and losers is socioeconomic class. The corporate class and owners of wealth, particularly in the Global North, are the primary beneficiaries of neoliberal globalization. Many workers around the world are among the losers, as is the environment. The rules governing the current globalization regime are designed to advantage rich countries in the Global North over poor ones in the Global South and to advantage corporations over workers, consumers, and the environment worldwide.

The chief exceptions to this pattern are nations that did not implement the neoliberal policies promoted by the Global North: China, India, and other nations in Southeast Asia. These countries, especially China, experienced exceptionally strong economic growth and large reductions in

262. Joseph E. Stiglitz, *The Dynamics of Social Inequities in the Present World* (New York: Roosevelt Institute, June 22, 2017), 17.

the number of extremely poor. Their success was not due to neoliberal policies but achieved by following their own path of economic development, including industrial planning, protecting their newly forming industries with tariffs, subsidizing their exports, and other practices and policies that are anathema to neoliberalism. However, these are the policies that were used by today's wealthy nations when they were developing their economies nearly two centuries ago.[263]

Global Poverty

Global income has risen quickly in recent decades, driven largely by high rates of economic growth in China and India. The number of people with income below $1.90 a day or $700 a year, the international definition of extreme poverty, has declined from 1.9 billion in 1990 (36 percent of the global population) to 689 million in 2017 (9 percent of the global population).[264] This is a very welcome achievement even if, as some very credible experts charge, the gains are overstated.[265] These numbers also antedate the coronavirus pandemic, which is exacerbating poverty.

But as the share of the population living in extreme poverty has fallen to near zero in China and 22 percent in India, further reductions in global poverty depend primarily on the rest of the world—the predominantly neoliberal world—where progress in poverty reduction is much slower. The rate

263. Ha-Joon Chang, *Bad Samaritans: The Myth of Free Trade and the Secret History of Capitalism* (New York: Bloomsbury, 2008).

264. World Bank, "PovcalNet," accessed November 19, 2020, http://iresearch.worldbank .org/PovcalNet/povOnDemand.aspx. These amounts are measured in international dollars, which adjust for differences in price levels and consumption in each country. Also see Marta Schoch, Christoph Lakner, and Samuel Freije-Rodriguez, "Monitoring Poverty at the US$3.20 and US$5.50 Lines: Differences and Similarities with Extreme Poverty Trends," *Data Blog*, World Bank, November 19, 2020, https://blogs.worldbank.org/opendata/ monitoring-poverty-us320-and-us550-lines-differences-and-similarities-extreme-poverty.

265. Thomas Pogge and Sanjay G. Reddy, "How Not to Count the Poor," in *Debates on the Measurement of Global Poverty*, ed. Sudhir Anand, Paul Segal, and Joseph E. Stiglitz, Initiative for Policy Dialogue (New York: Oxford University Press, April 30, 2010), 42–85; David Woodward, *How Poor Is "Poor"?* (London: New Economics Foundation, July 4, 2010); Thomas Pogge and Sanjay G. Reddy, "Unknown: The Extent, Distribution and Trend of Global Income Poverty," *Economic and Political Weekly* 41, no. 22 (January 2003): 41; Sanjay G. Reddy and Rahul Lahoti, "$1.90 Per Day: What Does It Say?," *New Left Review* 97 (January–February 2016): 106–27; Jason Hickel, *The Divide: Global Inequality from Conquest to Free Markets* (New York: W. W. Norton, 2017).

at which global extreme poverty is declining has more than halved in recent years, while the number of people living in extreme poverty in sub-Saharan Africa is actually increasing.[266]

To no longer be counted among the extremely poor, a person's income over the year must be sufficient to purchase (in their local currency) at least the amount that $700 ($1.90 per day) would buy *in the United States*.[267] This means a family of four with an income above $2,800 a year (four times $700) would not be classified as extremely poor. But this level of income would mean total destitution in the United States, and this is what it means in other countries also. By comparison, the US poverty line in 2019—$26,801 for a family of four and $13,300 for a single person—is $18 a day for each family member and $36 a day for a single person. Even these income levels, far higher than $1.90 a day, are entirely inadequate. According to the Food and Agriculture Organization of the UN, $1.90 a day is too little to buy even a healthy diet.[268]

Any reduction in the count of people living in officially defined extreme poverty is very good news. But it does not indicate that these neighbors are thriving. Global extreme poverty has fallen because people in the global bottom 50 percent saw their incomes nearly double, up *an average* of 94 percent between 1980 and 2016.[269] However, everyone in the bottom quarter of the global population still has income below $3.10/day ($1,132 a year)—some far below—and everyone in the bottom half lives on less than $6.15 per day ($2,245/year).[270] An escape from extreme poverty still leaves someone tragically poor. An income that is two or even three times the $1.90 extreme poverty level is still too little to escape deprivation.

266. World Bank, *Poverty and Shared Prosperity, 2020: Reversal of Fortune* (Washington, DC: World Bank, 2020), 32; Max Lawson et al., *Public Good or Private Wealth?* (Oxford: Oxfam International, January 2019).

267. Establishing international income comparisons is extremely imprecise. Moreover, there is no universal definition of poverty or extreme poverty.

268. Food and Agriculture Organization of the UN, *The State of Food Security and Nutrition in the World, 2020* (Rome: FAO, 2020).

269. Facundo Alvaredo et al., coords., *World Inequality Report 2018* (World Inequality Lab, 2018), table 2.1.1, https://www.hup.harvard.edu/catalog.php?isbn=9780674984554.

270. World Bank, "PovcalNet," accessed March 31, 2020, http://iresearch.worldbank.org/PovcalNet/povOnDemand.aspx. Also see Schoch, Lakner, and Freije-Rodriguez, "Monitoring Poverty."

We continue to see poverty's devastating consequences. Each day, 15,000 children die before reaching their fifth birthday—some 5.5 million each year—and nearly half of these deaths are due to undernutrition.[271] Moderate or severe stunting of bodily growth and possibly of brain development affects 22 percent of all children under age five and 45 percent of the poorest fifth of children.[272] An estimated 3 billion people could not afford a healthy diet in 2017.[273] Global poverty is immoral and also wasteful of people's potential gifts and contributions: "The world's greatest unexploited resource is not oil or gold but the minds of hungry children."[274] Poverty is a factor in about a third of all human deaths.[275]

As in the United States, poverty is much more than a shortage of income. Some 2.2 billion of the world's roughly 7.9 billion people do not have safe drinking water, 2 billion do not have the most basic sanitation services, and 3 billion lack basic handwashing facilities with clean water no more than thirty minutes away.[276] In the world's poorest countries, over one-third of hospitals and health centers lack running water and soap.[277]

Have Neoliberal Policies Reduced Global Poverty?

Neoliberal policies have been adopted by or imposed on most countries in the Global South, but they remain very controversial, charged with harming the poor, enriching the already wealthy, and increasing the power and wealth of corporations.[278] The decline in extreme poverty—from 36 percent to 9 percent of the global population over twenty-seven years—is one

271. UNICEF, "Malnutrition," March 2020, accessed September 22, 2020, https://data .unicef.org/topic/nutrition/malnutrition/#; UNICEF, *The State of the World's Children 2019; Children, Food and Nutrition: Growing Well in a Changing World* (New York: UNICEF, October 2019), 190–91.

272. UNICEF, *World's Children 2019*, table 8. Stunting is defined in children aged zero to fifty-nine months who are below minus two standard deviations from median height-for-age of the World Health Organization Child Growth Standards.

273. Food and Agriculture Organization, *Food Security 2020*.

274. Nicholas Kristof, "The World's Malnourished Kids Don't Need a $295 Burger," *New York Times*, June 12, 2019.

275. Thomas Pogge, "The Hunger Games," *Food Ethics* 1 (June 3, 2016): 9–27.

276. UNICEF and World Health Organization, *Progress on Household Drinking Water, Sanitation and Hygiene 2000–2017: Special Focus on Inequalities* (New York: UNICEF and WHO, 2019).

277. UNICEF, *Get the Facts on Handwashing* (New York: UNICEF, October 15, 2018).

278. See Naomi Klein, *The Shock Doctrine: The Rise of Disaster Capitalism* (New York: Henry Holt, 2007).

positive outcome often used to justify neoliberalism. Even if this figure overstates the decline as some charge, the numbers are impressive. But what are they really telling us?

Of all the people exiting from poverty, most lived in Asia, including 57 percent in China and 11 percent in India. However, China did not develop its economy using neoliberal, free market policies—just the opposite. Many of the largest companies in China are owned and run by the state, including banks and oil companies. The Chinese government manages the economy to support important industrial sectors and develop leading-edge technologies that will produce the high-tech products of the future. It manipulates the value of the currency on international markets to promote exports and create jobs. These are just some of the tools used in a strategy of comprehensive economic planning. The market is not free of government intervention and certainly not shaped by neoliberal policies. It is managed to produce desired national outcomes. India also uses a diverse set of economic policies, many of which are not neoliberal. Consequently, most of the poverty reduction in recent decades happened in countries that did not follow neoliberal orthodoxy. At best, neoliberalism was responsible for only a small share of the decline in global poverty.

Global Inequality

In most countries in most years, the economy grows. The economic pie gets larger. But in many countries, this growth provides only a small benefit to the poor because, like in the United States, it primarily flows to the highest-income households. Even China's huge reduction in poverty was not due to "pro-poor" growth. Between 1980 and 2016, the bottom 50 percent of Chinese received just 13 percent of China's growth in income, a smaller share than the 15 percent received by the top 1 percent.[279] The share of all national income received by the bottom 50 percent in China *fell* from 26.7 percent in 1980 to 14.8 percent in 2015.[280] Poverty was reduced due only to the massive rise in China's national income, up more than eightfold per adult over the period. This meant that even the 13 percent share of

279. Alvaredo et al., *World Inequality 2018*, table 2.1.2; and World Inequality Database, data for figures and tables, accessed August 4, 2020, https://wir2018.wid.world/methodology .html.

280. Alvaredo et al., table 2.7.1; and World Inequality Database, data for figures and tables, accessed August 4, 2020, https://wir2018.wid.world/.

growth received by the bottom half was a sizable increase. But China's high rate of growth over many years has not been matched in other countries, and in most countries, the small shares of national growth received by the poor mean little increase in income.

Between 1980 and 2016, the share of all the world's income received by the global bottom 50 percent rose from 8.0 percent to 9.7 percent.[281] This is a tiny increase over thirty-six years and a very small amount to be shared among the poorest half of the world's people. During the same period, the share of all global income received by the top 1 percent of the global population rose from 16.3 percent to 20.4 percent.[282] The *share* of all income received by the bottom 50 percent increased so little because they received so little of the *growth* in income—just 12 percent of the gains over the thirty-six years—while the top 1 percent received 27 percent, and half of that went to the top one-tenth of 1 percent (the highest-income 7.5 million people worldwide).[283] Over this period, for each additional dollar received by a person in the bottom half, someone in the top one-tenth of 1 percent received $542. The poor are slowly getting slightly less poor and the rich are quickly getting very much richer. In the Global South, income inequality is rising nearly everywhere.[284]

Income inequality means many people living in poverty see affluence all around them. As in the Global North, inequality inhibits participation in civic, political, and cultural life. It also slows a country's economic growth, retards efforts to reduce poverty, worsens social relations among people of differing socioeconomic backgrounds, weakens democracy, threatens social cohesion, and lessens individuals' sense of fulfillment and self-worth.[285]

---

281. Alvaredo et al., table 2.1.7; and World Inequality Database, data for figures and tables, accessed August 4, 2020, https://wir2018.wid.world/.

282. Since both the global bottom 50 percent and the top 1 percent had growing shares of global income, the rest of the global population—the upper-middle 49 percent—had a shrinking share. This group of "losers" includes most of the middle- and lower-income people in the Global North. See Branko Milanovic, *Global Inequality: A New Approach for the Age of Globalization* (Cambridge, MA: Belknap, 2016).

283. Alvaredo et al., *World Inequality 2018*, table 2.1.2.

284. Alvaredo et al., table 2.1.1a; UNDP, *Goal 10: Reduced Inequalities* (New York: UNDP), accessed December 2, 2021, https://www.undp.org/sustainable-development-goals#reduced -inequalities.

285. UNDP, *Sustainable Development Goals, Goal 10 Targets*; UNDP, *Humanity Divided: Confronting Inequality in Developing Countries* (New York: UNDP, November 2015).

Global wealth is even more unequally distributed than income. In 2018, the wealthiest 1 percent of global adults owned nearly half of all wealth, and the top 10 percent owned 85 percent.[286] The bottom half owned less than 1 percent. The wealthiest eight men in the world, multibillionaires all, own as much wealth as half the global population.[287]

Most wealth is owned by people in rich countries. The 4.8 percent of the world's adults who live in the United States own nearly one-third (31.0 percent) of global wealth. The 20 percent of global adults living in the United States, Western Europe, Canada, Japan, and Australia own over two-thirds (68.8 percent) of all the world's wealth.[288] Wealth inequality is extreme and will only get worse if current trends continue. Between 1980 and 2017, for each $1 in additional wealth that went to the bottom 99 percent, $19.53 went to the top one one-hundredth of 1 percent, and over $17.50 went to the rest of the top 1 percent.[289] The resources of the planet are being used, unsustainably, to generate wealth, but most of the benefits accrue to a small, already wealthy sliver of the global population.

I repeat: there is no economic inevitability about high inequality; it is a choice. The widening gaps in income, wealth, and other dimensions of well-being are not an unavoidable price we are forced to pay for economic growth or development in the Global North or South.[290] The public policies most important for creating these harmful outcomes include mismanaged neoliberal globalization designed to advantage multinational firms in the Global North; the neoliberal policy regime followed in most countries; weakened workplace protections and attacks on unions worldwide; the downsizing of public investments in critical sectors like health, education, and income support; and discrimination based on race, sex, ethnicity, religion, and country of origin.

286. Credit Suisse, *Global Wealth Databook 2018*, Zurich: Credit Suisse, October 18, 2018, table 3-4, accessed May 21, 2019, https://www.credit-suisse.com/media/assets/corporate/docs/about-us/research/publications/global-wealth-databook-2018.pdf.

287. Deborah Hardoon, *An Economy for the 99%* (London: Oxfam International, January 16, 2017).

288. Credit Suisse, *Global Wealth Databook 2018*, table 2-4.

289. Alvaredo et al., *World Inequality 2018*, table 4.1.2.

290. UNDP, *Humanity Divided*.

Debt

Poor countries face an ancient problem: debt. To meet the need for basic services like water, sanitation, health care, and education and to develop a more prosperous economy, a country can usually borrow money. But if a country cannot repay a loan, for whatever reason, there is no fair, systematic, transparent, and timely process—like bankruptcy—that allows the debtor to restructure unpayable sovereign debt. Instead, poor countries in a debt crisis are forced to participate in an ad hoc, inequitable, and disorderly process that provides too little debt relief that comes too late and has a strong bias toward preventing losses by lenders. In the wake of such a debt resolution process, a country is typically left with a heavier debt load and an even more difficult path of economic development and prosperity. Lenders are repaid, often in full, despite their risky or irresponsible practices, enabling them to make more loans without facing any consequences.[291]

Some debts should not be repaid. When lenders knowingly lend money for a bad project or if an unforeseen change in circumstances makes the loan unpayable, the lender must share in the cost of the failed loan as happens in the Global North. Or if the borrower is an illegitimate, unelected leader who represses the people and even directs some of the loan money to a secret personal bank account, the country's citizens should not be responsible for paying back the loan, which should never have been made. Or if a country faces the choice of repaying a loan or providing for the population's basic needs such as water or health care, life must be prioritized over loan payments.

In the late 1990s and 2000s, an international effort for a debt jubilee—debt cancellation—led by faith communities delivered $70 billion of debt relief to thirty poor countries.[292] Before the debt relief, twenty-six poor African countries paid more in debt service, on average, than they spent on health and education. After the debt relief, their spending on health,

---

291. Jubilee Debt Campaign, *Preventing and Resolving Sovereign Debt Crises: Stop Bailing Out Reckless Lenders* (London: Jubilee Debt Campaign, October 2019); European Network on Debt and Development, *We Can Work It Out: 10 Civil Society Principles for Sovereign Debt Resolution* (Brussels: Eurodad, September 2019).

292. UN Conference on Trade and Development, *From the Great Lockdown to the Great Meltdown: Developing Country Debt in the Time of Covid-19* (Geneva: UNCTAD, April 2020).

education, and other social services rose dramatically.[293] Debt cancellation was life giving and enabled people to thrive. However, many nations continue to have unpayable debt and high debt burdens. Debt service on developing countries' long-term debt cost an average of 10.3 percent of government revenues in 2018.[294] Some countries spend more than a quarter of all revenues on debt service.

Migrants and Refugees

The world has a growing migrant and refugee crisis. Economic hardship, climate change, and violence (which is often exacerbated by economic hardship and climate change) are forcing millions of people to leave their homes and their homelands. In 2019, nearly eighty million people were forced from their homes due to a fear of persecution, conflict, or violence; 40 percent were children.[295] Some forty-six million of these neighbors remained in their home countries as internally displaced people, four million sought asylum in another country, and nearly thirty million became refugees, unable to return home and typically living in camps in neighboring countries with minimal housing or food. Some 80 percent were hosted in developing regions.[296] The global number of refugees and asylum seekers increased by about thirteen million between 2010 and 2017.[297]

Migrants leave their homes by choice, although this choice may actually be forced by dire economic necessity. Poverty kills bodies and minds. Seeking a way out should not be a crime. Economic migrants often become legal or undocumented guest workers who face many forms of exploitation but are afforded few legal protections. In 2019, there were 272 million international migrants—3.5 percent of the global population and an increase

293. Alberto Espejo and Anna Unigovskaya, *Debt Relief Bringing Benefits to Africa* (Washington, DC: International Monetary Fund, February 25, 2008).

294. UN Conference on Trade and Development, *From the Great Lockdown*.

295. UN High Commissioner for Refugees, "Facts at a Glance," accessed August 4, 2020, https://www.unhcr.org/figures-at-a-glance.html.

296. Amnesty International, *The World's Refugees in Numbers* (London: Amnesty International), accessed April 3, 2020, https://www.amnesty.org/en/what-we-do/refugees-asylum-seekers-and-migrants/global-refugee-crisis-statistics-and-facts/.

297. Population Division, UN Department of Economic and Social Affairs, *Population Facts* (New York: UN DESA, September 2019), accessed April 3, 2020, https://www.un.org/en/development/desa/population/migration/publications/populationfacts/docs/MigrationStock2019_PopFacts_2019-04.pdf.

of fifty million people since 2010. The expectation that climate change will worsen both forced displacement and global migration requires a compassionate and coordinated response.

Religious Bodies Speak Out

A number of religious bodies have voiced their concerns with the current neoliberal globalization regime, especially its harmful impact on the Global South. The World Council of Churches avows, "Our faithfulness to God and to God's free gift of life compels us to confront idolatrous assumptions, unjust systems, the politics of domination and exploitation in the current world economic order. Economics and economic justice are always matters of faith as they touch the very core of God's will for creation."[298] The World Communion of Reformed Churches asserts that working to create a more just global economy is an essential obligation of the Christian faith: "We believe that the integrity of our faith is at stake if we remain silent or refuse to act in the face of the current system of neoliberal economic globalization."[299] According to Pope Francis, "As long as the problems of the poor are not radically resolved by rejecting the absolute autonomy of markets and financial speculation and by attacking the structural causes of inequality, no solution will be found for the world's problems or, for that matter, to any problems. Inequality is the root of social ills."[300]

A SUSTAINABLE ECONOMY

This is not a book about the environment. But it is a book about economics and faithful living, which today requires at least a brief exploration of how we live out our love of neighbor—neighbors in all places and of all species—in the midst of the existential threats of climate change,

298. World Council of Churches, *Alternative Globalization Addressing Peoples and Earth, a Background Document* (Geneva: WCC, 2005). The World Council of Churches represents more than five hundred million Christians in over 110 countries.
299. World Communion of Reformed Churches, *Accra Confession: Covenanting for Justice in the Economy and the Earth* (Geneva: WCRC, 2004). WCRC is composed of some 214 denominations and faith bodies of Reformed and United churches with a combined membership of seventy-five million people in 107 countries.
300. Francis, *Evangelii Gaudium*, 202.

environmental destruction, and species extinction. While God created and gifted us with a planet of abundance, a home flowing with milk and honey, we have overused, destroyed, and fouled God's gift. God's intentions for abundance and even for life itself are being thwarted. Recycling, taking reusable bags to the store to carry home our purchases, installing more energy-efficient lightbulbs, driving a hybrid vehicle, and similar practices are all good and necessary. But they are entirely inadequate to address the problem. Much more fundamental and comprehensive interventions are necessary to create an economy that is sustainable and life giving to human and nonhuman lives on planet earth for millennia into the future.

Climate change and the environment both affect and are affected by the economic system. We face not one but two existential threats stemming from our destruction of the environment. The first is climate change. We have filled the atmosphere with greenhouse gases (GHGs), largely emitted through the burning of fossil fuels and industrial agriculture, that are raising earth's temperature, worsening storms and droughts, reducing food production, melting glaciers, raising sea levels, and threatening the lives of plants, animals, and humans. Annual GHG emissions have grown 41 percent since 1990 and continue to climb.[301] Over half of the carbon from the burning of fossil fuels that has accumulated in the atmosphere since the start of the Industrial Revolution was emitted in the last thirty years, well after we were aware of the problem.[302]

The second threat is the destruction of the environment and subsequent loss of biodiversity. We have logged, burned, and destroyed the world's forests; degraded and denuded the fertile soil, allowing it to be blown away to leave a desert behind; fouled clean, fresh water and acidified the oceans making them toxic for living things; and encroached upon and destroyed the habitat used by other species. Dozens of species go extinct every day, and one million are threatened with extinction.[303]

301. Mengpin Ge and Johannes Friedrich, "4 Charts Explain Greenhouse Gas Emissions by Countries and Sectors," *Insights* (blog), World Resources Institute, February 6, 2020, https://www.wri.org/insights/4-charts-explain-greenhouse-gas-emissions-countries-and-sectors.
302. David Wallace-Wells, *The Uninhabitable Earth: Life after Warming* (New York: Tim Duggan, 2019), 4.
303. The Intergovernmental Science-Policy Platform on Biodiversity and Ecosystem Services, *Global Assessment Report on Biodiversity and Ecosystem Services* (Bonn, Germany: IPBES, 2019).

GHG emissions and thus responsibility for this problem are very unequal. Richer countries and richer households within countries produce more emissions per person than do the poor. Worldwide, the top 10 percent of household emitters produce 45 percent of GHGs; the bottom 50 percent emit 13 percent.[304] In the United States, industrial plants that emit harmful toxins into the air and water, the threat from the rising sea level, and even a lack of trees to provide shade and reduce temperatures are all more common in communities of color.[305] In the United States and globally, racism is entwined with the dire consequences of climate change. While poor people and poorer countries are more impacted by many of the harmful effects of climate change, they have less money with which to prevent and respond to changing realities and disasters.[306]

To date, many of the most severe adverse climate effects are happening in countries in the Global South. Deadly heat is a greater problem for those who work outside or lack air-conditioning at home (or even adequate shelter). Poor farmers have less access to irrigation and fewer defenses against drought. Lower agricultural yields will raise food prices, and it is the poorest who will be forced to eat less. Extreme weather events, land degradation and desertification, water scarcity, and rising sea levels are undermining global efforts to eradicate hunger. In twenty-two countries, mostly in North Africa and Asia, over 70 percent of the population currently faces water stress, indicating a likelihood of future water scarcity,[307] and by 2050, over 40 percent of the global population could be living in areas of severe water stress.[308]

304. Lucas Chancel and Thomas Piketty, "Carbon and Inequality: From Kyoto to Paris: Trends in the Global Inequality of Carbon Emissions (1998–2013) and Prospects for an Equitable Adaptation Fund" (working paper no. 2015/7, WID.world, Paris, 2015).

305. Sarah Kaplan, "Climate Change Is Also a Racial Justice Problem," *Washington Post*, June 29, 2020.

306. UN Development Program, *Human Development Report 2019: Beyond Income, Beyond Averages, Beyond Today; Inequalities in Human Development in the 21st Century* (New York: UNDP, 2019), chapter 5.

307. UN Department of Economic and Social Affairs, Statistics Division, "Goal Six: Ensure Availability and Sustainable Management of Water and Sanitation for All," in *Sustainable Development Goals Report 2018* (New York: UN DESA, 2018).

308. Sarah Whitmee et al., "Safeguarding Human Health in the Anthropocene Epoch: Report of the Rockefeller Foundation—Lancet Commission on Planetary Health," *Lancet* 386, no. 10007 (July 16, 2015); Andy Haines, "Addressing Challenges to Human Health in

The United States bears a heightened responsibility for climate change and environmental destruction. The United States uses more than its share of the world's resources. If everyone on earth used resources at the rate people in the United States do, sustainable living would require five planet earths, according to one estimate.[309] In 2017, China was the largest GHG emitter, accounting for 27 percent of the global total, while the United States was second, emitting 13 percent.[310] But China has 18.5 percent of the global population, while the United States has only 4.3 percent. Per capita emissions in China were 7.3 tons per person, while each person in the United States emitted over twice as much, 17.8 tons.[311] Countries in the European Union emitted from 6 to 11 tons per person; in Latin America, no country exceeded 5 tons per person; and in much of sub-Saharan Africa, emissions were below 1 ton per person. The United States has higher per capita GHG emissions than any other country.[312]

The United States has an extra responsibility for global emissions being produced now but also for those in the past. Greenhouse gases persist for centuries in the atmosphere. The majority of GHGs in the atmosphere today were emitted by the rich industrialized nations. Of all the gases accumulated since 1751, 26 percent originated in the United States, the largest single source.[313] The European Union (with a population nearly one and a half times that of the United States) is responsible for 22 percent. China is responsible for 13 percent. The United States and Europe have a special obligation today to reduce their emissions, since they are largely responsible for the problems we currently face.

As the global population increases, it uses more energy and consumes more food, water, and other goods and services. A very partial solution to addressing our environmental crisis is to slow population growth. But people

the Anthropocene Epoch—an Overview of the Findings of the Rockefeller/Lancet Commission on Planetary Health," *International Health* 9, no. 5 (September 1, 2017): 269–71.

309. Global Footprint Network, "Country Trends," accessed April 6, 2020, https://data.footprintnetwork.org/#/countryTrends?type=earth&cn=231.

310. UN Environment Program, *Emissions Gap Report 2019* (Nairobi: UNEP, November 2019), table 2.2.

311. Hannah Ritchie and Max Roser, *CO_2 and Greenhouse Gas Emissions*, OurWorldInData.org, last modified August 2020, https://ourworldindata.org/co2-and-other-greenhouse-gas-emissions.

312. UN Environment Program, *Emissions Gap*.

313. Ritchie and Roser, *CO_2 and Greenhouse Gas Emissions*.

have differing levels of consumption and therefore different impacts on the climate and environment. Each person in the United States has a disproportionately large, negative impact on both the use of resources and GHG emissions. Adults worldwide need access to the resources that allow them to control their reproduction. But the population that most needs to cease growing is our own, especially the upper-income segment of the population that uses the most resources.

The international community has recognized that climate change calls all countries to respond "in accordance with their *common but differentiated* responsibilities and respective capabilities and their social and economic conditions."[314] All countries must work toward sustainability, but those that make, and have made, the greatest contributions to the GHGs accumulated in the atmosphere today and those with excess resources potentially available to address the problem bear a heavier responsibility.

ACTING TO END OPPRESSION

Injustice is created and perpetuated by our economic system itself. It is built into the system and is not solely or even primarily due to individuals' acts. So justice requires fundamental changes in our economic system.

Failure to work for justice is to act in support of the status quo and of all the injustices described here. There are no innocent bystanders. Violations of God's will originate not only from the acts of the designers and perpetrators of systemic injustices but also from the complicity of those who fail to act. No one can work on all the issues that need redemption, but everyone can work on something: "What good is it, my brothers and sisters, if you say you have faith but do not have works? Can faith save you? If a brother or sister is naked and lacks daily food, and one of you says to them, 'Go in peace; keep warm and eat your fill,' and yet you do not supply their bodily needs, what is the good of that? So faith by itself, if it has no works, is dead" (Jas 2:14–17). In our democracy, our involvement must go far beyond works

---

314. UN Climate Change, Framework Convention on Climate Change, adopted at the United Nations Conference on Environment and Development, Rio de Janeiro, Brazil, June 3–14, 1992, https://unfccc.int/files/essential_background/background_publications _htmlpdf/application/pdf/conveng.pdf. Emphasis added.

of mercy, such as providing food and clothing to those who lack them. We must change the system that creates and perpetuates injustice.

In the simple living of their lives, people in the Global North engage in and benefit from the exploitation of their neighbors. I get up in the morning, take a quick shower (using more water than some families use in a day), get dressed (nearly certainly putting on clothes made in a sweatshop), and have some coffee and an orange (grown and harvested by people who cannot afford nutritious food for themselves and their families). This is just in the first hour I am out of bed, and it continues 24/7. My life is embedded in a system of abuse and exploitation of people, animals, and all creation. For many in the Global North, this is an original sin, a condition into which we are born and live our lives, the sin of willful ignorance and casual but deadly exploitation—and we are all such nice people! God have mercy. *Kyrie eleison.* We can possibly escape blame but not responsibility.[315] We are thankful that God *is* compassion (Luke 6:36),[316] and as Jesus promised, for God, all is possible (Matt 19:26; Mark 10:27; Luke 18:27). But take care: "Alas for those who lie on beds of ivory [sheets], and lounge on their couches . . . but are not grieved over the ruin of Joseph!" (Amos 6:4–6). We must change the economic system so we can live without routinely exploiting others. We must change the economic system so it promotes the well-being of all. As people of the Way, our primary allegiance is to God and to God's cosmic reign of justice and peace. With God's grace, we act.

Faith-based people too often get sidetracked with charitable efforts that are critically important, even lifesaving in the short term, but that are only way stations on the road to justice. There will always be emergencies, unexpected crises—hurricanes, house fires, floods, or other truly unforeseen events—that need an immediate charitable response. But episodically providing the poor a temporary escape from poverty is insufficient when a restructuring of the economy to prevent poverty is needed. Charity is too often a way to avoid more fundamental change.

One year before his death, Martin Luther King Jr. called us to restructure society: "On the one hand, we are called to play the good Samaritan on life's roadside, but that will be only an initial act. One day we must come to see that the whole Jericho Road must be transformed so that men and

---

315. Catherine Keller, *On the Mystery: Discerning Divinity in Process* (Minneapolis: Fortress, 2008).
316. "Compassion" is a better translation than "mercy." See Borg, *Jesus*, 176.

women will not be constantly beaten and robbed as they make their journey on life's highway. True compassion is more than flinging a coin to a beggar; it is not haphazard and superficial. It comes to see that an edifice which produces beggars needs restructuring."[317]

Charity is often debilitating. In ancient Palestine and in Jesus's day, reciprocal sharing and support were essential for thriving. Neighbors helped neighbors and knew that in the future when they needed help, they would receive it. But while reciprocal support is life giving for both givers and receivers and enhances egalitarian relationships, a flow of support that goes in one direction only—from the always rich to the always poor—is demeaning, is destructive of self-worth, and reinforces unequal social relations. Charity, while essential, is not enough. People need to be able to support themselves through their work. We will know the economy is just when the soup kitchens, food banks, homeless shelters, and other components of our charitable infrastructure are out of business because they have no clients.

According to the US Conference of Catholic Bishops, "As individuals, all citizens have a duty to assist the poor through acts of charity and personal commitment. But private charity and voluntary action are not sufficient. We also carry out our moral responsibility to assist and empower the poor by working collectively through government to establish just and effective public policies."[318]

Our call is to change our flawed institutions and structures, to create an economic system that protects the vulnerable and promotes the thriving of all. According to Walter Brueggemann's reading of the Bible, "Justice is not charity, nor is it romantic do-goodism. It is rather a mandate to order public policy, public practice, and public institutions for the common good and in resistance to the kind of greedy initiative that damages the community."[319]

The inequality, poverty, and economic exploitation that characterize life today in the United States and in most other countries are in direct violation of what could be considered the most important characteristic of a just

---

317. Martin Luther King Jr., "A Time to Break Silence," Address to clergy and laity concerned, Riverside Church, New York City, April 4, 1967, in *Testament of Hope: The Essential Writings and Speeches of Martin Luther King, Jr.*, ed. James Melvin Washington (New York: HarperCollins, 1986), 241.

318. US Conference of Catholic Bishops, *Economic Justice for All*, 93.

319. Brueggemann, *Theology of the Old Testament*, 423.

economy: the universal thriving of all. Seen through the lens of faith and biblical teaching, we must conclude the economy is failing to achieve its fundamental purpose. We are very far from God's vision of economic justice and, in many ways, are moving further away each year. Much more than small fixes around our economic edges are needed. In chapter 6, we explore some of the more fundamental necessary changes.

Chapter 6

MOVING TOWARD ECONOMIC JUSTICE

THE PATH TO A JUST ECONOMY

In 1946, the screenwriters of *It's a Wonderful Life* had insights into the impact of poverty, inequality, and unjust economic institutions that we seem to have forgotten.[1] In this Christmas classic, Jimmy Stewart plays George Bailey, a banker in the small town of Bedford Falls who has devoted his career to building a flourishing community where everyone thrives. During a moment when he questions the value of his life and considers suicide, his guardian angel, Clarence, shows him Bedford Falls (renamed Pottersville) as it would have developed in his absence, under the influence of his greedy and exploitative crosstown banking competitor, Mr. Potter.

In Pottersville, Mr. Potter is doing extremely well, but no one else is. Poverty and inequality are readily apparent, and so are anger, hate, fighting, gambling, alcoholism, prostitution, and despair. The same people live in Pottersville as in Bedford Falls, but the lives of the Pottersville residents have been twisted and stunted by poverty, inequality, and exclusion. Guardian angel Clarence shows George Bailey that the thriving citizens of Bedford Falls could have instead become the despairing inhabitants of Pottersville if they had lived under the policies and greedy practices of Mr. Potter.

Today, our failure to thrive as individuals and as a society and the prevalence of the diseases of despair may indicate that many people are living in

---

1. *It's a Wonderful Life*, directed by Frank Capra (1946; Culver City, CA: produced by Liberty Films [II], distributed by RKO Radio Pictures).

places that seem more like Pottersville than Bedford Falls. But Pottersville was not inevitable. Inequality and poverty are choices, whether in Bedford Falls, the United States, or our world. The economy is not totally under our control, but neither does it operate completely outside our direction. We can choose economic policies, institutions, and structures designed to achieve economic justice and reasonably expect to move toward that goal. We now explore those options.

This chapter is intended to be an early sketch of a road map that could guide us toward economic justice. We will concentrate on the broad, long-term changes that could be the focus of education, activism, and advocacy efforts over the next twenty to thirty years. These objectives can also shape our shorter-term efforts and ultimately lead us closer to where we are called to be.

We now examine ways to move toward achieving the four key components of a just economy:

- the thriving of all people and creation;
- a job for everyone who is available to work that pays a family-supporting wage;
- an economic system that is fair, is free of oppression, protects the vulnerable, and promotes the thriving of all and where justice-seeking people act to make and keep it so; and
- an economy operating sustainably in a manner that ensures abundant life for people and other beings indefinitely into the future.

EVERYONE THRIVES: ECONOMIC HUMAN RIGHTS

The foundation of a just economy is the thriving of all people and creation, the fullness of material life. But how can justice-seeking activists in the twenty-first century turn this concept into public policy and enforceable law? To begin, we must realize that the ancient obligation to ensure the material well-being of everyone is an alternative way of recognizing the modern concept of economic human rights. The language of economic human rights provides a way to express biblical concepts as public policy.

Of course, biblical writers and Jesus did not recognize human rights as we view them today. But the biblical law does include key components of economic human rights. The teachings recognized that everyone deserved and was *entitled* to a fair share of God's abundance, enough to support lives lived in wholeness. Society was *obligated* to alleviate poverty. The poor had *rights* to food. Workers had a *right* to livelihood, land (which meant food, shelter, clothing, fuel, and economic security), or a job that paid a living wage. These were not optional acts of charity but the commands of God, the requirements of justice.

Today we understand human rights to be those just claims inherent to every human being stemming solely from their personhood and human dignity. They are universal entitlements. For people of faith, human rights originate in the inherent sacredness of each person created in the image and likeness of God (Gen 1:26). The World Council of Churches calls us to work for human rights: "As Christians, we are called to share in God's mission of justice, peace and respect for all Creation and to seek for all humanity the abundant life which God intends. Within scripture, through tradition, and from the many ways in which the spirit illumines our hearts today, we discern God's gift of dignity for each person and their inherent right to acceptance and participation with the community. From this flows the responsibility of the churches as the Body of Christ, to work for universal respect and implementation of human rights."[2] The US Catholic Bishops speak of people's "rights to fulfillment of material needs. . . . These rights are bestowed on human beings by God and grounded in the nature and dignity of human persons. They are not created by society. Indeed society has a duty to secure and protect them."[3]

We also affirm that thriving, living in the fullness of life, is more than physical survival. The material resources that every person needs and deserves are those things that enable one to participate in society and engage in its usual customs and activities.

We distinguish rights, the fulfillment of justice, from charity. No person is a charity case. Everyone is a holder of rights that must be respected, protected, and fulfilled. Everyone has the right to a dignified life. Structures and policies that force people to rely on charity reveal an unjust economic system and a society of disrespect: "Every human being has a claim on

2. World Council of Churches, *Human Rights and the Churches: New Challenges, a Statement by the International Ecumenical Consultation* (Morges, Switzerland: WCC, June 23–27, 1998).
3. US Conference of Catholic Bishops, *Economic Justice for All*, 41.

whatever is necessary to fulfill his task of being human. Whenever what is necessary for this task is denied a person, his or her very humanity is denied, distorted, and ruined. Human rights are necessary to answer the creating/calling of every human being by God and are thus the basic requirements of the dignity of a person."[4] It is the responsibility of government to ensure rights are protected and not violated, respected by all entities in society, and fulfilled.

US law recognizes the political and civic rights of all citizens, even if at times these rights are not respected or fulfilled.[5] But US law fails to recognize a universal right to the material resources necessary for thriving. Freedom to speak, assemble, worship, vote, move about, and do all the other things we celebrate as our civil and political rights are vitally important. But true freedom is also freedom from hunger and homelessness. Freedom is the opportunity to work and support oneself and a flourishing family. Freedom means that not all our dreams will be endlessly deferred but that they can be freely pursued. Rights guaranteeing freedom *from* oppression are just half of our human inheritance. Rights that guarantee freedom *to* thrive must also be fulfilled. In international law, these are recognized as economic, social, and cultural rights. Economic human rights that are respected, protected, and fulfilled are a prerequisite for freedom and liberty.

Affirmative rights ensuring freedom to thrive are not foreign to Americans. In President Franklin D. Roosevelt's State of the Union message in 1944, when the end of World War II could be glimpsed on the horizon, he called for the United States to recognize economic human rights:

> We cannot be content, no matter how high that general standard of living may be, if some fraction of our people—whether it be one-third or one-fifth or one-tenth—is ill-fed, ill-clothed, ill housed, and insecure. . . . We have come to a clear realization of the fact that true individual freedom cannot exist without economic security and independence. "Necessitous men are not free men." . . . In our day these economic truths have become accepted as self-evident. We have accepted, so to speak, a second Bill of Rights under which a new

4. Meeks, *God the Economist*, 90.
5. When these rights are violated, the harmed individual can go to court seeking to have the law enforced.

basis of security and prosperity can be established for all regardless of station, race, or creed.[6]

Roosevelt then named a number of economic human rights: a job, housing, health care, education, economic security, and earnings sufficient to provide for a family's food, clothing, and recreation. He concluded, "All of these rights spell security. And after this war is won we must be prepared to move forward, in the implementation of these rights, to new goals of human happiness and well-being." But just fifteen months later, Roosevelt was dead and his economic human rights agenda was never pursued.

However, the ideas in the speech were an important source of inspiration for the United Nations Universal Declaration of Human Rights, a comprehensive statement inclusive of economic, social, cultural, political, and civil rights adopted by the UN General Assembly on December 10, 1948. It commits signatory nations to respect, protect, and fulfill all the human rights it describes. The United States was among the first nations to sign the declaration and endorse these rights.[7]

The Universal Declaration of Human Rights was followed by two covenants adopted by the UN in 1966: the International Covenant on Economic, Social and Cultural Rights and the International Covenant on Civil and Political Rights.[8] Unlike the Universal Declaration, when these covenants are ratified by a nation, they have the force of law. (In the United States, ratification happens by a majority vote of support in the US Senate.) The United States along with 173 other nations ratified the Covenant on Civil and Political Rights.[9] But unlike 170 other nations, the United States has never ratified the Covenant on Economic, Social, and Cultural Rights.

6. Franklin D. Roosevelt, "State of the Union Message to Congress," Washington, DC, January 11, 1944, American Presidency Project, https://www.presidency.ucsb.edu/documents/state-the-union-message-congress.

7. Judith Blau and Alberto Moncada, *Human Rights: Beyond the Liberal Vision* (Lanham, MD: Rowman & Littlefield, 2005), 41.

8. The full text of these treaties is available on the website of the UN: International Covenant on Economic, Social and Cultural Rights, https://www.ohchr.org/en/professionalinterest/pages/cescr.aspx; and International Covenant on Civil and Political Rights, https://www.ohchr.org/EN/ProfessionalInterest/Pages/CCPR.aspx.

9. UN High Commissioner for Human Rights, "Status of Ratification Interactive Dashboard," http://indicators.ohchr.org.

Economic human rights recognized in the covenant fall into seven areas. The following description includes language from the covenant:

- The right to a standard of living that includes adequate food, clothing, and housing and "to the continuous improvement of living conditions" in accordance with a nation's increasing prosperity.
- The right to a job, to safe, healthy working conditions, to fair wages and equal pay for equal work, and to form or join a trade union and to strike.
- The right to economic security, adequate income, and the enjoyment of all economic human rights even when someone is unable to work, whether due to unemployment, illness, disability, pregnancy, death of a spouse, child- or elder-care responsibilities, old age, or other circumstance.
- The right to food, to be free from hunger, and to have adequate nutrition. The right to food is the right to sufficient, nutritious food for an active, healthy life. It should also be understood primarily as the right to work to feed oneself rather than the right to be fed.[10] Income security programs must be sufficient to allow households to buy food for themselves.
- The right to the "highest attainable standard" of physical and mental health, given one's underlying health conditions, with special protections provided for a reasonable period before and after childbirth when working mothers should be accorded paid leave or leave with adequate social security benefits.
- The right to education to further the full development of the human personality and to enable all persons to participate effectively in a free society. Higher education shall be made equally accessible to all.
- The right to leisure, to rest from work, to a reasonable limitation of working hours, and to periodic paid holidays, including public holidays with pay.

These rights provide access to material resources essential to well-being. But federal law fails to recognize any of them as a right. Instead, our public policies provide access that is piecemeal, underfunded, and far from

10. UN High Commissioner for Human Rights, *Principles and Guidelines for a Human Rights Approach to Poverty Reduction Strategies* (New York: UNHCR, 2006), 28.

universal. US law has never recognized any governmental duty to provide even the most fundamental of these, a basic standard of living.[11] The failure to respect, protect, and fulfill these internationally recognized economic human rights is a choice we make as a society, a choice we make to stand aside as people fail to thrive. We largely view meeting human needs as an individual responsibility even though Jesus and the biblical writers teach that society is obligated to ensure the well-being of all.

An economic and social system structured to fulfill economic rights is very different from one that relies on charitable handouts. Such a system is designed to produce a particular outcome, and it can be evaluated in terms of those goals. Government is tasked with respecting, protecting, and fulfilling human rights, including economic rights, and it provides oversight of the system: "[Rights] are claims to a set of social arrangements—norms, institutions, laws, an enabling economic environment—that can best secure the enjoyment of these rights. It is thus the obligation of governments and others to implement policies to put these arrangements in place."[12]

How can American society move toward recognizing, respecting, protecting, and fulfilling economic human rights? A very long-term goal would be the addition of amendments to the US Constitution. But there are many steps we could take now that would begin a movement toward full recognition and fulfillment of economic rights in the United States.

Eradicate Poverty

As we have seen, biblical teaching calls for the eradication of poverty. In a just economy, everyone has the material resources necessary to thrive. Given the ups and downs of life, there will always be people who find themselves in poverty. But the nonpoor are obligated to help them. The Bible teaches that anyone who falls on hard times, for whatever reason, is to be given the things they need along with new opportunities and fresh starts. Society is to be structured so that poverty is a temporary setback, not a longer-term reality: "The biblical word is clear: We cannot seek our own salvation without seeking that of our neighbor, and we cannot minister to

11. Martha H. Good, "Freedom from Want: The Failure of United States Courts to Protect Subsistence Rights," *Human Rights Quarterly* 6, no. 3 (August 1984): 335–65.

12. UN Development Program, *Human Development Report 2000: Human Rights and Human Development* (New York: UNDP, 2020), 73.

the anguish of our neighbor's soul without ministering to the suffering of our neighbor's body."[13]

As we have seen, in the United States, poverty is seldom due to personal behaviors or individual failures but is due to failings of the economic and political systems and structures. We have two priorities. The first is to change the economic system so it is no longer producing poverty and material need. Everyone who is available to work must have a job, and all jobs must pay a family-supporting wage. Second, we need a safety net that lifts every person with material needs out of poverty by providing income and other services as needed. Structures must be in place to assist those who fall and return them to abundance. Poverty is a constant problem and must be addressed constantly and systematically. Everyone needs a guaranteed income received from either a job or a safety net program that is secure and sufficient for thriving.[14] It must be an entitlement, not dependent on charity or the uncertainty of the budgetary processes of Congress and state legislatures.

Strong safety net programs to bridge income gaps are like insurance policies, paid for with our taxes, which protect each one of us against future hardship. Individuals are harmed, society is weakened, and God's intentions are thwarted if we cannot rely on the community to ensure that all of us have all we need to thrive, no matter the ups and downs of our lives. We can live in the fullness of life only through the gift of God's abundance, made manifest in the commitment we make to one another. Economic security comes through community and only through community.

Sharing Our Resources

This book has made repeated references to the sharing of God's resources. On a practical level, sharing happens in two ways: (1) through the (universal) public provision of goods and services paid for with our taxes (e.g., health care, early childhood education, affordable housing, and a strong safety net)

---

13. Bruce C. Birch, *What Does the Lord Require? The Old Testament Call to Social Witness* (Philadelphia: Westminster, 1985), 62.

14. A negative income tax, which provides low-income individuals with an income supplement to ensure their income reaches a predetermined level, is preferable to a universal basic income program in which everyone regularly receives a specified amount of income.

and (2) through a more equal sharing of income realized primarily through a greater equalization of wages.

To obtain material resources through a market requires money; in the United States, most people get most of their material resources by buying them. Thus the distribution of income—which largely means the distribution of wages—hugely impacts how God's resources are shared. A just sharing of God's resources through a market requires much greater equalization of income and wages. Our current economic injustice and extremely unequal economic outcomes are due, in part, to how few material resources are provided publicly—unlike in some countries with universal health care, childcare, early childhood education, and other services—and, in part, to our very unequal distribution of wages.

A Personal Infrastructure

We all recognize that many services, including health care, childcare, and education at all levels, are essential for thriving. No individual and no family should ever be without them. These are not commodities to be available only to those who can afford to purchase them in a market. Access to these services is a human right. They are the essential framework, the *personal infrastructure*, which our lives depend on. In a just economy, everyone has access to these services.

We recognize the importance of the physical infrastructure—the structures, facilities, and services that are necessary for a flourishing society, including roads, bridges, bike paths, airports, the power grid, cell towers, a water system, sewers, the internet, and much more. Similarly, in a just economy and a just society, every human being has access to a personal infrastructure of essential structures and services that enable and support our journeys through life, making us healthier and happier, more capable and productive, and better citizens. This personal infrastructure benefits us all. We know our physical infrastructure is crumbling; we can see it happening. But many people find their personal infrastructure is in even worse shape.

Once we acknowledge that a personal infrastructure of services is a human right, we need to address how it should be provided. The best and least expensive systems are universal ones covering everyone, equally, for all needed services, paid for with taxes, managed by government based on expert and community input and oversight, and with services delivered by either public or private providers or both. Such a simplified system would

not only ensure universal coverage and high-quality programs for everyone
but also greatly reduce administrative costs. Universal programs like Social
Security and Medicare have far lower overhead expenses than similar private programs like personal retirement accounts (such as IRAs) and private
health insurance.[15]

Affordable, Livable Housing

A home is necessary for thriving. It is not a commodity available only to those
who can pay rent or a mortgage. Housing is a human right, but this right
is not recognized in the United States. The failure of our nation to provide
basic, affordable housing to a substantial share of the population is harmful
and shameful. Housing support for the poor is inadequately funded, and
there is little effort to ensure affordable housing is available to people of low
or middle incomes. Too many individuals and families pay more than they
can afford for their homes, suffer evictions, and are homeless.

The right to housing is more than the right to a roof over one's head,
which could be provided by a homeless shelter, one's car, or a tent. The right
to housing includes adequacy of the structure, affordability (defined as a
cost that is less than one-third of one's income), secure tenure without constant worry about eviction, physical safety and security, and adequate space
free of overcrowding.[16] In the United States, livable housing has functioning
fixtures and appliances, clean water and a sound sanitation system, adequate heating and cooling, a roof that doesn't leak, and no mold or cracked
and chipped lead paint.

The right to housing does not mean the government must give everyone
a home. It does, however, assign responsibility to the government to ensure
that all people have access to adequate housing.[17] If affordable housing is
not being built in sufficient quantities by private builders, the government
must step in. Everyone must have affordable, livable housing.

15. Emily Gee and Topher Spiro, "Excess Administrative Costs Burden the US Health Care
System," *American Prospect,* April 8, 2019; CBO, *Administrative Costs of Private Accounts in Social
Security* (Washington, DC: CBO, March 2004).
16. UN High Commissioner for Human Rights, *Principles and Guidelines,* 31.
17. National Homeless Law Center, *Housing Rights for All: Promoting and Defending Housing Rights
in the United States, Fifth Edition: A Resource Manual on International Law and the Human Right to Adequate Housing* (Washington, DC: NHLC, 2011). Also see the Housing is a Human Right Act
of 2020, H.R. 6308, 116th Cong.

Move Forward by Expanding Existing Legislation

Just because something is an economic human right does not mean that the government must automatically provide it. But public programs can fulfill a right if other measures fall short. Government assumes the ultimate responsibility to ensure human rights are respected, protected, and fulfilled.

Consider social programs and supports intended to help people in poverty. Under current law, many important programs provide benefits to just some of the people who need and qualify to receive them.[18] Here are some specific examples:

- Temporary Assistance for Needy Families (TANF), the nation's primary "welfare" program, provides cash assistance to poor families. In 2017, just 23 percent of families living in official poverty received TANF benefits. Moreover, the law carefully specifies that when the money runs out in any year, so do the benefits.[19]
- Federal rental assistance helps more than five million low-income households afford modest housing. But seventeen million households, three-quarters of all eligible households, and 77 percent of eligible households with children receive no federal rental assistance due to insufficient funds.[20]
- Head Start, the life-changing early childhood education program, serves just 46 percent of eligible three- and four-year-olds, and Early Head Start serves fewer than 5 percent of eligible infants and toddlers due to inadequate funding.[21]
- The Child Care and Development Block Grant is the primary federal program funding childcare assistance for low-income working

18. As this book goes to press, the Biden administration is seeking to pass legislation to address some of these shortfalls.

19. Liz Schott, Ife Floyd, and Ashley Burnside, *How States Use Funds under the TANF Block Grant* (Washington, DC: CBPP, April 2, 2018); Gene Falk, *The Temporary Assistance for Needy Families (TANF) Block Grant: A Primer on TANF Financing and Federal Requirements* (Washington, DC: Congressional Research Service, December 14, 2017). There is also a five-year lifetime limit on benefits.

20. David Reich and Chloe Cho, *Unmet Needs and the Squeeze on Appropriations* (Washington DC: CBPP, May 19, 2017); CBPP, *Three Out of Four Low-Income At-Risk Renters Do Not Receive Federal Rental Assistance* (Washington, DC: CBPP, August 2017).

21. Reich and Cho, *Unmet Needs*.

parents. In 2015, just 15 percent of children who qualified for child-care assistance got any help due to funding shortfalls.[22]

These programs are not legislated to be "entitlements." This means that when the money appropriated in a given year runs out, no additional eligible people can receive the service or benefit. In contrast, a program or service legally established as an entitlement serves everyone who meets the eligibility criteria without budgetary constraints. All programs that fulfill economic human rights must be established and funded as entitlements. Note that the tax expenditures described in the last chapter that primarily benefit higher-income households are all entitlements. Anyone who qualifies for the tax breaks receives them regardless of the adequacy of the federal budget.

The word *entitlement* has become a derogatory term implying a handout to the undeserving. Instead, we must celebrate entitlement programs as a recognition that people have rights that we are committed to respecting, protecting, and fulfilling. Our nation must ensure that the material resources necessary for thriving are available to everyone as entitlements. If essential material resources cannot be assured for everyone due to perceived funding limitations, then the last must be first. The needs of lower-income households must take precedence over the needs of those with higher incomes.

Dependency?

If the United States were to recognize and fulfill economic human rights, some people worry it would encourage laziness, create dependency, and destroy personal initiative. But a safety net—our personal infrastructure system—must be designed to serve as a springboard or trampoline that allows people to avoid material deprivation, social exclusion, shame, and despair and readies them to continue life as participating and contributing members of society. A vibrant safety net is more likely to encourage initiative rather than laziness and support independence rather than dependency. Without a robust springboard of support, people are forced to rely on charities like food pantries, thrift stores, community meals, and housing for the night in church basements. These relieve need, but they often cost beneficiaries their self-respect. Justice is not episodic but systemic, creating structures

22. Douglas Rice, Stephanie Schmit, and Hannah Matthews, *Child Care and Housing: Big Expenses with Too Little Help Available* (Washington, DC: CBPP, April 26, 2019).

and institutions that relieve poverty, provide opportunity, and allow people to work, care for themselves, and thrive.

Racism

We have reviewed some of the many ways that people of color are disadvantaged and exploited in our economy. Many of the largest gaps are between whites and African Americans. Scholars from Duke University's Samuel DuBois Cook Center on Social Equity assess the causes of the wealth gap between Blacks and whites, but their words also apply to various types of racial and ethnic gaps in income, employment, and other aspects of material well-being:

> The cause of the gap must be found in the structural characteristics of the American economy, heavily infused at every point with both an inheritance of racism and the ongoing authority of white supremacy. . . . There are no actions that black Americans can take unilaterally that will have much of an effect on reducing the . . . gap. For the gap to be closed, America must undergo a vast social transformation produced by the adoption of bold national policies, policies that will forge a way forward by addressing, finally, the long-standing consequences of slavery, the Jim Crow years that followed, and ongoing racism and discrimination that exist in our society today.[23]

A "vast social transformation" is unlikely to happen unless we first commit to acknowledging and seeking to understand the nation's history of slavery, lynching, terror, forced labor, and state-sanctioned discrimination and the ways that racism is embedded in our economic policies and structures. We must also confront our genocide of Native Americans, broken treaties, cultural destruction, and land theft and address their legacy. To date, a commitment to clearly face our history has not been made. Such a confrontation must include a discussion of reparations, restoration, and restitution. In each session of Congress since 1989, a bill has been introduced in the House of Representatives calling for a commission to study and develop proposals concerning reparations for African Americans. But

23. William Darity Jr. et al., *What We Get Wrong about Closing the Racial Wealth Gap* (Oakland, CA: Insight Center for Community Economic Development, April 2018), 3–4.

the bill has never received the support needed to move it to the House floor for consideration. We note that in the final days leading up to the exodus from Egypt, Moses, under Yahweh's direction, instructed the Israelites to ask their Egyptian neighbors for silver and gold, reparations for their long years of labor and oppression. The Egyptians gave as asked, recognizing the debt they owed to the Israelites (Exod 11:1–3).

According to Ta-Nehisi Coates,

> Reparations—by which I mean the full acceptance of our collective biography and its consequences—is the price we must pay to see our-selves squarely. . . . What I'm talking about is more than recompense for past injustices—more than a handout, a payoff, hush money, or a reluctant bribe. What I'm talking about is a national reckoning that would lead to spiritual renewal. . . . I believe that wrestling pub-licly with these questions matters as much as—if not more than—the specific answers that might be produced. An America that asks what it owes its most vulnerable citizens is improved and humane. An America that looks away is ignoring not just the sins of the past but the sins of the present and the certain sins of the future. More important than any single check cut to any African American, the payment of reparations would represent America's maturation out of the childhood myth of its innocence into a wisdom worthy of its founders.[24]

In the weeks and months following the death of George Floyd in 2020, the Black Lives Matter movement sparked a renewed national conversation and a process of white awakening that needs to continue and hopefully bring the changes that will allow all people of color and other marginal-ized neighbors to fully and equally participate in the economy and society. The "adoption of bold national policies" is essential if we are to begin to address the disadvantages faced by people of color, immigrants, and others on the margins of our economy who are not yet living lives of abundance as God intends.

24. Ta-Nehisi Coates, "The Case for Reparations," *Atlantic*, June 2014.

JOBS AND LIVING WAGES FOR ALL

The second characteristic of a just economy is full employment at living wages: everyone who is available to work has a job that pays a wage that enables a family to thrive. The biblical writers teach that a just economy rests on a two-way commitment: (1) everyone receives the material resources they need to thrive, and (2) everyone has work and contributes their talents to building the common good. Work is both an opportunity and a responsibility. Each of us has an obligation to work and the right to have a job. Work is not narrowly defined and may not be typical paid employment. Raising children, caring for elders, going to school, and training for a profession make social contributions and certainly are work.

Adults have a psychological and even a spiritual need to contribute the gifts of their labor to their neighbors. Harvard's Michael Sandel notes that religious leaders and philosophers over the ages "teach us that we are most fully human when we contribute to the common good and earn the esteem of our fellow citizens for the contributions we make."[25] We need to be needed by others. Engaging in labor (work of all kinds, not only paid employment) is how I develop, use, share, and find fulfillment in my God-given talents and creativity. Economic justice encompasses contributive justice, the opportunity for everyone to contribute their labor to fulfill the needs of others, thereby gaining social recognition and esteem.[26] Unemployment, with its economic, emotional, and physical toll, is destructive of flourishing people and a flourishing society.[27] If my offering of labor to society is blocked due to unemployment and a shortage of jobs, I may come to view myself as someone who, apparently, is so devoid of gifts as to be unable to make a contribution as others do. This is why having a job and not just an income is so essential to our well-being and is considered a human right. According to the great twelfth-century Jewish philosopher Maimonides, the highest form of aid that someone can give a poor person is to enable him to "earn an honest livelihood and not be forced [to] the dreadful alternative of

25. Sandel, *Tyranny of Merit*, 212.
26. Sandel, 206.
27. Deborah Belle and Heather E. Bullock, *The Society for the Psychological Study of Social Issues Policy Statement: The Psychological Consequences of Unemployment* (Washington, DC: SPSSI, 2010); M. W. Linn, R. Sandifer, and S. Stein, "Effects of Unemployment on Mental and Physical Health," *American Journal of Public Health* 75, no. 5 (1985): 502–6.

holding out his hand for charity."[28] Moreover, full employment is also smart. Society should not waste the talents and contributions of people who are able to work.

Since there is no economic factor that ensures the number of jobs matches the number of job seekers, without a societal commitment to full employment, there will always be people who are unemployed. Today there is also a huge shortfall of good jobs with living wages. Without a requirement for all jobs to pay a living wage, some working people will always be poor.

The nationwide shortage of jobs varies in severity over the years and across the regions of the country. Full employment requires a public program to supplement the existing labor market, to hire those who would otherwise be jobless, and to provide jobs in locations and at times when need is present.

There is no shortage of work that needs to be done but remains undone: caring for children and elders; rebuilding our crumbling roads and bridges; rehabilitating our aging housing stock to make it more livable, energy efficient, and lead-free; cleaning up brownfields and restoring despoiled rural areas; removing plastic from our waterways and oceans and trash from our land; creating and producing the next generation of green energy technology; replacing our ancient water pipes so they don't leak or poison us; constructing new schools; providing needed maintenance to our national parks; and building high-speed rail and other more energy-efficient, long-distance transportation options. The list is endless. For the most part, private firms are not doing these things, and governments at all levels are neglecting to make the investments in society that improve our lives, create jobs, and (research shows) boost private firms' productivity and profits as well.

A true living wage would be unaffordable for some employers if every worker or their employer paid for health care, childcare, education, early childhood education, and all the other essential services needed by each of us. But with a universal personal infrastructure in place, funded with tax dollars, a living wage in every job becomes a realistic goal.

During the Covid-19 pandemic, we were reminded that many low-wage workers do jobs that are essential to our lives and to society. These workers, like all workers, deserve wages that allow them to support a flourishing

---

28. Maimonides, "Selection XV," in *Selections from Jewish Literature*, ed. Central Conference of American Rabbis, part 2 of *Union Prayer Book for Jewish Worship* (New York: CCAR, 1956), 117–18.

family. All work that contributes to society has dignity; all workers deserve respect. Jesus was a low-wage worker but of infinite worth, just like all our low-wage workers today. When we pay all workers a family-supporting wage, we share God's abundance and the nation's resources.

Imagine this picture of the United States not too many years from now, a future that is both doable and affordable. No one has unmet material needs. Poverty happens, but the guarantee of a living-wage job, a personal infrastructure, and a robust safety net form a springboard that ensures a speedy return to well-being. Housing is affordable, safe, and livable. Everyone has sufficient income to meet their material needs as well as enjoy leisure activities in their time off work. Everyone has the resources to achieve economic security. It would be a different country than it is today, and we would be a different people.

THE ECONOMIC SYSTEM PROTECTS THE VULNERABLE AND PROMOTES UNIVERSAL THRIVING

We now turn to the third characteristic of a just economy: the economic system is fair and its interactions are free of fraud and corruption; it protects the vulnerable, promotes universal thriving, and can rely on the active engagement of justice-seeking people to make it so. Here are some ways to begin to address the problems identified in chapter 5.

Most fundamentally, workers and consumers need basic fairness. For example, wage theft must be policed, prosecuted, and penalized. Equal pay is owed for equal work. All workers need paid time off for illness, family responsibilities, and leisure. Legal but abusive financial agreements that primarily exploit the poor—including home purchases made through a contract for deed, high-interest payday loans, and auto title loans—must be thoroughly reformed. These changes and similar ones are necessary to establish even a minimal degree of economic fairness. We also examine three aspects of the economy where deeper structural change is needed: workers' bargaining power in the workplace, excessive corporate power and influence, and globalization.

Workers' Bargaining Power in the Workplace

A more equitable balance of power in the workplace will require strengthening workers' bargaining power and reining in corporate power. Many of the adverse changes workers have experienced over the past forty years are due not only to the rise of corporate power in the workplace but also to (1) workers' loss of bargaining power and (2) the changes in public policies affecting the workplace that have primarily benefited corporations. Workplace power needs to be rebalanced so workers receive a greater share of the nation's income.

We also need to address concerns related to immigrant workers, which the climate crisis will only worsen. Currently, weak labor laws combined with a lack of enforcement means native-born workers are in competition with undocumented ones. Most firms do not exploit workers, either immigrant or native born, but some do. If these companies can pay less than is required by law, violate safety standards, fire workers, or deport them if they try to form a union and do so with minimal penalties or none at all, then we will see more firms exploiting workers. Wages will continue to fall, benefits will continue to disappear, union membership will continue to decline, and American workers will become more financially insecure. The rich will get richer and the poor, poorer. The answer is not hostility to immigrants. Instead, we must strengthen and enforce workplace protections for *all* workers, provide undocumented workers with a path to legalize their status and gain citizenship, and engage with countries around the world to address the conditions that force workers to emigrate.

Unions

Workers need unions. There is no other way to achieve the workplace improvements that they need. But current laws governing union organizing and judicial interpretation of these laws are heavily skewed to favor corporations, which, through legal and illegal means, nearly always successfully block workers' efforts to organize. Sorely needed are more substantial penalties for violations of the right to organize; restrictions on what is currently considered legal activity during an organizing effort, including veiled threats to cut wages and benefits or shut a plant down entirely if workers form a union; and ending employers' right to permanently replace striking workers. Strengthening and protecting workers' rights to organize and strike will be key factors in reversing the trend toward greater inequality. This is why corporations have so strongly opposed unions and union organizing in recent decades. The needed changes are well known; beneficial bills have been introduced in Congress but face powerful opposition from corporate interests.[29]

Minimum Wage

The federal minimum wage must be raised to ensure it is a living wage that will support a family. The federal minimum wage, currently just $7.25 an hour, or $15,000 a year for a full-time worker, is the lowest wage that can legally be paid in most jobs. Congress last increased the minimum wage in 2009. By 2020, it had lost 17 percent of its buying power. Even working full time, minimum-wage workers are paid so little that their families may qualify for SNAP (formerly food stamps) and Medicaid. The value of the minimum wage peaked in 1968 (in terms of its buying power) and in 2020 was nearly one-third below that level, despite large increases in our nation's wealth and standard of living during the intervening fifty years. The federal minimum wage for a tipped worker—defined as anyone who receives $30 or more in tips per month—is a shockingly low $2.13 an hour, unchanged since 1991. Employers are required to augment a worker's pay if tips fail to fill the gap between $2.13 and $7.25 but this is very hard to police and enforce. Twenty-nine states have set their minimum wages higher than the federal level, but workers in twenty-one states are still protected by only the federal minimum.[30] Congress must raise the minimum wage to be a family-supporting wage with annual cost-of-living adjustments.

The purpose of the minimum wage and many of our nation's other labor protections is to close off potential avenues of exploitation. As we have seen, protecting the vulnerable from abusive contractual arrangements was an important focus of biblical teachings. Today, someone seeking employment may feel forced by necessity to take any job, even one that pays a wage too low to support a thriving family. The failure of Congress and state legislatures to raise the minimum wage to a living wage means it does not protect workers from exploitation.

29. For example, see the Protecting the Right to Organize Act of 2019, H.R. 2474, 116th Cong.; and McNicholas et al., *Unlawful*.

30. See the Raise the Minimum Wage resources from the National Employment Law Project at https://raisetheminimumwage.com/.

Exploitative Contractual Arrangements

The limits placed on contractual agreements by the biblical instructions are a recognition that poverty and the threat of material need destroy freedom and create an environment where coercion can flourish. In a just economy, exploitative arrangements are prohibited. But today, a growing number of employers are making profitable, exploitative contractual agreements a precondition of employment. These must be banned unless warranted by special circumstances.

Noncompete Agreements

Employers are increasingly requiring employees to sign noncompete agreements, which prohibit them from going to work for a competing business within a specified period of time after leaving a job.[31] Since changing jobs is often how workers get a raise, this is another factor causing wage stagnation. These clauses are more common among high-wage, high-skilled workers, but they are also being used among low-wage workers, including in fast food.[32] In 2017, roughly half of all firms used these agreements among some of their workers, and nearly one-third of firms required them of all workers. Congress should prohibit these agreements with a few exceptions for senior executives and to protect trade secrets.

Barriers to the Courts

A fundamental right in a just society is the option to go to court to adjudicate disputes and seek justice. But a growing number of corporations, enabled by the courts—including, in some cases, the Supreme Court—are blocking employees' ability to go to court and protect their rights in the workplace.

Mandatory arbitration of disputes is an increasingly common prerequisite for employment, especially for lower-wage workers and in industries that disproportionately employ women and people of color.[33] This contractual agreement mandates that all disputes between a worker and employer—including

31. Alexander J. S. Colvin and Heidi Shierholz, *Noncompete Agreements: Ubiquitous, Harmful to Wages and to Competition, and Part of a Growing Trend of Employers Requiring Workers to Sign Away Their Rights* (Washington, DC: EPI, December 10, 2019).

32. Rachel Abrams, "Why Aren't Paychecks Growing? A Burger-Joint Clause Offers a Clue," *New York Times*, September 27, 2017.

33. Alexander J. S. Colvin, *The Growing Use of Mandatory Arbitration* (Washington, DC: EPI, April 6, 2018).

the most egregious charges, such as racial discrimination, sexual harassment, or nonpayment of wages—be settled through arbitration, not the courts. However, arbitration is not a neutral process. The employer unilaterally defines how the process will work and selects and pays the arbitrator, an individual who is empowered to resolve the dispute by acting as both judge and jury. Arbitrators' findings are final and binding even though they are not required to issue decisions that follow the law or established precedent.[34] This "privatization of the justice system" tilts the playing field to advantage the employer.[35] Compared with going to court, an employee subject to mandatory arbitration is less likely to win their case, and if they do, they recover damages that average just one-fifth the amount awarded through judicial proceedings.[36] More than sixty million workers in 2017 were subject to mandatory arbitration. Congress needs to ban forced arbitration clauses from agreements related to employment, work conditions, and consumer protections.

Class-action lawsuits are also being restricted. A class-action lawsuit allows employees with a similar complaint to come together as a class to sue their employer. Some disputes between employers and employees involve relatively small amounts of money, making it financially unfeasible for each harmed individual to hire a lawyer to sue the firm. But it could be feasible for a group or *class* of harmed employees to do so. Individual losses might be small, but taken together they could be sizable, and the remedy could be large enough to provide financial relief to the wronged parties, pay attorneys' fees, and serve as an incentive for the firm to make changes in its practices and policies. But employers are closing off this access to the courts. In 2017, over twenty-four million employees were required to give up their right to participate in class actions as a condition of employment.[37] This practice was upheld by the US Supreme Court in a 5-to-4 decision in May 2018. Congress must restore the fundamental right of wronged workers and consumers to join together to sue by banning restrictions on class actions.

34. Stephanie Mencimer, "Have You Signed Away Your Right to Sue?," *Mother Jones*, March/April 2008.

35. Jessica Silver-Greenberg and Michael Corkery, "In Arbitration, a 'Privatization of the Justice System,'" *New York Times*, November 1, 2015. Statement is by Myriam Gilles, law professor at the Benjamin N. Cardozo School of Law, New York.

36. Colvin, *Mandatory Arbitration*.

37. Colvin.

Misclassifying Employees as Independent Contractors

Employers can save up to 30 percent of their labor costs by falsely classifying employees as independent contractors—that is, legally identifying them as workers who do not receive fringe benefits, who pay their own payroll taxes, and who lose the protections of core labor laws such as the minimum wage, overtime, antidiscrimination protections, workers' compensation for injuries on the job, and unemployment insurance.[38] Employment classifications are legally defined, but the law is unclear (a problem Congress could correct) and poorly enforced (another problem that could be corrected). Consequently, many workers who should be classified as employees—including janitors, home health aides, construction workers, cable installers, cooks, port truck drivers, and loading dock workers in distribution centers[39]—are instead often misclassified as independent contractors, thereby losing protections and money. Congress needs to clarify the definition of employees and enact enhanced enforcement provisions.

Corporate Power

The laws and regulations that govern corporate behavior are extensive, and many changes are needed. The proposals suggested here are not extreme or excessively idealistic. Most have been or currently are included in legislation that is pending in Congress but as yet lacks majority support.

Break Up Megacorporations

Megacorporations' dominance of many economic sectors has led to higher prices, lower wages, less innovation, and rising inequality. Unfortunately, the laws that could have preserved more vigorous competition have not been enforced in recent decades due, in part, to changes in judicial interpretation of the law, including by the US Supreme Court. Large firms with few competitors must be broken up. Increased funding of regulatory agencies and more aggressive enforcement are needed to ensure robust competition in all

38. National Conference of State Legislatures, *Worker Misclassification* (Denver: NCSL), accessed November 23, 2021, https://www.ncsl.org/research/labor-and-employment/employee-misclassification-resources.aspx.
39. David Weil, "Lots of Employees Get Misclassified as Contractors. Here's Why It Matters," *Harvard Business Review*, July 5, 2017.

sectors. Congress has not substantively updated antitrust law in more than sixty years. It must do so now, incorporating new economic insights that will address our current problems.[40]

Corporate Governance

Most large corporations today identify maximizing returns to shareholders as their primary purpose. This has come to mean a focus on short-term profits that often leads to insufficient investments in workers, new products and innovation, and a firm's long-term viability. It is one important cause of the nation's recent history of stagnant wages, high profits, and slow economic growth.

But a sole focus on shareholder value is much too narrow and omits other important stakeholders—workers, consumers, suppliers, and communities—whose interests must also be included in corporate decision-making. We need extensive revisions to corporate governance law and practice. Corporate boards of directors must comprise members representing all the firm's stakeholders; their fiduciary duty is not solely to shareholders but must be redefined to include all stakeholders.[41] Corporations are chartered to achieve specific purposes (which currently are usually very broadly and vaguely defined) and, to achieve their goals, are given special privileges. Diverse corporate boards, representing the broad interests of society, must ensure that corporations justify their privilege by operating in the interests of all stakeholders and making valuable contributions to the common good.

Financialization

The problem of financialization and corporations' focus on short-term profits, share buybacks, and shareholder value would be addressed, in part, by diverse corporate boards of directors representing all stakeholders, not just shareholders, as described above. We also need to address problems within the financial sector itself.

40. Fiona Scott Morton, *Reforming US Antitrust Enforcement and Competition Policy* (Washington, DC: Washington Center for Equitable Growth, February 18, 2020).

41. Lenore Palladino and Kristina Karlsson, *Towards "Accountable Capitalism": Remaking Corporate Law through Stakeholder Governance* (New York: Roosevelt Institute, October 4, 2018).

Banking

Banks are still too big, and the biggest banks need to be broken up. Banks also continue to take too many risks with government-insured money. We need to reestablish the wall between commercial banks that offer checking and savings accounts insured by the federal government and investment banks, which engage in much riskier financial transactions and activities. We need a twenty-first-century version of the Glass-Steagall legislation (enacted during the Great Depression) that safeguarded the banking system and the US economy until it was repealed in 1999, opening the way for the 2007–8 financial crisis and the Great Recession.

Private Equity

The reform of private equity must begin by making these firms jointly liable for the debt of companies they buy. The private equity firm should make money only if the companies they control flourish. These firms should also be made jointly responsible for workplace violations such as wage theft and unsafe working conditions.

Financial Transaction Tax

The financial transaction tax (FTT), called by some the Robin Hood tax, would restrict some of the worst excesses of financial markets while raising substantial sums of money from, primarily, the wealthiest households. This sorely needed tax is endorsed by Bill Gates, George Soros, Ralph Nader, Nobel Prize–winning economists Joseph Stiglitz and James Tobin, the former archbishop of Canterbury Rowan Williams, the former pope Benedict XVI, and the World Council of Churches.[42]

An FTT would levy a very small fee—say, one-tenth of 1 percent—on the sale of nearly every stock, bond, and financial instrument traded each business day, sales that total trillions of dollars. As we have noted, only about 15 percent of all these financial transactions are for the purpose of productive investments in the real economy. The rest are largely short-term speculative trades made for financial gain. The FTT would significantly reduce these trades, enhancing the stability of financial markets while reducing risk and volatility. It is an important way to begin to rein in financialization. The

---

42. Steven Greenhouse and Graham Bowley, "Tiny Tax on Financial Trades Gains Advocates," *New York Times*, December 6, 2011; World Council of Churches, *São Paulo Statement: International Financial Transformation for the Economy of Life* (Geneva: WCC, October 5, 2012).

tax would be paid primarily by the households that own most of the nation's wealth and engage in frequent trades. It is estimated to raise $777 billion over ten years.[43] The tax would be very small relative to the returns earned by investors with long-term time horizons.

Manufacturing

The United States today could have and needs to have a much larger manufacturing sector. Our goal must be the manufacture of high-value products that are created through our research, engineering, and innovation efforts and are produced by well-paid workers. Moreover, we must recognize that this goal, and a successful effort to rebuild our manufacturing sector, cannot be done under the financialization model of short-term profits.[44] Nor can it be done with a trade agenda focused on importing cheap consumer goods. We must use countervailing measures to respond to currency manipulation and support the interests of manufacturers and exporters in opposition to those of firms seeking cheap imports.

Globalization

In the last forty years, globalization has promoted inequality, the exploitation of workers, corporate power and profits, and the degradation of the environment. We must not turn away from globalization but institute a new globalization regime that serves and advances the well-being of all.[45]

For globalization to be beneficial, two criteria must be met. First, the rules must be fair, developed through open and transparent democratic processes. Second, the gains from globalization must be shared. Even when the rules are fair, there will be winners and losers. If globalization is to promote thriving, the winners must share some of their gains with those who lose their jobs or livelihoods, experience stagnant or declining wages, or suffer other hardships due to globalization. In the United States and most other countries, both criteria are violated by the current globalization regime.

---

43. CBO, *Options for Reducing the Deficit: 2019 to 2028* (Washington, DC: CBO, December 13, 2018).
44. Suzanne Berger, "How Finance Gutted Manufacturing," *Boston Review*, April 1, 2014; Berger with MIT Task Force on Production in the Innovation Economy, *Making in America*.
45. Stiglitz, *Globalization and Its Discontents*; Joseph E. Stiglitz, *Making Globalization Work* (New York: W. W. Norton, 2007); Chang, *Bad Samaritans*; Hickel, *Divide*.

Many sources provide detailed descriptions of the new globalization regime that is needed.[46] What follows is just a summary of factors that need to be comprehensively addressed.

Fair Rules

Fair treaties that promote the interests of all, especially the poor and also the 99 percent, must be negotiated and approved. Then they must be enforced and sanctions imposed for violations. The well-being of workers and consumers in the United States and around the world and the environment must be the primary focus of trade and investment agreements, not corporate profits. The strong social movement within the United States and internationally that is resisting the current regime of globalization can lead this effort.

Global economic policies must be determined by a body that represents the diversity of views: North and South; wealthy, middle class, and poor; workers, consumers, environmentalists, and Indigenous communities. The sovereign right of nations to shape their economies and public policies must be respected. All policies must have enforcement mechanisms and penalties that drive compliance. Here is a list of needed changes to international agreements:

- Protect workers' rights to organize, bargain collectively, and strike, free of retaliation, while prohibiting discrimination in employment, child labor, and forced labor.[47]
- Establish environmental protections, especially in regard to mining, logging, fishing, and fossil fuel extraction.
- Protect traditional landholders who, possibly for generations, occupied land that now may be sold, without their free and informed consent, to foreign governments and international businesses in a "land grab."
- Amend patent and copyright protections to (1) ensure that those who want to engage in follow-on innovation are not blocked, (2) prevent excessive rewards for multinational firms that dominate their markets, and (3) provide special provisions for poor countries, allowing

46. See organizations such as Tax Justice Network, Public Citizen's Global Trade Watch, the Citizen's Trade Campaign, Oxfam International, and Jubilee Debt Campaign.
47. These are also the four core labor rights of the International Labor Organization.

them to access drugs and other products that, under patent, would otherwise be unaffordable. Patents must not be applied to seeds, animals, plants, and other natural entities that have been used by Indigenous people for centuries.

- End the investor-state dispute settlement process that allows firms to sue a government if they project a loss of future profits due to new regulations.
- Open the markets of rich countries, unconditionally, to imports from poorer ones that meet product standards; middle-income countries also open their markets to imports from poorer ones and extend preferences to goods from other middle-income nations without also extending similar preferences to rich ones.[48]
- End US crop subsidies that primarily benefit the largest farmers, not small family farms;[49] reduce the prices of foods that make us sick; and harm farmers in other countries who produce without subsidies. An equitable agricultural system in the United States composed of farms raising diverse crops will continue to require government support.
- Enforce trade provisions that allow countries to take countervailing actions to offset currency manipulation.
- Establish an international tax structure to ensure that multinational firms pay appropriate taxes in all the countries in which they do business.[50]
- Establish an international regime of transparency and sharing of information to stop tax cheating by wealthy individuals and multinational corporations that use tax havens and shell companies to evade taxes.

Share the Gains

International trade creates winners and losers, even if, on the whole, such trade is beneficial to a country. The winners, for example, are industries with expanding markets and the firms and workers employed in those industries that experience increased sales, larger profits, and rising wages. But other

48. Stiglitz, *Making Globalization Work*.
49. Environmental Working Group, "Farm Subsidy Primer," accessed November 22, 2021, https://farm.ewg.org/subsidyprimer.php.
50. See Saez and Zucman, *Triumph of Injustice*; and Tax Justice Network, *The State of Tax Justice 2021* (Bristol, England: TJN, November 16, 2021).

industries will decline; these are the "losers." Wages will fall, workers will lose their jobs, and communities will suffer. But if the nation is benefiting from trade, the losses will be smaller than the gains. This means the winners can compensate the losers and still come out ahead. Everyone is better off.

For example, taxes could be assessed on the economic gains from trade and the revenue could be used to provide strong unemployment income support, retraining, new investment in locations with job losses, relocation support, and other measures to ease the pain and ensure a new, prosperous future for those whose jobs were lost and whose wages fell. But this positive outcome will happen only if it is national policy, implemented through tax law and fully funded programs to support those who are harmed. Over the recent decades of mismanaged globalization, the winners have kept their gains and often used them to further shape economic policy to their benefit. The losers and their pain were largely ignored; support was meager, inadequate, and delayed.[51] Trade adjustment assistance programs must be expanded and strengthened. The goal of globalization must be the greater well-being of the planet's people within a context of sustainability and protection for the environment and all creation. Growth in the Global South and also in the Global North must especially benefit the poor.

Debt

When poor countries are heavily burdened by unsustainable debt, there must be a process to address the problem, just as individuals and corporations may go through a bankruptcy process.[52] The goal is to restructure the debt and allow the country to emerge in a more financially viable condition, better positioned for economic development. Lenders must not be protected from losses arising from poor lending decisions or good decisions that encounter adverse circumstances that could not be anticipated. Lenders have an obligation to make responsible loans that the borrower can reasonably expect to repay.

International financial institutions, in partnership with poor countries, must establish binding standards for responsible lending and borrowing with an equitable process of debt restructure that appropriately holds lenders as well as creditors responsible for outcomes. If a country faces the choice of

51. Mark Muro and Joseph Parilla, *Maladjusted: It's Time to Reimagine Economic "Adjustment" Programs* (Washington, DC: Brookings Institution, January 10, 2017).
52. European Network on Debt and Development, *Work It Out*.

repaying a debt or meeting the basic needs of its people, the latter takes precedence. The needs of people for food, water, sanitation, health care, and education must come before debt service. Unsustainable and unjust debt must be canceled.

Foreign Aid

In 2018, US foreign aid totaled $47 billion, or 1.1 percent of the federal budget and 0.23 percent of GDP. For every $100 of national income, we shared 23 cents. Some 70 percent of this ($33 billion) was long-term development assistance and short-term humanitarian aid. The rest was military assistance. The United States provides far less foreign aid, measured as a share of national income, than most other major industrialized nations.

Foreign aid is controversial. Rather than advancing the goals of the poor recipient nations, it is too often used to promote US economic interests, enhance US geopolitical influence, or maintain friendly despots in power. Meanwhile, the neoliberal globalization regime continues to disadvantage poor countries. According to Yale University's Thomas Pogge, development assistance can be helpful, but it "cannot overcome the powerful headwind generated by a supranational institutional order designed by the rich for the rich."[53] But poor countries desperately need financial assistance. Aid could usefully expand a poor country's primary and secondary education systems, augment basic health care services and sanitation, and improve infrastructure that helps poor producers get their goods to markets. The Global South also needs and deserves much assistance to respond to climate change.

Economic Growth Is Not the Answer

There is one other huge flaw in the current economic regime. Within the neoliberal paradigm, the way to reduce poverty and boost incomes is faster economic growth. In this view, if the economic pie grows larger, poverty can be relieved, middle-class incomes can rise, and the affluent can become wealthier. And the faster the growth, the greater the gains. In this scenario, there is no need for difficult social debates and policy choices about who may benefit. Everyone can get more from the larger pie. The promise of faster economic growth—which, presumably, would benefit everyone—has been an important component of the campaign promises made by many

53. Thomas Pogge, "The End of Poverty?," Mark News, February 7, 2016.

candidates for high office. But as we have seen in the United States and most other countries, the neoliberal policy regime delivers most of the economic gains to the already very affluent, no matter the pace of growth. Faster growth alone, absent other more important and fundamental changes, will not solve our problems of poverty, inequality, and stagnant or falling wages.

For economic growth to benefit the people most in need of additional resources, countries must not rely on a neoliberal regime but must intentionally enact policies to promote the well-being of the poor. Pro-poor growth and the channeling of national resources to education, health care, sanitation, water, and job creation can reduce poverty and improve lives. Unfortunately, most of the poor in the Global North and South live in countries currently following neoliberal policies; further reductions in global poverty will happen very slowly.

If current trends in growth and inequality continue indefinitely into the future, extreme poverty in the world will eventually be eliminated *in about one hundred years*, when global per capita income exceeds $100,000 per person.[54] Given ecological constraints, this amount of growth is impossible. It is also too long to wait for too small a benefit. *The problem is not slow growth but who gets the increases.* The usual method of fighting poverty and stagnant income in both the Global South and the Global North—promoting economic growth—is ineffective unless additional policies such as those detailed in this book are in place to ensure the gains are directed to those who need more resources.

We will further examine economic growth below. But before moving on, we must remember an important and unambiguous lesson. As we saw earlier, between 1980 and 2018, per capita GDP in the United States rose 90 percent and productivity was up 70 percent. But the bottom 50 percent saw an average income gain of just 8 percent over the thirty-eight years, while the highest-income people had gains in the millions of dollars. The problem was not inadequate growth but who benefited from it. Faster growth will not solve our problems. We need to change the economic policies that allow high-income individuals to capture most of the gains. Moreover, our economy is already unsustainable. Faster growth increases the pace of environmental destruction and climate change.

---

54. David Woodward, "*Incrementum ad Absurdum*: Global Growth, Inequality and Poverty Eradication in a Carbon-Constrained World," *World Economic Review* 4 (2015): 43–62.

Good Government in a Flourishing Society

A well-functioning and well-funded government—of, by, and for the people—is an essential foundation of a strong, prosperous, and caring nation and a prerequisite for a just economic system. Hear again the opening of the Declaration of Independence and pay particular attention to the second sentence (we usually focus only on the first one): "We hold these truths to be self-evident, that all [people] are created equal, that they are endowed by their Creator with certain unalienable Rights, that among these are Life, Liberty and the pursuit of Happiness. *That to secure these rights, Governments are instituted among [people]*." Our forebearers knew what we have largely forgotten: our most fundamental rights, along with many other aspects of a good and just society, depend on government and all the things government does and provides. According to two best-selling political scientists, "It takes government—a lot of government—for advanced societies to flourish. . . . [Over the past 250 years] the United States got rich because it got government more or less right."[55]

Government is how we come together, decide what kind of society we want, and then make it happen. What power—other than the power of people together wielding the tools of government—can possibly overcome the force of wealth and abuses of greed? Covetousness, hoarding, and acquisitiveness (some of our "original" sins) truly are deadly. In recent decades, the steady attacks on government have been part of a special-interest strategy to denigrate and weaken the only institution that could constrain indiscriminate corporate profit making and wealth acquisition.

Let's start with political campaigns. Every politician, unless in possession of a huge private fortune, is *forced* to participate in the money chase in order to fund their campaigns. Democracy can only thrive when elections are publicly funded. TV and radio broadcasters who are licensed to use the *public* airways must be required to provide free air time for political purposes.[56] This would reduce the public money needed to fund campaigns. We also need to stop the revolving door that permits easy movement between public service jobs in government and private service jobs in corporations

55. Hacker and Pierson, *American Amnesia*, 1–2. I am grateful for their reminder about the second sentence in the Declaration of Independence.
56. Benjamin R. Barber, "A Political Revolution for Everyone: Take Back the Public Airwaves," Huffington Post, May 9, 2016.

and trade associations. Good bills with plans and strategies to accomplish these goals languish in congressional committees and lack majority support.

Democratic governance has been sidelined and overrun. Just as workers have lost their bargaining power in the workplace and consumers have lost protections in the marketplace, so also society has lost government's countervailing power to rein in the influence of wealth and greed and to act for the common good. A more just future enabled by good governance that addresses inequality, disparities of political power, and social exclusion will require mobilization, organizing, and more: "The task ahead requires much more than mobilizing voters and winning a Presidential election. It requires building and shifting power—in particular, the power of Black and brown communities and working families, where 'we the people' really does mean all of us. It also requires creating an entirely different infrastructure that can sustain and deepen this power, and make it tangible and real for people in their daily lives."[57]

Democratic government—if we are paying attention and involved—can reflect, enable, and promote our best collective aspirations. It can also embody our worst: greed, hoarding, hatred, fear, revenge, domination, and war. In a democracy, government is what we make of it. To discuss government, its necessity, and the good it can do requires an acknowledgment of the evil that is also possible. Abuses by law enforcement officials and the judicial system based in racism, classism, and sexism; surveillance, illegal treatment, and even assassination of dissidents in the United States; severe mistreatment of immigrants and asylum seekers; and the death and destruction wreaked abroad under false claims of national defense are beyond the purview of this study (but not our concern and careful attention) and surely must be addressed.

Government is certainly not an arena from which people of faith should withdraw their ideals, ideas, hopes, and dreams. Do not be misled into thinking that the separation of church and state bars our participation in the public arena. By law, government (the state) cannot support or suppress faith bodies and faith expression. But people of faith, called to love our neighbors and resist oppression, are also called to act, to help shape

---

57. Hollie Russon Gilman and K. Sabeel Rahman, "Civic Power: Reclaiming Democracy's Radicalism," *The Forge*, December 16, 2019. Also see K. Sabeel Rahman and Hollie Russon Gilman, *Civic Power: Rebuilding American Democracy in an Era of Crisis* (New York: Cambridge University Press, 2019).

our society, economy, political system, and government activities so they reflect our highest goals and aspirations. People of faith do not, cannot, and should not dictate and control outcomes. But neither are we free to hide our light under a bushel (Matt 5:15). We have good news to share, good news that can make the country and the world more life giving and life enhancing. We are called to act.

A JUST TAX SYSTEM TO FUND A JUST SOCIETY

A just economy that recognizes economic human rights will require an increased sharing of resources to fulfill our material needs, fund new investments in a transition to a sustainable future, and do all the other things that will enhance well-being and the common good. Fortunately, the nation is very wealthy and can afford this. Our goals for reforming the tax code are to raise much more revenue, increase progressivity, narrow inequality, reduce opportunities for tax avoidance and evasion, and reform tax expenditures. We now examine ways to achieve these goals.

Jesus taught us to give to Caesar the things that belonged to him and give to God the things that belong to God. Some of our tax dollars purchase the material necessities that everyone needs and that enrich all our lives. Paying these taxes is one way we share God's resources so everyone lives in abundance; it is the "sacred" portion of our resources (Deut 26:12–13). In the twenty-first century, it is how we give to God the things that belong to God. But some of our taxes support the domination system of Caesar. Our task is to distinguish between these and then structure our tax system and public expenditures to fully fund the needs of society and end support for Caesar.

The tax plan proposed here is not focused on numbers. There is no estimated cost of a society where all thrive. It is a matter of sharing and redistributing. It is achievable if we seek to do so. God's abundance is enough for all to thrive if we first seek God's reign. In a just economy, the amount of tax money needed is the amount that ensures that everyone has the material resources to thrive.

Individual Income Tax

To achieve our goals for society will require an increase in taxes levied on high-income households. As we saw in chapter 5, the average effective tax rate calculated across all types of taxes and among all taxpayers is 28 percent: 24 to 28 percent among low- and middle-income people and 28 to 30 percent among higher-income ones. The top four hundred taxpayers pay a remarkably low 23 percent. How much tax might high-income people pay?[58] What is equitable? Before answering that question, we need to remind ourselves of the huge differences in income and wealth across society. Each person in the top 1 percent receives $83 in income for each $1 received on average by each person in the bottom 50 percent. Each person among the wealthiest 1 percent owns $115 of wealth for each $1 owned by the average person in the bottom 90 percent.[59] Given these differences, it might be reasonable for the average effective tax rate paid by the top 1 percent—including all the types of tax we pay—to be twice the rate paid by the average taxpayer. If so, the top 1 percent would, on average, pay close to 60 percent. Lower-income households within the top 1 percent would pay somewhat less, while those at the highest reaches would pay somewhat more. This total could be achieved through some combination of ending tax breaks and levying higher taxes on labor and capital income and wealth.

In a more just tax system, the individual income tax rates assessed on labor income would also be assessed on capital gains and dividends, equalizing the tax rates assessed on these two forms of income. This change would create a fairer system and also a simpler one with fewer opportunities to avoid and evade taxes. The current tax break provided to capital income encourages schemes to make labor income appear to derive from investments. One such scheme is the carried interest loophole. In a private investment firm such as a private equity or hedge fund, a general partner typically receives a sizable share of the fund's profits each year in the form of "carried interest," which is taxed at the low capital gains rate of 20 percent, not the rate of 37 percent assessed on high earnings. In 2019, the highest-paid hedge fund manager made $2 billion (with a *b*) in one year.[60] The top ten of these managers averaged $864 million each. No one is worth so much money. But at least these ultrawealthy men (yes, they are all men) should not get a special low tax rate on their income.

58. The following discussion draws on Saez and Zucman, *Triumph of Injustice*, chapter 7.
59. Saez and Zucman, https://eml.berkeley.edu/~saez/SZ2019AppendixTables.xlsx, tables A1 and A2.
60. Stephen Taub, "The Rich List," *Institutional Investor*, April 30, 2019.

Corporate Tax

Corporations are obligated to help pay for the many benefits they receive from society that allow them to do business. Corporate tax rates must be raised, tax exemptions narrowed, and enforcement strengthened to reduce tax evasion.[61]

All profitable firms must pay taxes every year, possibly assessed on profits reported to investors and the Securities and Exchange Commission rather than the very different, lower amounts reported to the IRS. Alternatively, all profitable corporations could pay at least a minimum tax. The two tax expenditures identified in chapter 5 regarding stock options and accelerated depreciation need to be ended.

To address the problem of US multinational corporations using legal and illegal measures to avoid paying taxes in the United States, all multinational firms could be required to pay the same tax rate on offshore profits as they pay on domestic ones, making the tax fairer and also ending an incentive for firms to move offshore to lower-tax jurisdictions. Corporate taxes paid on offshore profits to foreign governments would be subtracted from what the firm owes in the United States. In other words, US firms doing business in low-tax locations would face a tax surcharge, ending the tax advantage.

Tax Expenditures

The system of tax expenditures must be thoroughly reexamined. Many should be eliminated and others converted into direct spending that is better targeted to meet the intended goal. All tax expenditures must be part of the annual budgeting process.

Wealth Tax

US households pay only one kind of wealth tax: property taxes on our homes. (Renters pay their landlords' property taxes via their rent payments.) For many of us, our home is our only or primary source of wealth, and we pay an annual tax on its value. But there is no direct tax on financial

61. Corporate tax policy quickly gets very complicated. For understandable discussions of tax reform options, see Gardner, Roque, and Wamhoff, *Corporate Tax Avoidance*; and Saez and Zucman, *Triumph of Injustice*.

assets like stocks, the primary type of asset owned by the very wealthy, and other forms of wealth other than real property. A wealth tax would reduce inequality, provide needed revenue, slow the growth of wealth held by the most affluent, and increase the progressivity of the tax system. Various policy experts and some politicians have proposed options for a very small tax, just 1 or 2 percent, to be assessed annually on the wealth owned by the very wealthiest households.[62] Congress should enact a tax on wealth.[63]

Estate Tax

Another factor contributing to the growth in inequality is the weakening of the estate tax, currently assessed on only those bequests that exceed $11.6 million for a single person or $23.2 million for a couple. On amounts above these levels, heirs are assessed a tax of 40 percent. In 2020, less than one-tenth of 1 percent of estates were expected to owe tax.[64] Over half of the nation's wealth (55 percent) is inherited, not earned by its owners.[65] The estate tax is important for moderating the accumulation of dynastic wealth and brings some leveling of the playing field between those who inherit wealth and those who depend primarily on earned income. The estate tax needs to be more robust with a higher tax rate, lower exemption threshold, and strengthened enforcement.[66]

62. See Emmanuel Saez and Gabriel Zucman, *Scoring of the Sanders Wealth Tax Proposal, September 2019* (Berkeley: University of California Press, September 22, 2019); and Emmanuel Saez and Gabriel Zucman, *Scoring of the Warren Wealth Tax Proposal, January 2019* (Berkeley: University of California Press, January 18, 2019).

63. Saez and Zucman, *Triumph of Injustice*; Steve Wamhoff, *The US Needs a Federal Wealth Tax* (Washington, DC: ITEP, January 23, 2019).

64. Tax Policy Center, *Briefing Book: Key Elements of the US Tax System* (Washington, DC: TPC), updated May 2020.

65. Facundo Alvaredo, Bertrand Garbinti, and Thomas Piketty, "On the Share of Inheritance in Aggregate Wealth: Europe and the United States, 1900–2010," *Economica* 84, no. 334 (2017): 239–60.

66. Richard Phillips and Steve Wamhoff, *The Federal Estate Tax: An Important Progressive Revenue Source* (Washington, DC: ITEP, December 6, 2018); Emmanuel Saez and Gabriel Zucman, "Progressive Wealth Taxation," *Brookings Papers on Economic Activity*, Fall 2019.

Taxes: Final Thoughts

The tax system is a key foundation of economic justice. Taxes fund resources that modify unjust economic outcomes and ensure the thriving of all. In a just economy, taxes fund a personal infrastructure of health care, education, childcare, and other necessary services that otherwise would not be affordable for all and that fulfill many of our economic human rights. Tax revenues fund the springboard of supports needed when someone is unable to work. Taxes pay for many of the goods and services we value, from city planning and fire protection to highways and parks. Taxes fund the work of government, which is essential to a just society. Each taxpayer willingly pays their portion, recognizing the value it provides to their neighbors and themselves, and is confident that each person is paying their share. An equitable tax system can move society toward greater income equality, strengthening both the economy and society.

Government must use care in spending these funds. Transparency, careful stewardship, regular audits, and periodic examinations to determine whether expenditures achieve their intended goals are essential. The role of the military must be reexamined and military spending greatly reduced. Our economy and our democracy are strengthened by these measures.

A SUSTAINABLE ECONOMY

We now examine how we could achieve the fourth characteristic of a just economy, sustainability. Although not included in biblical teachings, twenty-first-century discernment would certainly include this as an essential feature of a just economy within the reign of God.

The global average temperature in 2019 was 1.15°C (2.07°F) above pre-industrial levels.[67] To prevent severe disruption of life, the Intergovernmental Panel on Climate Change (IPCC) has urged the world to limit the rise to 1.5°C (2.7°F).[68] At the current rate of increase, the global temperature is

67. Rebecca Lindsey and LuAnn Dahlman, *Climate Change: Global Temperature* (Washington, DC: NOAA Climate.gov, August 14, 2020).
68. V. Masson-Delmotte et al., eds., *Global Warming of 1.5°C: An IPCC Special Report on the Impacts of Global Warming of 1.5°C above Pre-industrial Levels and Related Global Greenhouse Gas Emission Pathways, in the Context of Strengthening the Global Response to the Threat of Climate Change,*

likely to reach this point around 2040 and then shoot above it in the absence of rigorous abatement measures.[69] To slow the warming, the global community has committed to reach net-zero carbon emissions by 2050.[70] But this will require global emissions in 2030 to be 55 percent lower than in 2018, a goal that can be accomplished only if emissions *fall* by 7.6 percent every year between 2020 and 2030. This is an abrupt reversal from the previous decade, when global emissions *rose* at an average annual rate of 1.5 percent. According to the IPCC, achieving this goal will require "rapid and far-reaching transitions in energy, land, urban, infrastructure (including transport and buildings), and industrial systems."[71]

In the United States, greenhouse gas (GHG) emissions peaked in 2007 and have declined at an average rate of about 1 percent a year ever since (although emissions rose 3 percent between 2017 and 2018, the last years for which data are available).[72] So in the United States, the decline in emissions over the coming decade must be *more than seven times greater*, cumulatively each year, than in the recent past. Moreover, we must try to do even better to provide some flexibility for the Global South, where this goal will be even more difficult to achieve given their less developed technology, lower level of wealth, and greater needs. The cost to achieve zero emissions by 2050 is estimated by one economist to be about 2 percent of GDP a year, or some $400 billion in 2020, to both expand production of wind, solar, and geothermal energy and improve energy efficiency in transportation, buildings, and industrial production.[73]

Disruptive, System-Wide Reengineering

To achieve such a large reduction in GHG emissions, small incremental steps have not been and will not be enough. To begin, we will need a thorough overhaul of energy production and consumption, a "disruptive

Sustainable Development, and Efforts to Eradicate Poverty (Geneva: World Meteorological Organization, 2018).

69. Masson-Delmotte et al.

70. UN Environment Program, *Emissions Gap*.

71. Masson-Delmotte et al., *Global Warming of 1.5°C*.

72. US Environmental Protection Agency, *Inventory of US Greenhouse Gas Emissions and Sinks: 1990–2018* (Washington, DC: EPA, 2020).

73. Robert Pollin, "How Do We Pay for a Zero-Emissions Economy?," *American Prospect* 30, no. 5 (2019).

system-wide re-engineering."[74] Long-term planning and investments with the goal of net-zero emissions by 2050 are essential. Annual planning or even quadrennial planning in conjunction with a new presidential administration is inadequate and will fail to achieve our longer-term goal. We also need strong *global* planning, coordination, investment, and sharing of new technologies.

Prices Reflect True Costs

An efficient capitalist economy requires accurate prices that reflect the true cost of a product. The prices of carbon, meat, and all products with significant environmental impacts must rise to reflect the costs of storm damage, flooding of coasts and rivers, rising sea levels, falling aquifers, desertification, illness related to excessive heat and unhealthy air and water, wildfires, crop losses, and other climate impacts. This process can begin, most importantly, with a tax on carbon. We also must end all subsidies for fossil fuels. Together, these will raise the price of fossil fuels and everything produced with them. This is the goal. It will incentivize innovation, production, and consumption of alternative fuels and greater fuel efficiency. Since fossil fuels are used in nearly all products, it will be a regressive tax, falling most heavily (measured as a *share of income*) on lower-income households. But as incomes rise, people tend to use more fossil fuels (larger homes, more air travel, more purchases in general) so *dollars spent* on the tax rise with income. To offset the regressivity of the tax, one expert suggests the full amount of tax revenues collected could be rebated to all adults, with each person receiving an equal amount of money.[75] Lower- and lower-middle-income people would likely receive more than they spend on the tax, while upper-income people would likely receive less.

Economic Growth and the Environment

Over the last decade, the US economy has grown even as GHG emissions have gradually declined. But as we have seen, to meet the goal of net-zero

74. Enno Schröder and Servaas Storm, "Economic Growth and Carbon Emissions: The Road to 'Hothouse Earth' Is Paved with Good Intentions" (working paper no. 84, Institute for New Economic Thinking, New York, November 2018).

75. James K. Boyce, "Let's Pay Every American to Reduce Emissions," *Politico*, July 23, 2019.

emissions by 2050, the decline in emissions must be more than seven times greater. It is impossible to produce things without energy and natural resources. Can the economy continue to grow, can we continue to produce more each year, and also reduce emissions by the required amount? No one knows what new technologies may be developed in the future, but for now and the foreseeable future, the answer is no.[76] We cannot make the needed reductions in emissions while also growing the economy. Economic growth in the United States and throughout the Global North must cease, at least for a few decades. In the more distant future, greater efficiencies and new innovations may eventually allow some growth without negative environmental consequences.

But will zero economic growth condemn some people to poverty and freeze inequality in place? Not at all. Even if the economy is not growing, it must evolve.[77] The just economy of the future will be roughly the same size as it is today. But it will produce more of the things that people need and now lack: more health care and education, greater quantities of more nutritious food, and more affordable and energy-efficient housing. If we are to produce more of those things with no increase in total output, then we must produce fewer other, less necessary things. The economy will begin to more closely fulfill its purpose.

In the last forty years, economic growth in the United States has provided little help to those in need. The problem was not an absence of growth but who benefited from it. In the United States and nearly all nations, most of the gains from growth flow to the already affluent.[78] Nonetheless, growth—maximizing output and enlarging the economic pie as quickly as possible—continues to be held out as the solution to our economic woes, even as the Sabbath Day and Sabbath Year teach that maximizing output is not the goal of a just economy. Clearly, we need to rethink our strategy for ending poverty and creating material well-being for everyone. A focus on raising the pace of economic growth fails on two counts: it primarily

---

76. T. Parrique et al., *Decoupling Debunked: Evidence and Arguments against Green Growth as a Sole Strategy for Sustainability* (Brussels: European Environmental Bureau, 2019).

77. Herman E. Daly, *Beyond Growth: The Economics of Sustainable Development* (Boston: Beacon, 1996).

78. Do not confuse economic growth and the level of unemployment. Low unemployment sometimes accompanies more fast-paced growth. But low unemployment—full employment— must be a specific objective, a characteristic of a just economy, not a very occasional, fortuitous outcome.

benefits the wealthy and it is environmentally destructive. Instead, we need public policies designed to eliminate poverty, ensure jobs and living wages for all workers, and greatly reduce inequality while maintaining the current size of the economy.

The Green New Deal

The Green New Deal is described in legislation introduced in 2019 in the US House of Representatives and Senate.[79] A number of other organizations and individuals have created their own versions. All these plans share the goal of addressing both climate change and socioeconomic injustice. The Green New Deal proposes to shift the nation's energy use from fossil fuels to zero-emission renewables and achieve net-zero carbon emissions by 2050. It also proposes to overhaul the transportation system, increase the energy efficiency of residential and commercial buildings, restore ecosystems, and promote the international exchange of technology and expertise necessary to reduce emissions. These efforts would require the creation of millions of good jobs that pay a living wage, many of which would be located in depressed cities and regions. Everyone would have a guaranteed job, health care, affordable housing, economic security, a clean environment, education, training, and nutritious food.

This is a very ambitious plan and includes many elements—too many to list here—that mirror the characteristics of a just economy as described in this book. And it would be very expensive. But climate change, absent the extreme efforts included in the Green New Deal, is even more costly. For starters, what is the price of relocating New York City and Miami? Or do we just let the least resilient areas of the country sink below the waves along with the least resilient people? The cost of failing to meet the goal of zero emissions by 2050 may be our lives and society as we know it.

Our abundance—that is, God's abundance—including the gifts of our health, our lives and those of our descendants, and the lives of many other creatures on the planet, is utterly dependent on our response to the climate crisis and the ongoing destruction and degradation of the environment. There is no way to sugarcoat this existential threat. But if we act immediately, boldly, and comprehensively, the worst may be avoided. People in

79. Recognizing the duty of the Federal Government to create a Green New Deal, H.R. 109 and S.R. 59, 116th Congress.

the United States—those who have more than they need to thrive—must begin by realizing that *we* are the world's biggest problem. We have the highest per capita GHG emissions of any national population and the highest per capita use of resources, and our ancestors are responsible for the largest fraction of existing GHGs in the atmosphere. We need to provide leadership, financing, and expertise for the global effort to reduce emissions. Each of us has a different level of responsibility and ability to respond. In many cases, it correlates with our income. We have no excuses. We have the resources—material, financial, intellectual, and technological—to address this problem if we choose to do so. Yes, in some areas, our technological development is not where it needs to be. But we can make huge advances now with what is already available as we also work to develop the innovations needed in the future.

Climate Change, Economic Growth, and the Global South

The lives of billions of people in the Global South are stunted by poverty. To relieve the true scarcity experienced by so many, the Global South needs greater economic output produced through faster economic growth. To accommodate this growth and the GHGs it will produce, the Global North—and especially the United States—must reduce its GHG emissions below the average required among all countries. In the Global South, economic growth must benefit those who need it—the poor—not those who already have enough. The goal is economic growth, but growth that promotes human development, expanding the richness of human life rather than the richness of the economy.[80] A focus on human development would create the conditions under which people can grow into their full potential and lead lives they value. But as countries grow, they also must cut their carbon emissions. Coal and other fossil fuels are usually the cheapest and most readily available. The wealthy countries of the Global North must share the technology and funds to help support a transition to green energy in the Global South.

---

80. UN Development Program, *About Human Development* (New York: UNDP), http://hdr .undp.org/en/humandev.

OPPOSING INJUSTICE

People in the United States live in a very abusive economy within a system of domination. The biblical teachings indicate we have an obligation to God and to our neighbors to do something about it, nonviolently. So we step into our larger responsibilities. We name material want as a social evil, destructive of emotional, social, physical, and spiritual flourishing. Using all the nonviolent tools at our disposal, we work for an economic system that enables all to flourish and a tax structure that funds the material goods and services necessary for thriving.

We may too readily claim we have no time for social activism and political engagement. But God is calling. Jesus is coming to visit us as he did Zacchaeus, maybe even today (Luke 19:1–10). Even amid the threats and crises of Nazi Germany, Dietrich Bonhoeffer recognized that we must allow God to direct the use of our time: "We must be ready to allow ourselves to be interrupted by God. God will be constantly crossing our paths and canceling our plans by sending us people with claims and petitions. We may pass them by, preoccupied with our more important tasks. . . . When we do that we pass by the visible sign of the Cross raised athwart our path to show us that, not our way, but God's way must be done. . . . Do not assume that our schedule is our own to manage, but allow it to be arranged by God."[81]

How we use our time matters. Our choices also matter. The most important personal choices people in the United States will make regarding economic injustice and the existential threat posed by climate change and environmental destruction are the decisions made at the ballot box, closely followed in importance by the efforts we make to educate our neighbors about their ballot choices. Fundamental structural change is essential and it will only happen through political action and policy change.

But our daily activities and the ways we spend our money matter. What we buy—and whether we buy anything when we could do without—matters. The size of our homes and our closets and what is in them, what we drive and how much, whether and how we travel, and what we eat all matter.[82] Buying a "green" product is still consumption. These activities affect the

---

81. Bonhoeffer, *Life Together*, 99.
82. If cows were their own country, it would be the third-largest GHG emitter in the world. Sarah Kaplan, "Are My Hamburgers Hurting the Planet?," *Washington Post*, November 18, 2019.

economy, the climate, and the wider environment. And they affect us. My actions show me who I am and what I value. Whether I acknowledge it or not, my actions, my choices, and how I use my time are spiritual practices that bring me closer to (or farther from) God and God's vision and are today shaping the person I am becoming tomorrow.

CONCLUSION

AN IDEALIST VISION

The plan for a just economy proposed here is ambitious, even visionary. It cannot be otherwise if it even partially describes God's intentions for the economy. But while enacting some aspects of this plan may require decades of effort, the vision can be grasped now. The work can begin immediately. Having an idealistic vision cannot be an excuse for inaction. The commandments to love God, to love our neighbors as ourselves, and to love even our enemies are also incredibly idealistic. This does not mean we turn aside, give up, and no longer seek to fulfill those laws. We are imperfect humans. But we are each made in the image and likeness of God. We are called to perfection (Heb 6:1; Matt 5:48), relying on God's guidance and grace. We stumble and fall, often, but we get up and try again. God is love.

On a practical level, there are many next steps that could move us significantly toward greater economic justice. While these changes may be politically difficult, they are economically doable and, with work, could be achieved in the near term. They include the eradication of poverty; full employment; a guaranteed income; universal health care, childcare, and early childhood education; affordable postsecondary education; and improved protections for union organizing. All of these are on the edges or are even the central elements of very realistic policy proposals. Antitrust enforcement, breaking up and reining in the big banks, tax hikes on corporations and high-income households, and new taxes on wealth and financial transactions are also central components of many policy discussions. Substantial improvements in the lives of millions are achievable, even in the near term.

The hardest part of this vision of economic justice might be the change in worldview it describes. Our culture inculcates in us the values of the domination system, which close our eyes, stop our ears, and harden our hearts to the cries of our sisters and brothers, the torment of God's non-human creatures, and the destruction of our environment. Do we actually believe that everyone's economic human rights should be respected, protected, and fulfilled? Are we convinced that in the reign of God, no one is poor, the last are first, all people and beings live in the fullness of life, and everyone is deserving? These are essential elements of economic justice. They are also among the most central elements of Jesus's teachings and Christian beliefs.

THE ECONOMIC SYSTEM

This book proposes no particular form of economic system—not capitalism, socialism, or anything else. These words mean something different to nearly everyone who hears them, and often they are a source of confusion and fear instead of understanding. The best system is the one that moves society ever closer to a just economy with distributional fairness. Universal thriving and sustainability form the plumb line against which we measure where we are, the progress that has been made, and our unaddressed challenges. Whatever our type of economic system, it must be organized and run with the purpose of achieving universal thriving through living-wage jobs that affirm workers' dignity and with protections and support for those who find themselves on the margins. Poverty is eliminated. Creation thrives. These outcomes will require restrictions on the power and influence of moneyed interests and for corporations to be run in support of the common good. A just economy is not compatible with a radical free market dominated by the power of money. Whatever our system, the primary function of the economy must be the production of things that people and society actually need. Then we must ensure a just distribution of these resources. We must exert democratic sovereignty over the economy as well as our political system.

The main economic problems faced by the United States and the global community will be solved not through competition among individuals but by working together for the common good. We are all equal. We are all different. We need each other. We need a world based on solidarity, not greed. God's reign is one of abundance and sharing, not scarcity and competition.

OUR CALL

We are called to be advocates, marchers, learners, teachers, listeners, child-rearers, friends, voters, artists, musicians, writers, and preachers in the struggle for economic justice. The Spirit of the Lord is upon all of us, including you—*you*, who apparently felt called to read this book and have made it through to the conclusion. *You* have been anointed to bring good news to the poor—the economically poor as well as the poor in Spirit (Isa 61:1). You are called to oppose the forces of death, including poverty, inequity, violence, and oppression.

Our struggle is not with people but with the powers and principalities: the ideas, structures, systems, beliefs, and values that have fallen from their created purpose.[1] Against these "cosmic powers of this present darkness," these "spiritual forces of evil," we must employ the nonviolent, loving armor of God: the belt of truth, the breastplate of righteousness, shoes to proclaim the gospel of peace, the shield of faith, the helmet of salvation, the sword of the Spirit (which is the word of God), and constant prayer (Eph 6:12–18).

We are also called to ever more fully participate now, here, in the reign of God. In the United States, one of our most important spiritual practices will be to distinguish between our true needs and wants. As people of the Way, this is a lifelong journey of increasing faithfulness. How we use our money, time, and talents; how we care for the earth, our bodies, strangers, family, and friends; what we eat and buy; how much energy we use and what kind; and how we seek to influence our economic, social, and political systems are all spiritual practices, all steps along the Way. Each one takes us deeper in or draws us further from God's reign. We cannot allow our excess possessions to hinder our participation. Our path may seem difficult, but we have been promised the yoke is easy and the burden is light (Matt 11:30). Let

1. Wink, *Engaging the Powers*.

us not forget that, working within us, God can accomplish "abundantly far more than all we can ask or imagine" (Eph 3:20).

In creation, God formed the physical world. God also created and—as the ancient Israelites learned—cares deeply about the human world, our society. Just as evolution continues in the physical world, it also continues in the social world, the world of economics, politics, foreign policy, war and peace, poverty and wealth, discrimination and affirmation. We are called to actively oppose oppression and cocreate with God a society that reflects and embodies God's intentions. The future is left open; society and the economy are still evolving. God is taking a chance on humanity. The reign of God arrives not through power and domination but through conversion and transformation.

We also realize that the needed fundamental change—the redemption of our economic system—is beyond our ability to accomplish. But it is not beyond God's. Our work to form a more just economy, like the practices that shape our spiritual lives, does no more—but no less—than create the fertile soil where God may act. We do what we can while expectantly awaiting God's grace, which may further our efforts. We work and we wait, with hope, for God's transformation of ourselves and the whole society.

Our story tells of a loving God's gift of abundance—land flowing with milk, honey, and all we need, enough for all. Our story is of a God who seeks us endlessly and wants us to respond by placing God and God's vision before all else, a God whose desire is for us to thrive and to do so in loving relationship with the Creator, our neighbors, and all creation. We need material resources to live, and without them, we die. But am I willing to open my hands, to share, to risk, and to trust so that everyone, including myself, has enough for abundant life? Do I trust God to provide enough for all if I first seek the kingdom? Do I trust my neighbors to share enough? Can I live the story?

Too often and too easily, we underestimate what we are being called by God to do. We take our call too lightly. There is a message for us from Abba Joseph, a fourth-century CE Desert Father who lived many years in the Egyptian desert seeking God. One day a younger man, as yet less committed to his journey than Abba Joseph, came seeking advice, saying, "'Abba as far as I can I say my little office, I fast a little, I pray and meditate, I live in peace and as far as I can, I purify my thoughts. What else can I do?' Then the old man stood up and stretched his hands towards heaven. His fingers became like ten lamps of fire and he said to him, 'If you will, you can become all flame.'"[2]

Friends, we don't need to move to a desert or become a monastic. But let us trust God and respond to God's call. Let us seek to become all flame. Acting together and with God's grace, may we find salvation not only for ourselves but for the world.

2. Benedicta Ward, trans., *The Sayings of the Desert Fathers*, Alphabetical Collection (Kalamazoo, MI: Cistercian, 1984), 103.

Bibliography

Abbreviations

CBO   Congressional Budget Office
CBPP   Center on Budget and Policy Priorities
EPI   Economic Policy Center
ITEP   Institute on Taxation and Economic Policy
NBER   National Bureau for Economic Research
OECD   Organization for Economic Co-operation and Development
UN   United Nations
UNICEF United Nations Children's Fund

Abrams, Rachel. "Why Aren't Paychecks Growing? A Burger-Joint Clause Offers a Clue." *New York Times*, September 27, 2017.

Albertz, Rainer. *From the Beginning to the End of the Monarchy*. Vol. 1 of *A History of Israelite Religion in the Old Testament Period*. Translated by John Bowden. Louisville: Westminster John Knox, 1994.

Alexander, Michelle. *The New Jim Crow: Mass Incarceration in the Age of Color-blindness*. New York: New Press, 2010.

Alexander, Raquel Meyer, Stephen W. Mazza, and Susan Scholz. "Measuring Rates of Return for Lobbying Expenditures: An Empirical Case Study of Tax Breaks for Multinational Corporations." *Journal of Law and Politics* 25, no. 401 (2009). https://papers.ssrn.com/sol3/papers.cfm?abstract_id=1375082.

Alperovitz, Gar, and Lew Daly. *Unjust Deserts: How the Rich Are Taking Our Common Inheritance and Why We Should Take It Back*. New York: New Press, 2008.

Alstadsæter, Annette, Niels Johannesen, and Gabriel Zucman. "Tax Evasion and Inequality." *American Economic Review* 109, no. 6 (2019): 2073–2103.

Alvaredo, Facundo, Lucas Chancel, Thomas Piketty, Emmanuel Saez, and Gabriel Zucman, coords. *World Inequality Report 2018.* World Inequality Lab, 2018. https://wir2018.wid.world/.

Alvaredo, Facundo, Bertrand Garbinti, and Thomas Piketty. "On the Share of Inheritance in Aggregate Wealth: Europe and the United States, 1900–2010." *Economica* 84, no. 334 (2017): 239–260.

America for Sale? An Examination of the Practices of Private Funds: Hearings before the US House of Representatives Comm. on Financial Services. 116th Cong., November 18, 2019 (written testimony of Eileen Appelbaum). https://democrats-financialservices.house.gov/UploadedFiles/HHRG-116-BA00-Wstate-AppelbaumE-20191119.pdf.

American Legislative Exchange Council. *Strategic Plan 2016–2018.* Arlington, VA: ALEC, 2016.

Amnesty International. *The World's Refugees in Numbers.* London: Amnesty International. Accessed April 3, 2020. https://www.amnesty.org/en/what-we-do/refugees-asylum-seekers-and-migrants/global-refugee-crisis-statistics-and-facts/.

Andrzejewski, Adam. "How the Fortune 100 Turned $2 Billion in Lobbying Spend into $400 Billion of Taxpayer Cash." *Forbes,* May 14, 2019.

Appelbaum, Eileen, and Rosemary Batt. *Private Equity at Work: When Wall Street Manages Main Street.* New York: Russell Sage Foundation, 2014.

———. *Private Equity Pillage: Grocery Stores and Workers at Risk.* Washington, DC: Center for Economic and Policy Research, 2018.

Arias, Elizabeth, and Jiaquan Xu. "United States Life Tables, 2017." *National Vital Statistics Reports* 68, no. 7 (2019): 1–65.

Avila, Charles. *Ownership: Early Christian Teaching.* Eugene, OR: Wipf & Stock, 1983.

Bagenstos, Samuel. *Lochner Lives On: Lochner Presumption of Equal Power Lives in Labor Law and Undermines Constitutional, Statutory, and Common Law Workplace.* Washington, DC: EPI, October 7, 2020.

Baker, Bruce D. *Does Money Matter in Education?* 2nd ed., Washington, DC: Albert Shanker Institute, 2016.

Baker, Bruce D., Mark Weber, Ajay Srikanth, Robert Kim, and Michael Atzbi. *The Real Shame of the Nation.* New Brunswick, NJ: Education Law Center and Rutgers Graduate School of Education, 2018.

Banks, James, Michael Marmot, Zoe Oldfield, and James P. Smith. "Disease and Disadvantage in the United States and England." *Journal of the American Medical Association* 295, no. 17 (2006): 2037–2046.

Barber, Benjamin R. *Consumed: How Markets Corrupt Children, Infantilize Adults, and Swallow Citizens Whole*. New York: W. W. Norton, 2007.

———. "A Political Revolution for Everyone: Take Back the Public Airwaves." Huffington Post, May 9, 2016.

Barrera, Albino. *Biblical Economic Ethics: Sacred Scripture's Teachings on Economic Life*. Lanham, MD: Lexington, 2013.

Bauer, Lauren. *Who Was Poor in the United States in 2017?* Washington, DC: Brookings Institution, January 3, 2019.

Bean, Elise, Matthew Gardner, and Steve Wamhoff. *How Congress Can Stop Corporations from Using Stock Options to Dodge Taxes*. Washington, DC: ITEP, December 10, 2019.

Beatty, Jack. *The Age of Betrayal: The Triumph of Money in America, 1865–1900*. New York: Alfred A. Knopf, 2007.

Belle, Deborah, and Heather E. Bullock. *The Society for the Psychological Study of Social Issues Policy Statement: The Psychological Consequences of Unemployment*. Washington, DC: SPSSI, 2010.

Benmelech, Efraim, Nittai Bergman, and Hyunseob Kim. "Strong Employers and Weak Employees: How Does Employer Concentration Affect Wages?" Working Paper no. 24307, NBER, Cambridge, MA, February 2018.

Berger, Daniel, and Eric Toder. *Distributional Effects of Individual Income Tax Expenditures after the 2017 Tax Cuts and Jobs Act*. Washington, DC: Tax Policy Center, June 4, 2019.

Berger, Suzanne. "How Finance Gutted Manufacturing." *Boston Review*, April 1, 2014.

Berger, Suzanne, with MIT Task Force on Production in the Innovation Economy. *Making in America: From Innovation to Market*. Cambridge, MA: MIT Press, 2013.

Bergsten, C. Fred, and Joseph E. Gagnon. *Currency Conflict and Trade Policy: A New Strategy for the United States*. Washington, DC: Peterson Institute for International Economics, June 2017.

Berman, Joshua A. *Created Equal: How the Bible Broke with Ancient Political Thought*. New York: Oxford University Press, 2008.

———. "Supersessionist or Complementary? Reassessing the Nature of Legal Revision in the Pentateuchal Law Collections." *Journal of Biblical Literature* 135, no. 2 (2016): 201–222.

Bernhardt, Annette, Ruth Milkman, Nik Theodore, Douglas Heckathorn, Mirabai Auer, James DeFilippis, Ana Luz González, Victor Narro, and

Jason Perelshteyn. *Broken Laws, Unprotected Workers*. Berkeley: University of California, Los Angeles, Institute for Research on Labor and Employment, 2009.

Bhutta, Neil, Jesse Bricker, Andrew C. Chang, Lisa J. Dettling, Sarena Goodman, Joanne W. Hsu, Kevin B. Moore, Sarah Reber, Alice Henriques Volz, and Richard A. Windle. "Changes in US Family Finances from 2016 to 2019: Evidence from the Survey of Consumer Finances." *Federal Reserve Bulletin* 106, no. 5 (September 2020): 1–42.

Birch, Bruce C. *Let Justice Roll Down: The Old Testament, Ethics, and Christian Life*. Louisville: Westminster John Knox, 1991.

———. *What Does the Lord Require? The Old Testament Call to Social Witness*. Philadelphia: Westminster, 1985.

Birch, Bruce C., and Larry L. Rasmussen. *The Predicament of the Prosperous*. Philadelphia: Westminster, 1978.

Bivens, Josh. *Adding Insult to Injury: How Bad Policy Decisions Have Amplified Globalization's Costs for American Workers*. Washington, DC: EPI, July 11, 2017.

———. *The Decline in Labor's Share of Corporate Income since 2000 Means $535 Billion Less for Workers*. Washington, DC: EPI, September 10, 2015.

———. *Failure by Design: The Story behind America's Broken Economy*. An Economic Policy Institute Book. Ithaca, NY: ILR, 2011.

———. *Progressive Redistribution without Guilt: Using Policy to Shift Economic Power and Make US Incomes Grow Fairer and Faster*. Washington, DC: EPI, June 9, 2016.

Bivens, Josh, Lora Engdahl, Elise Gould, Teresa Kroeger, Celine McNicholas, Lawrence Mishel, Zane Mokhiber, Heidi Shierholz, Marni von Wilpert, Valerie Wilson, and Ben Zipperer. *How Today's Unions Help Working People: Giving Workers the Power to Improve Their Jobs and Unrig the Economy*. Washington, DC: EPI, August 24, 2017.

Bivens, Josh, Elise Gould, Lawrence Mishel, and Heidi Shierholz. *Raising America's Pay: Why It's Our Central Economic Policy Challenge*. Washington, DC: EPI, June 4, 2014.

Bivens, Josh, and Ben Zipperer. *The Importance of Locking in Full Employment for the Long Haul*. Washington, DC: EPI, August 21, 2018.

Blau, Judith, and Alberto Moncada. *Human Rights: Beyond the Liberal Vision*. Lanham, MD: Rowman & Littlefield, 2005.

———. *Justice in the United States: Human Rights and the US Constitution*. Lanham, MD: Rowman & Littlefield, 2006.

Blenkinsopp, Joseph. *Wisdom and Law in the Old Testament: The Ordering of Life in Israel and Early Judaism.* New York: Oxford University Press, 1983.

Board of Governors of the Federal Reserve System. *Report on the Economic Well-Being of US Households in 2018.* Washington, DC: Federal Reserve, May 23, 2019.

Bobo, Kim. *Wage Theft in America: Why Millions of Americans Are Not Getting Paid—and What We Can Do about It.* New York: New Press, 2009.

Boddupalli, Aravind, Frank Sammartino, and Eric Toder. "States Adopt Some Federal Tax Expenditures and Add Others." *TaxVox: State and Local Issues* (blog). Tax Policy Center, January 24, 2020. https://www.taxpolicycenter.org/taxvox/states-adopt-some-federal-tax-expenditures-and-add-others.

Boff, Leonardo. *Passion of Christ, Passion of the World.* Translated by Robert R. Barr. Maryknoll, NY: Orbis, 2001.

Bonhoeffer, Dietrich. *Life Together.* New York: Harper & Row, 1954.

Borg, Marcus J. *Jesus: Uncovering the Life, Teachings, and Relevance of a Religious Revolutionary.* New York: HarperCollins, 2006.

Borg, Marcus J., and John Dominic Crossan. *The First Paul: Reclaiming the Radical Visionary behind the Church's Conservative Icon.* New York: Harper-Collins, 2009.

———. *The Last Week: What the Gospels Really Teach about Jesus's Final Days in Jerusalem.* New York: HarperCollins, 2006.

Boyce, James K. "Let's Pay Every American to Reduce Emissions." *Politico,* July 23, 2019.

Bradley, Anne R. *Income Inequality and the Parable of the Talents.* Tysons, VA: Institute for Faith, Work, and Economics, May 24, 2012.

———. *Why Does Income Inequality Exist?—Part Two.* Tysons, VA: Institute for Faith, Work, and Economics, June 5, 2012.

Bradley, Anne R., and Art Lindsley, eds. *For the Least of These: A Biblical Answer to Poverty.* Grand Rapids, MI: Zondervan, 2014.

Brennan Center for Justice. *New Voting Restrictions in America.* New York: BCJ, November 19, 2019.

Bricker, Jesse, Sarena Goodman, Kevin B. Moore, and Alice Henriques Volz. "Wealth and Income Concentration in the SCF: 1989–2019." Board of Governors of the Federal Reserve System, FEDS Notes, September 28, 2020. https://doi.org/10.17016/2380-7172.2795.

Broshi, Magen. "The Role of the Temple in the Herodian Economy." *Journal of Jewish Studies* 38, no. 1 (1987): 31–37.

Brueggemann, Walter. *The Covenanted Self: Explorations in Law and Covenant.* Edited by Patrick D. Miller. Minneapolis: Augsburg Fortress, 1999.

———. *An Introduction to the Old Testament: The Canon and Christian Imagination.* Louisville: Westminster John Knox, 2003.

———. *The Land: Place as Gift, Promise, and Challenge in Biblical Faith.* Philadelphia: Fortress, 1977.

———. "The Liturgy of Abundance, the Myth of Scarcity." *Christian Century*, March 24–31, 1999.

———. *Money and Possessions.* Interpretation: Resources for the Use of Scripture in the Church. Louisville: Westminster John Knox, 2016.

———. *Theology of the Old Testament: Testimony, Dispute, Advocacy.* Minneapolis: Augsburg Fortress, 1997.

———. "Trajectories in Old Testament Literature and the Sociology of Ancient Israel." In *A Social Reading of the Old Testament*, edited by Patrick D. Miller, 13–42. Minneapolis: Augsburg Fortress, 1994.

———. "Voices of the Night—against Justice." In *To Act Justly, Love Tenderly, Walk Humbly: An Agenda for Ministers*, by Walter Brueggemann, Sharon Parks, and Thomas H. Groome, 5–28. New York: Paulist, 1986.

Burman, Leonard E. *Capital Gains Cuts Won't Cure the Covid-19 Economy.* Washington, DC: Tax Policy Center, May 11, 2020.

Burnside, Jonathan. *God, Justice, and Society: Aspects of Law and Legality in the Bible.* New York: Oxford University Press, 2011.

Callaway, Joseph A., and Hershel Shanks. "The Settlement in Canaan." In Shanks, *Ancient Israel*, 59–83.

Capaccio, Tony. "The Gun on the Air Force's F-35 Has 'Unacceptable' Accuracy, Pentagon Testing Office Says." *Time*, January 30, 2020.

Capra, Frank, dir. *It's a Wonderful Life.* Culver City, CA: Liberty Films, 1946.

Case, Anne, and Angus Deaton. *Deaths of Despair and the Future of Capitalism.* Princeton, NJ: Princeton University Press, 2020.

———. *Mortality and Morbidity in the 21st Century.* Washington, DC: Brookings Institution, March 23, 2017.

CBO. *Administrative Costs of Private Accounts in Social Security.* Washington, DC: CBO, March 2004.

CBO Budget and Economic Data. *The Budget and Economic Outlook: 2020 to 2030.* Washington, DC: CBO, January 28, 2020.

——— *The Distribution of Major Tax Expenditures in 2019.* Washington, DC: CBO, October 2021.

———. "Historical Budget Data, Table 4." Accessed April 24, 2020. https://www.cbo.gov/system/files/2020-01/51134-2020-01-historical budgetdata.xlsx.

———. "Increase Appropriations for the Internal Revenue Service's Enforcement Initiatives." In *Options for Reducing the Deficit: 2019 to 2028*. Washington, DC: CBO, December 13, 2018.

———. *Trends in the Internal Revenue Service's Funding and Enforcement*. Washington, DC: CBO, July 8, 2020.

CBPP. *Policy Basics: Supplemental Security Income*. Washington, DC: CBPP, February 6, 2020.

———. *Policy Basics: Temporary Assistance for Needy Families*. Washington, DC: CBPP, February 6, 2020.

———. *Policy Basics: Where Do Our Federal Tax Dollars Go?* Updated ed. Washington, DC: CBPP, April 9, 2020.

———. *Three Out of Four Low-Income At-Risk Renters Do Not Receive Federal Rental Assistance*. Washington, DC: CBPP, August 2017.

CBS News. "Mold, Lead Paint, and Rats: Military Families Complain of Unsafe Housing." February 13, 2019. https://www.cbsnews.com/news/senate-to-hold-hearing-on-military-families-housing-issues-mold-pests/.

Cellini, Stephanie Riegg, Signe-Mary McKernan, and Caroline Ratcliffe. *The Dynamics of Poverty in the United States: A Review of Data, Methods, and Findings*. Washington, DC: Urban Institute, January 2008.

Center for Responsible Lending. *Student Debt Cancellation Is Essential to Economic Recovery from COVID-19*. Washington, DC: Center for Responsible Lending, April 9, 2020.

Center for Responsive Politics. "Open Secrets, Business, Labor & Ideological Split in Lobbying Data." Accessed May 12, 2020. https://www.opensecrets.org/federal-lobbying/business-labor-ideological?cycle=2019.

———. "Open Secrets, Did Money Win?" Accessed May 12, 2020. https://www.opensecrets.org/elections-overview/did-money-win.

———. "Open Secrets, Donor Demographics." Accessed August 17, 2020. https://www.opensecrets.org/overview/donordemographics.php.

———. "Open Secrets, Election Overview, Sector Totals." Accessed September 22, 2020. https://www.opensecrets.org/elections-overview/sectors?cycle=2018.

———. "Open Secrets, Influence and Lobbying, Interest Groups." Accessed May 27, 2020. https://www.opensecrets.org/industries/.

————. "Open Secrets, Lobbying Data Summary." Accessed May 12, 2020. https://www.opensecrets.org/federal-lobbying.

Chancel, Lucas, and Thomas Piketty. "Carbon and Inequality: From Kyoto to Paris; Trends in the Global Inequality of Carbon Emissions (1998–2013) and Prospects for an Equitable Adaptation Fund." Working Paper no. 2015/7, WID.world, Paris, 2015.

Chang, Ha-Joon. *Bad Samaritans: The Myth of Free Trade and the Secret History of Capitalism.* New York: Bloomsbury, 2008.

Chetty, Raj, John N. Friedman, Emmanuel Saez, Nicholas Turner, and Danny Yagan. "Mobility Report Cards: The Role of Colleges in Intergenerational Mobility." Working Paper no. 23618, NBER, Cambridge, MA, July 2017.

Chetty, Raj, David Grusky, Maximilian Hell, Nathaniel Hendren, Robert Manduca, and Jimmy Narang. "The Fading American Dream: Trends in Absolute Income Mobility since 1940." *Science* 356, no. 6336 (April 28, 2017): 398–406.

Chicago Lawyers' Committee for Civil Rights. *2018 Fair Housing Testing Report.* Chicago: CLCCR, 2018. https://bit.ly/2CpI4rG.

Coates, Ta-Nehisi. "The Case for Reparations." *Atlantic*, June 2014.

Cohen, Shaye J. D. "Roman Domination: The Jewish Revolt and the Destruction of the Second Temple." In Shanks, *Ancient Israel*, 287–323.

Coleman-Jensen, Alisha, Matthew P. Rabbitt, Christian A. Gregory, and Anita Singh. *Household Food Security in the United States in 2018.* Economic Research Report no. 270. Washington, DC: US Department of Agriculture, Economic Research Service, September 2019.

Collyer, Sophie, David Harris, and Christopher Wimer. "Left Behind: The One-Third of Children in Families Who Earn Too Little to Get the Full Child Tax Credit." Center on Poverty and Social Policy at Columbia University. *Poverty & Social Policy Brief* 3, no. 6 (May 13, 2019): 1–4.

Colvin, Alexander J. S., and Heidi Shierholz. *Noncompete Agreements: Ubiquitous, Harmful to Wages and to Competition, and Part of a Growing Trend of Employers Requiring Workers to Sign Away Their Rights.* Washington, DC: EPI, December 10, 2019.

Compa, Lance. *Unfair Advantage: Workers' Freedom of Association in the United States under International Human Rights Standards.* New York: Human Rights Watch, 2000.

Cone, James H. *A Black Theology of Liberation.* 20th anniversary ed. Maryknoll, NY: Orbis, 1991.

Cooper, David, and Teresa Kroeger. *Employers Steal Billions from Workers' Paychecks Each Year*. Washington, DC: EPI, May 10, 2017.

Cooper, Preston. "Underemployment Persists throughout College Graduates' Careers." *Forbes*, June 8, 2018.

Craddock, Fred B. *Luke*. Interpretation: A Bible Commentary for Preaching and Teaching. Louisville: Westminster John Knox, 1990.

Crawford, Neta C. *United States Budgetary Costs and Obligations of Post-9/11 Wars through FY2020: $6.4 Trillion*. Costs of War. Providence, RI: Brown University Watson Institute, November 13, 2019.

Credit Suisse. *Global Wealth Databook 2018*. Zurich: Credit Suisse, October 18, 2018. https://www.credit-suisse.com/media/assets/corporate/docs/about-us/research/publications/global-wealth-databook-2018.pdf.

Cross, Frank Moore. *Canaanite Myth and Hebrew Epic*. Cambridge, MA: Harvard University Press, 1973.

———. *From Epic to Canon: History and Literature in Ancient Israel*. Baltimore: Johns Hopkins University Press, 1998.

Crossan, John Dominic. *The Birth of Christianity*. New York: HarperCollins, 1998.

———. *God and Empire: Jesus against Rome, Then and Now*. New York: HarperCollins, 2007.

———. *The Greatest Prayer: Rediscovering the Revolutionary Message of the Lord's Prayer*. New York: HarperCollins, 2010.

———. *The Historical Jesus: The Life of a Mediterranean Jewish Peasant*. New York: HarperCollins, 1991.

———. *How to Read the Bible and Still Be a Christian: Struggling with Divine Violence from Genesis through Revelation*. New York: HarperCollins, 2015.

Crossan, John Dominic, and Jonathan L. Reed. *Excavating Jesus: Beneath the Stones, behind the Texts*. New York: HarperCollins, 2001.

Crüsemann, Frank. *The Torah: Theology and Social History of Old Testament Law*. Translated by Allan W. Mahnke. Minneapolis: Augsburg Fortress, 1996.

Culpepper, R. Alan. "The Gospel of Luke: Introduction, Commentary, and Reflection." In *Luke, John*, vol. 9 of *New Interpreter's Bible*, edited by R. Alan Culpepper and Gail R. O'Day, 3–490. Nashville: Abingdon, 1995.

Daly, Herman E. *Beyond Growth: The Economics of Sustainable Development*. Boston: Beacon, 1996.

Darity, William, Jr., Darrick Hamilton, Mark Paul, Alan Aja, Anne Price, Antonio Moore, and Caterina Chiopris. *What We Get Wrong about Closing *the Racial Wealth Gap*. Oakland, CA: Insight Center for Community Economic Development, April 2018.

Dark, Taylor E. *The Unions and the Democrats: An Enduring Alliance*. Ithaca, NY: Cornell University Press, 1999.

Davies, James C. "Toward a Theory of Revolution." *American Sociological Review* 27, no. 1 (February 1962): 5–19.

Davis, Aidan. *Options for a Less Regressive Sales Tax in 2019*. Washington, DC: ITEP, September 26, 2019.

Davis, Carl. *State Itemized Deductions: Surveying the Landscape, Exploring Reforms*. Washington, DC: ITEP, February 5, 2020.

Defense Manpower Data Center. "Number of Military and DoD Appropriated Fund (APF) Civilian Personnel Permanently Assigned, September 30, 2021." https://dwp.dmdc.osd.mil/dwp/api/download?fileName =DMDC_Website_Location_Report_2109.xlsx&groupName= milRegionCountry.

Depalma, Anthony. "NAFTA's Powerful Little Secret: Obscure Tribunals Settle Disputes, but Go Too Far, Critics Say." *New York Times*, March 11, 2001.

DeParle, Jason. "How to Fix Child Poverty." *New York Review of Books*, July 23, 2020.

Desmond, Matthew. *Evicted: Poverty and Profit in the American City*. New York: Crown, 2016.

Dettling, Lisa J., Joanne W. Hsu, Lindsay Jacobs, Kevin B. Moore, and Jeffrey P. Thompson with assistance from Elizabeth Llanes. *Recent Trends in Wealth-Holding by Race and Ethnicity: Evidence from the Survey of Consumer Finances*. Washington, DC: Board of Governors of the Federal Reserve System, September 27, 2017.

Dever, William G. *Who Were the Early Israelites and Where Did They Come From?* Grand Rapids, MI: Eerdmans, 2003.

DiAngelo, Robin. *White Fragility: Why It's So Hard for White People to Talk about Racism*. Boston: Beacon Press, 2018.

Drutman, Lee. *The Business of America Is Lobbying: How Corporations Became Politicized and Politics Became More Corporate*. New York: Oxford University Press, 2015.

Dube, Arindrajit, and Ethan Kaplan. "Does Outsourcing Reduce Wages in the Low Wage Service Occupations? Evidence from Janitors and Guards." *Industrial and Labor Relations Review* 63, no. 2 (January 2010): 287–306.

Edelman, Gilad. "The Big Tech Hearing Proved Congress Isn't Messing Around." *Wired,* July 29, 2020.

Eisenbrey, Ross. *Middle Class Incomes Suffer without Collective Bargaining.* Washington, DC: EPI, March 4, 2015.

Elo, Irma T. "Social Class Differentials in Health and Mortality: Patterns and Explanations in Comparative Perspective." *Annual Review of Sociology* 35, no. 1 (2009): 553–572.

Environmental Working Group. "Farm Subsidy Database." Accessed June 8, 2020. https://farm.ewg.org/index.php.

EPI. "Family Budget Calculator." Accessed November 23, 2021. https://www.epi.org/resources/budget/.

————. *Top Charts of 2019.* Washington, DC: EPI, December 23, 2019.

EPI State of Working America Data Library. "Median/Average Hourly Wages." Last modified February 20, 2020. https://www.epi.org/data/#?subject=wage-avg.

————. "Productivity and Hourly Compensation." Last modified March 2020. https://www.epi.org/data/#?subject=prodpay.

————. "Unemployment." Last modified March 2020. https://www.epi.org/data/#?subject=unemp.

————. "Union Coverage." Last modified January 31, 2020. https://www.epi.org/data/#?subject=unioncov.

————. "Wages by Percentile and Wage Ratios." Last modified February 20, 2020. https://www.epi.org/data/#?subject=wage-percentiles.

————. "Wages for Top 1.0%, 0.1% and Bottom 90%." Last modified December 2019. https://www.epi.org/data/#?subject=wagegroup.

Epstein, Gerald, and Juan Antonio Montecino. *Overcharged: The High Cost of High Finance.* New York: Roosevelt Institute, July 2016.

Esler, Philip F., ed. *The Early Christian World.* 2nd ed., New York: Routledge, 2017.

Espejo, Alberto, and Anna Unigovskaya. *Debt Relief Bringing Benefits to Africa.* Washington, DC: International Monetary Fund, February 25, 2008.

Esteves, Junno Arocho. "Pope Francis: Labor Unions Are Essential to Society." *America Magazine,* June 28, 2017.

European Network on Debt and Development. *We Can Work It Out: 10 Civil Society Principles for Sovereign Debt Resolution.* Brussels: Eurodad, September 2019.

Everytown for Gun Safety. *Firearm Suicide in the United States.* New York: Everytown for Gun Safety, August 30, 2018.

Eviction Lab, Princeton University. "Why Eviction Matters, Affordable Housing Crisis." Accessed March 10, 2020. https://evictionlab.org/why -eviction-matters/#affordable-housing-crisis.

———. "Why Eviction Matters, Eviction Impact." Accessed March 10, 2020. https://evictionlab.org/why-eviction-matters/#eviction-impact.

Falk, Gene. *The Temporary Assistance for Needy Families (TANF) Block Grant: A Primer on TANF Financing and Federal Requirements.* Washington, DC: Congressional Research Service, December 14, 2017.

Faricy, Christopher G. *Welfare for the Wealthy.* New York: Cambridge University Press, 2015.

Faust, Avraham. *Israel's Ethnogenesis: Settlement, Interaction, Expansion and Resistance.* Oakville, CT: Equinox, 2006.

Federal Communications Commission. *International Broadband Data Report.* Report no. 6. Washington, DC: FCC, February 2, 2018.

Federal Reserve Economic Data, Federal Reserve Bank of St. Louis. "University of Groningen and University of California, Davis, Share of Labor Compensation in GDP at Current National Prices for United States." Accessed March 23, 2020. https://fred.stlouisfed.org/series/ LABSHPUSA156NRUG.

———. "US Bureau of Labor Statistics, All Employees, Manufacturing." Accessed January 13, 2021. https://fred.stlouisfed.org/series/MANEMP.

———. "US Bureau of Labor Statistics, All Employees, Total Nonfarm." Accessed January 13, 2021. https://fred.stlouisfed.org/series/PAYEMS.

———. "US Dept. of Commerce Bureau of Economic Analysis, Federal Government: Tax Receipts on Corporate Income." Accessed April 27, 2020. https://fred.stlouisfed.org/series/FCTAX.

———. "US Dept. of Commerce Bureau of Economic Analysis, Real Gross Domestic Product Per Capita." Accessed May 21, 2020. https:// fred.stlouisfed.org/series/A939RX0Q048SBEA.

———. "World Bank, 5-Bank Asset Concentration for United States." Accessed March 26, 2020. https://fred.stlouisfed.org/series/DDOI06 USA156NWDB.

Federal Trade Commission. *Consumer Information, Car Title Loans.* Washington, DC: FTC, July 2014.

Feeding America. *2019 Annual Report.* Chicago: Feeding America, 2020.

Feldman, Max, and Wendy Weiser. *The State of Voting 2018—Updated.* New York: Brennan Center for Justice, August 3, 2018.

Fiensy, David A. *Christian Origins and the Ancient Economy*. Eugene, OR: Cascade, 2014.

Finkelstein, Israel, and Neil Asher Silberman. *The Bible Unearthed: Archaeology's New Vision of Ancient Israel and the Origin of Its Sacred Texts*. New York: Simon & Schuster, 2001.

————. *David and Solomon: In Search of the Bible's Sacred Kings and the Roots of the Western Tradition*. New York: Free Press, 2006.

Fischer, Will, and Barbara Sard. *Chart Book: Federal Housing Spending Is Poorly Matched to Need*. Washington, DC: CBPP, March 8, 2017.

Floyd, Ife, Ashley Burnside, and Liz Schott. *TANF Reaching Few Poor Families*. Washington, DC: CBPP, November 28, 2018.

Foner, Eric. *Forever Free: The Story of Emancipation and Reconstruction*. New York: Alfred A. Knopf, 2005.

Food and Agricultural Organization of the UN. *Global Food Losses and Food Waste—Extent, Causes and Prevention*. Rome: FAO, 2011.

————. *The State of Food Security and Nutrition in the World, 2020*. Rome: FAO, 2020.

————. *Tackling Climate Change through Livestock: A Global Assessment of Emissions and Mitigation Opportunities*. Rome: FAO, 2013.

Foroohar, Rana. *Makers and Takers: The Rise of Finance and the Fall of American Business*. New York: Crown Business, 2016.

Foster, George. "Peasant Society and the Image of Limited Good." *American Anthropologist* 67, no. 2 (1965): 293–315.

Francis. *Evangelii Gaudium*. Rome: Libreria Editrice Vaticana, November 26, 2013.

Frank, Robert H. *Success and Luck*. Princeton, NJ: Princeton University Press, 2016.

Frankel, Todd C. "A Majority of the People Arrested for Capitol Riot Had a History of Financial Trouble." *Washington Post*, February 10, 2021.

Fretheim, Terence E. *Exodus*. Interpretation: A Bible Commentary for Teaching and Preaching. Louisville: Westminster John Knox, 1991.

Friedman, Thomas L. *The Lexus and the Olive Tree: Understanding Globalization*. Rev. ed. New York: Anchor 2000.

Friedman, Zach. "Student Loan Debt Statistics in 2019: A $1.5 Trillion Crisis." *Forbes*, February 25, 2019.

Funk, Robert W., Roy W. Hoover, and the Jesus Seminar. *The Five Gospels: The Search for the Authentic Words of Jesus*. New York: Macmillan, 1993.

García, Emma. *Schools Are Still Segregated, and Black Children Are Paying a Price.* Washington, DC: EPI, February 12, 2020.

García, Emma, and Elaine Weiss. *Education Inequalities at the School Starting Gate: Gaps, Trends, and Strategies to Address Them.* Washington, DC: EPI, September 2017.

García, Jorge Luis, James J. Heckman, Duncan Ermini Leaf, and María José Prados. "Quantifying the Life-Cycle Benefits of a Prototypical Early Childhood Program." Working Paper no. 23479, NBER, Cambridge, MA, June 2017, rev. February 2019.

Gardner, Matthew, Lorena Roque, and Steve Wamhoff. *Corporate Tax Avoidance in the First Year of the Trump Tax Law.* Washington, DC: ITEP, December 16, 2019.

Gardner, Matthew, and Steve Wamhoff. *Depreciation Breaks Have Saved 20 Major Corporations $26.5 Billion over Past Two Years.* Washington, DC: ITEP, June 2, 2020.

Ge, Mengpin, and Johannes Friedrich. "4 Charts Explain Greenhouse Gas Emissions by Countries and Sectors." *Insights* (blog). World Resources Institute, February 6, 2020. https://www.wri.org/insights/4-charts -explain-greenhouse-gas-emissions-countries-and-sectors.

Gee, Emily, and Topher Spiro. "Excess Administrative Costs Burden the US Health Care System." *American Prospect,* April 8, 2019.

Gettleman, Jeffrey, and Suhasini Raj. "Virus Closed Schools, and the World's Poorest Children Went to Work." *New York Times,* September 28, 2020.

Gilens, Martin, and Benjamin I. Page. "Critics Argued with Our Analysis of US Political Inequality. Here Are 5 Ways They're Wrong." *Washington Post,* May 23, 2016.

———. "Testing Theories of American Politics: Elites, Interest Groups, and Average Citizens." *Perspectives on Politics* 12, no. 3 (2014): 564–581.

Gilman, Hollie Russon, and K. Sabeel Rahman. "Civic Power: Reclaiming Democracy's Radicalism." *Forge,* December 16, 2019.

Giménez, Eric Holt. "We Already Grow Enough Food for 10 Billion People—and Still Can't End Hunger." Huffington Post, May 2, 2012, last modified December 18, 2014.

Global Footprint Network. "Country Trends." Accessed October 15, 2020. https://data.footprintnetwork.org/#/countryTrends?type=earth&cn=231.

Gnuse, Robert. *No Other Gods: Emergent Monotheism in Israel. Journal for the Study of the Old Testament* Supplement Series 241. Sheffield, England: Sheffield Academic, 1997.

—. *You Shall Not Steal: Community and Property in the Biblical Tradition.* Maryknoll, NY: Orbis, 1985.

Golden, Lonnie. *Part-Time Workers Pay a Big-Time Penalty.* Washington, DC: EPI, February 27, 2020.

Good, Martha H. "Freedom from Want: The Failure of United States Courts to Protect Subsistence Rights." *Human Rights Quarterly* 6, no. 3 (August 1984): 335–365.

Gordon, Colin. *Race in the Heartland.* Washington, DC: EPI, October 10, 2019.

Gottwald, Norman K. *The Tribes of Yahweh: A Sociology of the Religion of Liberated Israel, 1250–1050 BCE.* Maryknoll, NY: Orbis, 1979.

Gould, Elise. *No Matter How We Measure Poverty, the Poverty Rate Would Be Much Lower If Economic Growth Were More Broadly Shared.* Washington, DC: EPI, January 15, 2014.

—. *State of Working America Wages 2019.* Washington, DC: EPI, February 20, 2020.

Grabbe, Lester L. *Ancient Israel: What Do We Know and How Do We Know It?* New York: T&T Clark, 2007.

Graeber, David. *Debt: The First 5,000 Years.* Brooklyn, NY: Melville House, 2011.

Greenhouse, Steven, and Graham Bowley. "Tiny Tax on Financial Trades Gains Advocates." *New York Times,* December 6, 2011.

Guilford, Gwynn. "The Epic Mistake about Manufacturing That's Cost Americans Millions of Jobs." *Quartz,* May 3, 2018.

Gunaratna, Rohan. *Inside Al Qaeda: Global Network of Terror.* New York: Columbia University Press, 2002.

Gutiérrez, Gustavo. *On Job: God-Talk and the Suffering of the Innocent.* Translated by Matthew J. O'Connell. Maryknoll, NY: Orbis, 1987.

Hacker, Jacob, and Paul Pierson. *American Amnesia: How the War on Government Led Us to Forget What Made America Prosper.* New York: Simon & Schuster, 2016.

—. *Let Them Eat Tweets: How the Right Rules in an Age of Extreme Inequality.* New York: W. W. Norton, 2020.

Haines, Andy. "Addressing Challenges to Human Health in the Anthropocene Epoch—an Overview of the Findings of the Rockefeller/Lancet Commission on Planetary Health." *International Health* 9, no. 5 (September 1, 2017): 269–271.

Halle, Tamara, Nicole Forry, Elizabeth Hair, Kate Perper, Laura Wandner, Julia Wessel, and Jessica Vick. *Disparities in Early Learning and Development:*

Lessons from the Early Childhood Longitudinal Study—Birth Cohort. Bethesda, MD: Child Trends, June 2009.

Halpern, Baruch. "The Exodus from Egypt: Myth or Reality?" In *The Rise of Ancient Israel*, by Hershel Shanks, William G. Dever, Baruch Halpern, and P. Kyle McCarter Jr., 87–113. Washington, DC: Biblical Archaeology Society, 1992.

Hamilton, Darrick, Mark Paul, and William Darity Jr. "An Economic Bill of Rights for the 21st Century." *American Prospect*, March 5, 2018.

Hanson, K. C., and Douglas E. Oakman. *Palestine in the Time of Jesus*. 2nd ed. Minneapolis: Fortress, 2008.

Hanson, Paul D. *Political Engagement as Biblical Mandate*. Eugene, OR: Cascade, 2010.

Harding, Luke. "What Are the Panama Papers? A Guide to History's Biggest Data Leak." *Guardian*, April 5, 2016.

Hardoon, Deborah. *An Economy for the 99%*. London: Oxfam International, January 16, 2017.

Harrelson, Walter. *The Ten Commandments and Human Rights*. Rev ed. Macon: GA: Mercer University Press, 1997.

Hartung, William D., and Mandy Smithberger. "America's Defense Budget Is Bigger Than You Think." *Nation*, May 7, 2019.

Haught, John P. *The New Cosmic Story: Inside Our New Awakening Universe*. New Haven, CT: Yale University Press, 2017.

Heath, David, Mark Greenblatt, and Aysha Bagchi. "Dentists under Pressure to Drill 'Healthy Teeth' for Profit, Former Insiders Allege." *USA Today*, March 19, 2020.

Hedges, Chris. *America: The Farewell Tour*. New York: Simon & Schuster, 2018.

Hendricks, Obery M., Jr. *The Politics of Jesus: Rediscovering the True Revolutionary Nature of Jesus' Teachings and How They Have Been Corrupted*. New York: Three Leaves, 2006.

Herzog II, William R. *Jesus, Justice, and the Reign of God*. Louisville: Westminster John Knox, 2000.

———. *Parables as Subversive Speech: Jesus as Pedagogue of the Oppressed*. Louisville: Westminster John Knox, 1994.

Heschel, Abraham J. *The Prophets*. 2 vols. New York: Harper & Row, 1962.

Hickel, Jason. *The Divide: Global Inequality from Conquest to Free Markets*. New York: W. W. Norton, 2017.

Hirsch, Lauren. "Sears Sues Former CEO Eddie Lampert, Treasury Secretary Mnuchin and Others for Alleged 'Thefts' of Billions from Retailer." CNBC, April 18, 2019. https://www.cnbc.com/2019/04/18/sears-sues-eddie-lampert-steven-mnuchin-others-for-alleged-thefts.html.

Hoehner, Harold W. *Herod Antipas: A Contemporary of Jesus Christ.* Cambridge: Cambridge University Press, 1972.

Horsley, Richard A. *Covenant Economics: A Biblical Vision of Justice for All.* Louisville: Westminster John Knox, 2009.

———. "Jesus and Empire." In *In the Shadow of Empire,* edited by Richard A. Horsley, 75–96. Louisville: Westminster John Knox, 2008.

———. *Jesus and Empire: The Kingdom of God and the New World Disorder.* Minneapolis: Fortress, 2003.

———. *Jesus and the Spiral of Violence: Popular Jewish Resistance in Roman Palestine.* Minneapolis: Fortress, 1993.

Horsley, Richard A., and Neil Asher Silberman. *The Message and the Kingdom: How Jesus and Paul Ignited a Revolution and Transformed the Ancient World.* Minneapolis: Fortress, 1997.

Houseman, Susan N. "Understanding the Decline of US Manufacturing Employment." Working Paper no. 18-287, Upjohn Institute, Kalamazoo, MI, June 1, 2018.

Hout, Michel. "Social Mobility." Special issue, *Pathways* (2019): 29–32.

Howell, David R. "From Decent to Lousy Jobs: New Evidence on the Decline in American Job Quality, 1979–2017." Working paper, Center for Equitable Growth, Washington, DC, August 2019.

Hughes, Langston. *The Collected Works of Langston Hughes.* Vol. 3, *The Poems: 1951–1967.* Edited by Arnold Rampersad. Columbia: University of Missouri Press, 2001.

Ingraham, Christopher. "Wal-Mart Has a Lower Acceptance Rate Than Harvard." *Washington Post,* March 28, 2014.

Interfaith Worker Justice. *What Faith Groups Say about Worker Justice.* Chicago: IWJ, 2011.

Intergovernmental Science-Policy Platform on Biodiversity and Ecosystem Services. *Global Assessment Report on Biodiversity and Ecosystem Services.* Bonn, Germany: IPBES, 2019.

Internal Revenue Service, SOI Tax Stats. "Examination Coverage: Recommended and Average Recommended Additional Tax after Examination—IRS Data Book Table 9a." Accessed April 30, 2020. https://www.irs.gov/statistics/soi-tax-stats-examination-coverage-recommended-and

-average-recommended-additional-tax-after-examination-irs-data
-book-table-9a.

International Labor Organization. *Global Employment Trends for Youth 2020: Technology and the Future of Jobs*. Geneva: ILO, 2015.

———. *Global Wage Report 2016/17*. Geneva: ILO, December 15, 2016.

———. *Youth Unemployment in the Arab World Is a Major Cause for Rebellion*. Geneva: ILO, April 2011.

Isidore, Chris. "Buffett Says He's Still Paying Lower Tax Rate Than His Secretary." CNNMoney, March 4, 2013. https://money.cnn.com/2013/03/04/news/economy/buffett-secretary-taxes/index.html.

Jackson, Tim. *Prosperity without Growth: Economics for a Finite Planet*. Foreword by HRH The Prince of Wales. Washington, DC: Earthscan, 2011.

John Paul II. *Laborem Exercens*. Rome: Libreria Editrice Vaticana, September 14, 1981.

Johns, Andrew, and Joel Slemrod. "The Distribution of Income Tax Noncompliance." *National Tax Journal* 63, no. 3 (September 2010): 397–418.

Johnson, Chalmers. *Blowback: The Costs and Consequences of American Empire*. New York: Henry Holt, 2000.

Joint Center for Housing Studies of Harvard University. *The State of the Nation's Housing 2019*. Cambridge, MA: Harvard University Press, 2019.

Joint Committee on Taxation, US Congress. *Estimates of Federal Tax Expenditures for Fiscal Years 2019–2023*. JCX-55-19. Washington, DC: JCT, December 18, 2019.

Jubilee Debt Campaign. *Preventing and Resolving Sovereign Debt Crises: Stop Bailing Out Reckless Lenders*. London: Jubilee Debt Campaign, October 2019.

Kahlenberg, Richard D. *An Economic Fair Housing Act*. New York: Century Foundation, August 3, 2017.

Kaplan, Sarah. "Are My Hamburgers Hurting the Planet?" *Washington Post*, November 18, 2019.

———. "Climate Change Is Also a Racial Justice Problem." *Washington Post*, June 29, 2020.

Katz, Lawrence F., and Alan B. Krueger. "The Rise and Nature of Alternative Work Arrangements in the United States, 1995–2015." Working Paper no. 22667, NBER, Cambridge, MA, September 2016.

Katznelson, Ira. *When Affirmative Action Was White: An Untold History of Racial Inequality in Twentieth-Century America*. New York: W. W. Norton, 2005.

Keisler-Starkey, Katherine, and Lisa N. Bunch. *Health Insurance in the United States: 2019*. Report no. P60-271. Washington, DC: US Bureau of the Census, September 15, 2020.

Keller, Catherine. *On the Mystery: Discerning Divinity in Process*. Minneapolis: Fortress, 2008.

Kendi, Ibram X. *Stamped from the Beginning: The Definitive History of Racist Ideas in America*. New York: Nation, 2016.

Killebrew, Ann E. *Biblical Peoples and Ethnicity: An Archaeological Study of Egyptians, Canaanites, Philistines, and Early Israel, 1300–1100 BCE*. Leiden, Netherlands: Society of Biblical Literature, 2005.

King, Martin Luther, Jr. "A Time to Break Silence." Address to clergy and laity concerned, Riverside Church, New York City, April 4, 1967. In *Testament of Hope*, edited by James M. Washington, 231–244. New York: HarperCollins, 1986.

Klein, Naomi. *The Shock Doctrine: The Rise of Disaster Capitalism*. New York: Henry Holt, 2007.

Kloppenborg, John S. *Q, the Earliest Gospel: An Introduction to the Original Stories and Sayings of Jesus*. Louisville: Westminster John Knox, 2008.

Konczal, Mike, J. W. Mason, and Amanda Page-Hoongrajok. *Ending Short-Termism: An Investment Agenda for Growth*. New York: Roosevelt Institute, November 6, 2015.

Koskinen, John N. "Prepared Remarks of John A. Koskinen Commissioner Internal Revenue Service before the Urban-Brookings Tax Policy Center." Speech given at Urban-Brookings Tax Policy Center, Washington, DC, April 8, 2015.

Kota, Sridhar, and Tom Mahoney. "Reinventing Competitiveness: The Case for a National Manufacturing Foundation." *American Affairs Journal* 3, no. 3 (Fall 2019): 3–17.

Kristof, Nicholas. "The World's Malnourished Kids Don't Need a $295 Burger." *New York Times*, June 12, 2019.

Kuttner, Robert. *Can Democracy Survive Global Capitalism?* New York: W. W. Norton, 2018.

———. "Sears Didn't 'Die.' Vulture Capitalists Killed It." Huffington Post, October 15, 2018.

Lafer, Gordon. *The One Percent Solution: How Corporations Are Remaking America One State at a Time*. Ithaca, NY: ILR, 2017.

Lafer, Gordon, and Lola Loustaunau. *Fear at Work: An Inside Account of How Employers Threaten, Intimidate, and Harass Workers to Stop Them from*

Exercising Their Right to Collective Bargaining. Washington, DC: EPI, July 23, 2020.

Lai, K. K. Rebecca, Troy Griggs, Max Fisher, and Audrey Carlsen. "Is America's Military Big Enough?" *New York Times*, March 22, 2017.

Lawson, Max, Man-Kwun Chan, Francesca Rhodes, Anam Parvez Butt, Anna Marriott, Ellen Ehmke, Didier Jacobs, Julie Seghers, Jaime Atienza, and Rebecca Gowland. *Public Good or Private Wealth?* Oxford: Oxfam International, January 2019.

Lazonick, William. *Profits without Prosperity: How Stock Buybacks Manipulate the Market, and Leave Most Americans Worse Off.* New York: Institute for New Economic Thinking, April 2014.

Lenski, Gerhard E. *Power and Privilege: A Theory of Social Stratification.* Chapel Hill: University of North Carolina Press, 1984.

Lepore, Jill. *This America: The Case for the Nation.* New York: Liveright, 2019.

Levine, Amy-Jill. *The Misunderstood Jew: The Church and the Scandal of the Jewish Jesus.* New York: HarperCollins, 2006.

Lindsey, Rebecca, and LuAnn Dahlman. *Climate Change: Global Temperature.* Washington, DC: NOAA Climate.gov, August 14, 2020.

Linn, M. W., R. Sandifer, and S. Stein. "Effects of Unemployment on Mental and Physical Health." *American Journal of Public Health* 75, no. 5 (1985): 502–506.

Mack, Burton L. *The Lost Gospel of Q: The Book of Christian Origins.* New York: HarperCollins, 1993.

Maddison, Angus. *The World Economy.* Paris: OECD, 2006.

Magnan, Sanne. "Social Determinants of Health 101 for Health Care: Five Plus Five." *NAM Perspectives,* Discussion Paper, Washington, DC: National Academy of Medicine, October 9, 2017. https://doi.org/10.31478/201710c.

Magnuson, Katherine, and Elizabeth Votruba-Drzal. "Enduring Influences of Childhood Poverty." In *Changing Poverty, Changing Policies,* edited by Maria Cancian and Sheldon Danziger, 153–179. New York: Russell Sage Foundation, 2009.

Mahoney, Christine. "Why Lobbying in America Is Different." *Politico,* April 12, 2014.

Maimonides. "Selection XV." In *Selections from Jewish Literature,* part 2 of *Union Prayer Book for Jewish Worship,* edited by Central Conference of American Rabbis, 117–118. New York: CCAR, 1956.

Malina, Bruce J., and Richard L. Rohrbaugh. *Social-Science Commentary on the Synoptic Gospels.* Minneapolis: Fortress, 1992.

Marshall, Christopher D. *Compassionate Justice: An Interdisciplinary Dialogue with Two Gospel Parables on Law, Crime, and Restorative Justice*. Eugene, OR: Cascade, 2012.

Massachusetts Institute of Technology. "Living Wage Calculator." Accessed November 23, 2021. https://livingwage.mit.edu/.

Massey, Douglas S. *Categorically Unequal: The American Stratification System*. New York: Russell Sage Foundation, 2007.

Masson-Delmotte, V., P. Zhai, H.-O. Pörtner, D. Roberts, J. Skea, P. R. Shukla, A. Pirani, W. Moufouma-Okia, C. Péan, R. Pidcock, S. Connors, J. B. R. Matthews, Y. Chen, X. Zhou, M. I. Gomis, E. Lonnoy, T. Maycock, M. Tignor, and T. Waterfield, eds. *Global Warming of 1.5°C: An IPCC Special Report on the Impacts of Global Warming of 1.5°C above Pre-industrial Levels and Related Global Greenhouse Gas Emission Pathways, in the Context of Strengthening the Global Response to the Threat of Climate Change, Sustainable Development, and Efforts to Eradicate Poverty*. Geneva: World Meteorological Organization, 2018.

Mazar, Amihai. "The Patriarchs, Exodus, and the Conquest Narratives in Light of Archaeology." In *The Quest for the Historical Israel: Debating Archaeology and the History of Early Israel*, by Israel Finkelstein and Amihai Mazar, edited by Brian B. Schmidt, 57–65. Invited Lectures Delivered at the 6th Biennial Colloquium of International Institute for Secular Humanistic Judaism. Atlanta: Society of Biblical Literature, 2007.

Mbow, Cheikh, Cynthia Rosenzweig, Luis G. Barioni, Tim G. Benton, Mario Herrero, Murukesan Krishnapillai, Emma Liwenga, Prajal Pradhan, Marta G. Rivera-Ferre, Tek Sapkota, Francesco N. Tubiello, and Yinlong Xu. "Food Security." In *Climate Change and Land: An IPCC Special Report on Climate Change, Desertification, Land Degradation, Sustainable Land Management, Food Security, and Greenhouse Gas Fluxes in Terrestrial Ecosystems*, edited by P. R. Shukla, J. Skea, E. Calvo Buendia, V. Masson-Delmotte, H.-O. Pörtner, D. C. Roberts, P. Zhai, R. Slade, S. Connors, R. van Diemen, M. Ferrat, E. Haughey, S. Luz, S. Neogi, M. Pathak, J. Petzold, J. Portugal Pereira, P. Vyas, E. Huntley, K. Kissick, M. Belkacemi, J. Malley, chap. 5. Intergovernmental Panel on Climate Change, 2019. https://www.ipcc.ch/srccl/cite-report/.

McCormack, Richard, ed. *Remaking America*. Washington, DC: Alliance for American Manufacturing, 2013.

McFague, Sallie. *Life Abundant: Rethinking Theology and Economy for a Planet in Peril*. Minneapolis: Fortress, 2001.

McLaughlin, Michael, and Mark R. Rank. "Estimating the Economic Cost of Childhood Poverty in the United States." *Social Work Research* 42, no. 2 (June 2018): 73–83.

McNicholas, Celine, Zane Mokhiber, and Adam Chaikof. *Two Billion Dollars in Stolen Wages Were Recovered for Workers in 2015 and 2016—and That's Just a Drop in the Bucket.* Washington, DC: EPI, December 13, 2017.

McNicholas, Celine, Margaret Poydock, Julia Wolfe, Ben Zipperer, Gordon Lafer, and Lola Loustaunau. *Unlawful: US Employers Are Charged with Violating Federal Law in 41.5% of All Union Election Campaigns.* Washington, DC: EPI, December 11, 2019.

McNicholas, Celine, Samantha Sanders, and Heidi Shierholz. *What's at Stake in the States If the 2016 Federal Raise to the Overtime Pay Threshold Is Not Preserved—and What States Can Do about It.* Washington, DC: EPI, November 15, 2017.

Meeks, M. Douglas. *God the Economist: The Doctrine of God and Political Economy.* Minneapolis: Augsburg Fortress, 1989.

Mehta, Aaron, and Jen Judson. "The Pentagon Completed Its Second Audit. What Did It Find?" *Defense News*, November 16, 2019.

Meier, John P. *A Marginal Jew: Rethinking the Historical Jesus.* Vol. 4, *Law and Love.* Anchor Yale Bible Reference Library. New Haven, CT: Yale University Press, 2009.

———. *A Marginal Jew: Rethinking the Historical Jesus.* Vol. 5, *Probing the Authenticity of the Parables.* Anchor Yale Bible Reference Library. New Haven, CT: Yale University Press, 2016.

Meixell, Brady, and Ross Eisenbrey. *Wage Theft Is a Much Bigger Problem Than Other Forms of Theft—but Workers Remain Mostly Unprotected.* Washington, DC: EPI, September 18, 2014.

Mencimer, Stephanie. "Have You Signed Away Your Right to Sue?" *Mother Jones*, March/April 2008.

Mendenhall, George E. *The Tenth Generation: The Origins of the Biblical Tradition.* Baltimore: Johns Hopkins University Press, 1973.

Milanovic, Branko. *Global Inequality: A New Approach for the Age of Globalization.* Cambridge, MA: Belknap, 2016.

Milgrom, Jacob. *Leviticus 17–22: A New Translation with Introduction and Commentary.* Anchor Bible 3A. New York: Doubleday, 2000.

———. *Leviticus 23–27: A New Translation with Introduction and Commentary.* Anchor Bible 3B. New York: Doubleday, 2000.

Miller, Patrick D., ed. *A Social Reading of the Old Testament: Prophetic Approaches to Israel's Communal Life.* Minneapolis: Fortress, 1994.

————. *The Ten Commandments*. Interpretation: Resources for the Use of Scripture in the Church. Louisville: Westminster John Knox, 2009.

Mishel, Lawrence. *Low-Wage Workers Have Far More Education Than They Did in 1968, Yet They Make Far Less*. Washington, DC: EPI, January 23, 2014.

Mishel, Lawrence, Josh Bivens, Elise Gould, and Heidi Shierholz. *The State of Working America*. 12th ed. Ithaca, NY: Cornell University Press, 2012.

Mishel, Lawrence, Lynn Rhinehart, and Lane Windham. *Explaining the Erosion of Private-Sector Unions: How Corporate Practices and Legal Changes Have Undercut the Ability of Workers to Organize and Bargain*. Washington, DC: EPI, October 7, 2020.

Mishel, Lawrence, and Julia Wolfe. *CEO Compensation Has Grown 940% since 1978*. Washington, DC: EPI, August 14, 2019.

Montgomery, Peter. "Biblical Economics: The Divine Laissez-Faire Mandate." *Public Eye*, Spring 2015.

Moore, Megan Bishop, and Brad E. Kelle. *Biblical History and Israel's Past: The Changing Study of the Bible and History*. Grand Rapids, MI: Eerdmans, 2011.

Morrissey, Monique. *The State of American Retirement Savings*. Washington, DC: EPI, December 10, 2019.

Morton, Fiona Scott. *Reforming US Antitrust Enforcement and Competition Policy*. Washington, DC: Washington Center for Equitable Growth, February 18, 2020.

Mukunda, Gautam. "Profits without Prosperity: The Price of Wall Street's Power." *Harvard Business Review*, June 2014.

Muro, Mark, and Joseph Parilla. *Maladjusted: It's Time to Reimagine Economic "Adjustment" Programs*. Washington, DC: Brookings Institution, January 10, 2017.

National Academies of Sciences, Engineering, and Medicine. *A Roadmap to Reducing Child Poverty*. Consensus Study Report. Washington, DC: National Academies Press, 2019.

National Center for Health Statistics. *Health, United States, 2017*. Special Feature on Mortality. Hyattsville, MD: National Center for Health Statistics, 2018.

————. *Health, United States, 2018*. Hyattsville, MD: National Center for Health Statistics, 2019.

National Council of the Churches of Christ in the USA. *A 21st Century Social Creed*. Washington, DC: NCC, September 2007.

National Employment Law Project. *Raise the Minimum Wage*. https://raisetheminimumwage.com/.

National Health Care for the Homeless Council. *Homelessness and Health: What's the Connection?* Nashville: NHCHC, February 2019.

National Homeless Law Center. *Housing Rights for All: Promoting and Defending Housing Rights in the United States, Fifth Edition: A Resource Manual on International Law and the Human Right to Adequate Housing.* Washington, DC: NHLC, 2011.

National Low Income Housing Coalition. *Advocates Secure Increased Funding in Final FY20 Spending Bill.* Washington, DC: NLIHC, December 16, 2019.

———. *The Gap: A Shortage of Affordable Rental Homes.* Washington, DC: NLIHC, March 2019.

———. *Out of Reach 2019.* Washington, DC: NLIHC, 2019.

National Research Council and Institute of Medicine. *US Health in International Perspective: Shorter Lives, Poorer Health.* Edited by Steven H. Woolf and Laudan Aron. Washington, DC: National Academies Press, 2013.

Ngũgĩ wa Thiong'o. *Devil on the Cross.* Portsmouth, NH: Heinemann, 1987.

Oakman, Douglas E. *Jesus and the Peasants.* Eugene, OR: Wipf & Stock, 2008.

———. *Jesus, Debt and the Lord's Prayer: First-Century Debt and Jesus' Intentions.* Eugene, OR: Cascade, 2014.

———. *The Political Aims of Jesus.* Minneapolis: Fortress, 2012.

OECD. *Starting Strong 2017: Key OECD Indicators on Early Childhood Education and Care.* Paris: OECD, 2017.

OECD Data. "Health Spending." Accessed February 11, 2020. https://data.oecd.org/healthres/health-spending.htm.

———. "Net ODA." Accessed November 16, 2020. https://doi.org/10.1787/33346549-en.

OECD iLibrary. "Poverty Rate." Accessed April 26, 2019. https://doi.org/10.1787/0fe1315d-en.

Open Markets Institute. "America's Concentration Crisis." Accessed March 26, 2020. https://concentrationcrisis.openmarketsinstitute.org/.

OpenSecrets.org. *2020 Election to Cost $14 Billion, Blowing Away Spending Records.* Washington, DC: Center for Responsive Politics, October 28, 2020.

Orfield, Gary, Erica Frankenberg, Jongyeon Ee, and Jennifer B. Ayscue. *Harming Our Common Future: America's Segregated Schools 65 Years after Brown.* Civil Rights Project. Los Angeles: University of California Press, May 10, 2019.

Ostry, Jonathan, Andrew Berg, and Charalambos G. Tsangarides. "Redistribution, Inequality, and Growth." Staff discussion note. Washington, DC: International Monetary Fund, 2014.

Oxfam International. *Reward Work, Not Wealth*. Oxford: Oxfam International, January 2018.

Palladino, Lenore, and Kristina Karlsson. *Towards "Accountable Capitalism": Remaking Corporate Law through Stakeholder Governance*. New York: Roosevelt Institute, October 4, 2018.

Parrique, T., J. Barth, F. Briens, C. Kerschner, A. Kraus-Polk, A. Kuokkanen, and J. H. Spangenberg. *Decoupling Debunked: Evidence and Arguments against Green Growth as a Sole Strategy for Sustainability*. Brussels: European Environmental Bureau, 2019.

Patrick, Dale. *Old Testament Law*. Atlanta: John Knox, 1985.

Pew Charitable Trusts. *Auto Title Loans: Market Practices and Borrowers' Experiences*. Philadelphia: Pew, March 25, 2015.

———. *The Precarious State of Family Balance Sheets*. Philadelphia: Pew, January 29, 2015.

Philbrick, Nathaniel. *Mayflower: Voyage, Community, War*. New York: Viking, 2006.

Philippon, Thomas. "The US Only Pretends to Have Free Markets." *Atlantic*, October 29, 2019.

Phillips, Matt. "Apple's $1 Trillion Milestone Reflects Rise of Powerful Megacompanies." *New York Times*, August 2, 2018.

Phillips, Richard, and Steve Wamhoff. *The Federal Estate Tax: An Important Progressive Revenue Source*. Washington, DC: ITEP, December 6, 2018.

Piketty, Thomas. *Capital in the Twenty-First Century*. Translated by Arthur Goldhammer. Cambridge, MA: Harvard University Press, 2014.

Piketty, Thomas, Emmanuel Saez, and Gabriel Zucman. "Distributional National Accounts: Methods and Estimates for the United States." *Quarterly Journal of Economics* 133, no. 2 (2018): 553–609.

Pincus, Walter. "Defense Procurement Problems Won't Go Away." *Washington Post*, May 2, 2012.

Pogge, Thomas. "The End of Poverty?" Mark News, February 7, 2016. http://www.themarknews.com/2016/02/07/the-end-of-poverty/.

———. "The Hunger Games." *Food Ethics* 1, no. 1 (June 3, 2016): 9–27.

———. *World Poverty and Human Rights*. 2nd ed., Malden, MA: Polity, 2008.

Pogge, Thomas, and Sanjay G. Reddy. "How Not to Count the Poor." In *Debates on the Measurement of Global Poverty*, edited by Sudhir Anand, Paul Segal, and Joseph E. Stiglitz, 42–85. Initiative for Policy Dialogue. New York: Oxford University Press, April 30, 2010.

————. "Unknown: The Extent, Distribution and Trend of Global Income Poverty." *Economic and Political Weekly* 41, no. 22 (June 2006): n.p.

Polakow-Suransky, Shael. "How to End the Child-Care Crisis." *New York Times,* May 24, 2019.

Pollin, Robert. *Greening the Global Economy.* Cambridge, MA: MIT Press, 2015.

————. "How Do We Pay for a Zero-Emissions Economy?" *American Prospect* 30, no. 5 (December 5, 2019): n.p.

Rahman, K. Sabeel, and Hollie Russon Gilman. *Civic Power: Rebuilding American Democracy in an Era of Crisis.* New York: Cambridge University Press, 2019.

Rank, Mark R. "The Cost of Keeping Children Poor." *New York Times,* April 15, 2018.

————. *One Nation, Underprivileged: Why American Poverty Affects Us All.* New York: Oxford University Press, 2005.

Rank, Mark R., Thomas A. Hirschl, and Kirk A. Foster. *Chasing the American Dream: Understanding What Shapes Our Fortunes.* New York: Oxford University Press, 2014.

Rank, Mark R., Hong-Sik Yoon, and Thomas A. Hirschl. "American Poverty as a Structural Failing: Evidence and Arguments." *Journal of Sociology & Social Welfare* 30, no. 4, art. 2 (2003): n.p.

Reagan, Ronald. "Inaugural Address." Washington, DC, January 20, 1981. https://www.reaganfoundation.org/ronald-reagan/reagan-quotes -speeches/inaugural-address-2/.

Reddy, Sanjay G., and Rahul Lahoti. "$1.90 Per Day: What Does It Say?" *New Left Review* 97 (January–February 2016): 106–127.

Reed, Jonathan L. *Archaeology and the Galilean Jesus: A Re-examination of the Evidence.* Harrisburg, PA: Trinity International, 2002.

Reich, David, and Chloe Cho. *Unmet Needs and the Squeeze on Appropriations.* Washington, DC: CBPP, May 19, 2017.

Reich, Robert B. "The Monopolization of America: The Biggest Economic Problem You're Hearing Almost Nothing About." *Robert Reich* (blog). May 6, 2018. http://robertreich.org/post/173655842990.

————. *Saving Capitalism: For the Many, Not the Few.* New York: Alfred A. Knopf, 2015.

Rice, Douglas, Stephanie Schmit, and Hannah Matthews. *Child Care and Housing: Big Expenses with Too Little Help Available.* Washington, DC: CBPP, April 26, 2019.

Ritchie, Hannah, and Max Roser. *CO_2 and Greenhouse Gas Emissions*. Our-WorldInData.org, last modified August 2020. https://ourworldindata .org/co2-and-other-greenhouse-gas-emissions.

Rohrbaugh, Richard L. "The Jesus Tradition: Gospel Writers' Strategies of Persuasion." In *The Early Christian World*, 2nd ed., edited by Philip Esler, 169–196. New York: Routledge, 2017.

———. "A Peasant Reading of the Talents/Pounds: A Text of Terror." *Biblical Theology Bulletin* 23, no. 1 (1993): 32–39.

Roosevelt, Franklin D. "State of the Union Message to Congress." Washington, DC, January 11, 1944. American Presidency Project. https://www .presidency.ucsb.edu/documents/state-the-union-message-congress.

Rosenfeld, Jake. *What Unions No Longer Do*. Cambridge, MA: Harvard University Press, 2014.

Rosenthal, Steven M., and Lydia S. Austin. "The Dwindling Taxable Share of US Corporate Stock." *Tax Notes*, May 16, 2016.

Rothstein, Richard. *The Color of Law: A Forgotten History of How Our Government Segregated America*. New York: Liveright, 2017.

Ruetschlin, Catherine, and Amy Traub. *A Higher Wage Is Possible at Walmart*. New York: Demos, 2014.

Saez, Emmanuel, and Gabriel Zucman. "Progressive Wealth Taxation." *Brookings Papers on Economic Activity*, Fall 2019, 437–533.

———. *Scoring of the Sanders Wealth Tax Proposal, September 2019*. Berkeley: University of California Press, September 22, 2019.

———. *Scoring of the Warren Wealth Tax Proposal, January 2019*. Berkeley: University of California Press, January 18, 2019.

———. *The Triumph of Injustice: How the Rich Dodge Taxes and How to Make Them Pay*. New York: W. W. Norton, 2019.

Sandel, Michael J. *Justice: What's the Right Thing to Do?* New York: Farrar, Straus & Giroux, 2009.

———. *The Tyranny of Merit: What's Become of the Common Good?* New York: Farrar, Straus & Giroux, 2020.

Saramago, José. *Raised from the Ground*. Translated by Margaret Jull Costa. Boston: Houghton Mifflin Harcourt, 2012.

Sarin, Natasha, and Lawrence H. Summers. "Shrinking the Tax Gap: Approaches and Revenue Potential." *Tax Notes*, November 18, 2019.

———. "Understanding the Revenue Potential of Tax Compliance Investment." Working Paper no. 27571, NBER, Cambridge, MA, July 2020.

Sarna, Nahum M., and Hershel Shanks. "Israel in Egypt." In Shanks, *Ancient Israel*, 35–57.

Savell, Stephanie. "Where We Fight." *Smithsonian*, January 2019.

Schoch, Marta, Christoph Lakner, and Samuel Freije-Rodriguez. "Monitoring Poverty at the US$3.20 and US$5.50 Lines: Differences and Similarities with Extreme Poverty Trends." *Data Blog*. World Bank, November 19, 2020. https://blogs.worldbank.org/opendata/monitoring-poverty-us320 -and-us550-lines-differences-and-similarities-extreme-poverty.

Schott, Liz. "State Assistance for Poor Childless Adults Shrinking." *Off the Charts* (blog). CBPP, July 13, 2015. https://www.cbpp.org/blog/state -assistance-for-poor-childless-adults-shrinking.

Schott, Liz, Ife Floyd, and Ashley Burnside. *How States Use Funds under the TANF Block Grant*. Washington, DC: CBPP, April 2, 2018.

Schröder, Enno, and Servaas Storm. "Economic Growth and Carbon Emissions: The Road to 'Hothouse Earth' Is Paved with Good Intentions." Working Paper no. 84, Institute for New Economic Thinking, New York, November 2018.

Schulz, William. *Tainted Legacy: 9/11 and the Ruin of Human Rights*. New York: Nation, 2003.

Scott, Robert E. *We Can Reshore Manufacturing Jobs, but Trump Hasn't Done It*. Washington, DC: EPI, August 10, 2020.

Semega, Jessica, Melissa Kollar, Emily A. Shrider, and John Creamer. *Income and Poverty in the United States: 2019*. Report no. P60-270. Washington, DC: US Bureau of the Census, September 2020.

Shanks, Hershel, ed. *Ancient Israel: From Abraham to the Roman Destruction of the Temple*. 3rd ed. Washington, DC: Biblical Archaeology Society, 2011.

Shierholz, Heidi. *More Than Eight Million Workers Will Be Left behind by the Trump Overtime Proposal*. Washington, DC: EPI, April 8, 2019.

Smithberger, Mandy. "The Pentagon Budget Is Out of Control." *Nation*, March 3, 2020.

Social Security Administration. *Fast Facts & Figures about Social Security, 2020*. Washington, DC: SSA, July 2020.

———. *Income of the Aged Chartbook, 2014*. Pub. no. 13-11727. Washington, DC: SSA, April 2016.

Sorkin, Andrew Ross. "Bridgewater's Ray Dalio Tops the List of Hedge Fund Manager Compensation." *New York Times*, April 30, 2019.

Speth, James Gustave. *The Bridge at the Edge of the World: Capitalism, the Environment, and Crossing from Crisis to Sustainability*. New Haven, CT: Yale University Press, 2008.

Springmann, Marco, Michael Clark, Daniel Mason-D'Croz, Keith Wiebe, Benjamin Leon Bodirsky, Luis Lassaletta, Wim de Vries, Sonja J. Vermeulen, Mario Herrero, Kimberly M. Carlson, Malin Jonell, Max Troell, Fabrice DeClerck, Line J. Gordon, Rami Zurayk, Peter Scarborough, Mike Rayner, Brent Loken, Jess Fanzo, H. Charles J. Godfray, David Tilman, Johan Rockström, and Walter Willett. "Options for Keeping the Food System within Environmental Limits." *Nature* 562 (October 25, 2018): 519–525.

Stanley, Jason. *How Fascism Works: The Politics of Us and Them*. New York: Random House, 2018.

Steffen, Will, Katherine Richardson, Johan Rockström, Sarah E. Cornell, Ingo Fetzer, Elena M. Bennett, and Reinette Biggs, Stephen R. Carpenter, Wim de Vries, Cynthia A. de Wit, Carl Folke, Dieter Gerten, Jens Heinke, Georgina M. Mace, Linn M. Persson, Veerabhadran Ramanathan, Belinda Reyers, and Sverker Sörlin. "Planetary Boundaries: Guiding Human Development on a Changing Planet." *Science* 347, no. 6223 (February 13, 2015): 735–746.

Stegemann, Ekkehard W., and Wolfgang Stegemann. *The Jesus Movement: A Social History of Its First Century*. Translated by O. C. Dean Jr. Minneapolis: Fortress, 1999.

Steinbaum, Marshall, Eric Harris Bernstein, and John Sturm. *Powerless: How Lax Antitrust and Concentrated Market Power Rig the Economy against American Workers, Consumers, and Communities*. New York: Roosevelt Institute, March 27, 2018.

Stiglitz, Joseph E. *The Dynamics of Social Inequities in the Present World*. New York: Roosevelt Institute, June 22, 2017.

———. *Globalization and Its Discontents, Revisited: Anti-globalization in the Era of Trump*. New York: W. W. Norton, 2018.

———. *The Great Divide: Unequal Societies and What We Can Do about Them*. New York: W. W. Norton, 2015.

———. *Making Globalization Work*. New York: W. W. Norton, 2007.

———. *People, Power, and Profits: Progressive Capitalism for an Age of Discontent*. New York: W. W. Norton, 2019.

———. *The Price of Inequality: How Today's Divided Society Endangers Our Future*. New York: W. W. Norton, 2012.

———. *Rewriting the Rules of the American Economy: An Agenda for Growth and Shared Prosperity*. New York: W. W. Norton, 2016.

———. *The Welfare State in the Twenty-First Century*. New York: Roosevelt Institute, June 20, 2017.

Strauss, Mariya. "'Faith-Washing' Right-Wing Economics: How the Right Is Marketing Medicare's Demise." *Public Eye*, Fall 2015, 4–10.

Sunstein, Cass R. *The Second Bill of Rights*. New York: Basic Books, 2004.

Tanner, Kathryn. *Economy of Grace*. Minneapolis: Fortress, 2005.

Tarrance, V. Lance. *Despite US Economic Success, Financial Anxiety Remains*. Washington, DC: Gallup, July 12, 2019.

Taub, Stephen. "The Rich List." *Institutional Investor*, April 30, 2019.

Tavernise, Sabrina, and Abby Goodnough. "American Life Expectancy Rises for First Time in Four Years." *New York Times*, January 30, 2020.

Tax Justice Network. *The State of Tax Justice 2021*. Bristol, UK: TJN, November 16, 2021.

Tax Policy Center. *Briefing Book: Key Elements of the US Tax System*. Washington, DC: TPC, May 2020.

———. "Effective Tax Rate by AGI, 1935–2015." Accessed October 20, 2020. https://www.taxpolicycenter.org/file/182421/download?token=oPN7UniL.

———. "Table 20-0037: Average Effective Federal Tax Rates, by Expanded Cash Income Percentile, 2019." February 26, 2020. Accessed October 20, 2020. https://www.taxpolicycenter.org/model-estimates/baseline-share -federal-taxes-february-2020/t20-0037-average-effective-federal-tax.

Tepper, Jonathan, with Denise Hearn. *The Myth of Capitalism: Monopolies and the Death of Competition*. Hoboken, NJ: Wiley, 2019.

Theoharis, Liz. *Always with Us? What Jesus Really Said about the Poor*. Grand Rapids, MI: Eerdmans, 2017.

Tikkanen, Roosa, and Melinda K. Abrams. *US Health Care from a Global Perspective, 2019: Higher Spending, Worse Outcomes?* New York: Commonwealth Fund, January 30, 2020.

Townsend, Peter. *Poverty in the United Kingdom: A Survey of Household Resources and Standards of Living*. Berkeley: University of California Press, 1979.

Trawick, Paul, and Alf Hornborg. "Revisiting the Image of Limited Good: On Sustainability, Thermodynamics, and the Illusion of Creating Wealth." *Current Anthropology* 56, no. 1 (February 2015): 1–27.

Treasury Inspector General for Tax Administration. *High-Income Nonfilers Owing Billions of Dollars Are Not Being Worked by the Internal Revenue Service*.

Ref. no. 2020-30-015. Washington, DC: US Department of the Treasury, May 29, 2020.

Trisi, Danilo, and Matt Saenz. *Economic Security Programs Cut Poverty Nearly in Half over Last 50 Years*. Washington, DC: CBPP, November 26, 2019.

Turner, Adair. *Between Debt and the Devil: Money, Credit, and Fixing Global Finance*. Princeton, NJ: Princeton University Press, 2015.

UN Climate Change. Framework Convention on Climate Change, adopted at the United Nations Conference on Environment and Development, Rio de Janeiro, Brazil, June 3–14, 1992. https://unfccc.int/files/essential _background/background_publications_htmlpdf/application/pdf/ conveng.pdf.

UN Conference on Trade and Development. *From the Great Lockdown to the Great Meltdown: Developing Country Debt in the Time of Covid-19*. Geneva: UNCTAD, April 2020.

———. "Investment Dispute Settlement Navigator, Investment Policy Hub." Accessed June 6, 2020. https://investmentpolicy.unctad.org/ investment-dispute-settlement.

UN Department of Economic and Social Affairs, Population Division. *Population Facts*. New York: UN DESA, September 2019.

UN Department of Economic and Social Affairs, Statistics Division. "Goal Six: Ensure Availability and Sustainable Management of Water and Sanitation for All." In *Sustainable Development Goals Report 2018*. New York: UN DESA, 2018. https://unstats.un.org/sdgs/report/2018/goal-06/.

UN Development Program. "About Human Development." Human Development Reports. Accessed November 23, 2021. http://hdr.undp.org/ en/humandev.

———. *Human Development Report 2000: Human Rights and Human Development*. New York: UNDP, 2000.

———. *Human Development Report 2016: Human Development for Everyone*. New York: UNDP, 2016.

———. *Human Development Report 2019: Beyond Income, Beyond Averages, Beyond Today; Inequalities in Human Development in the 21st Century*. New York: UNDP, 2019.

———. *Humanity Divided: Confronting Inequality in Developing Countries*. New York: UNDP, November 2015.

———. "Goal 10 Reduced Inequality." Sustainable Development Goals. Accessed November 23, 2021. https://www.undp.org/sustainable -development-goals#reduced-inequalities.

UN Environment Program. *Emissions Gap Report 2019*. Nairobi: UNEP, November 2019.

UN High Commissioner for Human Rights. *Principles and Guidelines for a Human Rights Approach to Poverty Reduction Strategies*. New York: UNHCR, 2006.

———. "Status of Ratification Interactive Dashboard." http://indicators .ohchr.org/.

UN High Commissioner for Refugees. "Facts at a Glance." Accessed August 4, 2020. https://www.unhcr.org/figures-at-a-glance.html.

UNICEF. *Get the Facts on Handwashing*. New York: UNICEF, October 15, 2018.

———. "Malnutrition." March 2020. Accessed October 20, 2020. https:// data.unicef.org/topic/nutrition/malnutrition/#.

———. *The State of the World's Children 2019; Children, Food and Nutrition: Growing Well in a Changing World*. New York: UNICEF, October 2019.

UNICEF and World Health Organization. *Progress on Household Drinking Water, Sanitation and Hygiene 2000–2017: Special Focus on Inequalities*. New York: UNICEF and WHO, 2019.

US Agency for International Development. "Foreign Aid Explorer, Activities." Accessed November 16, 2020. https://explorer.usaid.gov/.

US Bureau of the Census. "Historical Poverty Tables: People and Families—1959 to 2018, Table 2." Accessed March 23, 2018. https:// www2.census.gov/programs-surveys/cps/tables/time-series/historical -poverty-people/hstpov2.xls.

———. "Poverty Thresholds." Accessed March 13, 2020. https://www2 .census.gov/programs-surveys/cps/tables/time-series/historical -poverty-thresholds/thresh19.xls.

US Conference of Catholic Bishops. *Economic Justice for All: Pastoral Letter on Catholic Social Teaching and the US Economy*. Washington, DC: US Catholic Conference, 1986.

US Department of Agriculture, Food and Nutrition Service. "Annual Summary of Food and Nutrition Service Programs." Accessed December 2, 2021. https://www.fns.usda.gov/sites/default/files/resource-files/annual -10.xls.

———. "Supplemental Nutrition Assistance Program Participation and Costs." Accessed December 2, 2021. https://www.fns.usda.gov/sites/ default/files/resource-files/SNAPsummary-11.pdf.

———. *What Is FNS Doing to Fight SNAP Fraud?* Washington, DC: USDA, June 27, 2019.

US Department of Housing and Urban Development. *The 2019 Annual Homeless Assessment Report to Congress, Part 1*. Washington, DC: US Department of HUD, January 2019.

US Department of Labor, Bureau of Labor Statistics. *Employee Benefits in the United States—March 2020*. Washington, DC: BLS, 2020.

———. "Employment Projections: Table 1.4." Accessed March 28, 2020. https://www.bls.gov/emp/tables.htm.

———. "Retirement Benefits: Access, Participation, and Take-Up Rates." In *National Compensation Survey: Employee Benefits in the United States, March 2021* (Washington, DC: BLS, September 2021), table 1, https://www.bls.gov/news.release/ebs2.t01.htm. Accessed November 23, 2021.

US Department of Labor, Employee Benefits Security Administration. *Private Pension Plan Bulletin, Historical Tables and Graphs, 1975–2017*. Washington, DC: DOL, September 2019.

US Environmental Protection Agency. *Inventory of US Greenhouse Gas Emissions and Sinks: 1990–2018*. Washington, DC: EPA, 2020.

US Government Accountability Office. *Most Large Profitable US Corporations Paid Tax but Effective Tax Rates Differed Significantly from the Statutory Rate*. GAO-16-363. Washington, DC: GAO, published March 17, 2016, publicly released April 13, 2016.

———. *Tax Gap: IRS Needs Specific Goals and Strategies for Improving Compliance*. GAO-18-39. Washington, DC: GAO, published October 31, 2017, publicly released November 30, 2017.

US Interagency Council on Homelessness. *Deploy Housing First Systemwide*. Washington, DC: US Interagency Council on Homelessness, August 15, 2018.

Van Biema, David, and Jeff Chu. "Does God Want You to Be Rich?" *Time*, September 10, 2006.

Ventry, Dennis J., Jr. "Why Steven Mnuchin Wants a Stronger IRS." *New York Times*, March 27, 2017.

Vogel, David. *Fluctuating Fortunes: The Political Power of Business in America*. New York: Basic Books, 1989.

Vogel, Steven K. "America Needs an Industrial Policy—Now More Than Ever." *The Hill*, October 13, 2020.

Wakabayashi, Daisuke. "Google's Shadow Work Force: Temps Who Outnumber Full-Time Employees." *New York Times*, May 28, 2019.

Walker, Robert, Grace Bantebya Kyomuhendo, Elaine Chase, Sohail Choudhry, Erika K. Gubrium, Jo Yongmie Nicola, Ivar Lødemel,

Leemamol Mathew, Amon Mwiine, Sony Pellissery, and Yan Ming. "Poverty in Global Perspective: Is Shame a Common Denominator?" *Journal of Social Policy* 42, no. 2 (April 2013): 215–233.

Wallace-Wells, David. *The Uninhabitable Earth: Life after Warming*. New York: Tim Duggan, 2019.

Walzer, Michael. *Exodus and Revolution*. New York: Basic Books, 1985.

———. *In God's Shadow: Politics in the Hebrew Bible*. New Haven, CT: Yale University Press, 2012.

Wamhoff, Steve. "Emmanuel Saez and Gabriel Zucman's New Book Reminds Us That Tax Injustice Is a Choice." *Just Taxes* (blog). ITEP, October 15, 2019. https://itep.org/emmanuel-saez-and-gabriel-zucmans-new-book -reminds-us-that-tax-injustice-is-a-choice/.

———. *The US Needs a Federal Wealth Tax*. Washington, DC: ITEP, January 23, 2019.

Wamhoff, Steve, and Matthew Gardner. *Federal Tax Cuts in the Bush, Obama, and Trump Years*. Washington, DC: ITEP, July 11, 2018.

Wamhoff, Steve, and Richard Phillips. *The Failure of Expensing and Other Depreciation Tax Breaks*. Washington, DC: ITEP, November 19, 2018.

Ward, Benedicta, trans. *The Sayings of the Desert Fathers*. Alphabetical Collection. Kalamazoo, MI: Cistercian, 1984.

Weil, David. "Lots of Employees Get Misclassified as Contractors. Here's Why It Matters." *Harvard Business Review*, July 5, 2017.

Weinfeld, Moshe. *Social Justice in Ancient Israel and in the Ancient Near East*. Minneapolis: Fortress, 1995.

Western, Bruce, and Jake Rosenfeld. "Unions, Norms, and the Rise in US Wage Inequality." *American Sociological Review* 76, no. 4 (2011): 513–537.

Whitlock, Craig, and Bob Woodward. "Pentagon Buries Evidence of $125 Billion in Bureaucratic Waste." *Washington Post*, December 5, 2016.

Whitmee, Sarah, Andy Haines, Chris Beyrer, Frederick Boltz, Anthony G. Capon, Braulio Ferreira de Souza Dias, Alex Ezeh, Howard Frumkin, Peng Gong, Peter Head, Richard Horton, Georgina M. Mace, Robert Marten, Samuel S. Myers, Sania Nishtar, Steven A. Osofsky, Subhrendu K. Pattanayak, Montira J. Pongsiri, Cristina Romanelli, Agnes Soucat, Jeanette Vega, and Derek Yach. "Safeguarding Human Health in the Anthropocene Epoch: Report of the Rockefeller Foundation—Lancet Commission on Planetary Health." *Lancet* 386, no. 10007 (July 16, 2015): 1973–2028.

Wiehe, Meg, Aidan Davis, Carl Davis, Matt Gardner, Lisa Christensen Gee, and Dylan Grundman. *Who Pays: A Distributional Analysis of the Tax Systems in All 50 States*. 6th ed. Washington, DC: ITEP, 2018.

Wilkinson, Richard, and Kate Pickett. *The Inner Level: How More Equal Societies Reduce Stress, Restore Sanity and Improve Everyone's Well-Being*. New York: Penguin, 2019.

———. *The Spirit Level: Why Greater Equality Makes Societies Stronger*. New York: Bloomsbury, 2009.

———. "The Spirit Level Authors: Why Society Is More Unequal Than Ever." *Guardian*, March 9, 2014.

Wink, Walter. *Engaging the Powers: Discernment and Resistance in a World of Domination*. Minneapolis: Fortress, 1992.

———. *The Human Being: Jesus and the Enigma of the Son of Man*. Minneapolis: Fortress, 2002.

Wirth, Eugen. *Agrargeographie des Irak*. Hamburg: Instituts für Geographie und Wirtschaftgeographie der Universität Hamburg, 1962.

Wolff, Edward N. "Household Wealth Trends in the United States, 1962–2016: Has Middle Class Wealth Recovered?" Working Paper no. 24085, NBER, Cambridge, MA, November 2017.

Wolin, Sheldon S. *Democracy Incorporated: Managed Democracy and the Specter of Inverted Totalitarianism*. Princeton, NJ: Princeton University Press, 2008.

Woodward, David. *How Poor Is "Poor"?* London: New Economics Foundation, July 4, 2010.

———. "*Incrementum ad Absurdum*: Global Growth, Inequality and Poverty Eradication in a Carbon-Constrained World." *World Economic Review* 4 (2015): 43–62.

Woolhandler, Steffie, and David U. Himmelstein. "The Relationship of Health Insurance and Mortality: Is Lack of Insurance Deadly?" *Annals of Internal Medicine* 167, no. 6 (September 19, 2017): 424–431.

Workman, Simon, and Steven Jessen-Howard. *Understanding the True Cost of Child Care for Infants and Toddlers*. Washington, DC: Center for American Progress, November 15, 2018.

World Bank. "Data." Accessed November 23, 2021. https://data.worldbank .org/indicator/SI.POV.GINI.

———. "PovcalNet." Accessed March 31, 2020. http://iresearch.worldbank .org/PovcalNet/povOnDemand.aspx.

―――. *Poverty and Shared Prosperity, 2020: Reversals of Fortune*. Washington, DC: World Bank, 2020.

World Communion of Reformed Churches. *Accra Confession: Covenanting for Justice in the Economy and the Earth*. Geneva: WCRC, 2004.

World Council of Churches. *Alternative Globalization Addressing Peoples and Earth, a Background Document*. Geneva: WCC, 2005.

―――. *Human Rights and the Churches: New Challenges; A Statement by the International Ecumenical Consultation*. Morges, Switzerland: WCC, June 23–27, 1998.

―――. *São Paulo Statement: International Financial Transformation for the Economy of Life*. Geneva: WCC, October 5, 2012.

Yoffie, David, and Joseph L. Badaracco Jr. "A Rational Model of Corporate Political Strategies." Working paper, Division of Research Harvard Business School, 1984.

Zucman, Gabriel. *The Hidden Wealth of Nations*. Chicago: University of Chicago Press, 2015.

―――. *Taxing Multinational Corporations in the 21st Century*. Economics for Inclusive Prosperity, February 2019. https://econfip.org/policy-briefs/taxing-multinational-corporations-in-the-21st-century/.

Index

Scripture Index